W9-BVG-928

But They All Come Back

Also of interest from the Urban Institute Press:

Juvenile Drug Courts and Teen Substance Abuse, edited by Jeffrey Butts and John Roman

Prisoners Once Removed: The Impact of Incarceration and Reentry on Children, Families, and Communities, edited by Jeremy Travis and Michelle Waul

But They All Come Back

Facing the Challenges of Prisoner Reentry

Jeremy Travis

THE URBAN INSTITUTE PRESS
Washington, D.C.

THE URBAN INSTITUTE PRESS
2100 M Street, N.W.
Washington, D.C. 20037

Editorial Advisory Board

Jeffrey Butts	George E. Peterson
Kathleen Courrier	Robert D. Reischauer
William Gorham	John Rogers
Jack Hadley	Raymond J. Struyk
Demetra S. Nightingale	

Copyright © 2005. The Urban Institute. All rights reserved. Except for short quotes, no part of this book may be reproduced or utilized in any form or by any means, electronic or mechanical, including photocopying, recording, or by information storage or retrieval system, without written permission from The Urban Institute Press.

Library of Congress Cataloging-in-Publication Data

Travis, Jeremy.
  But they all come back : facing the challenges of prisoner reentry / Jeremy Travis.— 1st ed.
     p. cm.
  Includes bibliographical references and index.
   ISBN 0-87766-750-0 (alk. paper)
   1. Prisoners—Rehabilitation—United States. 2. Imprisonment—United States. 3. Prisoners—United States—Social conditions. 4. Prisoners' families—Effect of imprisonment on—United States. I. Title.
   HV9304.T68 2005
   364.8'0973—dc22
                                                                    2005001340

ISBN 0-87766-750-0 (paper, alk. paper)

Printed in the United States of America
10 09 08 07 06   2 3 4 5

BOARD OF TRUSTEES

Joel L. Fleishman, Chairman
Robert M. Solow, Vice Chairman
Dick Thornburgh, Vice Chairman
Robert D. Reischauer, President
Michael Beschloss
John M. Deutch
Richard C. Green Jr.
Fernando A. Guerra, MD
Robert S. McNamara
Charles L. Mee Jr.
Robert E. Price
Louis A. Simpson
Judy Woodruff

LIFE TRUSTEES

Joan T. Bok
Warren E. Buffett
James E. Burke
Joseph A. Califano Jr.
Marcia L. Carsey
Carol Thompson Cole
William T. Coleman Jr.
Anthony Downs
George J. W. Goodman
William Gorham
Aileen C. Hernandez
Carla A. Hills
Vernon E. Jordan Jr.
Bayless A. Manning
David O. Maxwell
Arjay Miller
J. Irwin Miller
Robert C. Miller
Sol Price
Lois D. Rice
William D. Ruckelshaus
Herbert E. Scarf
Charles L. Schultze
William W. Scranton
Mortimer B. Zuckerman

 THE URBAN INSTITUTE is a nonprofit policy research and educational organization established in Washington, D.C., in 1968. Its staff investigates the social, economic, and governance problems confronting the nation and evaluates the public and private means to alleviate them. The Institute disseminates its research findings through publications, its web site, the media, seminars, and forums.

Through work that ranges from broad conceptual studies to administrative and technical assistance, Institute researchers contribute to the stock of knowledge available to guide decisionmaking in the public interest.

Conclusions or opinions expressed in Institute publications are those of the authors and do not necessarily reflect the views of officers or trustees of the Institute, advisory groups, or any organizations that provide financial support to the Institute.

Weeping

Bright Blue

I knew a man who lived in fear
it was huge it was angry
it was drawing near
Behind his house a secret place
was the shadow of the demon
he could never face.

He built a wall of steel and flame
and men with guns to keep it tame
Then standing back he made it plain
that the nightmare would never ever rise again
But the fear and the fire and the guns remain.

It doesn't matter now it's over anyhow
He tells the world that it's sleeping
But as the night came round I heard
it slowly sound
it wasn't roaring it was weeping
it wasn't roaring it was weeping.

And then one day the neighbours came
they were curious to know about the smoke and flame
They stood around outside the wall
But of course there was nothing to be heard at all
"My friends," he said, "we've reached our goal
the threat is under firm control
As long as peace and order reign
I'll be damned if I can see a reason to explain
Why the fear and the fire and the guns remain."

It doesn't matter now it's over anyhow
He tells the world that it's sleeping
But as the night came round I heard
it slowly sound
it wasn't roaring it was weeping
it wasn't roaring it was weeping.

It doesn't matter now it's over anyhow
He tells the world that it's sleeping
But as the night came round I heard
it slowly sound
it wasn't roaring it was weeping
it wasn't roaring it was weeping.

Written in 1986 during the state of emergency in South Africa, "Weeping" became an anthem for those engaged in the struggle against apartheid. Words and music by Peter Cohen, Ian Cohen, Tom Fox, and Dan Heymann. Copyright © 1998 Gallo Music Publishers. All rights for Gallo Music Publishers controlled and administered by Music of Windswept. All rights reserved. Used by permission.

To my parents, Harriet and Willard Travis,
whose devotion to public service, zest for life,
and passion for learning continue to inspire me

Contents

Preface

In the spring of 1999, Attorney General Janet Reno pulled me and my colleague Laurie Robinson aside after a meeting to ask a simple question: "What are we doing about all the people coming out of prison?" Laurie was then the assistant attorney general for justice programs and I was the director of the National Institute of Justice, positions that arguably should have prepared us for a good answer to the attorney general's question. We answered honestly—we did not know what was being done for returning prisoners. Ms. Reno directed us to get back to her in two weeks with a better answer.

That two-week assignment has turned into a five-year journey for me. Soon after the meeting with Ms. Reno, I convened the senior staff at the National Institute of Justice to get a basic understanding of the issue. At our first meeting, we learned that a large number of people were leaving the nation's prisons—about 585,000 a year at that time. For most of the people in the room—all seasoned criminal justice experts—this number was a shock. We also learned that not all of these returning prisoners were supervised upon release. For many (including me) who were familiar with state systems where every released prisoner was placed on parole, this was a revelation. We discovered that a large percentage of prisoners were being sent back to prison on parole revocations, a remarkable fact that changed our whole understanding of the period following release from prison. We discussed the hodgepodge of sentencing policies that had developed around the country.

Early on in our discussions, we realized that, in order to answer the attorney general's question, we could not focus simply on the parole system, since so many people were being released from prison without parole supervision. I suggested we use the word "reentry" to capture the experience of being released from custody, and the word quickly became convenient shorthand for our inquiry.* An examination of "prisoner reentry," we hoped, would allow us to set aside debates over sentencing policy and avoid the pitfalls of defending or critiquing parole. We hoped that the topic "prisoner reentry" would be broad enough to allow conservatives and liberals, pro- and antiprison advocates to come together with pragmatic answers to Janet Reno's question.

Now, five years later, I have a much better understanding of the phenomenon of prisoner reentry. My thinking on the topic has been shaped by a rich mix of research projects, pilot programs, and collegial interactions. While still at the National Institute of Justice, I wrote a paper that proposed creating "reentry courts" as new managers of the reentry process. On October 14, 1999, Ms. Reno and I held a press conference announcing a call for proposals from communities interested in developing reentry courts. Eight were selected as test sites. Working with my colleagues Larry Meachum, director of the Corrections Program Office, and Joe Brann, director of the Office of Community Oriented Policing Services, we launched the first Reentry Partnerships in another five sites, bringing together police, corrections agencies, and community leaders to improve reentry planning.

In April 2000, I left the National Institute of Justice to join the Urban Institute as a senior fellow. Over the next four years, my colleagues and I built a robust portfolio of research projects exploring different dimensions of the prisoner reentry phenomenon. The most ambitious project is called *Returning Home,* a four-state longitudinal study of the experience of leaving prison from the perspectives of prisoners, their families, and the communities to which they return.

Our first step in building our portfolio was to create the Reentry Roundtable, a group of researchers, practitioners, policymakers, former prisoners, community leaders, victim advocates, and service providers who met eight times over four years. Our mission was to "unpack" pris-

---

*I later learned that the word "reentry" had been used years before (Irwin 1970).

oner reentry by examining the phenomenon through different policy lenses. At our first two meetings, we defined the topic, surveyed the state of knowledge, and designed a research agenda. Then we held a series of topical meetings on the intersection of prisoner reentry and civil society, public health, families and children, employment, housing and home-lessness, youth development, and community policing. For each of these meetings we commissioned discussion papers from the best academics in the country, invited practitioners working at the cutting edge of inno-vation, brought together different points of view, and held two days of lively discussion. Because the Roundtable meetings were held "in the round" before an audience of as many as 100 observers, these discussions resonated through a broad range of policy and research networks.

In the summer of 2001, after the first two Roundtable meetings and following the successful launch of *Returning Home,* the Urban Institute Press invited me to write a book about prisoner reentry. For the next three years, as the Roundtable meetings were being convened and the results of *Returning Home* were coming in, I was drafting the chapters that now make up this book.

Now, as I complete this five-year journey, I am profoundly grateful to the many individuals and institutions that provided support and guid-ance along the way. First, I applaud Janet Reno, Laurie Robinson, and my former colleagues at the Department of Justice for their willingness to take on a complicated new topic of national importance. The crimi-nal justice team in the Clinton administration's Department of Justice was a magical collection of talented, generous, and public-spirited indi-viduals. Second, I cannot imagine a better home for this exploration of prisoner reentry than the Urban Institute. As a high-quality research organization of unquestioned integrity, the Institute quickly became recognized as an authoritative source for solid, timely research on the topic of prisoner reentry. Two presidents of the Institute were unwaver-ing advocates—Bill Gorham, the founding president who invited me to join the Institute, and Bob Reischauer, his successor who consistently supported my work and my unique role at the Institute. Two directors of the Justice Policy Center—Adele Harrell and Terry Dunworth—were staunch allies. The Urban Institute Press, under the leadership of Kathy Courrier, provided incomparable editorial support, encouragement, and guidance.

All I know about the issue of prisoner reentry I have learned from oth-ers, too many to name in this space. However, I would like to single out a few who have been particularly valuable. Joan Petersilia has been the cochair of the Reentry Roundtable. With infectious enthusiasm, she brings wisdom and objectivity to any discussion of these issues. My initial thinking on this topic was informed by the deliberations of the Executive Session on Sentencing and Corrections, a group that met twice a year from 1996 to 1999 to explore new approaches to sentencing and corrections. In addition to Joan Petersilia, the Executive Session included Michael Tonry, Michael Smith, Mark Moore, Tony Fabelo, Marty Horn, John Larivee, Kay Pranis, Richard Gebelein, Tom Ross, Neil Bryant, Ronnie Earle, Dennis Maloney, Ronald Angelone, Harold Clarke, Walter Dickey, John Gorczyk, Kathleen Sawyer, Joe Lehman, Larry Meachum, Dora Schriro, and Reginald Wilkinson. For me, the Executive Session tilled the intellectual ground that made possible this sustained examination of the prisoner reentry issue.

The work on this book was supported by a number of institutions. First and foremost is the Urban Institute, which made an investment in my colleagues and me as we built the reentry portfolio. This investment was particularly important in the early years when outside funding was not yet available. The Reentry Roundtable, which generated many of the ideas and perspectives that are now reflected in this book, was supported by a number of foundations and government agencies, including the Open Society Institute, the Annie E. Casey Foundation, the Joyce Foundation, the Robert Wood Johnson Foundation, the California Endowment, the Hewlett Foundation, the Rockefeller Foundation, the Centers for Disease Control and Prevention, the Office of Community Oriented Policing Services, and the Fannie Mae Foundation. The *Returning Home* project has been supported by a broad spectrum of foundations, including the John D. and Catherine T. MacArthur Foundation, the George Gund Foundation, the JEHT Foundation, the Health Foundation of Greater Cincinnati, the Houston Endowment, the Abell Foundation, the Smith Richardson Foundation, and the Cleveland Foundation, as well as the states of Maryland, Illinois, and Ohio. I am particularly grateful for the support of the JEHT Foundation, and its president, Bob Crane. Without the support of the JEHT Foundation, which provided direct assistance for the research activities needed to complete this project, there would be no book.

As I worked on the book, a small army of colleagues provided research assistance, critical reviews, and emotional support when the project seemed daunting. Louise van der Does served ably as research assistant as I was beginning to collect my thoughts. She helped me structure each chapter and provided background research for a variety of topics. Elizabeth Cincotta McBride played a critical role in organizing the final push to complete the manuscript. I deeply appreciated her editorial skills, organizational acumen, and analytical abilities. Each chapter had one or more research assistants who helped me understand the literature on a variety of different topics. I am grateful to all of them for their enthusiasm and professionalism: Asheley Van Ness, Allison Hastings, Lisa Feldman, Noah Sawyer, Erica Lagerson, Sinead Keegan, Alyssa Whitby, Karen Beckman, Meagan Funches, Tony Hebert, and Sam Wolf.

As each chapter was taking shape, I convened a group of colleagues at the Urban Institute to give their unvarnished reactions. These luncheon discussions were lively, constructive, and enormously valuable. I thank Christy Visher, Amy Solomon, Nancy La Vigne, Sarah Lawrence, Sue Popkin, Embry Howell, Marge Turner, Caterina Roman, Avi Bhati, Matt Stagner, Janine Zweig, and Michelle Waul Webster for their generosity in offering their reactions to the early, rough versions of the book chapters.

After the chapters had moved closer to a final version, I sent each one to substantive experts outside the Institute for their review and comment. I am deeply grateful to Al Blumstein, Joan Petersilia, Rick Rosenfeld, Marty Horn, Margaret Love, Chris Uggen, Harry Holzer, Bob Greifinger, Ted Hammet, Tom LeBel, Donald Braman, Sabra Horne, Creasie Finney Hairston, Sylvia Oberle, Shadd Maruna, Todd Clear, Steve Garvey, Mindy Tarlow, Alan Mobley, Ed Rhine, and Carol Shapiro for the time they took from their own work to offer suggestions and criticisms. These are generous colleagues and friends. A number of chapters appeared in earlier versions in other books or Urban Institute reports. I thank the editors of those books—Marc Mauer, Meda Chesney-Lind, Mary Pattillo, Bruce Western, and David Weiman—and my coauthor Sarah Lawrence for their contributions to those previous versions. Finally, I would like to express my appreciation to the two anonymous reviewers who provided the Urban Institute Press with comments on the draft manuscript. They offered perspectives on the whole book—its structure, argument, and consistency—that were immensely important as the manuscript moved into final production.

Although I appreciate the many contributions of these colleagues over the years, I still accept full responsibility for the final work. This statement, quite traditional in book prefaces, is particularly applicable in this book, which aspires to push our thinking to explore new ways of conducting the work of the agencies of justice. Some readers of early versions of the book were quite clear they disagreed with my policy proposals, so they should all be absolved of any responsibility for the book's recommendations.

I cannot adequately express my gratitude to my wife, Susan, and our daughters, Aliza and Zoe. For nearly three years, I have spent many evenings and weekends working on the book—time that by all rights I could have spent with them. They have been patient and understanding as I have wrestled with the demands of this project. They have encouraged me during the difficult phases, shared in the celebrations of the breakthroughs, and helped me keep this work in proper perspective.

As I leave the Urban Institute to assume the presidency of John Jay College of Criminal Justice, I know that the national focus on prisoner reentry will continue to expand. Many forces are lined up to guarantee this result, including the energy coming from communities that have confronted these complex issues, the national leadership displayed by President Bush and members of Congress from both parties, the innovations in the world of practice, and the pivotal role of the nation's foundations. My fondest hope is that, in this fertile soil, some of the ideas presented in this book will take root and grow so that we can have better answers to one of the oldest challenges facing the criminal justice system: What are we doing about all the people leaving prison?

Introduction

Reentry and Reintegration

The steady growth of imprisonment in America over the past generation has created an unprecedented challenge for our society: the reintegration of thousands of individuals who have spent time in our prisons. Just as the rate of incarceration in America has increased fourfold, the number of people leaving prison each year has also quadrupled. In 2002, more than 630,000 individuals (1,700 per day) left federal and state prisons—compared with the 150,000 who made a similar journey 30 years ago. Sadly, the challenge of prisoner reintegration has been largely overlooked amid intense political and philosophical debates over America's punishment policies. As we have embarked upon one of the greatest social experiments of our time—the expansive use of prisons as our response to crime—we have forgotten the iron law of imprisonment: they all come back. Except for those few individuals who die in custody, every person we send to prison returns to live with us.

It has not always been so. In the "Golden Age" of indeterminate sentencing, which began in the early 20th century and lasted to the mid-1970s, the goal of prisoner reintegration occupied a prominent place in the rhetoric and practice of American jurisprudence (Tonry 1999). Under the indeterminate sentencing model, judges are given wide discretion to sentence defendants to prison terms with low minimum and high maximum limits. Parole boards then decide the actual time of release, basing their decisions in part on prisoners' readiness to return to the community.

Parole agents then supervise released prisoners during the remainder of their sentences, during which time parolees are expected to meet certain conditions designed to reestablish positive connections with their families, the world of work, and other supportive institutions of civil society.

The reintegration of returning prisoners as well as reductions in their criminal behavior are the explicit objectives of this system of supervised transition from prison to community. The rehabilitation of offenders is a stated purpose of sentencing. Judges, corrections officials, parole board members, and parole agents are given wide discretion to make decisions based on their assessments of offenders' readiness to return to a law-abiding life. For more than half a century, every state in the Union, the District of Columbia, and the federal government operated within an indeterminate sentencing framework and subscribed to these ideals. Of course, the reality of practice during the "Golden Age" did not always match the lofty aspirations of the indeterminate sentencing model. This shortcoming, however, does not obscure the fact that both the rhetoric of our sentencing jurisprudence and our rationale of imprisonment pointed to prisoner reintegration as an important objective of the criminal justice system.

The seismic changes in sentencing policy that began to take hold in the 1970s fundamentally altered the landscape of punishment in America. The indeterminate sentencing model came under attack from both the left and the right. Civil rights activists and defense lawyers, citing evidence of widespread racial and class disparities in sentencing and correctional administration, called for limiting the discretion of judges, prison administrators, and parole authorities. At the same time, political conservatives, pointing to rising crime rates and research findings questioning the effectiveness of rehabilitation programs, advocated limits on discretion as a means to enforce tougher standards and crack down on criminals.

As the indeterminate sentencing model lost its intellectual and political dominance, federal and state legislatures adopted a dizzying succession of sentencing reforms. Legislatures enacted mandatory minimums, truth-in-sentencing laws, and "three strikes and you're out" schemes. States abolished their parole boards, enacted sex offender registration requirements, and created sentencing commissions to set limits on judges' sentencing power. Correctional practice changed as well. Educational programs and other activities deemed to be "frills" were eliminated from prisons. Drug testing following release from prison became routine. Electronic surveillance kept track of people under community supervision. Additionally, state and federal legislatures created a vast network of collateral sanctions for individuals with felony convictions, denying them access to jobs, public housing, welfare benefits, the ballot box, and even their children. The reality of punishment in America has changed, perhaps forever, in fundamental ways.

True, indeterminate sentencing (including the use of parole boards as release mechanisms and parole officers as supervisory agents) still exists in many states. But the concepts of rehabilitation and reintegration no longer hold the majority market share in the competition for ideas that provide an intellectual foundation for our sentencing jurisprudence. Other concepts—just desserts, retribution, and incapacitation for crime control purposes—now dominate discussions of sentencing policy in America. As a result, at the turn of the 21st century, a patchwork of sentencing philosophies and practices has emerged. The American consensus has given way to a variety of state-level experiments. The unifying ideals of the indeterminate sentencing model no longer frame our penal policy. We now live in an era resembling the Tower of Babel—we speak no common language when we discuss the purposes of punishment.

Present Realities

Thus, as we begin our exploration of the challenges of prisoner reentry, we face two defining realities. First, we live in an era of "mass incarceration," a phrase used by a number of commentators (e.g., Drucker 2002; Mauer and Chesney-Lind 2002; Pattillo, Weiman, and Western 2004). Although there are indications that the prison building boom may now be over, as well as hints that the number of state prisoners may actually decline in the coming years (particularly as the states face unprecedented fiscal constraints), these developments cannot obscure the sobering realization that our prisons now hold a million more people than they did a generation ago. It is hard to imagine the current political environment combining with legislative reform and public demand in a way sufficient to return America to a level of imprisonment significantly closer to that seen in the 1970s.

The reality of mass incarceration translates into a reality of reentry. If progress toward significant reductions in our prison population is unlikely, then America must face up to the fact that large numbers of its citizens will serve time in prison. Because a wide network of prisoners' children, families, and neighbors now feels the harmful effects of high rates of incarceration and reentry, the era of mass incarceration calls for a sustained effort within public and private institutions to embrace policies that promote reintegration, not retribution.

Second, we have not created a new unifying penal philosophy that could take the place of indeterminate sentencing. Granted, noteworthy innovations in sentencing policy are sprouting up all over the country. Based on a fundamentally different concept of the proper response to crime, restorative justice programs hold enormous promise. Researchers and policymakers are touting an emerging consensus that prison-based rehabilitation programs can indeed reduce future criminal behavior. Parole and probation practitioners are fundamentally rethinking the mission of community supervision. Judges are experimenting with reentry courts, a promising idea that envisions a role for the judiciary in supervising the reintegration process. Yet, for the moment, these efforts must be viewed as tender seedlings struggling for light in the dark forest of robust retributivism dominating our discourse on sentencing policy.

The challenge we face, therefore, is to develop a jurisprudence of reintegration that can comfortably coexist with the disparate philosophies governing sentencing practice in modern America. If our nation is serious in pursuing the reintegration ideal, then its sentencing laws must be significantly reformed. This new sentencing framework does not require that America resolve its many debates on punishment philosophy, because all sentencing policies result in prisoners being sent to prison and then being sent home. But it does require legislative action. Then, once a reintegrative sentencing framework is in place, reform of the systems that carry out penal policy can be implemented in ways that measurably improve reintegration outcomes.

This book argues that neither the reality of mass incarceration nor the absence of a new sentencing ideal should stand in the way of a renewed focus on prisoner reentry and reintegration challenges. Stated affirmatively, the book argues that a focus on the reality of reentry and the goal of reintegration creates a new common ground for developing criminal justice policy. There, the philosophical differences that have created the current cacophony of sentencing policies can be put to one side. There, policies designed to improve outcomes for returning prisoners, their families, and their communities can gain broad support.

I quickly make two qualifying observations. First, the decision to accept the state of imprisonment in America as a given is not an endorsement of that reality. For a number of reasons, ranging from moral to pragmatic, I agree with those who believe that our current level of incarceration is unacceptably high. In fact, this book documents some of the deep harms attributable to our current imprisonment policies. It is my hope that this discussion provides empirical support for a fundamental reexamination of the wisdom of those policies.

Second, the future is not bleak. On the contrary, over the five years that I have undertaken this examination of prisoner reentry, I have been deeply impressed by the level of energy, innovation, and intellectual engagement I have seen around the country. For the past three decades, it has been hard to be optimistic about the state of political discourse on crime and punishment issues in America. Now, however, with crime rates at their lowest in a generation and prison populations leveling off, practitioners and policymakers are remarkably willing to open up the discussion, to focus on the consequences of our experiment with mass incarceration, and to challenge some assumptions that have governed the definition of what is possible. So, I am optimistic. Indeed, this book addresses some of the innovations that I find most promising.

In short, I have come to the conclusion that, by acknowledging that more than 630,000 individuals leave prison each year and by observing that our sentencing policy has lost its focus on the goal of prisoner reintegration, we create a new discussion in the midst of our long-standing debates on punishment policy. By recognizing that they all come back, we may find it easier to meet the challenges of prisoner reentry.

The Reentry Framework

The book uses a "reentry framework" to analyze the challenges we face in this unprecedented era of mass incarceration. Reentry is the process of leaving prison and returning to society. Reentry is not a form of supervision, like parole. Reentry is not a goal, like rehabilitation or reintegration. Reentry is not an option. Reentry reflects the iron law of imprisonment: they all come back. While the concept of reentry applies to release from any type of incarceration—jails, federal prisons, or juvenile facilities—this book focuses on the reentry of state prisoners back to the community. These prisoners are those individuals who are sent to prison for serious offenses under sentencing schemes that reflect the changes in American penal policy over the past generation.

The reentry framework views sentencing and corrections policies from the perspectives of the individuals who pass through America's prisons as well as the perspectives of their families and the communities to which they return. We can use this framework as a prism to refract, in new ways, some age-old debates in the criminal justice field. For example, a reentry perspective can be used to refocus the role of prisons in our society. Since, with rare exceptions, everyone comes home, the policy question that we must address in every aspect of prison management is, "How can prisoners best be prepared for their inevitable return?" This question leads to a series of new goals for corrections professionals. For example, providing drug treatment in prison is certainly commendable, but such programs are quite incomplete unless we develop ways to reduce the high rates of postrelease relapse found among individuals with substance abuse histories. Similarly, facilitating family contacts for prisoners may be desirable, but visitation programs miss the larger challenge of helping prisoners and their families work through the complex dynamics of the prisoners' return home. Finally, encouraging participation in job readiness programs may be good correctional practice, but creating concrete links to the world of work on the outside is the ultimate test of program success.

The reentry framework redefines the social responsibilities of prison managers in an even more fundamental sense. Now, about one-fifth of the more than 630,000 prisoners released annually from America's state and federal prisons are released unconditionally. These prisoners are not on parole, are under no legal obligations to meet special conditions following their release, and do not report to a parole officer. In a very real sense, prison administrators have discharged their social obligations when these individuals leave prison. Yet, from a reentry perspective, prison administrators have a broader social obligation to prepare these prisoners for the inevitable return home. The prisoners leaving under no supervision, as well as their families and communities, have the same interest in successful reentry as do those who leave with supervision. The fact that unsupervised prisoners are not subject to legal constraints may impede the state's ability to enforce certain behaviors, but the larger social interest in reconnecting prisoners to positive and productive activities in their communities still exists.

The reentry framework also serves as a basis for questioning sentencing policies. As discussed above, this bridge between sentencing policy and prisoner reintegration is an established but underappreciated aspect of the indeterminate sentencing model. The possibility of early release theoretically creates incentives for prisoners to participate in rehabilitative programs and arrange for housing, employment, and family support. Parole boards are supposed to ensure that appropriate conditions of supervision have been met and the prisoner's return to the community presents low risk of failure. But determinate sentencing laws, by eliminating parole boards as the gatekeeper between prison and community, do not offer a substitute mechanism for promoting prisoner reintegration. Similarly, sentencing reforms that eliminate parole supervision after release simply allow prisoners to leave confinement without any conditions. These comparisons between different sentencing schemes raise a fundamental question: "Does the state have a responsibility to minimize the harmful effects of the transition from prison to community?" One answer might be no—the risks of failure are borne entirely by the prisoner, his family, his social network, and the public at large. For some motivated prisoners with a solid base of human and social capital, that laissez-faire policy might indeed be the appropriate societal response. But for others— imagine, for example, a violent, mentally ill, drug-addicted prisoner who has completed his fixed sentence—a sentencing policy that simply shows them the door makes little sense.

As these examples illustrate, the reentry framework creates a natural linkage to a related, important discussion about the goals of the criminal sanction. Reduced recidivism is certainly a core objective for criminal justice interventions, imprisonment included. Yet another objective quickly comes into focus—successful reintegration of those who have violated the law. At times, these goals overlap; more often, they are quite distinct. For example, connecting a former prisoner with a job may or may not reduce the likelihood that he will violate the law. But the same job also serves reintegration purposes. It connects him to the habits of work, provides economic benefits to his family, adds his taxes to the public coffers, and gives him status in the community. Similarly, assisting a returning prisoner in establishing a healthy relationship with his family upon return from prison may or may not reduce his propensity to reoffend. But a successful familial reintegration may also have a number of positive effects on the overall well-being of the former prisoner's family. Too often, criminal justice interventions are assessed solely on their effectiveness at reducing reoffending without consideration for the societal impact of reintegrating those who have violated the law and served time in prison.

Finally, the reentry perspective also sheds light on social policies outside of the traditional criminal justice domains of sentencing, corrections, and the role of the criminal sanction. In the chapters that follow, we will explore the nexus between the modern reentry phenomenon and our nation's policies regarding employment, public health, families and children, housing, community strengthening, and civic participation. When viewed through the reentry prism, these policy domains take on different dimensions and contours. Indeed, a high degree of overlap exists between these domains and criminal justice policy. Consider the following three policy questions. In some communities, a large percentage of minor children have a parent in prison. Should educators, foster care providers, and youth-serving agencies in those communities try to mitigate the harmful effects of parental incarceration on those children? Many low-skilled workers (particularly minority males) have spent time in prison. Should workforce development agencies and private businesses work to improve the employment prospects of returning prisoners? A large portion of those Americans with various communicable diseases passes through a correctional facility each year. Should public health officials collaborate with their prison health counterparts to increase the level of inoculation, screening, and treatment for these prisoners, particularly treatment extending into the community? Stated differently, the reentry framework defines a common ground of overlapping policy interests between unlikely allies in different arenas of public policy. This analytical framework holds the potential for creating new partnerships between criminal justice practitioners and their counterparts in other areas of social policy.

This Book—Research and Purpose

The book begins in Part 1 by looking back at the dissolution of the American consensus on sentencing policy and then describes three new realities of punishment—the growth in incarceration, the extended reach of supervision, and the expanded universe of invisible punishment. Part 2 examines the nexus between prisoner reentry and seven policy domains—public safety, families and children, work, housing, public health, civic identity, and community capacity. Each of the chapters in Part 2 ends with a discussion of new policy directions. Part 3 builds on these new ideas, proposing five principles for successful reentry and five building blocks for a new jurisprudence of prisoner reintegration.

Throughout the book, reference is made to promising programs, innovate practices, and ongoing interventions. Where possible, the book cites evaluations of those initiatives to assess their effectiveness at producing desired outcomes. But the sobering truth is that very few of these initiatives have been subjected to rigorous evaluations using random assignment. The purpose of this book, however, is far broader than merely producing a review of the research. Rather, its purpose is to promote new ways of thinking, encourage innovation, challenge existing orthodoxy, and spur policy reform. Therefore, although the recommendations found in each policy chapter could easily be collected into a master list, the larger hope is that the reader will be convinced to pursue a more fundamental set of reforms. The principles of successful reentry and the building blocks for a jurisprudence of prisoner reintegration could serve as guideposts for a national effort to face the challenge of prisoner reentry in an era of mass incarceration.

A Note on Language

Throughout the book I will generally refer to those who are in prison as "prisoners," and those who have left prison as "former prisoners," or "people who have formerly been incarcerated." Through an enlightening series of conversations with former prisoners (including some who comprise a group of "convict criminologists," or former prisoners who have earned PhDs), I have come to realize the importance of the words we use to refer to these citizens who have violated the law. In their view, the term "inmate" improperly lumps prisoners with mental patients. The term "offender" may be appropriate at the time of the criminal offense, but bears little meaning years later. "Ex-offender" implies that this former status is forever the defining characteristic of a person. Moreover, all of these labels tend to diminish the humanity of individuals who have violated the law.

In justice reform circles, the preferred terminology to refer to someone who has been in prison is just that—a "formerly incarcerated individual." That phrase, though accurate and preferable to some alternatives, is somewhat unwieldy, particularly in written text. Accordingly, throughout this book, I will principally refer to those who journey from prison to home as former prisoners, or formerly incarcerated persons. Yet because not all law violators have been in prison, even this linguistic solution has its limits. So in discussing this larger population, I still resort to such words as "ex-offender" or "ex-felon." Perhaps someday our language will better accommodate this complicated reality.

The title of this book reflects the certainty of prisoner reentry, the fact that "they all come back." In choosing these words, I intend to capture the dilemma of sentencing: As a society, we send people to prison, but fail to recognize the reality that (with few exceptions) they all return. Even as we embrace different sentencing reforms, we cannot escape the challenges of prisoner reintegration.[1] The title also implicitly recognizes the public's denial of this fact: The word "but" demonstrates that all debates over sentencing policy should lead to a discussion of what happens after prison, but they rarely do. Therefore, every sentencing proposal, whether retributive or rehabilitative, should include consideration of the realities of reentry—"but" they all come back. In choosing the word "they" to describe returning prisoners, I also intend to invoke the tendency, in public discourse, to characterize those who violate the law as "others." We use many linguistic devices to separate ourselves from these "others"—we call them cons, ex-cons, career criminals, sociopaths, predators, and worse. By adopting this "us-them" dichotomy in the title, I hope to illustrate, not embrace, that impulse. In fact, I argue in this book that one of the goals of a successful reentry model should be to break down the artificial construct of "us" versus "them."

Finally, the "challenges" referenced in the book's subtitle are both individual challenges facing returning prisoners, their families, and extended social networks, and the societal challenges our country faces as a result of the fourfold increase in incarceration and reentry rates. Others have written insightfully and eloquently, sometimes from personal experience, of the personal challenges facing returning prisoners. I could not possibly add to those accounts. It is my hope that this book will prompt a new consideration of the best ways American society can face the complex and profound challenges inherent in the new reality that more than 630,000 individuals leave prison each year to return home.

NOTES

Parts of this introduction appeared as "Reentry and Reintegration: New Perspectives on the Challenges of Mass Incarceration" in *Imprisoning America: The Social Effects of Mass Incarceration,* edited by Mary Patillo, David Weiman, and Bruce Western (New York: Russell Sage Foundation, 2004). The text is reprinted with permission.

1. A version of this phrase appeared in an article by Attorney General Homer Cummings entitled "They All Come Out," originally delivered as a speech on May 23, 1938, subsequently published in the October 1938 issue of *Federal Probation* (vol. 2, no. 4), and reprinted in the June 2003 issue of *Federal Probation* (vol. 67, no. 1). The editors prefaced the reprint with the statement: "As we grapple today with what we now call 'prisoner reentry' issues, readers may be interested to read an important public figure speaking on a similar issue 65 years ago."

PART I
The New Realities of
Punishment in America

Introduction

Entering the "Hidden World of Punishment"

O n August 9, 2003, Anthony M. Kennedy, associate justice of the
U.S. Supreme Court, delivered a remarkable keynote address to
the annual meeting of the American Bar Association. In an eloquent,
reflective rumination on the state of justice in America, Kennedy
declared that the nation had closed its eyes to the realities of punishment,
particularly the world inside its prisons. He called upon the members of
the legal profession, and the American people, to accept responsibility
for "what happens after a prisoner is taken away," and to remember that
"the prisoner is a person; [a] part of the family of humankind."

Justice Kennedy encouraged his audience to take a close look at the
"hidden world of punishment." Once we enter this world, he asserted,
"we should be startled by what we see." America's inmate population has
climbed to more than 2 million. Compared with nations in Europe,
where incarceration rates are about 1 in 1,000, America's rate is about 1
in 143. Kennedy described a system that disproportionately incarcerates
African Americans and, in some cities, places over half of all young
African-American men under criminal justice supervision. He also
observed that the cost of maintaining the nation's prison system has
risen to more than $40 billion a year. Kennedy reached this stark con-
clusion: "Our resources are misspent, our punishments too severe, our
sentences too long."

Justice Kennedy's speech contained a number of specific criticisms and proposals. For example, he advocated less punitive federal sentencing guidelines, called mandatory minimum sentences "unwise and unjust," and argued that sentencing discretion should be the province of the judiciary, not the prosecutors. Yet his indictment of the state of justice in America was more than a lawyerly critique of the mechanics of our sentencing practices. His speech reflected a sense of compassion for the human beings involved in our justice system. He reminded his audience that "the more than 2 million inmates in the United States are human beings whose minds and spirits we must try to reach."

Kennedy's critique of the American justice system was particularly noteworthy because, as a conservative member of the Court (appointed by President Reagan in 1988), he had typically voted to uphold the very same sentencing practices that he now found so troubling. Coming from another source, his observations would have attracted little public notice. Coming from a conservative Supreme Court justice, however, they garnered national attention. One of the nation's preeminent conservative jurists had added his voice to a growing chorus of citizens who believe our country's pursuit of justice has lost its intellectual, political, and moral moorings.

The four chapters that follow describe the "hidden world of punishment" in America and trace the historical developments leading up to the realities that Justice Kennedy described. Chapter 1 documents the rise and fall of the indeterminate sentencing model, the coherent approach to sentencing policy that dominated our jurisprudence for a half century and one that has since been replaced by a potpourri of disconnected sentencing practices. Chapter 2 describes how, following a 50-year period of relative stability, incarceration rates in America have quadrupled over the past three decades. Chapter 3 details the dramatic shifts in policies that govern release from prison, changes that consequently leave prisoners now less likely to be released by parole boards, more likely to be supervised following release, and significantly more likely to be sent back to prison for violating supervision rules. Chapter 4 documents the expansion of collateral sanctions, those barriers and restrictions that flow from a felony conviction.

Taken together, these chapters paint a picture of American justice that is quite troubling. In Justice Kennedy's words, "we should be startled by what we see." In simplest terms, we have witnessed a significant expansion of state power over the lives of hundreds of thousands of individuals who, in an earlier time, would not have been imprisoned, supervised by a government agency, or hobbled in their efforts to regain a footing following a felony conviction. The instrument for this expansion of state power has been the criminal justice system.

As we take this close look at the "hidden world" of punishment, we should not forget that these new realities, for the most part, reflect policy choices made by our elected officials, acting on behalf of the American public. New sentencing schemes, which have resulted in longer sentences and increased incarceration rates, were enacted by legislatures, commissions established by legislatures, or the citizens themselves (for example, California's "three strikes" laws). Reductions in discretionary release from prison, the expansion of supervision, and, to some extent, increases in parole violations have all resulted from legislative reforms. Furthermore, the expanded universe of collateral sanctions, by definition, has been created by state and federal legislatures.

In short, our legislators, acting in our name through a series of reforms large and small, have dramatically transformed our justice system over the last quarter-century. Unfortunately, this transformation has largely occurred out of public sight, as we have constructed a hidden world of punishment. Accordingly, the first step in reclaiming our justice system is to foster a public discussion about the current realities of punishment in America, particularly as experienced by the millions of prisoners, their families, and the communities to which they return. As Justice Kennedy concluded, "It is the duty of the American people to begin that discussion at once." The following chapters contribute to this important public inquiry.

1
The Rise and Fall of the Indeterminate Sentencing Ideal

The modern American correctional system can be traced to reforms instituted in colonial Pennsylvania under the leadership of the colony's founder, William Penn. Quaker reformers sought to replace such barbaric forms of punishment as pillories, gallows, and branding irons with more humane punishments, such as hard labor, fines, and forfeiture. The cornerstone of these reforms was the workhouse, a building where offenders would be held. The first workhouse, the High Street Jail, was constructed in Philadelphia in 1682. A century later, in 1790, the Quakers of Philadelphia successfully petitioned the Pennsylvania legislature to expand Philadelphia's Walnut Street Jail by adding a group of single cells that could hold convicted felons. These felons would be separated from minor offenders, separated from each other, and forbidden to speak to the other prisoners. The Quakers hoped that this form of isolation would give the felons an opportunity to reflect on their sins, repent, and return to free society less likely to violate communal norms. For this reason, these institutions were called "penitentiaries," or places where penitents could realize the error of their ways. This experiment laid the foundation for the belief that prisons should be places where criminals can be reformed (Friedman 1993).

Over the next few decades, this innovation shaped the direction of a new American institution, the penitentiary or prison. Two kinds of prisons followed the experiment in Philadelphia. The Auburn Prison, built in 1816 in New York State, included many of the core elements of the Walnut

Street Jail model. Initially, prisoners were completely isolated from each other and a regime of silence was strictly enforced. Then in 1823, after a number of suicides and self-mutilations, these extreme practices were abolished and replaced with a system isolating prisoners in their cells only at night, allowing for silent labor in congregate workshops during the day.

A second kind of prison emerged in Pennsylvania. A new prison, called the Western Penitentiary and completed in 1818, represented the first full realization of the Walnut Street Jail experiment. In the Western Penitentiary, each inmate was confined to a single cell for the entire period of his sentence. The prison resembled the spokes on a wheel, with seven cellblocks radiating from the hub. Each prisoner had a small workbench on which to make handicrafts. In addition, each cell had its own yard where the prisoner could exercise for an hour each day. Two years later, Pennsylvania built the Eastern Penitentiary, a second prison based on this isolation model.

The Auburn system ultimately prevailed, largely because this kind of prison was cheaper to build, and served as the model used to accommodate the rapid increase in imprisonment in America. In the 50 years following the opening of Auburn Prison, more than 30 state prisons were built, all using the Auburn model. Between 1840 and 1870, the number of prisoners across the country skyrocketed from 4,000 to 33,000, and the per capita rate of imprisonment more than tripled from 24 per 100,000 population to 83 per 100,000 population, a rate of prison growth similar to that seen recently (American Correctional Association 1983).

The basic architectural outlines of the American prison were fully developed by the early 19th century, and have not changed much since then. Then and now, we house individuals convicted of serious crimes in large, secure facilities with congregate eating and working environments, using solitary confinement for disciplinary purposes. What has changed, however, is the conceptual "architecture" of imprisonment. Specifically, the framework for deciding the length of a prison sentence, the method for deciding when a prisoner can be released, and the relationship between a released prisoner and the state have all undergone significant transformations.

The Origins of the Indeterminate Sentencing Model

In the mid-1800s, sentences to state penitentiaries were "flat" (i.e., for defined periods of time). Today, we would call them "determinate" sentences—prison terms established by judges at the time of sentencing that could not be altered. The first chink in the armor of the determinate sentencing model, as practiced in the 19th century, was the adoption of the concept of "good time." A number of prison administrators, believing that prisoners (the "penitents" in the penitentiary) would respond favorably to incentives for good behavior, asked state legislatures to enact "good time" provisions so that well-behaved inmates could see their sentences reduced. New York enacted such a law as early as 1817, but most "good time" laws were passed after 1850. By 1869, 23 states had enacted these laws (Friedman 1993, 159).

Influence from Abroad

Interestingly, the origins of the American system of indeterminate sentencing, the mainstay of our jurisprudence for a century, can be traced to two prison reformers, not judicial reformers—neither of them an American. Captain Alexander Maconochie, a Scotsman, worked as a prison warden in Australia during the mid-1800s and was responsible for Norfolk Island, the worst of England's penal colonies (Morris 2002). Maconochie came to the conclusion that the flat sentence—in which a convict was sentenced to a fixed term—was counterproductive. Therefore, he developed a different approach, a "mark system," in which an inmate could earn his freedom before the end of his prison term providing he worked hard and demonstrated good behavior. In Maconochie's own words: "When a man keeps the key of his own prison, he is soon persuaded to fit it to the lock" (Barnes and Teeters 1959, 418).

Sir Walter Crofton, director of prisons in Ireland, shared Maconochie's critique of determinate sentencing. If penitentiaries are designed for repentance, he argued, why not release prisoners when they achieve the goal of repentance? Crofton adapted Maconochie's ideas and developed what he called the "indeterminate system" of punishment, also called the "Irish system." Under this system, an inmate could progress through a series of stages, beginning with solitary confinement, moving to group work, and then progressing to a kind of halfway house where the prisoner could work unsupervised and spend time in the community. Prisoners who completed these stages, and found employment, would subsequently be released to the community on a conditional pardon, called a "ticket of leave."[1]

Crofton made a particularly significant addition to Maconochie's idea of early release. He devised a system of supervision for the released prisoner in which he enlisted a group of upstanding citizens called "moral instructors" to oversee the released prisoner's conduct. If the prisoner failed to meet the conditions established for his release, his "ticket of leave" could be revoked and he could be returned to prison, up to the maximum period of the original sentence. With these ingredients, Sir Walter Crofton's Irish system first embodied the two critical elements of the modern system of indeterminate sentencing: (1) a prisoner could earn his freedom through work and good behavior, and (2) he could be released fully if he maintained good behavior while on conditional release.

Early Reform Movements

The new thinking of Maconochie and Crofton attracted the attention of American prison administrators and reformers. In the mid-19th century, the conditions in America were right for testing new ideas about prison management. Prison populations had soared, rising 72 percent between 1860 and 1870. Nearly every state had a penitentiary, but most were overcrowded. In the 1860s, a private watchdog group in New York commissioned Rev. Enoch Wines and Theodore Dwight to conduct an inspection of American and Canadian prisons. Their study, *Report on the Prisons and Reformatories of the United States and Canada* (1867), concluded, "there is not a prison system in the United States . . . which seeks the reformation of its subjects as a primary object" (Wines and Dwight 1867, 62). Just a few years after this report was released, cries for prison reform were resounding around the world.

Wines called for an international conference of prison reformers, which met in Cincinnati in 1870 as the National Congress on Penitentiary and Reformatory Discipline. Delegates came from 24 states, Canada, and South America. Wines began the conference by presenting his report on prison conditions in North America. Sir Walter Crofton then presented a paper describing the "Irish system" of earned release and postprison supervision. Zebulon R. Brockway, a prison administrator from Detroit interested in developing scientific principles of prison management, also gave a speech urging that reformation, not punishment, should be the goal of imprisonment. This historic conference resulted in the adoption of the "Declaration of Principles," a revolutionary document that provided the framework for American sentencing and correctional policies for the next century. Among other things, the Declaration called for a program of full industrial training in prison, the abolition of the system of contract labor, more judicious exercise of the pardoning power, improved prison architecture, a system of uniform prison statistics, and pointed to the necessity of making society at large realize its responsibility for crime conditions. The foundation for the Declaration was the belief that crime was "a sort of moral disease" and, therefore, the "great object [of] . . . the treatment of criminals . . . should be [their] moral regeneration . . . the reformation of criminals, not the infliction of vindictive suffering" (Wines 1871, 541).

Two key provisions of the Declaration of Principles are important for this discussion of the rise of indeterminate sentencing in America. Overshadowed by the Declaration's grand statements of the moral justifications for imprisonment were two rather technical recommendations regarding the best way to determine the length of a prison term. First, in Principle III, the National Congress of Penitentiary and Reformatory Discipline proposed that "progressive classification of prisoners, based on character and worked on some well-adjusted mark system, should be established" (Wines 1871, 541), meaning that prisoners could earn their release and serve part of their sentence in the community on a "ticket of leave." Second, in Principle VIII, the Congress recommended that "pre-emptory [determinate] sentences ought to be replaced by those of indeterminate length. Sentences limited only by satisfactory proof of reformation should be substituted for those measured by mere lapse of time" (541–42). With these two recommendations, the prison administrators and reformers gathered in Cincinnati ratified the concepts of earned early release, now called parole,[2] and indeterminate sentencing.[3] For the next 100 years, the framework of the Cincinnati conference defined American thinking on sentencing and correctional issues.

Early Legislation

It did not take long for the concept of indeterminate sentencing to find its way into legislation. In 1877, New York State passed a law stating that judges could not "fix the limit or duration" of sentences for young offenders sent to a reformatory. Rather, reformatory administrators would grade prisoners' behavior and, once the young people had accumulated the requisite "marks," they could be released. Other states soon followed suit and extended this concept into the adult system. In 1885, Ohio enacted one of the first parole programs in the nation, allowing for prisoners to be released before completing their sentences. Decisions regarding inmate releases were to be made at the discretion of a prison's board of managers, and parolees would remain under the parole board's legal custody (Friedman 1993). By 1900, five states had adopted the indeterminate sentencing approach. And by 1920, just 50 years after the Cincinnati conference, every state except Florida, Mississippi, and Virginia had a parole system. By 1923, approximately half of the inmates in state prisons had received an indeterminate sentence, and about half of all prison releases were releases to parole supervision.

The transformation of American sentencing and corrections policies was nearly complete. It had taken place quickly. Moreover, the consensus supporting these reforms was broad. As historian David Rothman noted:

> The rapidity with which these transformations occurred, the fact that criminal justice assumed a new character within twenty years, reflected the broad nature of the supporting coalition. State after state passed probation and parole legislation with little debate and no controversy. Concerned citizens, settlement house workers, criminologists, social workers, psychologists, and psychiatrists stood together with directors of charitable societies, judges, district attorneys, wardens and superintendents. To find a common goal uniting such a diverse group is itself surprising. When one remembers the stake that many of these groups had in existing practices, the harmony of views becomes still more astonishing. Judges were supporting a procedure that transferred their sentencing power to a parole board; wardens were almost unanimously in favor of measures that appeared to be anti-institutional. Traditionally hard-line, "no-coddling-the-criminal" types such as district attorneys also backed programs that could be seen as being distinctly soft on the offender. And that settlement house workers and social workers agreed with directors of charitable societies was no less unprecedented. (1980, 44–45)

The early "tickets of leave" experiments by Maconochie and Crofton, embedded in the revolutionary concept of indeterminate sentencing articulated at the Cincinnati conference, had profoundly restructured the conceptual "architecture" of American imprisonment. In this new way of thinking, one quite foreign to Philadelphia's Quaker reformers, prisoners could now earn their way out of prison, and serve a portion of their sentence under supervision in the community. A link had been created between the purposes of imprisonment and life in the community following imprisonment. This connection would survive until indeterminate sentencing itself came under attack by another generation of reformers.

The Indeterminate Sentencing Model in Operation

The indeterminate sentencing model that emerged from the reforms of the 19th century is fairly straightforward. In establishing the criminal code for the state, the state legislature sets broad ranges of possible sentences for criminal offenses. When sentencing an offender found guilty of a particular offense, the judge determines a "range within the range," sentencing the offender to a period of years with a lower and upper limit. If the offender receives a prison sentence, a parole board later reviews the prisoner's progress toward rehabilitation and assesses his readiness to return to society. If these conditions are met, the board is authorized to release him from confinement. The former prisoner then serves the remainder of his sentence in the community, but can be returned to prison if he fails to observe the conditions that the parole board placed on his liberty.

By the early 1920s, nearly every state in the union, the federal government, and the District of Columbia operated under an indeterminate sentencing model, yet these sentencing regimes were not necessarily identical. There were, in fact, important differences. First, the ranges established by the states showed substantial variation. For instance, the Idaho legislature provided that an offender convicted of first-degree burglary could be sentenced to probation or a prison term of 1 to 15 years.[4] New York's legislature, by contrast, provided that an offender convicted of the same crime could receive a sentence of probation or a prison term of 3 to 25 years.[5] Next, sentencing judges within the same state demonstrated significant variation in their sentence practices. Because judges were granted broad discretion, a lenient judge and a stringent judge could mete out quite different sentences when facing the same set of facts. Finally, the release decisions made by parole boards—the decisions that ultimately determined the actual length of the prison sentence—varied among the states, varied over time, and varied from prisoner to prisoner. As we shall see, critics of indeterminate sentencing seized upon these discrepancies in sentencing policy and practice as ammunition in a broader intellectual and political assault on the indeterminate sentencing framework. These differences should not detract, however, from the fact that, for about 50 years, all 50 states, as well as the federal system and the District of Columbia, subscribed to the same fundamental principles in their sentencing systems. These years made up Tonry's (1999, 4) "Golden Age" of American sentencing jurisprudence.

The Three Pillars of Sentencing Philosophy

THE SEPARATION OF POWERS

This remarkable consensus reflected more than agreement on the mechanics of sentencing; it also reflected an appreciation of three bedrock principles: the separation of powers, the role of official discretion, and the purposes of the criminal sanction. Deeply embedded in the indeterminate sentencing framework is a particular theory of governance, a view of the proper relationship among the branches of government in the imposition of criminal sanctions. In this view, the legislature is responsible for articulating the substantive criminal law and criminal procedure for the state and for establishing a broad range of possible penalties for crimes. The judicial branch is responsible for overseeing criminal trials, monitoring the integrity of criminal proceedings, and—when an individual has been found to have violated the law—imposing an appropriate sentence. Judges are expected to determine, within the broad range of permissible sentences, which sentence is most appropriate for the individual offender. In making this decision, the sentencing judge is expected to consider the seriousness of the offense, the nature and extent of the offender's prior criminal history (if any), the offender's social history, and the likelihood that the offender could be rehabilitated. The executive branch also plays a critical role in the criminal justice system. In addition to its responsibility for arresting and prosecuting offenders, the executive branch, through its corrections department, manages the institutions that hold prisoners. Another executive branch agency, the parole board (whose members are usually appointed by the governor), then decides whether and when to release the prisoners, thereby determining the end date of the sentence's prison portion. Finally, parole agencies (sometimes located within state departments of corrections, sometimes established as separate executive branch agencies) supervise those individuals released from prison, determine whether they are meeting their conditions of parole, and decide whether to "violate" (i.e., deem in violation of parole) those who have failed to meet parole conditions and recommend to the parole board their return to prison.

The key point here *is not* that the indeterminate sentencing model makes broad allocations of responsibility across the three branches of government—any sentencing system would expect legislatures to define the criminal law and authorize punishments, judges to pronounce sentence, and corrections agencies to house and supervise offenders. Rather, what *is* noteworthy is the balance struck between the articulation of general punishment levels and the specification of actual punishment levels for individual offenders. In the indeterminate framework, legislatures are supposed to do the former; judges (and, to some extent, parole boards) are supposed to do the latter. In reality, this balance allows elected representatives to appear to be tough on crime without determining actual punishments for criminal offenders (Zimring, Hawkins, and Kamin 2001). Legislators can rightfully claim credit for passing sentencing laws that allow long prison sentences to be imposed for crimes that worry the public. At the same time, legislators can rightfully point out that the lower end of the sentencing range allows for more lenient treatment, making it possible for judges to go easier on first-time offenders or those the public might think deserve leniency. This balance also allows legislators to distance themselves from a particular sentencing decision that ignites public controversy. A legislator (or other public official) could criticize a judge for being too lenient (or even too harsh), saying that a particular sentence was too short (or too long). Similarly, a legislator could criticize a parole board's decision to release a prisoner at a particular time, but could not challenge the right of the parole board to make the decision. Implicit in this political posturing is a tacit recognition of the principle of the separation of powers: Legislators create the broad framework of punishments, but judges have the final authority to make decisions, subject to parole board review.

THE ROLE OF DISCRETION

A second characteristic of the indeterminate sentencing framework is its reliance on government officials' exercise of discretion. Judges are expected to consider various factors in determining an appropriate punishment, including, among others, the crime's severity, the extent of any prior criminal convictions, the offender's family circumstances, and his or her prospects for rehabilitation. Parole boards are expected to examine another set of factors in determining whether to release the prisoner on parole, including, among others, his or her progress toward rehabilitation, behavior in prison, job prospects in the community, family support, remorse, and prospects for a successful return home. Finally, parole administrators are expected to determine what combination of services and supervision would promote continued rehabilitation and, if a release condition is breached, whether the facts warrant recommending the parolee's return to prison. All of these decisions require the exercise of enormous discretion and envision a system of individualized justice. A system of indeterminate sentencing inherently relies on the sound professional judgment of judges, parole boards, and parole officers, all of whom must make critical decisions affecting an offender's liberty with remarkable latitude.

THE PURPOSES OF THE CRIMINAL SANCTION

The third characteristic of the indeterminate sentencing model—and the one most closely related to this discussion of the pathways of prisoner reentry—is the recognition that, in most cases, time in prison is merely the midpoint between a criminal conviction and a return to free society. A major purpose of the criminal sanction is rehabilitation, not punishment. However, the operating mechanisms of indeterminate sentencing also embody a concern about life after prison. Judges are expected to determine an offender's likelihood of rehabilitation. Parole boards are expected to assess a prisoner's preparation for release—both by determining whether the prisoner participated in programs designed to facilitate success on the outside, and by ensuring that the prisoner had arranged for a job, housing, and family support in the community. Finally, parole officers are seen as the link between life in prison and life in the community. Their job, under the classic indeterminate sentencing model, is to help the returning prisoner find a job, work on improving personal skills and abilities, stay away from negative community influences, attend treatment programs if needed, and move toward successful reintegration.

The Pillars Weaken

As the indeterminate sentencing system came under attack in the 1970s, these three pillars of American sentencing philosophy weakened as well. None was eliminated from our modern sentencing architecture. While legislative, judicial, and executive branches still play quite different roles, the balance of power has shifted significantly. In most states and the federal government, legislatures, legislatively created sentencing commissions, and even the general public (acting through voter initiatives and public referenda) have now severely restricted the role of judges in determining the extent of criminal punishment. Judges still exercise some discretion, but the scope of that discretion is a pale version of its former self. Justice is still individualized—in the sense that sentencing judges may consider an offender's background characteristics—but the sentencing equation is now weighted by the severity of the current offense and the extent of the prior criminal record. Finally, as the architecture of indeterminate sentencing weakened, our sentencing practices lost their focus on life after prison. Parole boards still operate in many states, but other states have abolished them, thereby eliminating an important link between life in prison and life on the outside. Although attention to prisoner reintegration is still a factor in the operations of American sentencing and corrections policy, the dominant philosophy today is retribution, not rehabilitation—just desserts, not prisoner reintegration.

The Attack on Indeterminate Sentencing

Beginning in the early 1970s, the reigning philosophical framework of American sentencing and corrections policy came under attack from both the left and right ends of the political spectrum. Over a relatively short period, each of the three pillars of indeterminate sentencing—the separation of powers, the role of discretion, and the purpose of the criminal sanction—was weakened, called into question at the most fundamental level. The practice of assigning significant sentencing responsibilities to the judicial branch was criticized as an inappropriate exercise of unchecked, unguided, and unreviewable power. Reliance on the exercise of discretion by judges, corrections administrators, parole boards, and parole officers was criticized as arbitrary, racially discriminatory, and fundamentally unfair. The belief in the individualization of justice, the potential for redemption, and the goal of rehabilitation was roundly characterized as tantamount to coddling criminals. In addition, concern for offenders' reintegration was seen as the idealistic view of social engineers who minimized the offenders' propensity to cause harm.

How did the "Golden Age" of American sentencing jurisprudence so quickly come to an end? No single event or conceptual breakthrough changed our approach to sentencing and corrections policy. Rather, the convergence, in a relatively short time, of a set of mutually reinforcing critiques and counterproposals weakened the reigning sentencing ideology. In rapid succession, a blue ribbon commission issued a fundamental challenge to accepted sentencing ideals, a Quaker committee challenged the notion of voluntary treatment in the criminal justice system, a respected federal judge attacked the exercise of judicial discretion, and a team of respected academics concluded that no programs had been proven effective in rehabilitating offenders.

In 1971, the Field Foundation and the New World Foundation, two New York City philanthropies, created the Committee for the Study of Incarceration. Liberal Republican Charles E. Goodell, the former United States Senator from New York, chaired the committee. In his introduction to the committee's final report, Goodell stated the group's purpose as follows:

> There was growing disenchantment with prisons, and with the disparities and irrationalities of the sentencing process. Yet reformers lacked a rationale to guide them in their quest for alternatives, save for the more-than-century-old notion of rehabilitation that had nurtured the rise of the penitentiary. The purpose of our study was to consider afresh the fundamental concepts concerning what is to be done with the offender after conviction. (von Hirsch 1976, xv)

The new rationale developed by the committee represented a significant departure from the prevailing wisdom. Another expert, Andrew von Hirsch (1976), went on to argue that punishment should be based on the principle of "just desserts" or, in his words, "commensurate desserts." According to this principle, the severity of the sentence should be directly proportional to the severity of the crime. Hirsch argued that a mild sentence undermined the seriousness of the crime committed, therefore denigrating the violated law's importance.

Indeterminate sentencing practices drew harsh criticism from the left as well. In 1971, the American Friends Service Committee, an antiwar Quaker organization, published a report decrying class and racial biases apparent among the disparate sentences handed down for similar offenses. The committee's report proposed to remedy these discrepancies with more uniform sentencing rules and guidelines. Albeit for different reasons, Marvin Frankel, a respected federal judge, came to similar conclusions about the failings of American sentencing jurisprudence. He described judicial sentencing discretion as wielding "almost wholly unchecked and sweeping powers . . . terrifying and intolerable for a society that professes devotion to the rule of law" (1973, 5). Like von Hirsch, Frankel also attacked the rehabilitative ideal underpinning the indeterminate sentencing framework, concluding that most criminals committed crimes out of cold, rational calculations of reward and risk and, therefore, made poor candidates for rehabilitative "treatment." Most notably, Frankel proposed a basic framework for sentencing commissions that many states soon adopted in their efforts to limit judges' discretion when imposing sentences.

Robert Martinson (1974) and his colleagues landed a devastating blow to the rehabilitative ideal with a controversial report on the effectiveness of prison programs. Their report surveyed 231 studies examining the relationship between adult prison education programs and recidivism rates. Due to the bold nature of their conclusion—that these programs had little effect on inmate recidivism—the Martinson report gained national fame as articles appeared in major newspapers, magazines, and journals trumpeting the conclusion, "Nothing works!" As a result, many conservative voices cited Martinson's report as a rationale for harsher sentencing policies.

These attacks on the pillars of American penal policy ultimately carried the day. By the end of the decade, forces of reform had been set loose in the country, breaking out of the restraints of the reigning ideology and rearranging the contours of American jurisprudence and penal policy. Both the reality and the rhetoric of American sentencing policy were transformed. Although it is true that the outlines of the indeterminate sentencing framework can still be found in many American states, the intellectual ground has shifted, and the Golden Age is over. No new framework has taken the place once occupied by indeterminate sentencing.

In some states, a modern observer would find few significant differences between sentencing policy in 2000 and the one that existed a generation ago. Nevertheless, variety is the norm and the pace of sentencing reform has been dizzying. In 1976, Maine became the first state to abandon the indeterminate sentencing model with its abolishment of parole; California and Indiana followed shortly thereafter (Petersilia 2003). In the late 1970s, Minnesota became the first state to create a sentencing commission, as recommended by Judge Frankel. This commission established guidelines, the first of which took effect in 1980, restricting the exercise of judicial discretion in sentencing criminals. Since then, 25 states and the federal government have followed this example (Tonry 1996). In 1984, Washington became the first state to adopt "truth-in-sentencing" legislation, which required that individuals convicted of certain offenses (typically violent crimes) must serve 85 percent of their sentences before being eligible for parole. These laws severely restricted both judicial and parole board discretion, and effectively lengthened average prison terms. Since then, aided by the infusion of $1.9 billion in federal funds, 29 states have emulated this example with minor variations (Sabol et al. 2002).[6] In 1994, the voters of California passed a referendum requiring that offenders convicted of multiple felonies serve a life sentence. Since then, Georgia, Washington, Florida, and the federal government have enacted similar "three strikes and you're out" laws, although none is as draconian as the California model. A number of states have enacted laws imposing mandatory minimum sentences, thereby depriving judges of the community supervision option and generally increasing the size of the prison population.

These waves of sentencing reform have had far-reaching consequences. As will be discussed in greater detail later in Part 1, the prison population has increased dramatically after a 50-year period of relative stability, methods for releasing individuals from prison and supervising their return home have changed significantly, and the network of collateral sanctions that accompany felony convictions has grown in complexity as never before. As we consider next these new realities of punishment in modern America, we recall that our nation has been the crucible for new ideas about the role of the criminal sanction, specifically the role of prisons, as part of society's response to crime. One hundred and thirty years ago, the concept of indeterminate sentencing emerged during an era of prison expansion and reformers' calls for a new approach to criminal sentencing. Today, we have witnessed another era of prison expansion and hear a cacophony of new proposals for the justice system's response to crime. Whether a new idea for our sentencing jurisprudence emerges from the modern era of mass incarceration remains to be seen.

NOTES

1. See Friedman (1993, 161).

2. The word "parole" was first used by the Boston penologist Samuel G. Howe in 1846. It comes from the French language, literally meaning "word of honor" (Giardini 1959, 9).

3. Interestingly, the concept of indeterminate sentencing endorsed by the Congress meant that a prisoner should be kept in prison until he had reformed. As Rev. Wines stated at the Congress, "imprisonment ought to be continued till reformation has been effected, and, if that happy consummation is never attained, then during the prisoner's natural life." If a prisoner never reformed, he should be kept there until he died. One is reminded of Capt. Maconochie's declaration: The keys to the prison door were held by the prisoner himself—all he had to do was repent and reform—even if he died first. Ironically, the Declaration of Principles took the reformation ideal to its extreme conclusion.

4. *Idaho Code,* sec. 18-1403, 19-2601.

5. NYS Penal Law 40-85.

6. Under the Violent Offender Incarceration and Truth-in-Sentencing Incentive (VOI/TIS) Grant Program, approximately $1.9 billion was available from fiscal year 1996 through fiscal year 1999.

2

The Growth in Incarceration

I n 1973, Professors Alfred Blumstein and Jacqueline Cohen published "A Theory of the Stability of Punishment." The article begins by recognizing the work of Emile Durkheim (1893), who postulated that crime is a normal attribute of stable societies and that there will always be crime because there will always be people who fail to internalize the norms and values of the group, what he called the "collective conscience." Blumstein and Cohen built upon Durkheim's insight by positing that stable societies also maintain stable levels of punishment. They theorized that if the level of criminal behavior declined, society would respond by redefining previously minor infractions as punishable crimes. If, on the other hand, criminal behavior became more widespread, society would become more lenient and would not impose harsher punishment. In Blumstein and Cohen's view, the alternative—defining a large portion of the population as criminal and thereby alienating that group from mainstream society—would threaten the social fabric. Furthermore, they argued, the costs of increased incarceration would be too high and the public would be unwilling to bear the burden.

As evidence supporting their theory, Blumstein and Cohen cited the American experience with imprisonment.[1] Between 1920 and 1970, the per capita rate of incarceration in America remained stable at about 110 state and federal prisoners per 100,000 residents. This level of punishment prevailed in times of unprecedented economic expansion as well as during the Great Depression. It endured during two world wars, when hundreds of thousands of men were sent overseas and families were left to struggle with new challenges. It prevailed during the Prohibition era, and when the nation reversed course and again allowed alcohol to flow. Given this history, Blumstein and Cohen predicted that American society would maintain an equilibrium of punishment—if crime rates went down, then society would respond by developing more "rigid thresholds" and punishing people for lesser crimes; if crime rates went up, society would relax the boundaries of the criminal law and impose less punishment. In either scenario, the level of imprisonment would remain stable.

The Prison Boom

Things turned out quite differently, however. As already discussed, American crime policy, particularly its sentencing policy, began to lose its moorings in the late 1960s. These were turbulent times. The urban riots of that decade represented to many a display of wanton lawlessness. In 1968, Richard Nixon ran for president on a law-and-order platform. Crime policy, once the domain of criminal justice professionals, became dominated by electoral politics. Legislative mandates constrained official discretion, long the hallmark of our justice system. The judgment of experts was questioned by the voice of the people. American crime policy was now shaped by a new mix of "punishment and democracy" (Zimring, Hawkins, and Kamin 2001).

Sentencing policy was particularly affected. Beginning in the 1970s, the consensus around indeterminate sentencing fell apart and the center could not hold. The aftershocks of this "earthquake" could best be observed in the growth of America's prison population. Beginning in 1973 (the year Blumstein and Cohen's article appeared), the imprisonment rate in America started to increase at about 6 percent a year (figure 2.1). Since then, it has increased every year, for 30 years, and the growth of America's prison population has seemed inexorable. When crime rates declined, first in the early 1980s and then again, more dramatically, in the late 1990s, the rate of imprisonment increased. When crime rates soared, as in the late 1980s, the rate of imprisonment also increased. The United States prison population increased by half in the 1990s, a time of unprecedented economic expansion and historically low rates of poverty and unemployment. Furthermore, during the recessions of the early

Figure 2.1. *Incarceration Rates in the United States, 1930–2002*

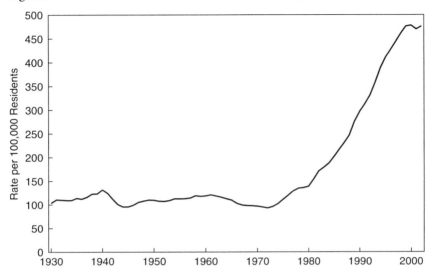

Sources: U.S. Bureau of Justice Statistics, *Prisoners in State and Federal Institutions on December 31*, annual, and *Correctional Populations in the United States*, annual. http://www.census.gov/statab/hist/02HS0024.xls.

1980s and early 1990s, the country built more prisons. Whether times were good or bad, whether crime was on the rise or on the decline, we put more people in prison.

The results have been dramatic. In 1973, there were slightly more than 200,000 people in prison; by 2003, 1.4 million individuals were in prison in America. In 2002, the per capita rate of imprisonment stood at 476 per 100,000, more than quadruple the prevailing rate between 1925 and 1973. Including jails in the calculation increases the rate to 700 people per 100,000 (Harrison and Beck 2003), making America the global leader in the use of imprisonment, slightly ahead of Russia (601), Belarus (554), South Africa (402), and Thailand (401), and far ahead of England and Wales (132), Canada (102), France (85), and Japan (48) (International Centre for Prison Studies n.d.).

For the past generation, the level of punishment has certainly not been stable. Rather, as the new politics of crime policy have taken hold, American society has expanded the use of punishment—particularly imprisonment, but including criminal justice supervision and the network of collateral sanctions discussed in the next two chapters—to unprecedented levels. According to the Bureau of Justice Statistics, about 5.6 million U.S. residents—or 1 in every 37 adults—have served time in prison (Bonczar and Beck 2003). As some observers of criminal justice policies in America have concluded, we now live in an era of "mass incarceration" (Drucker 2002; Mauer and Chesney-Lind 2002).

This growth in the prison population has profound consequences for our society. The racial disparities are particularly striking. In 2002, slightly more than 10 percent of African-American men between the ages of 25 and 29 years old were in prison, compared with 2.4 percent of Hispanic men and 1.2 percent of white men. Assuming no changes in incarceration rates, nearly one in six Hispanic men and one in three African-American men will be sentenced to state or federal prison at some point in their lives (figure 2.2). Although their chances of incarceration are much lower, African-American women still face a 5.6 percent lifetime probability of going to prison, nearly the same as white men (5.9 percent) (Bonczar and Beck 2003). As we will discuss later, the disparate racial impact stemming from mass incarceration causes ripple effects throughout minority communities—particularly the African-American community—weakening the family, diminishing earnings levels, and reducing participation in the electoral process. At a very fundamental level, the realities of mass incarceration undermine America's pursuit of racial justice.

The fiscal consequences are also substantial. Between 1973 and 2000, the number of state prisons nearly doubled—from 592 to 1,023 (Lawrence and Travis 2004). The federal and state governments now spend $60 bil-

Figure 2.2. *Lifetime Likelihood of Incarceration in the United States, 2001*

Black males	32.2%	1 in 3
Hispanic males	17.2%	1 in 6
White males	5.9%	1 in 17
Black females	5.6%	1 in 18
Hispanic females	2.2%	1 in 45
White females	0.9%	1 in 111

Source: Bonczar and Beck (2003).
Note: These percentages reflect likelihood of incarceration if current incarceration rates remain unchanged.

lion a year to house 1.4 million individuals in prison (Bauer and Owens 2004). Except for Medicaid, corrections expenditures have been the fastest-growing portion of state budgets, approaching the $74 billion the states spent on higher education in 2000 (Justice Policy Institute 2002). Between 1977 and 1999, state and local expenditures for corrections rose by 946 percent, far outpacing the growth in outlays for education (370 percent), hospitals and health care (411 percent), and public welfare (510 percent) (Gifford 2002). Even the simplest managerial challenges related to managing the far-flung prison systems seem daunting. State and federal governments are now responsible for 1,668 correctional facilities, with approximately 750,000 employees (Bauer and Owens 2004).

The new realities of mass incarceration have resulted in troubling distortions in traditional governmental responsibilities for maintaining prisons. In 2002, for example, almost 94,000 state and federal prisoners were housed in facilities run by private corporations, raising issues about the proper exercise of state power over the management of institutions of confinement (Harrison and Beck 2003). In addition, to accommodate prison overcrowding in one state and underutilization in another, state corrections agencies have entered into interstate compacts whereby states agree to house each other's prisoners. This situation raises questions about which state is truly responsible for overseeing punishments for violations of its laws. Furthermore, pursuant to the 1994 Crime Act, the federal government provided $2.7 billion in grants to the states (through the Violent Offender Incarceration and Truth-in-Sentencing [VOI/TIS] Incentive Grant Program) to help defray prison construction costs conditional on the states enacting certain sentencing reform measures. This initiative brings up important questions about the federal government's role in state criminal justice policies (Sabol et al. 2002). Finally, because the U.S. Census counts prisoners in the jurisdiction where they are incarcerated, the growth of prisons in suburban and rural communities across the country has resulted in distortions of the very meaning of "resident." In 13 counties in the 10 states with the highest rates of prison growth, more than 20 percent of the counties' "residents" were actually housed in prisons in 2000. Because many federal funding programs allocate money according to the census count, these counties receive a windfall of federal financial aid (Lawrence and Travis 2004). And, because apportionment of political representation is also based on the census, these counties stand to gain political power by representing "residents" who cannot vote.

The rest of this chapter describes the growth of America's prison population, with a special focus on the factors relating to prisoner reentry. In particular, it examines the dynamics of the prison expansion, identifying the critical reasons for such an increase. Special attention is paid here to the rise in drug arrests and the increased average length of stay in prison. The category of prisoners called "churners" (Lynch and Sabol 2001)—namely those prisoners who are released from prison, placed under criminal justice supervision, then sent back to prison for violating the conditions of their release—is then discussed. Next, we identify dimensions of the new reality of incarceration in America that particularly affect returning prisoners' likelihood of succeeding in the community. A profile of the reentry cohort—a snapshot of who is coming home in the era of "mass incarceration"—is then presented. The chapter concludes with some thoughts about the nexus between the current levels of incarceration and the challenges prisoners face when they return to free society.

Understanding the Dynamics of the Prison Expansion

There is no single explanation for the dramatic growth in America's prison population. Many factors have contributed to this massive shift in criminal justice policy, including changes in the crime rate, shifts in sentencing policy, new approaches to drug enforcement, and tougher policies regarding supervision following release from prison. In this section, we will attempt to discern the distinct contributions of these social forces and policy shifts. In so doing, we will see that no consistent narrative exists for the 30 years that have marked the steady growth in our incarceration rate. The relative importance of these contributing factors has shifted markedly over time; therefore, the reasons for America's high rate of incarceration at the beginning of the 21st century are quite different from the reasons for the growth of imprisonment 30 years ago. Furthermore, the complicated history of the nation's prison expansion makes it even more difficult to predict the future of imprisonment in America.

Changes in Crime Rates

We begin our analysis of the growth in imprisonment by disaggregating the overall increase, examining the increase by distinct types of criminal behavior. This allows us to isolate, for special attention, the role of drug enforcement policies in the growth of our nation's prisons. Figure 2.3 illustrates how the incarceration rate for each of the six major crime categories rose between 1980 and 2001. For five of those crime types, the growth was significant but not dramatic. The incarceration rate for murder increased 201 percent, for sexual assault 361 percent, for robbery 65 percent, for assault 306 percent, and for burglary 66 percent.[2] For drug offenses, however, the growth was dramatic. The per capita incarceration rate for drug offenses in America grew by more than 930 percent from 1980 to 1996, reflecting the nation's decision to launch a "war on drugs."

Two trends in the nation's enforcement practices account for this dramatic surge in the incarceration rate for drug offenses. First, we have witnessed significant increases in the drug arrest rate. In 1980, there were fewer than 300 arrests for drug crimes per 100,000 adults. By 1996, the drug arrest rate more than doubled to almost 700 arrests per 100,000

Figure 2.3. *Incarceration Rates by Crime Type, 1980–2001*

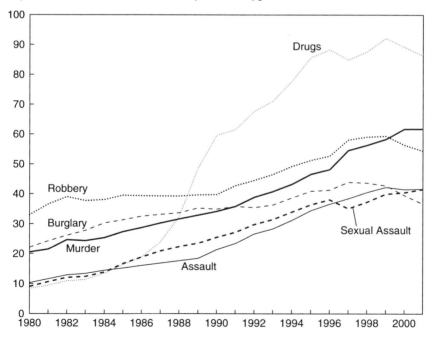

Sources: Beck (2000); Beck and Harrison (2001); Beck and Mumola (1999); Blumstein and Beck (1999); Harrison and Beck (2002, 2003); U.S. Census Bureau (2000, 2002).

adults. Second, we have experienced even more pronounced increases in the share of these arrests that have resulted in prison sentences. In 1980, there were 2 prison admissions for every 100 arrests for drug crimes. By 1990, that number had quintupled, rising to 10 admissions per 100 drug arrests. By 1996, the rate had fallen to 8 admissions per 100 arrests, but a number still four times the 1980 rate (Blumstein and Beck 1999). In short, in a relatively brief time, the nation significantly "ramped up" the use of arrests and imprisonment as our response to drug offenses.

The implications for the prison population were profound. As admissions to prison rose steadily between 1980 and 1996 (see below), the proportion of prison admissions that were the result of drug crimes more than tripled. In 1981, 9 percent of prison admissions were for drug crimes; by 1996, the share of admissions that were drug offenders had risen to 30 percent (Austin and Irwin 2001). Notably, the time served by incarcerated drug offenders varied over this period. In 1980, the estimated time served by drug offenders was just under 2 years. By 1987, average time served dropped to 1.3 years; between 1987 and 1998, however, when the war on drugs was in high gear, the estimated time served increased by a full year. From a reentry perspective, the implications of these trends are quite clear: substantially larger numbers of the cohort of prisoners returning home in the latter part of the 20th century were incarcerated for drug offenses for longer periods of time.

Next we examine the impact of drug enforcement policies through a different lens—the differential impact on African Americans (figure 2.4). If we disaggregate the prison admissions for drug convictions according to the race of the prisoner, we see that the numbers of admissions for whites, blacks, and Hispanics were remarkably similar for the first seven years of the 1980s. Beginning in 1987, however, the number of admissions for blacks resulting from drug offenses skyrocketed, nearly quadrupling in three years, then increasing steadily until it reached in 2000 a level more than 26 times the level in 1983. Over this same period of time, from 1983, the number of whites and Hispanics admitted on drug convictions increased as well, but less dramatically. The number of whites admitted for drug offenses in 2000 was only eight times the number admitted in 1983. For Hispanics, the number of 2000 drug admissions was 22 times the number of 1983 admissions.

What happened in the mid-1980s that might explain this staggering shift? Crack cocaine exploded upon the streets of urban America, drawing large numbers of inner-city youth, mostly minorities, into the new drug trade, with the attendant risks of apprehension, prosecution, and

Figure 2.4. *Prison Drug Admissions by Race, 1983–2000*

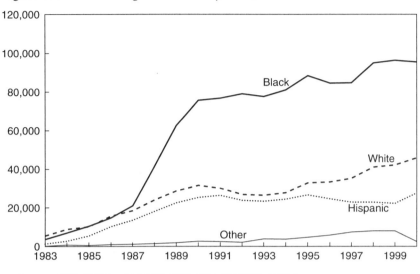

Sources: 1983–1998: Iguchi (2001); 1999–2000: BJS (1999, 2000b).

imprisonment (Blumstein and Wallman 2000). Not only did the black and Hispanic communities bear the brunt of increased violence and drug addiction associated with the emergence of crack, these communities also lost tens of thousands of men and women to prison each year.

Tougher Sentencing Policies

The second step in our analysis is to determine whether the overall increase in incarceration can be attributed to changes in the crime rate, improvements in the rate of criminal convictions, or increases in the length of sentences served by those sent to prison. In their review of these questions, Blumstein and Beck (1999) found that only 22 percent of the growth in imprisonment between 1990 and 1996 could be attributed to increases in the crime rate. Furthermore, only 15 percent of the growth in the prison population could be attributed to increases in sentence length, or more specifically, to increases in the amount of time served in prison, including time served on recommitment following a parole violation. Most of the rise in incarceration—63 percent—could be attributed to an increase in the level of prison commitments per arrest. In other words, during this period, the criminal justice system had simply become much more punitive, sending a higher percentage of people to prison relative to the number of arrests made by the police. This important shift principally reflects tougher sentencing policies, and in particular the increased use of mandatory minimum sentences.

Figure 2.5 illustrates the combined effects of two decades of these "tough on crime" sentencing policies. Between 1991 and 1997, the percentage of soon-to-be-released prisoners who reported serving five years or more almost doubled, rising from 13 to 21 percent. The percentage who had served between one and five years decreased from more than 60 percent to slightly more than 50 percent. On the other hand, the share of exiting prisoners who had served one year or less declined from 33 percent in 1991 to 17 percent in 1997. The overall effect of these shifts was a 27 percent increase in time served—from an average of 21 months for those released in 1993 to 28 months for those released in 1998 (Lynch and Sabol 2001).

These same policies have had another effect, with profound long-term consequences for the management of American penal institutions. In

Figure 2.5. *Time Served by Soon-to-Be-Released Inmates, 1991 and 1997*

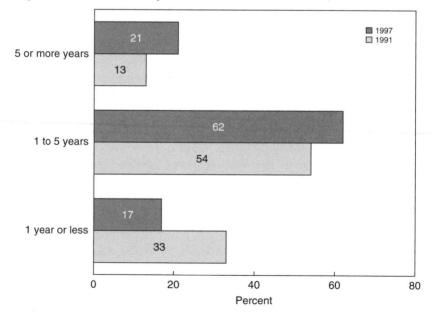

Source: Lynch and Sabol (2001).

1992, 69,845 individuals were serving a life sentence in American prisons; 17.8 percent of these (12,453) had been sentenced to life without parole. In 2003, that number had increased 83 percent—127,677 persons were serving life sentences, one-quarter (26.3 percent) of whom (33,633) were not eligible for parole (Mauer, King, and Young 2004). As this population ages, American prisons will become home to an increasing number of geriatric prisoners for whom the possibility of reentry into society is remote at best.

As a result of these shifts in the dynamics of prison expansion in the 1990s, the profile of the cohort of prisoners coming home shifted as well. Between 1990 and 1998, the portion of released prisoners who had been convicted of drug crimes increased (26 percent vs. 32 percent). However, the portion convicted of property crimes decreased (36 percent vs. 32 percent) and the share convicted of violent crimes remained constant (24 percent vs. 25 percent). Most telling is the fact that fully one-third (36 percent) of the prisoners released in 1998 had been reincarcerated for violating the conditions of their supervision following an earlier prison sentence. This population reflects a failed effort at reentry. These prisoners—ones who are returned to prison because they failed on parole the last time they were released, stay in prison a short time, and then face a high risk of being returned to prison—have been aptly called "churners" (Lynch and Sabol 2001). Because understanding this phenomenon is central to meeting the new challenges of prisoner reentry, we now turn our attention to a closer examination of "churning."

Churning and Incarceration

For many prisoners, being sent to prison is not a new experience. In fact, almost half (44 percent) of the people released from our state prisons in 1997 had been in prison before (Langan and Levin 2002). On one level, this trend is perhaps not surprising—the recidivism rate of former prisoners has historically been high and many of them commit crimes that warrant a new prison term. Over the past 20 years, however, the trip back to prison has taken a quite different turn. In 1980, about 27,000 individuals sent to America's prisons—or 17 percent of all prison admissions—were parole violators. This means that these individuals were still under legal supervision for their most recent felony conviction, had likely served time in prison, and were being sent back to prison for violating a condition of their supervision. Some had been arrested for new crimes; others had violated "technical" conditions of supervision, such as failing to observe a curfew, missing appointments with the parole officer, or moving to a new address without permission. Twenty years later, more than one-third (35 percent) of prison admissions resulted from parole violations. In absolute terms, more than 200,000 parole violators were sent back to prison, a staggering seven-fold increase over 1980. In other words, about as many people were returned to prison for parole violations in 2000 as were admitted in 1980 for all reasons (Travis and Lawrence 2002a).

Two major factors have combined to create this new reality. First, as we will discuss in more detail in chapter 3, the number of prisoners being released to supervision each year increased since 1980, swelling the ranks of parolees. The equation is simple: because we have placed more people under supervision, more are eligible for parole revocation and return to prison. Second, as we shall discuss in chapter 5, this rapid return to prison of large numbers of individuals also reflects the high rates of re-arrest in the months immediately following release. According to a Bureau of Justice Statistics study, about 30 percent of released prisoners in its sample were rearrested within 6 months of release (Langan and Levin 2002). Within a year, 44 percent were rearrested. It stands to reason, then, that with the larger number of prisoners being released, a larger number would return to prison.

For these reasons primarily, of all prisoners, almost half—the churners— have been incarcerated before, sometimes quite recently. Todd Clear (2004) refers to this phenomenon as "reentry cycling." By whatever appellation, the consequences of this large-scale movement in and out of prison are far-reaching. From a management perspective, the population returned for parole violations is hard to handle. New prison terms among this population are typically very short, meaning that program participation and treatment options are restricted. Yet, prison managers must still treat these inmates the same as the others, including administering expensive health screening, watching for possible suicides, and integrating them into daily prison life. Because parole boards can revoke a parolee's liberty with less due process than is required for criminal convictions, the removal of these prisoners from their communities has been more abrupt than for others who come to prison after awaiting trial and conviction on new offenses.

From the perspective of the prisoners' families and social networks, the return to prison for a short period of time may be a benefit (if the individuals were causing harm) or a loss (if they were providing financial and emotional support) or both. From a larger perspective, however, churning has added a new dimension to the incarceration picture in modern America. In some ways, prisons have become more like jails, accepting a significant share of the incoming population for a very short period of time. Yet the volume of churners has artificially kept prison populations high. If, for example, the level of prison admissions for parole violators in 2000 reflected the realities of 1980 (17 percent rather than 35 percent of admissions), then about 100,000 fewer individuals would have been sent to prison.

From a reentry perspective, churning presents a difficult challenge to reformers in the reentry field—namely, managing reentry for people coming out of prison the second or third (or more) time. Particular attention must be paid to prisoners who have been serving short revocation sentences, and especially those who complete their sentences in prison and are released without supervision. Churners are an identifiable group at high risk for failure. Individuals who have failed on parole before are considerably more likely than others to be returned to prison for a parole violation or a new crime. Of those prisoners released in 1994 who had previously failed on parole, only 20 percent were successfully discharged. The remaining 80 percent were returned to prison as a result of a parole violation or a new crime (Lynch and Sabol 2001). This reality of elevated risk is further complicated by the fact that many individuals returned to prison on parole revocations complete their sentences in prison and are released without supervision. At this time, no criminal justice agency is responsible for reducing the risk these individuals pose and providing appropriate supports. Finally, because churners are typically returned to prison for short revocation sentences measured in months rather than years, the logistical barriers to the development of a sensible reentry plan are daunting. It is highly ironic that our criminal justice system is so hobbled in its ability to successfully manage the reentry of a high-risk population, individuals presumably returned to prison because they have demonstrated difficulty observing societal norms.

Before we conclude this overview of the changing nature of incarceration in America, we should step back from an analysis of the drivers and dynamics of the prison buildup to focus squarely on one certain consequence of these developments: as more people are sent to prison, more come home. By bringing a reentry perspective to this phenomenon, we face the iron law of corrections: with the exception of those who die in custody, all prisoners return to free society. As figure 2.6 illustrates, the size of both the reentry and the admissions cohorts have steadily increased

Figure 2.6. *Sentenced Prisoners Admitted to and Released from Federal and State Prisons, 1978–2001*

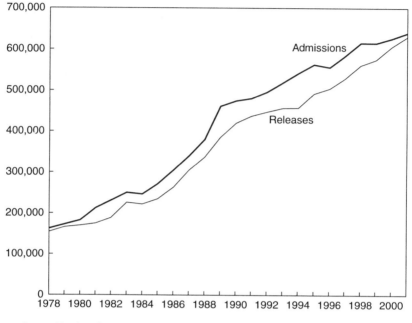

Source: Travis, Solomon, and Waul (2001).

since 1978. The difference between these two trends can be attributed to the increase in the average time served. The reentry cohort has quadrupled since 1978, so that approximately 630,000 individuals—or about 1,700 a day—are now leaving America's prisons to return home. These individuals—and the families and communities affected by increased levels of reentry—are the focus of our inquiry.

Profile of the Reentry Cohort

Before considering the implications of the growth in incarceration and reentry in America, we should briefly describe the population that is coming out of prison today. The profile reveals a population facing a significant number of challenges and shortcomings that might make a safe return home quite difficult. Most prisoners (91 percent) coming home from state prisons are men, although the share of women is growing rapidly (Harrison and Beck 2003). About one-third of reentering prisoners are white, 47 percent are African-American, and 16 percent are Hispanic. The average age of the reentry cohort is 34 years for state prisoners, although the number of released prisoners over age 55 more than doubled during the 1990s—to 44,000 in 1999 (Petersilia 2003).

The level of human capital in the reentry population is quite low, particularly with regard to educational attainment. In 1997, nearly half (41 percent) of all state prison inmates did not have a high school diploma or general equivalency diploma (GED) credential. About 17 percent had an 8th grade education or less. According to one report (Harlow 2003), the number of incoming prisoners in state prisons without a high school diploma increased by 44 percent between 1991 and 1997. About half (56 percent) were employed full-time at the time of their arrest; another 12.5 percent were employed part-time (BJS 2000a).

These prisoners have left extensive family networks behind. More than half (55 percent) of the men and nearly two-thirds (65 percent) of the women in state prisons report having minor children. About one-quarter of parents in state prison are married. One in five are divorced (Mumola 2000). They also bring with them a range of health burdens. About three-quarters of state prisoners report significant alcohol or drug abuse (Mumola 1999). At least 16 percent have mental illness, about 3 percent carry the HIV virus, 18 percent are infected with Hepatitis C, and 7 percent are infected with tuberculosis. In fact, the prevalence rates for these diseases are significantly higher in the prison population than in society as a whole (NCCHC 2002).

Finally, individuals leaving prison have extensive prior involvement with the criminal justice system. In 2002, the Bureau of Justice Statistics documented the recidivism rate of 272,111 prisoners released from the prisons of 15 states in 1994. Of these prisoners, 93 percent had previously been arrested, 81 percent had a prior conviction, and 44 percent had previously served time for another offense (Langan and Levin 2002).

This profile underscores some of the challenges presented by the reentry issue. The population under discussion faces significant hurdles as they leave prison. Most incarcerated individuals leave prison with low educational levels, extensive family obligations, histories of substance abuse, prior criminal involvement, and poor ties to the workforce. When the additional burdens of stigma associated with their criminal past and, for some, racial discrimination, are considered, the obstacles to successful reentry may seem formidable. In the chapters of Part 2, we will look in depth at different dimensions of the reentry profile to ascertain what our society could do—during imprisonment, but particularly following release—to lessen those obstacles to success.

Looking Forward

The growth in America's prison system has seemed unstoppable. Through all kinds of economic and political conditions, across all states, and during high- and low-crime eras, the prison network has grown. Yet there is reason to believe that the prison-building boom of the last quarter-century may be over. With the exception of the federal prison system, which is growing rapidly, the population in our state prisons has virtually leveled off. After decades of annual increases averaging 6 percent, the state prison population grew only 2.6 percent between 2001 and 2002. In nine states, prison populations actually declined between 2001 and 2002. And in fact, Alaska, Illinois, and Delaware each saw their populations decline by more than 3 percent (Harrison and Beck 2003).

As we look forward from the current state of affairs, the question at hand is whether, over the next quarter-century, the prison population will remain stable, increase, or decline, and, if so, by how much. There are reasons to believe the population might decrease. Certainly the current historically low crime rates in America will lead to lower per capita rates of arrest, conviction, and imprisonment than during the high crime rates of the 1980s. But the "peace dividend" from low crime rates seems quite illusory. In fact, the sharp decline in violence seen during the mid- to late 1990s did not translate directly into equally sharp reductions in prison commitments. In short, we should not expect that the return to the crime rates of the 1970s will result in imprisonment rates found in the 1970s. Policy reforms, not declines in crime rates, are needed to bring about substantial reductions in the prison population.

The analysis presented in this chapter has identified policy opportunities for those who advocate for fewer prisons. We learned that the current high level of incarceration reflects three distinct contributory factors, each of which is subject to policy reform. First, much of the nation's prison growth can be attributed to an increase in the average length of stay in prison. This reflects, in turn, decisions by state legislatures to increase prison sentences, primarily for convictions for violent offenses. These policy choices could be reversed. Second, the high rate of imprisonment has been sustained to a large extent by prison sentences for drug offenses, particularly drug selling. These policy choices, especially those made at the onset of the crack cocaine epidemic in the mid-1980s, could be reversed. Given the decline in the epidemic, a review of the enforcement policies adopted during a time of national crisis seems appropriate. Finally, our prison population now reflects the influx of large numbers of churners, particularly parole violators, who move in and out of prison and stay for relatively short periods, only to return home. State legislatures could reverse the parole supervision and revocation policies that have resulted in this remarkable state of affairs.

A number of states have, in fact, examined each of these three policy domains to find ways to reduce prison populations. In recent years, three states have changed their "truth-in-sentencing" formulas so that prisoners convicted of violent crimes are released earlier (Butterfield 2003b). According to a study by the Vera Institute of Justice, in the last few years, five states have eliminated or modified their mandatory minimum sentences for drug offenses so that more offenders convicted of these crimes can serve their sentences in the community. In addition, six states have reformed their parole policies so that fewer parolees will be sent back to prison for technical violations (Wool and Stemen 2004).

These reforms will certainly affect prison populations, but those reductions will likely be modest compared with the growth in imprisonment in America over the past generation. To bring the population closer to earlier levels would require a significant change in the American approach to punishment, which, in turn, would require a new consensus on crime policy. We would have to develop a presumption against incarceration, which would require far stronger community sanctions than currently exist. It seems quite unlikely, however, that we could develop sentencing policies that disfavor incarceration given the nation's 30-year march in the other direction. In particular, efforts to enhance community sanctions, though promising in their own right, are too often overshadowed by the dominant retributivist philosophy.

To bring our prison populations down significantly, we would have to radically restrict the use of imprisonment as the dominant weapon in the war against drugs. A number of states, most notably California through Proposition 36, have embraced innovative strategies to offer treatment instead of incarceration, but the jury is still out on the effectiveness of those reforms. To reduce imprisonment for drug convictions, we would have to implement effective alternatives to our current drug enforcement strategies, and there are as yet few sustained efforts to explore these alternatives. In short, the drug policy reforms currently being tested are likely to fall short of substantially reversing the result of the past 20 years, a period that witnessed a nine-fold increase in the nation's incarceration rates for drug offenders in state and federal prisons.

Other realities of incarceration in America also give us serious cause for concern. As an analysis by the Urban Institute (Lawrence and Travis 2004) pointed out, the prison network now extends far throughout the American landscape. In the 10 states that experienced the greatest growth of prisons between 1979 and 2000, the share of counties that had at least one prison rose from 13 percent to 31 percent (Lawrence and Travis 2004). The extent of prison expansion into a large percentage of America's counties and the financial and political benefits that flow from prisons have created powerful incentives to maintain the status quo. In essence, the prison network has become a separate reality, distinct from the operations of the criminal justice system, with strong proponents who have a vested interest in its continued existence. One need only recall the political turmoil caused by the mere suggestion of military base closures to imagine the political opposition that would form against a serious proposal to close a significant percentage of America's prisons.

This book takes our current high incarceration rate as a reality, a historical truth that underscores our need to face squarely the challenges posed by our experiment in mass incarceration. Perhaps our current incarceration rate will fall somewhat in years to come; perhaps it will decline significantly. Or perhaps we have achieved, to borrow the phrase of Blumstein and Cohen (1973), a new stability of punishment. But while we wait to see which of these predictions comes true, about 630,000 people still leave prison each year and we must ask ourselves whether they—and the broader society—are prepared for their return. We turn next to an examination of the way they are released, and the world of supervision that awaits them in the community.

NOTES

1. They also found some stability in the imprisonment rates in Norway, which fluctuated from 40 to 75 prisoners per 100,000 residents between 1880 and 1964.

2. Blumstein and Beck (1999) reported the changes in the incarceration rate by crime type between 1990 and 1996. These figures are updated here with data available through 2001 (Beck 2000; Beck and Harrison 2001; Beck and Mumola 1999; Harrison and Beck 2002, 2003).

3

The Extended
Reach of Supervision

The massive increase in America's prison population has had one
certain consequence—more people than ever before are being
released from prison to return home. We already know that in 2002
more than 630,000 individuals made that journey, a fourfold increase
over the 150,000 who left state and federal prisons a quarter-century
earlier. This chapter examines three dimensions of the new realities of
prisoner reentry: How are these prisoners released? How, if at all, are they
supervised by the agencies of the criminal justice system once they are
released? And what happens when they fail to meet the conditions of
their supervision?

Our examination leads to a simple and striking conclusion: The classic model of parole, developed by American reformers at the turn of the
20th century as the preferred method for determining which individuals
should be released from prison and how they should be supervised in the
community, has been significantly transformed. That original model
bears little resemblance to the haphazard way we now make those critical
determinations about liberty, punishment, and reintegration for the hundreds of thousands of individuals who pass through our prisons each year.

As originally conceived by criminal justice reformers a century ago,
the parole system was the cornerstone of the indeterminate sentencing
model that dominated American jurisprudence for most of the 20th century (Bottomley 1990). In this model, still operating in many states

today, the parole system plays three critical roles. First, parole boards determine the actual length of a prison sentence. Second, parole agencies supervise former prisoners in the community for the remainder of their sentences. Third, parole administrators are authorized to revoke a parolee's conditional liberty and return him or her to prison after finding that the parolee has failed to observe one or more release conditions.

As indeterminate sentencing came under intense scrutiny in the 1970s, so did the parole system (Reitz 1998). Judicial discretion was challenged as arbitrary, lenient, and unfair, and parole board discretion was subjected to similar critiques. As the goal of rehabilitation gave way to "just desserts," or retribution, parole's mission to support prisoner reintegration was called into question. As rising crime rates fueled public calls for tough anticrime measures, parole supervision became more closely aligned with the law enforcement community. And as our entire criminal justice system came to reflect the "tough on crime" posture of the public and elected officials, parole systems struck an awkward balance between parole's twin missions of supervision and support. In short, beginning in the 1970s, as the landscape of sentencing philosophy shifted and public confidence in rehabilitation dropped, the institution of parole lost its sense of mission (Rhine, Smith, and Jackson 1991). As a result, today's parole system differs significantly from the "classic" model designed by criminal justice reformers a century ago.

Thus our examination of the processes of release and supervision for prisoners leaving America's prisons today is, in large part, an inquiry into the substantial shifts in the operations of our parole system. These shifts have affected all three components of the classic parole model. First, the role of parole boards in deciding when (and whether) prisoners get out of prison has declined significantly. In 1999, parole boards released only 24 percent of the individuals getting out of prison, down from 65 percent in 1976. Second, a far greater percentage of released prisoners are now placed on parole supervision. Today, more than 80 percent of individuals leaving prison are placed on parole, up from 60 percent in 1960. Third, the growth in parole revocations has been explosive. Over the past 20 years, as the number of people sent to prison on new convictions has increased threefold, the number sent back to prison for parole violations has increased sevenfold. We now send as many people back to prison for parole violations each year as the total number of prison admissions in 1980.

Yet, a narrow focus on parole operations in modern America, as important as it is, only raises larger questions about how we should face the challenges of prisoner reentry. How should release decisions be made? Who should be supervised after release, by whom, for how long, under what conditions, and for what purposes? And how should we respond to the antisocial acts, particularly criminal acts, committed by those among us who have been in prison and are released under criminal justice supervision? These questions raise even more profound questions about the pathways of prisoner reentry and the relationship between former prisoners, the public, and the state. This chapter begins with an analysis of the shifting landscape of parole in America and ends with a discussion of those larger questions.

The Evolution of Prison Release Methods

Who decides when a prisoner should be released from prison? There are two fundamental release mechanisms in the American sentencing system. Under the first, which we shall call "discretionary release," a parole board makes the decision. As described earlier, the sentencing judge, operating under an indeterminate sentencing statute, decides that the offender should serve a term of years in prison with an upper and lower boundary, say 5 to 15 years. The prisoner is then eligible to appear before the state's parole board after serving the minimum amount of that sentence and petition the parole board to be released from prison.[1] The second release mechanism, which we shall call "mandatory release," does not involve a parole board at all. Mandatory release decisions are made by operation of law: The prison term comes to an end and the corrections authorities have no choice but to release the prisoner.[2] In some of these cases, the exact term of imprisonment is set at the time of sentencing. For example, the judge imposes a one-year sentence and the prisoner is released when the one-year term expires. In other cases, the prisoner is serving an indeterminate sentence but has not been released by the parole board. For example, a prisoner may have applied for parole and been denied release by the parole board; when the prison term comes to an end, however, the prisoner must be released. Other prisoners choose not to apply for parole, preferring to spend the entire prison sentence in confinement.[3]

The balance between discretionary and mandatory releases from prison has shifted substantially over time. The first use of discretionary release can be traced to 1877 when New York State enacted the country's first indeterminate sentencing statute. By 1890, 20 states had adopted a parole system. By the time Mississippi enacted a parole statute in 1942, every state and the federal government had embraced discretionary release as part of sentencing policy (Rhine et al. 1991).[4]

Despite the widespread acceptance of this parole concept, however, not all prisoners were released this way. The reports of three landmark national examinations of the American criminal justice system tell the story of an idea that never fully dominated practice. First, according to a survey conducted by the National Commission on Law Observance and Enforcement (1931) (also known as the Wickersham Commission), 44,208 prisoners were released from state prisons and reformatories in 1927; however, only 49 percent of these were released by parole boards. Forty-two percent were released when their maximum terms expired, and the remaining 9 percent were released through other means, such as commutations and pardons. Next, when United States Attorney General Herbert Brownell convened a 1956 national conference on parole, the attendees learned that situation had not changed much. About half of prisoners released in 1955 had been discharged mandatorily, when their sentence expired. Third, in the mid-1960s, when the President's Commission on Law Enforcement and the Administration of Justice examined the balance between mandatory and discretionary release in America, it found some progress: more than 60 percent of adult prisoners were released by parole boards (Rhine et al. 1991). By 1970, parole reached its high watermark: 70 percent of prison releases in America were discretionary, decided by a parole board (Cahalan and Parsons 1986).

In the 1970s, as the system of indeterminate sentencing came under attack from both ends of the political spectrum, parole boards became a lightning rod for criticism. In 1971, the American Friends Service Committee, a Quaker organization, called for the abolition of parole. In 1975, the Citizens' Inquiry on Parole and Criminal Justice reviewed the decisions of New York State's parole board and found them to be arbitrary, secretive, cursory, and inherently unfair. At the same time, practitioners who ran parole systems, with support from the academic community, were beginning a sustained effort to develop parole release guidelines designed to reduce the disparities in decisionmaking and bring greater transparency to the release process itself (Gottfredson, Wilkins, and Hoffman 1978). The U.S. Parole Commission adopted such guidelines in 1972, and by 1986, 18 paroling authorities reported they used guidelines (Rhine et al. 1991). However, these efforts to counter charges of arbitrariness and secrecy did little to protect the institution of parole release from public attack.

These challenges to the philosophical underpinnings of the parole system found a sympathetic audience in state legislatures. In 1976, Maine became the first state to eliminate parole release. A year later, California and Indiana abolished their indeterminate sentencing systems and provided that future release decisions would be mandated by law, not made by a parole board. By the turn of the 21st century, the "abolish parole" movement had reached its peak. In fact, by 2002, 16 states had abolished discretionary release by a parole board, only 16 states still retained parole boards with full power to make release decisions, and the remaining states had either restricted the parole board's jurisdiction or abolished discretionary parole altogether (Petersilia 2003).

There are many ways to understand this profound shift in American sentencing practice. First, on the most pragmatic level, parole is no longer the dominant method for making release decisions. In 1976, about two-thirds (65 percent) of prisoners released in America were released by discretionary means; by 1999, that share had dropped to one-quarter (24 percent) (figure 3.1).[5] Because this shift took place during a time when the reentry population quadrupled, the consequences in absolute numbers were quite dramatic. In 1980, the state prisons in America released approximately 150,000 prisoners, by both mandatory and discretionary means. Nearly 20 years later, our state prisons released approximately 380,000 prisoners by mandatory means alone; none of these prisoners was released by a parole board.

Figure 3.1. *The Growth in Mandatory Prison Releases between 1976 and 1999*

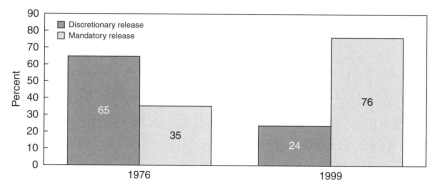

Source: Travis and Lawrence (2002a).

The decline in parole as a release mechanism can also be viewed as a realignment of relationships between the three branches of government. Under the indeterminate sentencing philosophy, the judicial and executive branches of government exercised substantial discretion over the length of a prison sentence. Within broad ranges of possible sentences, judges imposed a minimum and maximum prison term, and the parole board, an executive branch agency, decided the actual moment an inmate was to be released from prison. The movement toward determinate sentencing has restricted the role of the judiciary. Furthermore, the abolition or curtailment of parole boards has restricted the role of the executive branch. In both instances, the legislature has emerged as a more powerful factor in sentencing policy. Legislatures, the branch of government most responsive to public concerns about crime, have increasingly determined the appropriate prison terms for broad classes of offenses and offenders.[6]

The Expansive Reach of Postrelease Supervision

After the decision is made to release an offender from prison—either by exercise of a parole board's discretion, or as mandated by statute—the next step is to determine whether the offender will be placed on supervision in the community. This legal status is commonly referred to as "parole supervision," although a number of states have adopted other terms, such as "community punishment," "supervised release," and "controlled release." For purposes of this discussion, we will use "conditional release" to refer to all forms of post-prison supervision. As we shall see, not all prisoners are released conditionally. Many—now about one in five—are released unconditionally. They have no parole officer, no special legal status, and no restrictions other than those that flow from their criminal convictions, such as prohibitions against certain kinds of employment. They are simply shown the door and sent on their way.

Under the classic parole model, the parole board served as a bridge between the prison and the community; it had oversight responsibility for both the release decision and the supervisory infrastructure in the community. When New York's pioneering indeterminate sentencing scheme was implemented at the Elmira Reformatory in 1877, the components of indeterminate sentencing and parole were links in a logical chain. An inmate was sentenced to a minimum term of years. Once he earned enough credits, or "marks," by participating in educational programs, taking religious instruction, and generally behaving well, he would become eligible to appear before the equivalent of the parole board. The board, in consultation with the reformatory superintendent, would decide whether he should be released. If the inmate was released, the superintendent retained jurisdiction over him. If, after six months back in the community, the board determined there was a "strong and reasonable probability" that the parolee would "live and remain at liberty without violating the law" and that "his release [was] not incompatible with the welfare of society," the board could recommend that the governor grant the parolee an "absolute release from imprisonment" (Rhine et al. 1991, 9). From intake at the prison's front door to the release decision, oversight of community supervision, and the final dispensation of the sentence, the system of punishment, rehabilitation, and reintegration was managed by the prison administrator, in conjunction with the parole board.

During the 1960s and 1970s, as the institution of parole release was being called into question, the links in this logical chain also started to come apart. At an organizational level, the relationship between the agency making the parole decision and the agency supervising parolees shifted considerably. In 1966, parole boards were also responsible for community supervision in 31 states. By 1972, a short six years later, that number had dropped to 18. By 2000, parole boards would have responsibility for supervising parolees in only 10 states (Petersilia 2003). In the remaining 40 states, one entity (the parole board) would make release decisions and establish release conditions, while another entity (the parole supervision agency), typically housed in the department of corrections, would be responsible for enforcing those conditions (Petersilia 2003; Rhine et al. 1991, 102). A structural link in the logic chain of parole had been weakened.

Even more significant was the decoupling of the decision to release from the decision to supervise. As was noted previously, beginning in the 1970s, the use of discretionary release declined significantly to the point where, today, only one in four prisoners is released by parole board decision. As this aspect of the classic parole model was in decline, the second dimension of that model—supervision in the community—was on the rise. As figure 3.2 illustrates, from 1923 to the mid-1960s, between 50 and 60 percent of all prisoners were released to community supervision. Between 1960 and 1990, however, the share of conditional prison releases grew from 56 percent to a high of 87 percent before declining somewhat to 82 percent in 1999.

Figure 3.2. *Growth in Share of Prison Releases to Parole Supervision, 1923–1999*

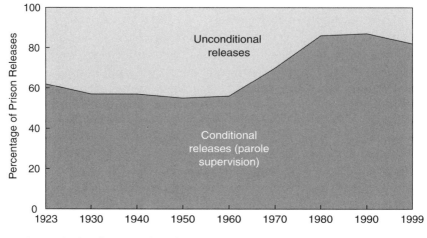

Source: Travis and Lawrence (2002a).

When viewed in light of the collapse of consensus regarding indeterminate sentencing, these trends prompt two observations. First, during the era when that consensus was strong, nearly half of all prisoners were released without supervision. In other words, there was a significant gap between theory and practice regarding postprison supervision. Second, as states moved away from indeterminate sentencing models, the use of parole supervision increased. This result is highly ironic. At the same time that legislatures placed severe restrictions on discretion exercised by judges and parole boards, they greatly expanded the realm of official discretion by placing more people than ever before under the supervision of parole officers, government employees with far more discretion and far less accountability for the exercise of that discretion than judges and parole board members.

Yet, in a larger sense, the significant expansion of parole supervision over the past few decades is consistent with the tenor of our times. Just as America has expanded the use of prisons, placing more and more people under direct state control, the country has also expanded supervision of former prisoners, placing more and more people under another form of control (Simon 1993). In 1980, there were 220,000 individuals supervised by parole agencies across the country. By 2000, that number had risen to 725,000, an all-time high. This dramatic expansion of criminal justice supervision for former prisoners has been merely one dimension of a more fundamental shift in the landscape of punishment.[7]

The Explosion of Parole Revocations

When a prisoner is released and placed under the supervision of a parole agency, he or she must observe certain conditions of supervision. A survey of parole conditions in 51 jurisdictions conducted by the Parole Task Force of the American Correctional Association found a remarkable diversity in the conditions imposed (Rhine et al. 1991). According to this survey, more than 90 percent of the supervision agencies require that the parolee obey all laws, report to the parole officer when directed, answer all reasonable questions, refrain from carrying a firearm or other dangerous weapon without permission, and remain within the jurisdiction and notify the parole officer of any change of residence. About three-quarters of these agencies require the parolee to maintain gainful employment and obey agency rules. About half require the parolee to pay fines and restitution, meet family responsibilities, support dependents, and undergo treatment. About one-third require payment of supervision fees. Only one in six require the parolee to attend educational or vocational training programs or perform community service (Rhine et al. 1991).

When these (or other) conditions are not met, the parole officer may report a violation. Perhaps no action will be taken at the time, or the conditions of supervision may be changed. A parolee who fails a mandated drug test may be required to attend more drug treatment classes. A parolee who is seen associating with known felons at an illegal drug market late at night may be ordered to observe a curfew. A parolee who threatens an intimate partner may be directed to move to another address. In more serious cases, however, the parolee's liberty may be revoked and he or she may be returned to custody. In most instances, these parolees are returned to the state prison system; in some jurisdictions, they are returned to local jails. Under applicable court rulings, this revocation of liberty requires a due process hearing at which the evidence of the violation is weighed. Typically, these hearings are held before an administrative law judge employed by the parole board or the parole board itself (Runda, Rhine, and Wetter 1994).

The number of parole violators returned to state prison has increased dramatically over the past 20 years. In 1980, state prisons admitted approximately 27,000 parole violators.[8] In 2000, those same states admitted approximately 203,000 parole violators, a remarkable sevenfold increase (figure 3.3). The magnitude of this shift in sentencing policy is staggering. In 1980, state prisons admitted 169,000 individuals for any reason, including conviction for a new offense and parole revocation. Twenty years later, our state prisons admitted slightly more than that number (203,000) for parole violations alone (Travis and Lawrence 2002a). In 1980, only 17 percent of the prisoners admitted to state prisons were parole violators. The remaining 83 percent were new court admissions—offenders sentenced for new crimes. By 1999, the percentage of prison admissions for parole violations had grown to 35 percent, more than twice the rate two decades earlier (figure 3.4). Stated differently, the dramatic growth in parole revocations has changed the composition of the nation's incoming prison population.[9]

What do we know about why more than 200,000 individuals are sent back to prison each year as parole violators? Remarkably little. The Bureau of Justice Statistics records parole revocations in two broad categories— revocations resulting from "new crime" violations and revocations result-

Figure 3.3. *Increases in the Number of Parole Violators Returned to Prison, 1977–2000*

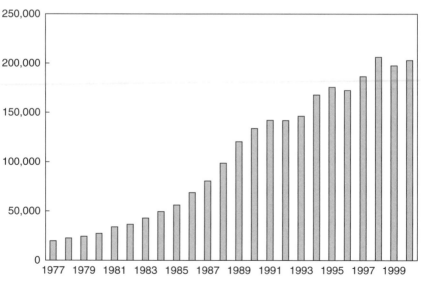

Source: Travis and Lawrence (2002a).

Figure 3.4. *Growth in Parole Violators as a Share of Prison Admissions, 1980–1999*

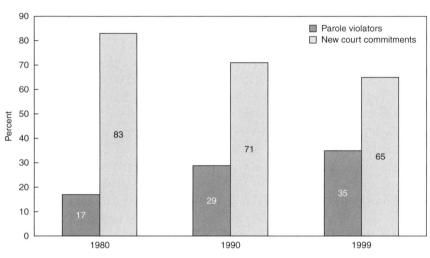

Source: Travis and Lawrence (2002a).

ing from "technical" violations. Since all parole agencies require that a parolee obey the law, the first category is fairly self-explanatory. A new crime violation occurs when a parolee has been arrested and prosecuted in court for a new violation of the criminal law. The second category is, how-ever, more difficult to define. A technical violation involves disobeying any other condition of supervision—failing a drug test, failing to maintain employment, moving without permission, or missing appointments with the parole officer. Of all parole violators returned to prison in 2000, nearly one-third (about 65,000) were returned for a new conviction and two-thirds (about 135,000) were returned for technical violations (Travis and Lawrence 2002a).

We also know little about the underlying behavior of parole violators. Most states do not keep detailed records on activities that led to a par-ticular violation, much less the reasoning that led to the decision to return the parolee to prison. In particular, the available research does not answer a critical question, namely whether the increase in parole revo-cations is due to an increase in crimes committed by those under super-vision. A closer examination of one state—California, which sends more parole violators back to prison than any other—suggests that, at least in this state, the growth in parole revocations is more a reflection of policy shifts than increases in the criminal behavior of parolees. Over the decade of the 1980s, the rate of return to prison for California's parolees (the number of parole revocations divided by the number of individuals on parole supervision) increased sharply, from about 25,000 per 100,000 to more than 80,000 per 100,000. Then, almost as sharply, the rate decreased in the early 1990s to 60,000 per 100,000 before settling in the range of 65,000 to 75,000 returns to prison per 100,000 parolees (Travis and Lawrence 2002b). Over these two decades, however, the rate of returns to prison for new crimes remained virtually constant—about 20,000 a year—while the rate of technical violations fluctuated wildly. Other states have similar stories. Studies by the Urban Institute in Maryland, Illinois, Ohio, New Jersey, and Texas have all documented dramatic upward and downward shifts in the percentage of revocations attributable to technical violations (La Vigne and Thomson 2003; La Vigne, Mamalian, et al. 2003; La Vigne, Kachnowski, et al. 2003; Travis, Keegan, and Cadora 2003; Watson et al. 2004).

These single-state studies suggest that the use of technical parole revocations is highly susceptible to shifts in policy. Some experts justify increasing parole revocations for technical reasons by claiming that sending more parolees back to prison is good crime policy. Taking parolees off the streets, even for technical reasons, the argument goes, might reduce crime. Certainly any policy that incapacitates hundreds of thousands of individuals who have high recidivism rates will avert some number of crimes. Perhaps a policy of strictly enforcing conditions of supervision, and the resulting high rates of parole revocation such enforcement brings, has both general and specific deterrent effects along with decreased offending rates and increased overall compliance with supervision. So far, however, there is no research that analyzes the extent of these policies' crime control effects.

Nor is there any research that examines the costs of these policies. Of course, incarceration costs can be calculated and certainly amount to billions of dollars a year. In California alone, about 20 percent of the state's prisoners are being housed on parole violations. Yet these policies incur deeper costs. Just as incarceration costs generally should be assessed in terms of prison's effects on a number of social indicators, parole revocation policies should be evaluated in terms of the disruption they bring to families, jobs, social networks, and community life. Parole revocations for technical reasons should also be evaluated for their impact on the attitudes of parolees and their families toward the criminal justice system. Arguably the deprivation of liberty for months due to a "technical" reason, such as a failed drug test or missed curfew, could result in increased cynicism toward the rule of law, an outcome that should be included in calculating costs and benefits. These critical questions should be at the top of the nation's research agenda as we come to terms with the new realities of imprisonment through parole revocations.

Our increased reliance on parole revocations as punishment also raises basic questions about our sentencing philosophy. By placing more people under supervision and sending many more parolees back to prison, we have, in essence, created a system of "back-end" sentencing. We deprive hundreds of thousands of citizens of their liberty with a minimum of due process, and imprison them for significant amounts of time, often for minor infractions of administrative rules or for low-level criminal conduct. The processes by which these decisions are made are not subject to the same level of scrutiny as those in the "front-end" sentencing system, with its legislative framework, sentencing guidelines, and open adversarial proceedings. The exercise of discretion by parole officers and parole boards is not scrutinized in the same way as the exercise of discretion by police officers, prosecutors, and judges, even though the parole system is responsible for one out of every three prison admissions in America. It is remarkable that the attention devoted over the past generation to reducing sentencing disparities, limiting discretion, promoting "truth in sentencing," and assuring that prison sentences are reserved for serious offenses has overlooked back-end sentencing from parole revocations.

This path from parole back to prison has not received much scrutiny in the research literature. New research could shed light on the critical decisions that constitute the parole revocation process. In particular, we should delineate the distinction between a technical violation and a new crime violation. We should better understand the decisionmaking process parole boards employ when they return a parolee to custody. We should be able to answer the critical policy question, "Does parole supervision reduce crime?"—a question that so far has not been answered conclusively by the research community. (See chapter 5 for a longer discussion of the current state of research on this question.)

But the most important task that lies ahead is to ask the fundamental questions that flow from this discussion of the state of parole in America: How should prisoners be released? Should they be supervised by the criminal justice system after release, and, if so, why and how? And, if conditions are attached to their supervision, what should happen when those conditions are not met? In short, does the parole model still serve the nation well? In the final section of this chapter, we examine a proposal for new answers to those questions, answers that create the foundation for a new approach to meeting the challenges of prisoner reentry.

Looking Forward

I have come to the conclusion, paraphrasing the rallying cry of the welfare reform movement, that it is time to end parole as we know it. The following discussion outlines a new approach that would abolish parole as a release mechanism, reconceptualize the purposes and operations of parole supervision, and sharply limit the use of imprisonment to respond to violations of supervision conditions. The section ends with the framework for a new vision of postrelease supervision that would redefine the relationship between the returning prisoner, the justice system, and community stakeholders interested in promoting successful prisoner reentry.

A New Approach to Parole

We noted in the first section of this chapter a significant decline in the share of prisoners who are released by parole boards. As America has turned away from indeterminate sentencing, fewer and fewer prisoners have been released through this discretionary means. Yet, indeterminate sentencing still has its proponents. Even Jerry Brown, who as the governor of California in 1976 signed the law abolishing indeterminate sentencing, now as the mayor of Oakland ascribes his city's high levels of violent crime to former prisoners who return angry and unprepared, and has called for a return to indeterminate sentencing (DeFao 2003). Joan Petersilia (2003, 187–88), the nation's preeminent scholar on parole, has argued that "we should reinstitute discretionary parole release in the 16 states that have abolished it." She argues persuasively that "eliminating discretionary release reduces the incentives for inmates to try to rehabilitate themselves while incarcerated." Furthermore, she notes, discretion can also be exercised in favor of keeping more violent and dangerous prisoners in custody longer. She recommends that the parole release mechanism be retained, or reinstituted, with stronger guidelines governing the exercise of discretion and greater reliance on risk assessment instruments to predict the likelihood that a particular prisoner will return to crime following release. She also recommends insulating parole boards from political interference by establishing professional qualifications for board members.

Petersilia's call for a return to parole release reflects an important insight. By significantly reducing the role of parole boards in making release decisions, our sentencing reforms over the past 25 years have eliminated a valuable role these boards played, namely overseeing the process of preparing prisoners for release. Because parole boards place a value on positive behavior in prison—including program participation and a clean disciplinary record—they promote rehabilitation. Because parole boards give credit for a prisoner's connections in the community—including job availability, stable housing, and transition services—they promote successful reintegration.

Yet it is hard to imagine a political scenario under which discretionary release through parole boards could be revived in this country. Sixteen states have abolished parole release. Others have cut back on the types of prisoners who are eligible for parole release. At this point, parole boards release only one-quarter of the prisoners released in America, a percentage that will likely decline further, reflecting changes in our sentencing statutes. Simply put, parole release has lost market share in the competition of ideas.

"GOOD-TIME" CREDIT

The challenge, then, is to construct a system that includes the benefits of parole release—which principally means incentives for prisoners while in prison—while navigating the tricky waters of public opposition. Interestingly, the best vehicle for providing incentives is the widespread but undervalued system of awarding "good-time" or "earned release" credits. Under this system, which has received little attention in the debate over discretionary parole release, a prisoner with a record of good discipline and program participation is eligible for a reduction in his or her prison term, in some states up to 50 percent of the sentence.

Evidence that good-time credit positively influences prisoner behavior, however, remains limited and inconclusive. Good-time systems vary enormously across the states (Jones, Connelly, and Wagner 2001). As a result, good-time policies can be criticized for many of the same reasons that parole policies are denounced—prisoners are released pursuant to arcane rules or poorly understood regulations that operate outside public view with little opportunity for external review. Indeed, as Jacobs

(1982) points out, it is ironic that good-time policies have survived in states that have abolished discretionary parole release.

For purposes of this discussion, however, the fact that good-time policies exist in states with determinate sentencing systems *and* those with indeterminate systems is critically important. Precisely because these policies have survived the national schism over indeterminate sentencing, they provide a vehicle for creating, under all sentencing schemes, an incentive system rewarding program participation and good behavior. Furthermore, the weaknesses in these policies could be addressed through reform legislation that would ensure that good time is awarded based on an objective set of measures, administered in a manner open to public scrutiny, and subject to judicial review. Appropriate legislative reforms could ensure that this early release mechanism, unlike parole, would not reflect a de novo assessment of the crime of conviction, could not be influenced by prosecutors or victims, would not be based on a prediction of future behavior, and would be impervious to manipulation for administrative convenience. This system's sole purpose would be to create incentives for behavior that promotes safer prisons, program participation, and preparation for release. If the prisoner satisfies the statutory requirements for earned release, then he or she should then be legally entitled to release. All in all, to the extent that discretion in release decisions is deemed necessary in motivating desired in-prison behavior, we have a mechanism—good-time credit—that can, with critical reforms, provide that discretion while avoiding some of the flaws of our current parole release system.

UNIVERSAL SUPERVISION

However prisoners are released, we face a critical question: Which released prisoners, if any, should be supervised? As was discussed earlier in this chapter, in 2001, about one-fifth of all returning prisoners— approximately 120,000—were *not* placed on supervision upon their release. They reported to no parole officer; they observed no special conditions; they cannot now be sent back to prison for a parole violation. For some individuals like these, the fact they are released without supervision is the result of legislative action—their sentences did not mandate a postrelease supervision period. For others, lack of supervision is a consequence of a parole board decision that had previously denied them early release, which means they were required to serve out their sentences in prison. In other cases, the prisoner—not the legislature or the parole board—decides to leave prison without supervision. He or she has not exercised the option to seek parole, preferring to "max out" his or her sentence and therefore leave prison totally free.

This state of affairs is highly troubling. Dangerous prisoners can be released with no supervision. Prisoners can decide whether they will be supervised. Parole boards, in the name of public safety, can deny a violent prisoner early release, but in doing so they effectively deny the community the right to have that prisoner supervised after the prison gates close. A violent prisoner who has been in solitary confinement for months and has been denied parole must ultimately be released, but will not be supervised. A strong public safety argument can be made that, at a minimum, our sentencing system should require postrelease supervision for all violent prisoners.

Yet perhaps some prisoners require neither supervision nor transitional services. We can imagine a prisoner who finishes a one-year mandatory minimum and has family, job, home, and a supportive network waiting for him. Maybe he should get no transitional support and should be allowed to leave prison with his debt to society fully paid. Martin F. Horn (2001), former corrections secretary for Pennsylvania and parole director for New York State, has, in fact, proposed that supervision be abolished totally, and that all former prisoners be granted vouchers to allow them to choose and purchase the services necessary to make their transition back into the community. Horn argues that given (1) the absence of research showing that supervision is indeed effective at reducing crime and (2) the demonstrated increase in parole revocation for technical violations, we should drop the pretense that parole supervision cuts crime and empower (and subsidize) returning prisoners to make their own choices regarding transitional services.

Although Horn's free market approach to determining the allocation of reentry services is intuitively appealing—and his candid assessment of parole effectiveness refreshing—the reentry perspective advocated throughout this book calls for an articulated set of obligations between the government and the returning prisoner. Our challenge is to define those mutual obligations in ways that recognize the distinct interests of the returning prisoner *and* society. The prisoner's interests are clear— connecting with family, health care, employment, housing, and community institutions. Society has important interests as well—reducing crime, promoting successful family reunification, and securing employment and improving health outcomes for the population of former prisoners. To entrust the responsibility for managing the transition period entirely to the returning prisoner, even with financial assistance in the form of vouchers, would relieve government of its responsibility to promote positive reentry outcomes. In a free market system of brokered transition services, it would be too easy for government agencies to place blame solely on the former prisoner when the transition plan falls apart. The proper question, then, is not whether government is interested in successful transitions from prison, but whether our current supervision system effectively achieves those outcomes.

LIMITS TO SUPERVISION

To advance these interrelated individual and society interests, we should favor a presumption of universal supervision for every returning prisoner, subject to two limitations. First, the supervision period should be reduced for good behavior, and, second, supervision conditions should be few in number, tailored to the specific needs of and risks associated with the returning prisoner, and enforced parsimoniously. Both limitations reflect a careful balance of societal and individual interests. Prolonged periods of supervision for someone who has made a successful transition back into the community accomplishes little for society. In fact, the opportunity to earn release from supervision might also promote prosocial behavior. Furthermore, a criminal justice system that rewards successful reintegration and celebrates the establishment of prosocial identities for ex-offenders serves a broad societal interest in reducing the distance between those who have violated the law and the rest of society (see chapter 10).

We turn next to a more extensive discussion of the second limitation, that the requirements of the supervision period be minimal, specific, and parsimoniously enforced. On what grounds may the government deprive someone of liberty after he or she has been released from prison? Under the indeterminate sentencing scheme, the answer is simple: During the period of conditional supervision, the prisoner still "owes" time to the state such that, if the conditions of supervision are breached, all bets are off and the parolee can be sent back to prison.

We need to rethink the connection between violations of supervision conditions and incarceration in a state prison. Once an individual has been released from state prison, he or she should be deprived of liberty in only two situations. First, if the former prisoner has committed a new crime, then that crime should be prosecuted like any other crime, not under the guise of a parole violation. States should also enact penalty enhancements for particular crimes committed during parole. Second, if a parolee has repeatedly failed to abide by a critical component of a transition plan, such as attending a drug treatment program, avoiding an intimate partner if there has been a history of abuse, working at an approved job, or staying drug free, then he or she could be subject to a short period of incarceration.

But what is the appropriate penalty for these failures? As was noted earlier, a four-month prison stay resulting from failing a drug test seems out of proportion to the misconduct. The State of Washington has taken an approach that faces these dilemmas squarely. Under laws enacted in 1999, a parolee in that state can be incarcerated for no more than 60 days for a technical parole violation. In addition, technical parole violators are detained in county jails, not state prisons, and the money the state saves in foregone prison costs is rebated to the counties to cover this new expense (Little Hoover Commission 2003).

The implications of this shift in our approach to parole revocations are far-reaching. If Washington's statutory scheme were in place across America, we would no longer send 130,000 individuals—the two-thirds of parole revocations resulting from technical violations—back to state prison each year. We would reduce prison intake levels to fewer than 500,000 a year, realizing substantial savings in state corrections budgets. These savings could in turn pay for increased county detention costs. More important, as is discussed in greater detail below, a system that shares state corrections savings with local jurisdictions could create incentives to fund programs that support prisoner reintegration at the community level.

A New Vision for Supervision

Creating a system based on universal supervision, with incentives for early release and limited use of sanction power to promote successful reintegration, will require a new organizational structure, far removed from the parole system found in modern America. Devolution—the concept of moving responsibility for government functions closer to the people affected by them—provides a useful framework for reorganizing the supervision function. In the current system, parole supervision is typically considered the state's responsibility. Because a prison term for a felony conviction is "owed" to the state, the remainder that is not served in a state prison—the period of parole supervision—is still considered time owed to the state. Hence, parole is a state function, as compared with probation, another form of community supervision, which is typically a function of local or county government.

Viewed through the devolution lens, this notion of state responsibility for prisoner reintegration is antiquated, counterproductive, and inefficient. Eric Cadora, Charles Swartz, and Mannix Gordon (2003) illustrate the power of the devolution concept as applied to postprison supervision. They examined the distribution of community supervision in Bedford Stuyvesant, a Brooklyn neighborhood, using the outlines of the 79th and 81st police precincts as arbitrary boundaries. About 1,200 people living in those precincts are under the supervision of the Division of Parole, a state agency. Another 1,800 residents are under the supervision of the Department of Probation, a city agency. If we add those who are on juvenile probation, or under pretrial supervision, the total supervision caseload approaches 4,000 individuals, in a community with a population of 44,500 residents over age 18.

From a community perspective, these legal and organizational distinctions make little sense. Why should the dozens of individuals on one block who are under criminal justice supervision report to three or four different agencies? Why should they be supervised by more than a dozen different supervision officers? More important, from a theoretical perspective, this way of organizing community supervision misses a critical point, namely, that the best way of accomplishing the purposes of supervision— promoting positive behavior, preventing crime and other antisocial behavior, and supporting reintegration processes—is to draw heavily on the resources of community (families, churches, local employers) and be acutely attentive to the risks of community (drug markets, gangs, family violence, crime opportunities). If responsibility for supervision were devolved to an entity much closer to the dynamics of community life, then perhaps supervision could be transformed into a vehicle for reintegration rather than a period of time owed to the state.

COMMUNITY JUSTICE CORPORATION

The first step in reorganizing postprison supervision to accomplish the social goals of reintegration and crime reduction is to create a new entity, located in the community, to oversee all community supervision—perhaps called the Community Justice Corporation (CJC). The CJC could be a public agency or a private nonprofit corporation. It would act on behalf of the criminal justice system, leveraging the assets and navigating the risks found in the community, acting in a problem-solving mode to help offenders, particularly those returning from prison, achieve adherence to supervision conditions and reintegration. The CJC would be funded partially by money now spent on traditional supervision, augmented by savings from reduced incarceration as fewer parole violators (see below) are returned to prison, and further enhanced by blending funds from housing, drug treatment, workforce development, and social service programs. This is a justice version of devolution—the transfer of responsibility for a critical function from the state to a community-based organization.[10]

REENTRY COURT

One final question must be answered as we reconstruct the parole function: What governmental entity should oversee the reintegration process and decide when to revoke the liberty of those under supervision? Some states, such as California, that have abolished parole boards as releasing authorities have retained parole boards to oversee the revocation process. There are undoubtedly some benefits to this arrangement. For example, an administrative entity such as a parole board can adopt guidelines to ensure consistency in the handling of revocation cases. For several reasons, however, I have come to believe that this function is best lodged in the judicial branch of government, not the executive branch, in the form of a "reentry court." Since I first developed this concept in 1999 (Travis 2000), reentry courts have been established on an experimental basis in several jurisdictions around the country. Briefly stated, a reentry court provides judicial oversight of the reintegration process, just as a drug court provides judicial oversight of a drug addict's treatment process. In a reentry court, the parole officer essentially serves as a case manager, working with the court and the parolee on a reentry plan. Prisoners are brought before the reentry court judge at the time of release and then appear in court on a monthly basis, reporting on their progress in meeting the conditions of their reentry plan. The judges are able to marshal community resources, and wield both "carrots" and "sticks" in their efforts to promote successful reintegration. The carrots are services, positive reinforcement, family and community support, and a forum for the acknowledgement of success. The sticks are enhanced levels of supervision (such as curfews, more intensive drug treatment, or more frequent drug testing), and ultimately short periods of incarceration, typically measured in days rather than months.

The reentry court offers many advantages over the current organizational structure for parole supervision. It is an open forum, fostering a public discussion of the purposes of supervision, the parolee's expectations, and the reasons for supervision changes, if necessary. This format reflects the principles of "procedural justice" (Tyler 1988, 1990) that have been demonstrated to enhance the legitimacy of rule-enforcing institutions. Reentry courts can provide forums for acknowledging the new civic identities of ex-offenders who have completed the desistance process. Such courts can impose, modify, and lift legal sanctions that flow from felony convictions. Finally, reentry courts serve a very important public purpose: they bring into public view the hidden system of back-end sentencing called parole revocations. (See chapter 10 for more on reentry courts.)

A century after American criminal justice reformers defined the parole system as a way to make release decisions and supervise those who have been released, few voices are arguing for keeping the status quo. The system has been contorted beyond recognition by decades of ideological skirmishing, legislative reform, political posturing, and managerial neglect. The time has come to end parole as we know it. This does not mean that discretionary release should be abandoned. On the contrary, a system of rewarding prosocial prisoner behavior should be rescued from America's fragmented sentencing policy. Nor should supervision be abolished or retained in its current form. Rather, the time is right for a total rethinking of the supervision function that balances societal and individual goals. This rethinking process should be open to new ideas about the allocation of responsibilities among the branches of government (with more functions given to the judiciary); among the levels of government (with more functions devolving from the state to the local units of government); and between the government and the private sector (with the creation of a new justice intermediary). With this new alignment of responsibilities for overseeing the reentry process, we stand a better chance of promoting successful prisoner reintegration.

NOTES

1. There is a second discretionary dimension to the release decision, the system for awarding "good-time" credits. In calculating a prisoner's eligibility to appear before the parole board for a possible release decision, corrections administrators can award credit that, in effect, reduces the prison sentence as recognition for good behavior.

2. The actual release date may reflect the award of "good-time" credits, a discretionary means for advancing a release date.

3. According to Piehl (2002), 32 percent of eligible prisoners in Massachusetts (4,744 prisoners) waived their right to a parole hearing in 1999, choosing for whatever reason to bypass the possibility of discretionary early release and leave prison without a period of parole supervision in the community.

4. Of those 20 states, 11 had also adopted an indeterminate sentencing scheme (Rhine et al. 1991, 10).

5. This national perspective, however, does not begin to capture the disparities in release practices among the 50 states. In states such as Florida, Pennsylvania, and Washington, more than 95 percent of prisoners released in 1998 were released as a result of a parole board decision. In California, Illinois, Indiana, and Minnesota, by contrast, fewer than 1 percent were parole board releases. Between these two extremes, a number of states have developed mixed systems. For example, in Ohio, about half of released prisoners were released mandatorily by statute and half by the parole board (Travis and Lawrence 2002a).

6. Advocates for the abolition of parole release argued that parole boards were "soft on crime." Measured against this yardstick, the movement to abolish parole release has not been a success. According to an analysis by the Bureau of Justice Statistics, prisoners released by parole discretion served an average of 35 months; those released mandatorily served 33 months (Hughes, Wilson, and Beck 2001). Ironically, for prisoners convicted of violent offenses—presumably the group that advocates of parole abolition thought should be serving more time in prison—the differences were most pronounced. Men convicted of violent offenses and released by parole boards served 60 months on average; those with mandatory release served an average of 48 months. Women convicted of violence and released by parole boards served 45 months in prison; those with mandatory release served 36 months. If the movement from discretionary to mandatory release was intended to keep prisoners off the streets longer, the movement did not succeed.

7. Just as the states have experimented with different balances between discretionary and mandatory release mechanisms, they have also been laboratories for experimentation with different approaches to postprison supervision. Some states, such as Oregon, Rhode Island, and California, place virtually all of their released prisoners under some form of postprison supervision. Other states have decided that only certain offenders are required to be supervised on parole, based on various factors such as commitment offense or time served. For example, in Massachusetts, Florida, and Oklahoma, more than half of their prisoners are released without any supervision requirements (Travis and Lawrence 2002a).

8. Technically, these are "admissions" to prison, not individuals admitted to prison. A parolee can be returned to prison, released, and returned again within the same year. This would be counted as two admissions. There are no reliable national estimates on the numbers of individuals who are returned to prison more than once in the same year on the same case.

9. As with our analysis of the shifts in release decisions and parole supervision over the past generation, we also see remarkable state-level variation in the flow of parole violators back to state prisons. In some states, such as Florida, Mississippi, Indiana, West Virginia, and Alabama, fewer than 10 percent of prison admissions are parole violators.

At the other end of the spectrum, in states such as Montana, Louisiana, and Utah, more than half of prison admissions are parole violators. California tops the list: Fully two-thirds (67 percent) of that state's prison admissions are parolees who are being sent back to prison for failing to meet their supervision conditions.

10. To borrow another analogy, this proposal constitutes the community corrections version of the community policing experiment. Bringing this government function closer to the community, and engaging the community in problem-solving activities regarding prisoner reentry much as community policing involved the community in crime strategies, would restore the public's confidence in this dimension of our criminal justice system, just as public confidence in the police has been enhanced under community policing (Skogan 2003).

4

The Expanded Universe of
Invisible Punishment

I n the three preceding chapters, we documented the stunning rise in the rate of imprisonment in America and the enormous extension of criminal justice supervision. In a traditional assessment of the state of criminal punishment in America, the analysis typically ends there, with an accounting of prisons and supervision. However, there is a third form of punishment that we rarely consider when we assess the weight of the criminal sanction on American society and particularly on the lives of those we punish. In this chapter, we consider a range of punishments that are nearly invisible to the public eye—the various legal restrictions that diminish the rights and privileges of those convicted of crimes, both in and out of prison. At the same time that our state and federal legislatures have enacted tougher sentencing statutes, they have also decreed that criminal convictions carry additional penalties. Depending on the precise circumstances, some felons are now ineligible for public assistance, education loans, driving privileges, public housing, and food stamps. Some will find they can no longer vote, are more likely to have their parental rights terminated, must register with the police for the remainder of their lives, and may even be deported. Although these criminal sanctions are not as obvious as some others, they may in fact be more pernicious because they make it more difficult for ex-felons to gain a foothold in free society.

In considering the challenges of prisoner reentry, we must focus squarely on the criminal sanctions that apply after the prison gates close, and after the period of supervision is over. There is little research on the impact of these sanctions; however, from the perspective of returning prisoners, they pose steep hurdles on the road to reintegration. Long after the prison time has been served and parole has been completed, the ex-felon is frequently reminded that his debt has not been paid as society continues to extract a price for violating its laws.

In a recent publication (Travis 2002), I coined the phrase "invisible punishment" to describe this unique set of criminal sanctions. These restrictions certainly constitute "punishment": they are legislatively defined penalties imposed on individuals convicted of crimes, resulting in serious, adverse consequences.[1] Such sanctions are "invisible" in three ways. First, they operate largely beyond public view. By contrast, prisons are highly visible instruments of punishment. Prisons and prisoners can be counted, the costs for prisons can be tallied, and the effectiveness of prison programs can be measured. Community supervision is also quite visible. The number of individuals on parole and probation can be counted, and supervision itself can be evaluated. By contrast, invisible criminal sanctions that deprive ex-offenders of the rights and privileges of citizenship take hold in ways that the public poorly understands. Nor can researchers adequately measure their effectiveness, impact, or even "implementation" through the myriad of private and public entities that are authorized to enforce these new rules.

Second, these forms of punishment are invisible in the sense that they typically take effect outside the traditional sentencing framework. In other words, they are imposed by operation of law rather than by decision of the sentencing judge. Consequently, they are invisible players in the sentencing drama that plays out in courtrooms across America each day.[2] Finally, these sanctions are rarely visible in the legislative debates on sentencing policy. They are not typically enacted by the same legislative committees that determine a state's sentencing statutes. Often they are added as riders to other major pieces of legislation and therefore are given scant attention in the public debate over the main event.[3] They are not even codified with other criminal sanctions, which makes it difficult to grasp the full range of consequences that flow from a felony conviction. Some defy traditional notions of federalism by importing federal penal policy into state sentencing statutes so that a conviction for a state law violation triggers federal consequences.

In short, this universe of criminal sanctions has been hidden from public view, ignored in our national debate on punishment policy, and generally excluded from research on the life course of ex-offenders or the costs and benefits of the criminal sanction. This chapter argues that these punishments subvert reintegration goals by forcing returning prisoners to carry the stigma of past mistakes well beyond the prison gates. It documents the recent history of collateral sanctions in America, including the emergence of a sustained reform effort in the mid–20th century designed to curtail the impact of these sanctions and the sharp reversal that occurred when the nation significantly expanded the reach of these sanctions. It also explores the impact of the network of invisible punishments on returning prisoners, their families, and communities—where such sanctions are anything but invisible—and discusses the distinctive character of the collateral sanctions enacted in the past two decades.

The chapter ends with a series of recommendations that would, if followed, bring these punishments into open view. Specifically, these punishments should be made visible as critical elements of state and federal sentencing statutes. They should be recognized as visible players in the sentencing drama played out in courtrooms every day, with judges required to inform defendants that these consequences flow from a finding of guilt or plea of guilty. Finally, they should be incorporated in our sentencing jurisprudence, subjected to rigorous research and evaluation, and openly included in our debates over punishment policy and prisoner reentry.

The Swinging Pendulum of American Policy on Invisible Punishment

Early Legislation

From the beginning, America has enacted legislation denying convicted offenders certain rights and benefits of citizenship. The American colonies, for example, passed laws denying criminal offenders the right to enter into contracts, automatically dissolving their marriages, and barring them from a wide variety of jobs and benefits. American legislatures were simply following a long tradition, reaching back to ancient Greece, which deemed criminals to be less than full citizens (see chapter 10).

In the modern era, this view has found expression in federal legislation of the 1980s and 1990s, which denies certain felons access to welfare benefits. Before discussing the current situation, however, we should first consider a remarkable era in American history when criminal justice reformers attempted to oppose the tradition of excluding ex-offenders from full citizenship. In the mid–20th century, the country witnessed an extraordinary burst of criminal justice reforms. A landmark presidential commission called for a "revolution in the way America thinks about crime" (President's Commission on Law Enforcement and Administration of Justice 1967). Congress passed the Bail Reform Act of 1968, which reduced pretrial detention for poor people. The Supreme Court issued a series of constitutional rulings granting new rights and protections to those accused of committing a crime. The American Law Institute adopted the Model Penal Code. Rehabilitation was understood to be the goal of corrections.

Reform Actions

Not surprisingly, reformers in this era focused attention on the collateral consequences of criminal convictions (Demleitner 1999). In its 1955 Standard Probation and Parole Act, the National Council on Crime and Delinquency (NCCD) proposed that an offender's civil rights be restored upon completion of his criminal sentence. A year later, the National Conference on Parole concluded, "The present law on deprivation of civil rights of offenders is in most jurisdictions an archaic holdover from early times and is in contradiction to the principles of modern correctional treatment" (NCCD 1962, 97–98). The Model Act proposed by the NCCD included a provision to allow for the expungement of criminal records, meaning that an individual could be restored to his legal status prior to his conviction (NCCD 1962).

In 1967, the President's Commission on Law Enforcement and Administration of Justice noted that "there has been little effort to evaluate the whole system of disabilities and disqualifications that has grown up. Little consideration has been given to the need for particular deprivations in particular cases" (1967, 88). In 1973, the National Advisory Commission on Criminal Justice Standards and Goals recommended fundamental changes in voter disqualification statutes, arguing that reintegration required no less: "Loss of citizenship rights . . . inhibits reformative efforts. If corrections is to reintegrate an offender into free society, the offender must retain all attributes of citizenship. In addition, his respect for law and the legal system may well depend, in some measure, on his ability to participate in that system" (National Advisory Commission on Criminal Justice Standards and Goals 1973, 593).

In 1981, the American Bar Association (ABA) promulgated the Standards on Civil Disabilities, a document that seems quaint from a contemporary perspective. Asserting that the automatic imposition of civil disabilities on persons convicted of a crime were inconsistent with the goal of offender reintegration, the ABA recommended that no such disabilities be automatically imposed, except those related directly to the offense (for example, revoking the driver's license of a repeated drunk driver); that disabilities be imposed on a case-by-case basis, upon a determination that it was "necessary to advance an important governmental or public interest;" and that they be imposed only for a limited time, and then with adequate avenues for early termination upon appropriate review (ABA 1981, chapter 23, part VIII).

The reform spirit touched state legislatures as well. In the 1960s and 1970s, the number of state laws imposing collateral consequences declined (Demleitner 1999). The same period witnessed an increase in the number of laws requiring the automatic restoration of an offender's civil rights, either upon completion of his or her sentence or passage of a certain amount of time. A comprehensive review of all state statutes, conducted in 1986, concluded that "states generally are becoming less restrictive of depriving civil rights of offenders" (Burton, Cullen, and Travis 1987, 60).

Restrictive State Legislation

This reform movement peaked in the 1980s. Then, just as sentencing policy generally became more punitive, state legislatures rediscovered collateral sanctions. A new analysis of state statutes, conducted in 1996, documented the reversal (Olivares, Burton, and Cullen 1996). Compared to 1986, there were increases in the number of states (a) permanently denying convicted felons the right to vote (from 11 to 14 states); (b) allowing termination of parental rights (from 16 to 19); (c) establishing a felony conviction as grounds for divorce (from 28 to 29); (d) restricting the right to hold public office (from 23 to 25); and (e) restricting rights of firearm ownership (from 31 to 33).[4]

The largest increase came in the area of criminal registration. In 1986, only 8 states required released offenders to register with the local police. Following some well-publicized crimes committed by parolees, a tidal wave of registration laws, spurred on by federal funding, swept across the country.[5] By 1998, every state had enacted legislation requiring that convicted sex offenders register with the police upon release from prison, an increase of 42 states in 12 years. Forty states mandate lifetime registration for some sex offenders, and a small number of states mandate lifetime registration for all sex offenders (Center for Sex Offender Management 1999). As of 2001, 386,000 sex offenders were listed in the state registries (BJS 2002).

States also increased the number of occupational barriers for people with various criminal convictions. For example, prohibitions against hiring teachers, child care workers, and related professionals with prior criminal convictions expanded. In addition, checking criminal records became easier because of new technologies, expanded access to criminal records, and an increase in the number of employers checking criminal records of prospective employees (Hebenton and Thomas 1993). One's criminal past became both more public and more exclusionary, limiting the universe of available work.

Federal Sanctions

Congress followed suit, but with a telling twist. As with the state legislatures, Congress ratcheted up the levels of punishment generally, and specifically enhanced the range of collateral consequences for those convicted of violating federal criminal laws. But Congress went even further. As illustrated below, Congress created a web of collateral sanctions that transformed a conviction for certain state crimes into ineligibility for federal benefits.[6] Furthermore, it used the power of the federal purse to encourage states to extend the reach of collateral sanctions.

Consider the following examples: The most blatant form of social exclusion is the deportation of criminal aliens, akin to the ancient practice of exile. Foreigners with criminal convictions are generally excluded from admission into the United States, but beginning with the Immigration Reform and Control Act of 1986 and the Illegal Immigration Reform and Immigrant Responsibility Act of 1996, Congress significantly expanded the categories of crimes that would subject an alien to deportation. Congress even authorized deportation for past crimes.[7] As a result, the number of deportations of aliens with criminal convictions rose from 7,338 in 1989 to 56,011 in 1998 (Schuck and Williams 1999, 384–85).

Congress also enacted legislation to cut offenders off from the remnants of the welfare state. The welfare reform law of 1996 ended individual entitlement to welfare and replaced that scheme with block grants to the states known as Temporary Assistance for Needy Families (TANF). One provision of that law requires that states permanently bar individuals with drug-related felony convictions from receiving federally funded public assistance and food stamps during their lifetime.[8] (States can opt out of or narrow the lifetime ban, and more than half have done so.) The welfare reform law also stipulates that individuals who violate their probation or parole conditions are "temporarily" ineligible for TANF, food stamps, or Social Security Income (SSI) benefits, and public housing (Rubenstein 2001).

Congress also authorized the exclusion of certain offenders from federally supported public housing. Statutes enacted in the late 1990s permit public housing agencies and providers of Section 8 housing to deny housing to individuals who have engaged in "any drug-related or violent criminal activity or other criminal activity which would adversely affect the health, safety, or right to peaceful enjoyment of the premises [by others]"[9] (see chapter 10 for further discussion). Those convicted of drug crimes can reapply for housing after a three-year waiting period and must show they have been rehabilitated.[10] Anyone subject to lifetime registration under a state sex-offender registration statute is ineligible for federally assisted housing.[11]

Congress separated offenders from other benefits as well. The Higher Education Act of 1998 suspends eligibility for a student loan or other assistance for someone convicted of a drug-related offense.[12] (Eligibility can be restored after meeting certain conditions, including two unannounced drug tests.) In the 2000–2001 academic year, about 9,000 students were found ineligible under this provision.[13] The Adoption and Safe Families Act of 1997 prohibits individuals with certain criminal convictions from being approved as foster or adoptive parents. It also accelerates the termination of parental rights for parents whose children have been in foster care for 15 of the most recent 22 months, a provision that particularly affects incarcerated mothers.[14]

Finally, Congress used the power of the purse to encourage states to pass laws restricting offenders' rights. In 1992, Congress passed a law requiring states to either revoke or suspend the driver's licenses of people convicted of drug felonies or lose 10 percent of their federal highway funds.[15] Similarly, the 1994 Crime Act required each state to enact a sex-offender registration law within three years or lose 10 percent of its federal funding for criminal justice programs.[16] A final example: the Public Housing Assessment System, established by the federal government, creates financial incentives for public housing agencies to adopt strict admission and eviction standards to screen out individuals who have engaged in criminal behavior.[17]

The Resurgence of Retributivism

In sum, over the space of a few decades, America has witnessed a dramatic shift in the public discourse on the use of collateral sanctions as a form of punishment. From the 1950s to 1980s, collateral sanctions were strongly criticized by legal reformers and restricted by state legislatures. Then, beginning in the mid-1980s, these sanctions experienced a surge in popularity. As the nation embarked on a steady buildup of prisons and extended the reach of criminal justice supervision, America's new punitive attitude also led to an expansion in the network of invisible punishment. Taken together, the laws enacted by the states and Congress during this resurgence of collateral sanctions constructed substantial barriers to participation in American society. These laws became instruments of the "social exclusion"[18] of people with criminal convictions.

In some respects, this development is no more than a further articulation of the retributive impulse that determined most criminal justice policies in the latter part of the 20th century. In other ways, however, these sanctions seem cut from a different cloth. We can detect a social impulse distinct from the robust retributivism that has fueled harsher sentencing policies over the past 25 years. When sex offenders are subjected to lifetime parole supervision, drug offenders are denied student loans, families are removed from public housing, and legal immigrants with decades-old convictions are deported from this country, even the harshest variants of "just desserts" theories cannot accommodate these outcomes.

The enactment of laws imposing invisible punishment is an exercise in unchecked retributivism. Because these punishments are invisible to the public, to sentencing judges, and to traditional legislative processes, they are not subject to some of the realities that have constrained the growth in imprisonment and supervision. If an elected official wants to "do something" about crime and thereby curry public favor, enacting laws denying ex-offenders the rights and privileges of citizenship is a virtually cost-free exercise in symbolic politics. Taxpayers bear no direct costs; on the contrary, there may be savings in public benefits. There are no sentencing commissions asking tough questions about proportionality or adverse racial impacts. There are no judges interposing their own discretion and deciding that a particular punishment might not be right for a particular offender. There are no political battles over the siting of prison facilities. In short, this strategy's political appeal is strong, particularly when, as in the 1980s and 1990s, public posturing over "get tough" strategies brought political dividends.

As we consider the impact of these sanctions at the individual and community levels, we must remember this political reality. The swing in the pendulum was so extreme because enactment of these sanctions met little political opposition. Restoring a more balanced approach will require public awareness of the social costs of these sanctions.

Assessing the Impact of Invisible Punishment

At the beginning of the 21st century, the realities of invisible punishment are quite different from those of any earlier era. First and foremost, because of the dramatic rise in arrests and criminal convictions, these sanctions simply affect more people than ever before. More than 47 million Americans (or one-quarter of the adult population) now have criminal records on file with federal or state criminal justice agencies (BJS 1993). An estimated 13 million Americans are either currently serving a sentence for a felony conviction or have been convicted of a felony in the past (Uggen, Thompson, and Manza 2000). This means that more than 6 percent of the adult population has been convicted of a felony. One in eight African-American adult males between the ages of 25 and 29 is currently in prison or jail (Mauer 2003). Invisible punishments reach deep into American life.

Beyond these statistical observations, however, gauging the precise impact of these punishments on individual returning prisoners is difficult. For some consequences of felony convictions, analysis is relatively straightforward. For example, we know that the laws of 48 states and the District of Columbia deny prisoners the right to vote while they are in prison (Kalogeras 2003). Therefore, we could survey prisoners, determine how many were registered to vote prior to imprisonment, calculate the likelihood that they would have voted had they not been imprisoned, and project the diminished voter participation attributable to these state laws (Uggen and Manza 2002). In like fashion, we can estimate the impact of statutes that bar 4 million convicted felons from voting. For example, according to Uggen and Manza's detailed analysis (2002) of the impact of felon disenfranchisement (discussed in greater detail in chapter 10), if felons had been allowed to vote, Democrats would likely have retained control of the Senate in the 1990s and Al Gore would have been elected president in 2000.

Assessing the impact of other collateral sanctions is far more complicated, however. Tracking the consequences of statutes that disqualify criminals from education loans, public housing, welfare benefits, or parental rights would be extraordinarily difficult. Counting the number of individuals punished through these laws approaches impossibility. Agencies administering these sanctions are far flung, have little or no connection with the criminal justice system, may or may not keep records of their decisions, and have no incentive to report on these low-priority exercises of discretion.

An evaluation of the impact of collateral sanctions should extend beyond an analysis of individual-level effects. Of course, as is traditional with other forms of punishment, we would ask whether denying rights, privileges, and benefits to individuals convicted of certain offenses actually has a deterrent effect on those who might otherwise engage in illegal behavior. The frame of inquiry, however, should also include an analysis of these sanctions' impact on communities with high rates of incarceration and reentry. To continue the voting rights discussion, for example, we should inquire whether the disenfranchisement of a large percentage of citizens living within a small community has the effect of undermining the legitimacy of the political process. Similarly, a comprehensive assessment of the laws excluding individuals convicted of drug-related crimes from public housing would gauge the impact on families living there. Or, an evaluation of the laws denying food stamps and public assistance to certain felons would measure these sanctions' impact on the health and well-being of felons' families. In short, a comprehensive research agenda would examine the long-lasting consequences of this constellation of punishments for the vitality of families, labor markets, and civic life in poor communities. Although an empirical analysis of the individual- or community-level effects of this new strain of invisible punishments is difficult, we can still easily discern that these punishments are qualitatively different from collateral sanctions of an earlier era. Taken together, recent enactments, many of them passed by Congress, chip away at critical ingredients of the support systems vital to poor people in this country. Under these new laws, offenders can be denied public housing, welfare benefits, the mobility necessary to access jobs that require driving, child support, parental rights, the ability to obtain an education, and, in the case of deportation, total access to the opportunities that bring immigrants to this country. For many offenders, the social safety net has been severely damaged.

These modern punishments affect more than the benefits of the welfare state. They also make it harder to exercise the individual autonomy that is taken for granted by others in society—being a parent, living in public housing with one's family, moving freely without notice to the police, and establishing a residence without suffering the rejection of one's neighbors. In this brave new world, punishment for the original offense is no longer enough; one's debt to society is never paid. Some commentators, seeing parallels with practices from another era when convicts were sent to faraway lands, refer to this form of punishment as "internal exile" (Demleitner 1999). Others liken this extreme labeling to "the mark of Cain" (Hubbell 2001), the effects of these sanctions as relegating the offender to the status of "non-citizen, almost a pariah" (Jacobs 1983, 30).

In his framework for describing the evolution of the concept of citizenship, Marshall (1964, 65–71) traces three phases: the expansion of "civil rights" in the 18th century (e.g., the rights to free speech and religion, to own property and enter into contracts); "political rights" in the 19th century (e.g., the right to vote); and "social and welfare rights" in the 20th century (e.g., entitlements to shelter, welfare, and food).[19] The strain of invisible punishments that emerged at the end of the 20th century represents an intrusion into this third dimension of citizenship. In the modern welfare state, these restrictions on the universe of social and welfare rights amount to a kind of "civil death," in which the offender is deemed unworthy of societal benefits and excluded from the social compact.

Looking Forward

Invisible punishment constitutes a form of criminal sanction that in many ways cuts deeper into American life than do imprisonment and supervision. The scars of imprisonment are certainly felt for a lifetime. The effects of supervision are long-lasting. Collateral sanctions, however, serve as a constant reminder that one's criminal past carries over into one's future. These sanctions define a relationship between citizen and state that is forever altered.

The new forms of invisible punishment that emerged in the latter part of the 20th century are particularly disturbing because they exacerbate the division between "us," the law-abiding, and "them," the law-breakers. By enacting welfare reform and dismantling the six decades' old safety net for the poor, Congress has determined that the poor with criminal histories are less deserving than others. Interjecting itself into criminal justice policy domains traditionally reserved for the states, Congress has not hesitated to use federal benefits to enhance punishments or provide federal funds to encourage new state criminal sanctions. In an era when the symbolic denunciation of criminals has been politically rewarding, the opportunity to deny offenders the benefits of the welfare state has been just too tempting. However, federal and state legislatures have not acted alone. Just as changes in sentencing policies have led to the increased use of imprisonment and the expansion of criminal supervision, so has the expansion of collateral sanctions been carried out in the public's name, with the tacit if not explicit support of the electorate. In this kind of environment, the people who come through our criminal justice system—mostly poor, urban, minority males who are often denied the right to vote because of their felony convictions—have few friends in high places.

The policy challenge we face, then, is to find ways to constrain this form of punishment, to establish limiting principles, and to reverse the movement toward social exclusion of prisoners returning home. There are several encouraging developments that provide a basis for optimism. A number of states have rolled back their laws disqualifying felons from voting (see chapter 10 for a detailed discussion). Congress is considering rolling back the reach of the law banning drug offenders from education loans.[20] In fact, Representative Barney Frank (D-MA) has sponsored a bill (H.R. 685) that would repeal restrictions on college loans for students convicted of a drug crime. In addition, the Department of Housing and Urban Development has tempered its policies regarding the exclusion of felons from publicly supported housing.

Perhaps most significant is the leadership shown by the American Bar Association (ABA). At its August 2003 meeting, the ABA approved new guidelines—*ABA Standards for Criminal Justice: Collateral Sanctions and Discretionary Disqualification of Convicted Persons, Third Edition.*[21] In these remarkable recommendations, the ABA calls for restricting the reach of invisible punishment by limiting collateral sanctions to those that relate directly to the offense charged, and prohibiting sanctions that "without justification, infringe on fundamental rights, or frustrate a convicted person's chances of successfully reentering society" (ABA 2004, BL-1). The ABA also recommends that state legislatures codify these sanctions and that defendants be notified of these consequences and their avenues for relief before offering a guilty plea. Taken as a whole, these standards powerfully articulate the injustice of invisible punishments and offer promising and just solutions. As previously discussed, at that ABA conference, Supreme Court Justice Anthony M. Kennedy called for a complete reexamination of the country's approach to sentencing and corrections. In his eloquent and compelling speech, Justice Kennedy (2003) succinctly identified the problems with our current punitive justice system: "Our resources are misspent, our punishments too severe, our sentences too long." Taking up his challenge to "find more just solutions and more humane policies," the ABA created a special commission—named after Justice Kennedy—charged to review sentencing policies in America, including policies that hinder reintegration. In keeping with the spirit of the new ABA standards, we conclude this chapter by considering some concrete recommendations that would, if followed, constrain the impulse to punish those who violate our laws by diminishing their rights and privileges.[22]

Making Invisible Punishments Visible

The critical first step in a reform agenda is to make invisible punishments visible. We should begin by changing our language to recognize that these are indeed punishments—they are legislatively authorized sanctions imposed on individuals convicted of criminal offenses. As a next step, state and federal legislatures should codify the collateral sanctions that are scattered throughout their respective statutes. A criminal defendant or his counsel should be able to find, in one place, all of the potential consequences of a criminal conviction. In a parallel action, collateral sanctions should be reviewed by the legislative committees with jurisdiction over state sentencing policies, or by a state's sentencing commission. The final step would require defendants to acknowledge that they are aware of the potential consequences of a guilty plea or a determination of guilt.[23] One need not recite in open court *all* collateral sentences; that would be impossible. Yet, judges should be required to ask a defendant whether counsel has explained the collateral consequences, and perhaps list some that might be pertinent to the defendant's situation.[24] It is ironic that the truth-in-sentencing movement, which promotes certainty in the imposition of prison sentences, values open decisionmaking about the terms of punishment, and denigrates the exercise of discretion in sentencing, has not yet discovered that the "secret sentences" (Chin and Holmes 2002) that constitute the universe of invisible punishment violate these three principles.

Applying Sentencing Principles

Once the universe of invisible punishment is brought into open view, we should seek to apply these sanctions according to general sentencing principles. One such bedrock principle of our sentencing jurisprudence holds that the severity of the criminal sanction should be limited by the seriousness of the offense and the offender's relevant attributes. Sentencing grids, featuring charge severity on one axis and prior criminal record on the other, and limiting departures for mitigation or aggravation, are concrete expressions of this principle. Yet the collateral sanctions under discussion here do not reflect this principle of proportionality. A felon convicted of the lowest felony loses his right to vote, as does a serial murderer. A minor drug offender can be evicted from public housing just like a major drug dealer. A sex offender convicted of statutory rape for a consensual act may be subject to lifetime registration along with a repeated child molester. A de novo review of collateral sentences would begin by asking the questions posed in other sentencing contexts: How does this sanction further the purposes of sentencing, to whom should it be applied, and with what consequences? A state's sentencing commission might also carry out this complicated review. These quasi-independent entities have a track record of reviewing punishments in an effort to diminish disparities among similarly situated defendants. They could provide a similar service to the legislature and the judiciary by developing guidelines regarding the imposition of collateral sanctions.

Another bedrock principle of sentencing is that sanctions should be individualized. In applying this principle, we should recognize that some collateral sanctions might appropriately be automatic. For example, barring convicted felons from jury eligibility automatically may well be reasonable to protect the integrity of criminal trials. However, the vast majority of collateral sanctions cannot be justified this way. Within the established legislative ranges, these sentences should be imposed in ways that tailor the punishment to the circumstances. Is a bar from a particular kind of employment appropriate for a given offender? Does it relate to the offense charged? A new approach to collateral sanctions would operate under the presumption that these sanctions should be applied by sentencing judges to individual defendants, to fit their unique circumstances, rather than applied automatically by operation of law.

Providing for Judicial Relief

A third principle should guide a revision of our approach to collateral sanctions—we need clear avenues for judicial or administrative relief if a sanction causes undue hardship. Under the current situation, it is unclear where a convicted felon turns to challenge the imposition of a particular sanction. Who tells him what his options are? When a drug offender is barred from living in public housing with his mother, what is his redress? Granted, some of the statutes discussed in this chapter provide avenues for relief; for example, a drug offender denied a student loan may be restored to eligibility after passing two unannounced drug tests. In addition, many states allow individuals to petition a court for relief from these "civil disabilities." These are cramped expressions of legal remedy, however. We should allow a convicted offender to return to the sentencing court and argue that a collateral sanction should not apply to him. We should allow the offender to bring housing agency officials to this same court to explain the decision to exclude him from his apartment. We should require the courts to inform offenders of their rights to seek relief.

Adopting a New Sensibility

The most important recommendation—indeed, more a hope—is that our nation should reverse the current cultural sensibility about those who have violated our laws and adopt a goal of reintegration, not exclusion. We need to find concrete ways to reaccept and re-embrace offenders who have paid their debt for their offense. In chapter 10, which discusses the "identity" of those who have violated the law, we will explore the importance of a new ethos of reintegration. The concluding chapter outlines a new jurisprudence of reintegration. The language of reintegration can certainly be relevant to a discussion of the realities of imprisonment and supervision, but the reintegration imperative is nowhere as compelling as in this discussion of invisible punishment.

These concrete recommendations for reforming the universe of invisible punishment may not comport with the punitive attitudes that often characterize our political discourse. Yet they are firmly rooted in both traditional notions of sentencing philosophy and modern innovations such as truth in sentencing. The mere act of proposing them to legislative bodies would have this advantage: these recommendations would make such punishments visible and raise searching questions about why we have chosen these responses to the wrongdoing of our fellow citizens. Discussing the impact of these sanctions on the lives of hundreds of thousands of returning prisoners—and their families and communities—would force a public discussion of the challenges of reintegration. By asking how we expect returning prisoners to become productive members of their community when our elected officials have placed so many roadblocks in the way, we are implicitly asking fundamental questions about the relationship between society and those who have violated society's laws.

NOTES

A version of this chapter entitled "Invisible Punishment: An Instrument of Social Exclusion" first appeared in *Invisible Punishment: The Collateral Consequences of Mass Imprisonment,* edited by Marc Mauer and Meda Chesney-Lind (New York: The New Press, 2002). The text is reprinted by permission of The New Press.

1. These forms of punishment have been defined as "civil" rather than "criminal" in nature, as "disabilities" rather than punishments, as the "collateral consequences" of criminal convictions rather than the direct results. These linguistic distinctions miss the central point, which is that these sanctions are intended to punish those who violate the law, and are experienced as punitive. For a critique of the legal doctrine distinguishing direct from collateral consequences, see Chin and Holmes (2002).

2. Little wonder, then, that defense lawyers cannot easily advise their clients of all of the penalties that will flow from a plea of guilty. Indeed, the courts have held that it is not a breach of the principle of effective assistance of counsel for a defense lawyer to fail to inform his client, for example, that a plea of guilty to a certain offense will expose him to the risk of deportation. This constitutional interpretation stands in contrast to the standards of the American Bar Association that provide: "To the extent possible, defense counsel should determine and advise the defendant, sufficiently in advance of the entry of a plea, as to the possible collateral consequences that might ensue from entry of the contemplated plea" (ABA 1997, Standard 14-3.2(f)).

3. The provision to exclude individuals with drug convictions from eligibility for welfare was debated for two minutes in the U.S. Congress. See Rubenstein and Mukamal (2002).

4. The study found no change in three other categories—disqualification for jury duty, restrictions on public employment, and application of concept of civil death (Olivares, Burton, and Cullen 1996).

5. In 1994, Congress passed the Jacob Wetterling Crimes Against Children and Sexually Violent Offender Registration Act (42 U.S.C.A. § 14071) requiring states to create registries of child molesters and sexually violent offenders. States that fail to comply with the Wetterling Act are subject to a 10 percent reduction in Byrne formula grant funding (The Edward Byrne Memorial State and Local Law Enforcement Assistance Programs [42 U.S.C. § 3750]). In 1996, Megan's Law (Public Law 104-145, *U.S. Statutes at Large* 110 (1996): 1345) was passed as an amendment to the Wetterling Act requiring states to release relevant information on convicted sex offenders. The Pam Lyncher Sexual Offender Tracking and Identification Act of 1996 (42 U.S.C. § 14072) further amended the Wetterling Act by instructing the FBI to develop a national database of names and addresses of sex offenders released from prison.

6. In 1991, a report of the Office of National Drug Control Policy found that offenders could lose 462 benefits from 53 federal agencies. See Demleitner (1999), footnote 86.

7. This provision was declared unconstitutional by the Supreme Court in *INS v. St. Cyr.* (121 S. Ct. 2271 [2001]).

8. *U.S. Code* 42, sec. 862a.

9. *U.S. Code* 42, sec. 13662(c). A 1988 amendment to the 1986 Drug Abuse Act also authorizes the eviction of a family member who was involved in certain drug offenses, even if the case did not result in a conviction (*U.S. Code* 42 [1999], sec. 1437[d][1][6]).

10. *U.S. Code* 42, sec. 13662(c).

11. *U.S. Code* 42, sec. 13663(a).

12. *U.S. Code* 20, sec. 1091(r).

13. In the 2000–2001 academic year, about 67,000 of the 7.5 million applicants for student aid said they had been convicted of selling or possessing drugs. About 11,000 left the question blank. See Curry (2001).

14. Public Law 105-89.

15. *U.S. Code* 23, sec. 159. As of 2001, 17 states, the District of Columbia, and Puerto Rico had enacted legislation conforming to the federal law requiring driver's license suspensions and revocations. Thirty-three states filed a certification from the governor and resolution by the state legislature expressing opposition to the federal policy. Filing these documents places the state in compliance with the Department of Transportation's policy so the state is not subject to loss of federal highway funds. Brian Dover, Department of Transportation, personal communication with the author, September 19, 2001.

16. The Edward Byrne Memorial State and Local Law Enforcement Assistance Program (*U.S. Code* 42, sec. 3750) provides formula grants to states to improve the functioning of the criminal justice system with an emphasis on initiatives targeting violent crime and serious offenders. Under the Wetterling Act, states had three years to comply with the provisions (September 13, 1997) and the option to apply for a two-year extension before losing 10 percent of the state Byrne formula grant. In fiscal year 2000, nearly $500 million was available to states through the Byrne formula grant program. All but 14 of the 56 states and territories applied for the two-year extension.

17. 24 CFR 966.203(b) and 966.4(l)(5)(vii).

18. The Blair government in the United Kingdom has pledged to overcome the distances created between mainstream society and those who live at society's margins. In this category are included the homeless, runaways, truants, pregnant teenagers, and former prisoners. "Social exclusion" is defined as "what can happen when people or areas suffer from a combination of linked problems such as unemployment, poor skills, low income, poor housing, high crime, bad health, and family breakdown" (Social Exclusion Unit, Office of the Deputy Prime Minister 2001, 10).

19. I am indebted to Demleitner (1999, 154) for this insight.

20. Jenny Collier, director of the National Policy and State Strategy Legal Action Center, personal communication with the author, April 6, 2004. The 2005 budget proposed by the Bush administration calls for limiting the law's application to drug crimes committed while in school.

21. The ABA defines "collateral sanction" as "a legal penalty, disability, or disadvantage, however denominated, that is imposed on a person automatically upon that person's conviction for a felony, misdemeanor, or other offense, even if it is not included in the sentence" (ABA 2004, BL-1). "Discretionary disqualification" refers to the same punishments that flow from a civil conviction.

22. In formulating these recommendations, I have benefited from my participation in the American Bar Association's Task Force on Collateral Sanctions, which was established in 2001 to review the ABA standards on this issue. I acknowledge the contributions of my fellow members.

23. The Supreme Court recognized this reality in *INS v. St. Cyr* (121 S. Ct. 2271 [2002]), holding that avoiding the collateral consequence of deportation is "one of the principal benefits sought by defendants deciding whether to accept a plea offer or instead proceed to trial."

24. This approach was recently embraced by the Delaware Supreme Court in *State v. Berkley* (Del. 724 A. 2d 558 [1999]), holding that a state law requiring that a convicted person forfeit his driver's license could not be enforced where the offender did not know it was a consequence of a guilty plea.

PART II
Defining the Policy Challenges of Prisoner Reentry

Introduction

The Policy Dimensions of Prisoner Reentry

A criminal justice expert transported in time from 1970 to the early 21st century would scarcely recognize the modern landscape of punishment in America. In the intervening decades, our country added 1 million people to its prisons, quadrupling the rate of imprisonment. Through legal reforms and shifting penal philosophy, we dramatically transformed the parole release and supervision system. At this point, far fewer prisoners are released by parole boards, and America now sends as many people to prison for parole revocations as were sent to prison for any reason in 1970. Our observer would be puzzled by the maze of legal hurdles now facing the nation's felons as they move down the path of reintegration. Particularly striking is the federal government's expanded role in adding new burdens to the quantum of punishment meted out by the states. Our expert would wonder why the nation had become so disenchanted with relying on judges, parole boards, and parole officers to exercise discretion; why our legislatures had felt compelled to specify the dimensions of punishment; and why modern-day criminal justice experts had lost sight of rehabilitation as their primary goal.

Perhaps most unsettling would be the realization that the criminal justice system now reaches deep into the fabric of American society. One-quarter of America's adult population—47 million people—have criminal records (BJS 1993b). Approximately 13 million have been convicted of a felony (Uggen, Thompson, and Manza 2000). By 2001, an estimated 5.6 million U.S. residents—or one in 37 adults—had served some time in prison (Bonczar and Beck 2003). If rates of first incarceration remain constant, then nearly 1 in 15 persons born in 2001 will be imprisoned during his or her lifetime. The nation's incarceration rate is five to eight times higher than the rates of industrialized nations similar to the United States, including Canada and western Europe (Mauer 2003). Our expert from 1970 might readily agree with modern scholars who conclude that we now live in an era of "mass incarceration" (Mauer and Chesney-Lind 2002), that we are now "imprisoning America" (Pattillo, Weiman, and Western 2004).

This expert would speculate about how this dramatic increase in the use of imprisonment affects American society. This inquiry would begin logically with questions about the impact of high incarceration rates on the prisoners themselves, then expand to examinations of how incarceration influences their families, communities, and the wider society. Our observer would be stunned to see the ripple effects of the nation's shift in criminal justice policy. Certainly in those neighborhoods that are home to large numbers of prisoners, virtually every aspect of community life has undergone profound changes. The dynamics of family life have been transformed. The rhythms of finding work and building a career are quite different. The public health and public safety risks facing a community are now assessed differently, as so many individuals presenting those risks now spend time in prison. Society's efforts to provide safe and affordable housing must now accommodate the realities of incarceration. At a broader level, the American experiment in democracy and pluralism has been tested, as millions of American citizens are denied the right to vote, African Americans and Latinos disproportionately carry the stigma of criminal justice involvement, and the nation lives uneasily with a large population of ex-felons.

The following seven chapters explore these dimensions of the new realities of punishment in America. They view the experiment in mass incarceration through the lens of seven distinct social policy domains. Rather than view these new situations simply as matters of concern to criminal justice experts, these chapters analyze how our incarceration policies affect the work of practitioners, advocates, and community leaders in other policy arenas. Chapter 5 examines the public safety risk posed by returning prisoners, asking how high levels of imprisonment have affected community efforts to reduce crime rates. Chapter 6 assesses the impact of incarceration on families and children, documenting the consequences for relationships between men and women in urban communities, for prisoners' children, and for the social service agencies responsible for child and family welfare. Chapter 7 documents incarceration's influence on the labor markets of America, particularly on the low-skilled male workers who are having difficulty improving their economic circumstances in the modern economy. Chapter 8 views incarceration from the perspective of public health practitioners, assessing whether the high prevalence of communicable diseases, mental illness, and substance abuse among the imprisoned population mandates different approaches to prison health care. Chapter 9 explores the intersection between incarceration, reentry, and housing policy, focusing in particular on the high rate of homelessness in the reentry cohorts. Chapter 10 explores the relationship between society and its former felons, especially with regard to limits on voting rights, legal privileges, and other attributes of civic identity. Finally, chapter 11 views the era of mass incarceration from the ground up, looking at the ways in which these new realities have affected the well-being of the communities hardest hit by the nation's decision to increasingly use imprisonment as a response to crime.

These chapters reflect a common analytical framework—the reentry perspective—as a way of exploring the nexus between the new realities of punishment and each of the seven policy domains. They document, from different vantage points, the consequences of imprisonment—but with a twist, namely, recognizing that reentry is the inevitable reality of imprisonment. In other words, these chapters view our punishment policies as creating a motion picture, not a snapshot. When a convicted offender is sentenced to prison, he or she leaves a life behind. That life may (or may not) include children, intimate partners, peer groups, coworkers, employers, partners in crime, or classmates. All of these dimensions of community life may benefit or suffer from the prisoner's absence. After entering the prison gates, the prisoner enters a new community, with its own cultural norms and social structure. In this new life, prison inmates may (or may not) work, participate in the civic life of the prison, have their health needs addressed, learn new skills, develop new partners in crime, or further their education. This time in prison may benefit the prisoner in some ways; it may damage him or her in others. Finally, when the moment of reentry occurs, the returning prisoner may (or may not) reconnect with family, peer groups, and the community in positive ways. He or she may (or may not) secure employment, housing, and health care. The return to the free society left behind may or may not be successful.

In short, the reentry perspective—the motion picture—reflects the fact that our imprisonment policies not only send people to prison, but they also create ripple effects that undermine our society's efforts to promote safety, child and family welfare, strong labor markets, safe and affordable housing, healthy individuals, civic participation, and vibrant neighborhoods.

Following an exploration of the intersection among incarceration, reentry, and a particular policy domain, each of these chapters concludes with a section entitled "Looking Forward." These short essays build upon some of the themes developed in the main body of the chapter but suggest new areas for research and policy development. The goal is to prompt the reader to imagine different policy strategies that would recognize the realities of punishment in America yet attempt to mitigate some of the harshest effects of those realities. The reader is challenged to ask whether our nation must necessarily accept high levels of rearrest among the reentry cohort, suffer a generation of harmed children, consign former prisoners to lifetimes of lower earnings, accept returning prisoners with unattended health risks that endanger themselves and others, tolerate a marginalized population that cannot exercise the rights and privileges of citizenship, and undermine the valiant efforts of churches, banks, foundations, and government agencies to strengthen the capacity of our poorest communities. We *must* face the challenges of prisoner reentry, particularly in this era of mass incarceration. The following chapters are intended to prompt new thinking about the best ways to meet those challenges.

5

Prisoner Reentry and Public Safety

The odds against successful reentry are daunting. According to the Bureau of Justice Statistics (BJS), two-thirds of released prisoners will be rearrested for one or more crimes, including felonies and serious misdemeanors, within three years after they get out of prison. Nearly half will be convicted of a new crime. One-quarter will be returned to prison for these new convictions (Langan and Levin 2002). In crafting public policies to improve the chances of successful reentry, we must confront this stubborn fact: under current conditions, most prisoners will fail to lead law-abiding lives when they return home.

The public safety issue has the potential to shape and distort most policy debates on how best to meet the challenges of prisoner reentry. Referring to research showing that a particular program or policy is effective at reducing crime rarely resolves these debates. Evaluations showing, for example, that halfway houses, drug treatment programs, work release facilities, transitional housing, or electronic monitoring cut recidivism rates are often overshadowed by anecdotes of prisoners who participated in these programs and still committed new crimes. Policymakers must debate and resolve difficult and pressing issues regarding prisoner reentry in a charged atmosphere where risks are unavoidable and public sentiment is volatile.

Accordingly, a discussion of the nexus between public safety and prisoner reentry is best conducted on two levels. On the one hand, we must step back from this heightened public sensitivity to take an objective, empirical look at the scope of the safety risks that returning prisoners pose. Policy choices must be made and programs must be implemented; decisions regarding those policies and programs are best informed by the available evidence. On the other hand, we must recognize the validity and importance of the public's concerns about those risks. After all, the public is correct in believing that most returning prisoners will commit new crimes. The challenge, then, is to engage the public in a sustained discussion that begins by acknowledging the reentry reality—they all come back—and moves toward adopting policies that demonstrably reduce the levels of criminal behavior within the population of returning prisoners.

The public's understanding of the crime problem associated with returning prisoners is often shaped by individual, high-profile incidents. A single incident of a horrible crime committed by someone recently released from prison can easily overwhelm dispassionate analysis based on rigorous research. To illustrate this point, this chapter begins by recounting a story from New York State showing that, when developing policies that effectively promote prisoner reintegration, even the best programs may not be able to withstand the public's outrage when a program participant gets rearrested for a horrific crime. We next extract a larger lesson from the New York story about the unique attributes of crimes committed by ex-offenders who are under criminal justice supervision. We then examine the risk of new crimes committed by recently released prisoners, exploring the significance of the BJS finding that two-thirds of returning prisoners will be rearrested in three years. This is followed by an examination of supervision policies and their role in reducing crime. The chapter ends with a discussion of a new way to frame the relationship between prisoner reentry and public safety, including a new strategy that might reduce the seemingly intractable odds that returning prisoners will commit new crimes.

One Crime Too Many

For many reasons, programs that allow carefully selected prisoners to spend time in the community are considered sound correctional policy. Under these programs, prisoners are placed in facilities that allow them to attend school, go to a job, or connect with their families during the day, and return to the correctional facility at night. Prisoners living in these facilities are not formally on parole; technically, they are still in correctional custody, but they are granted restricted privileges to spend time in the community. One premise for these programs—which include halfway houses, work release facilities, furloughs, and education release programs—is that they reduce crime. Indeed, a number of studies have shown that prisoners who participate in conditional release programs commit very few crimes while on release and have lower recidivism rates following program completion (Seiter and Kadela 2003).

Program Failures

Yet public support for programs such as these hangs by a slender thread. Even though the prisoners may pose a minimal crime risk while they are in the program, the risk is still not zero. One crime committed by one program participant may be one crime too many. In New York State, the thread of public support snapped in the spring of 1977 when four prisoners assigned to temporary release programs escaped. One had been convicted of notorious murders. The other three went on horrific crime sprees that made headlines in New York's tabloids (Heffernan 1977; Raftery 1977; Raine 1977). In the withering heat of the public outrage over these escapes, the state's policies on prisoner reentry fell apart.

The first case had quite a history. On the night of August 30, 1959, Salvador Agron, the 16-year-old leader of the Vampires, a Puerto Rican gang, stabbed three unarmed teenagers sitting in a playground on Manhattan's West Side. Two of the victims died. Agron quickly became known as "the Capeman" because of the black cape he wore on the night of the murders (Gonzalez 1997). He was arrested, convicted, and sentenced to death, the youngest man on death row in New York State history. Agron's conviction received national attention and prominent citizens in the community, including Eleanor Roosevelt, voiced their disapproval over the sentence's severity. In 1962, Governor Nelson A. Rockefeller commuted Agron's sentence from death to life imprisonment, citing diminished mental capacity. While incarcerated at Green Haven Correctional Facility, Agron earned an associate's degree from Dutchess County Community College. In 1976, Governor Hugh Carey commuted Agron's life sentence, making him eligible for parole. Agron was then transferred to Fishkill Correctional Facility, a medium-security facility, where, under an education release program, he attended college classes five days a week on the campus of New Paltz State College. In many respects, Agron was a poster child for the rehabilitation ideal. Yet on April 16, 1977, just eight months before his parole date, and nearly 18 years after his arrest, the 34-year-old convicted murderer absconded from his educational release program. Two weeks later, he was taken into custody in Phoenix, Arizona.

On May 1, 1977, less than three weeks after "the Capeman" absconded from Fishkill, Richard Gantz was out on a day pass from the Lincoln Correctional Facility in Manhattan, a work release facility for prisoners who had less than a year left on their sentences. Gantz, who was serving a sentence for robbery, left Lincoln to attend classes at Kingsborough Community College. He abducted a 19-year-old Baruch College student who was sitting in her car near the Kings Plaza Shopping Center in Brooklyn. He drove around the neighborhood, held up multiple gas stations, and took his victim to a motel where he repeatedly raped her. Three days later, on May 4, 1977, Harry Elmore, another resident of the Lincoln Correctional Facility, was also released on a one-day pass. He then murdered 45-year-old Ethel Loney. The next day, Jerry Williams, a trucker's helper at one of New York's work release facilities, was arrested for the March 10 rape of a 20-year-old nurse at her Brooklyn apartment.

Headlines from the *Daily News,* a New York tabloid, captured the public outrage: "Sal Agron, the Capeman Killer, Is on the Loose," "State Prisoners in Escapist Mood," "Woman Slain, Accuse Convict on Jail Leave," "Rape Rap Hits 3rd Con on Release." Within a month, New York's Corrections Commissioner Benjamin Ward was on the hot seat before the State Senate's Crime and Corrections Committee. Ward presented the strongest possible policy arguments in defending his department's action. He told the Senate that these programs were an integral part of the reintegration process. Thousands of prisoners had participated in work programs since 1970, he testified, earning nearly $1 million in wages, paying taxes, and saving money to help with their transition from prison. Ward noted that there had only been 114 absconders out of the 3,053 prisoners participating in release programs, a remarkably low failure rate of 3.7 percent (Kihss 1977). He pointed out that the rate of new crimes committed by released prisoners was higher in the months after they were released on parole than during their time on work or educational release. His last argument surely reverberated in a state that had just six years earlier endured the violent prison riots at Attica. If the work release program were abolished, as the legislators proposed, Commissioner Ward predicted he would face "an extremely violent situation" in the prisons.

Policy Changes

Despite Commissioner Ward's plea, on July 15, 1977 (just three months after Agron's escape), the legislature approved sweeping changes in the state's temporary release and parole policies. The controversial release program would be kept alive for a year, an extension made necessary, according to the *New York Times,* for very practical reasons: "There was no other place to put the 3,000 prisoners now in the community under these conditions" (Kihss 1977, 22). In the future, eligibility for furloughs would be severely restricted. Only prisoners with serious medical problems that could not be addressed in prison, or prisoners whose closest relative was near death, would be considered. Furthermore, prisoners convicted of violent crimes or sexual assault could only be assigned to work release or educational release with the personal approval of the corrections commissioner. To ensure that parole decisions would be made by an agency outside the commissioner's control, the Parole Board was removed from the Department of Corrections to become a separate entity. In August, Governor Carey signed these bills into law.

The changes were immediate and dramatic. Commissioner Ward bridled at the statutory requirement that he personally approve the assignment of every prisoner to a work release program. He ordered a complete review of the nearly 1,000 cases then on work release, spending hours each day reading their files before deciding whether the prisoner should remain in the program or be sent back to a secure facility. In late August, he ordered special Corrections Emergency Response Teams (CERT) into the state's work release facilities to remove 140 of the program participants and return them to prison.[1] Participation levels in the state's conditional release programs dropped dramatically, decreasing from 766 participants in September to 386 in December. Between 1979 and 1984, the portion of the state's inmate population permitted to participate in temporary release programs dropped from 1.60 to .02 percent (BJS 1979).[2] Martin F. Horn, who served on the commissioner's staff and later ran New York State's parole agency and the departments of corrections in Pennsylvania and New York City, recalls the process of rewriting the program's procedures manual: "Under the old policy, the philosophy was to run temporary release programs that would benefit the inmate. Under the new policy, the primary goal was to promote public safety."[3]

Not All Crimes Are Alike

In 1977, there were 1,919 homicides and 5,272 forcible rapes in New York State, yet the murder of Ethel Lomey and the rapes committed by Gantz and Williams prompted a public outcry and resulted in a dramatic reversal in public policy. Why?

A crime committed by a recently released prisoner is different from other crimes, not because the crime is different, but because the criminal is different. Some, and perhaps most, members of the public feel that a former prisoner who is still under state supervision is someone who could be in prison but is not. After all, that individual was indeed convicted of a felony and sentenced to prison. Yet, because of the parole board's decision, the correctional agency's conditional release policies, the judge's leniency, or legal technicalities, that former prisoner is back on the streets—free to murder, rape, assault, or steal.

Seen from this perspective, every crime committed by an inmate on conditional release or a former prisoner on parole is a crime that should not have happened. One can argue that (1) when a judge sentences an offender to an indeterminate sentence, and states a minimum and maximum term, no one expects the entire maximum term to be served in prison; (2) conditional release programs are good for society because they help prisoners make a more structured transition to life in the community; (3) parole supervision is a smart way to provide both surveillance and services to prisoners returning home; or (4) these policies reduce crime. However, these arguments carry little weight when confronted with the harsh facts of a brutal crime committed by someone who arguably could have been in prison but was not.

Because these crimes are different, the victims of these crimes occupy a unique status in public debates on crime policy. They are victims not only at the hands of criminals; they are also victims of our government's failure to protect its citizens from harm. These victims can direct their anger—and the public's anger—toward an identifiable target, namely the government policy that allowed the prisoner's release. These victims' voices can be enormously powerful. Their stories provide fuel to coalitions of politicians, law enforcement representatives, editorial writers, and other advocates for "get tough" crime policies. The murder of Polly Klaas by Richard Allen Davis, a state parolee with a long criminal history, led to a groundswell of public outrage in California that culminated in the enactment of that state's "three-strikes-and-you're-out" law. Megan Kanka's rape and murder by Jesse Timmendequas, a convicted sex offender with two prior convictions for sexual abuse, spurred a national movement to enact "Megan's laws," which require sex offenders to register their locations. As we saw in the New York vignette, advocacy on behalf of these victims can trump any arguments that particular criminal justice policies save money, promote successful reentry, or, ironically, reduce crime.

These stories of dramatic shifts in criminal justice policy following high-profile crimes committed by released prisoners underscore the conundrum of prisoner reentry and public safety. Because a large percentage of released prisoners commit new crimes after their release, there is always a risk that someone right out of prison, but still under supervision, will commit a horrific crime. The public will think, with some justification, that this crime could have been prevented. However, society cannot keep people in prison forever. Our notions of proportionality dictate that, because the punishment must fit the crime, most prison sentences must be limited in time. Because reentry is inevitable for all but the few individuals who die in prison, and because the probability of new crimes is high, all programs that oversee returning prisoners must accept the risk that a program participant may commit the crime that sparks a firestorm of public outrage.

Crime Rates among Returning Prisoners

Faced with such horrific crimes as those committed by Gantz, Elmore, Davis, and Timmendequas, it is difficult to take an objective view of the public safety risk posed by returning prisoners. It is hard to step back from the harsh probability that many newly released prisoners will commit crimes, sometimes brutal ones, that could have been avoided had the prisoner never been released. Yet, if crime policy is to be responsive to the public safety risks associated with prisoner reentry, then we must disentangle fact from fiction, distinguish data from emotion, and place priorities on policies that reduce those risks.

Rearrest Rates and Types of Crime

As a first step we should ask, "How much risk do released prisoners pose to public safety?" Recidivism studies or data that tell us how often prisoners were rearrested after their release from prison provide a partial answer.[4] In 2002, BJS published the most recent and most comprehensive study of recidivism rates among released prisoners (Langan and Levin 2002). The bureau collected data on a sample of 272,111 prisoners released in 1994 in 15 states (figure 5.1).[5] Within three years of their release, 67.5 percent of these individuals were rearrested at least once for a new offense. Nearly half (46.9 percent) were convicted of a new crime and 25 percent were returned to prison for a new conviction.[6]

The released prisoners in the BJS sample were arrested for a wide range of crimes. Within three years, they were charged with violent offenses (21.6 percent), property offenses (31.9 percent), drug offenses (30.3 percent), and offenses against the public order (28.3 percent).[7] Many were arrested for crimes in more than one of these categories. In fact, they averaged four new crimes per person over the three years of the study.

Figure 5.1. *Rearrest Rates of Prisoners Released from Prisons in 15 States, 1994*

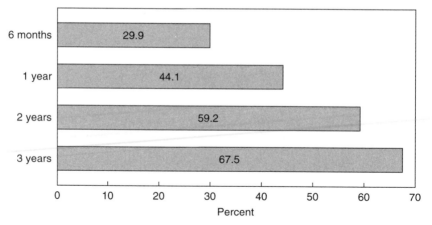

Source: Langan and Levin (2002).

Note: Percentages are cumulative by time period in which prisoners were rearrested after release.

A listing of the crimes for which they were arrested is quite chilling. Over a three-year period, these 272,111 prisoners were charged with an estimated

- 2,900 homicides,
- 2,400 kidnappings,
- 2,400 rapes,
- 3,200 other sexual assaults,
- 21,200 robberies,
- 54,600 assaults,
- 13,900 other crimes of violence,
- 40,300 burglaries,
- 16,000 motor vehicle thefts,
- 79,400 drug possession violations,
- 46,200 drug trafficking charges, and
- 26,000 weapons offenses.

These arrests were not evenly distributed over the three-year period of the study. Nearly 30 percent of the released prisoners were arrested within the first six months after leaving prison. The cumulative total rose to about 44 percent within the first year and almost 60 percent within the first two years following release (Langan and Levin 2002). Clearly the months and years right after the release from prison present the highest risk to public safety.

This study seems to confirm the public's concerns about returning prisoners: As a group, they pose a significant risk to public safety; many return quickly to criminal behavior after their release; and a significant portion will be returned to prison for a new crime. In fact, compared with the general population, recently released prisoners are 20 to 50 times more likely to be arrested (Raphael and Stoll 2004). The BJS study also lends support for crime control initiatives that focus enforcement and surveillance attention on newly released prisoners, for the simple reason that their rate of offending is so high. Indeed, it is hard to imagine another identifiable group of people who exhibit such a high rate of criminal behavior.

We should be cautious, however, before leaping from these recidivism studies to full-blown public safety policies that promise substantial crime reductions by focusing on returning prisoners. The fact that returning prisoners have high recidivism rates does not tell us much about their contributions to America's overall crime rates. If most crimes were committed by people who had *not* recently been released from prison, we would not expect much public safety gain from even the most effective efforts to reduce recidivism among returning prisoners. So we need to ask a second question, "What portion of all crime, as measured by arrests, can be attributed to recently released prisoners?"[8]

Proportion of All Arrests

To answer this more complex question, we turn again to the BJS study. The bureau calculated the crimes of the 1994 release cohort as a proportion of all criminal arrests in the selected states. Examining index crimes (murder, rape, robbery, aggravated assault, burglary, larceny, and motor vehicle theft; arson is not included in the study) in 13 states, the researchers found that these released prisoners accounted for 140,534 arrests between 1994 and 1997.[9] Dividing this number by the total number of adult arrests for these crimes during the same period (2,994,868), BJS found the released prisoners in their study accounted for only 4.7 percent of all the arrests from 1994 to 1997 (Langan and Levin 2002).[10]

This statistic provides only a partial answer to our question, however, because it reflects only those arrests attributed to the 1994 release cohort in the years 1994 through 1997. In each of those three years, more prisoners were released and committed crimes that contributed to the overall crime rates. Additionally, some prisoners who were released in the years before the 1994 cohort were still arrested for crimes committed in the years covered by the study. If we make the reasonable assumption that those released in years just prior to and after 1994 display recidivism rates similar to those of prisoners released in 1994, then we can make a more realistic estimate of the percentage of arrests for which recently released prisoners were responsible. Following this logic, Rosenfeld, Wallman, and Fornango (forthcoming) determined that, for the years 1994 to 1997 in the 13 states in the BJS study, prisoners who had been released in the three preceding years accounted for between 13 and 16 percent of arrests (figure 5.2).[11] Rosenfeld et al. (forthcoming) also projected the 1994 cohort's recidivism rates for cohorts released between 1995 and 2001 and found that, by 2001, the arrests of prisoners released within the previous three years accounted for more than 20 percent of all arrests, up from 13 percent in 1994. This increase was not the result of increased recidivism rates, but instead because this seven-year period witnessed two important trends in America—a rise in the number of prisoners being released and a decrease in the number of arrests. Because

Figure 5.2. *The Contribution of Multiple Release Cohorts to Total UCR Arrests, 1994–2001*

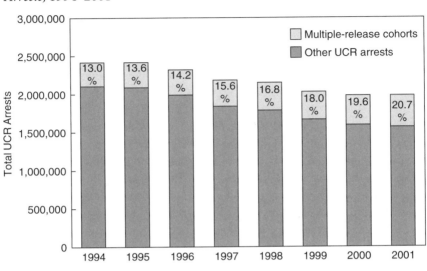

Source: Based on analyses conducted by Rosenfeld et al. (2004).
Note: UCR = Uniform Crime Reports.

these two trends occurred simultaneously, the percentage of arrests attributable to recently released prisoners rose steadily.

Prisoners Presenting the Greatest Risk

Additional analysis of the BJS data reveals that asking three different questions—Which prisoners are rearrested? Where are they rearrested? And when are they rearrested?—provides important insights that can shape the policy response to the safety risks that the reentry cohort poses. For example, BJS found that the 6.4 percent of the release cohort who committed 45 or more crimes were responsible for 14 percent of the 4.9 million pre- and postrelease arrest charges attributable to the cohort. Prisoners with 25 or more crimes in their past (24 percent of the release cohort) accounted for 52 percent of all arrests (Langan and Levin 2002). These findings demonstrate that the release cohort does not pose a uniform risk of reoffending. Some returning prisoners are significantly more dangerous than others, and examining their criminal histories provides a starting point for identifying the differential risks. When combined with other factors that predict future criminal behavior, such as the crime of conviction and the prisoner's age at release, it becomes possible to differentiate the categories of prisoners who pose the greatest risk to public safety (Blumstein et al. 1986).

Variation among the States

Rosenfeld et al.'s analysis of BJS data (forthcoming) shows that location also matters in assessing returning prisoners' contribution to crime rates. In California, for example, individuals released from prison within the three years preceding 1994 accounted for nearly one-quarter (24.1 percent) of all arrests for drug crimes and 16 percent of arrests for violent crimes. In Ohio, by contrast, recently released prisoners accounted for 45 percent of all arrests for violent crimes. Even more striking is their finding that these release cohorts made only small contributions to all arrests in Michigan (7.7 percent of all violent arrests, 6.8 percent of all property arrests, and 3.7 percent of all drug arrests) and Minnesota (10.9 percent of all violent arrests, 7.7 percent of all property arrests, and 3.5 percent of all drug arrests). Thus, policies developed to reduce crimes committed by released prisoners should be quite different among these four states. Policymakers in Ohio seeking to reduce violence would be well advised to focus substantial attention on the reentry cohort. Michigan and Minnesota, by contrast, would find little safety yield from targeting returning prisoners. Even great successes in reducing recidivism rates among returning prisoners in these states would not make much difference in the state's overall arrest rates. On the other hand, given the high rate of drug arrests among its release cohort, California could potentially reduce its level of drug arrests by implementing strategies to address drug use and sales among returning prisoners. This provocative interpretation of the BJS data raises a number of intriguing questions about state-level differences. At a minimum, this analysis suggests that a single national picture of recidivism rates masks enormous state-to-state variation in the nexus between prisoner reentry and public safety.

National Trends

Disaggregating the data by crime type also reveals distinct trends with important public safety implications (figure 5.3). By 2001, prisoners released in the three preceding years accounted for approximately 30 percent of the arrests for violent crime, 18 percent of the arrests for property crime, and 20 percent of the arrests for drug offenses.

Figure 5.3. *The Contribution of Multiple Release Cohorts to Total UCR Arrests, by Type of Crime, 1994–2001*

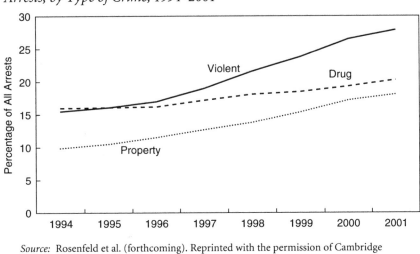

Source: Rosenfeld et al. (forthcoming). Reprinted with the permission of Cambridge University Press.
Note: UCR = Uniform Crime Reports.

This final calculation highlights the unique relationship between prisoner reentry and public safety at the beginning of the 21st century. Today, as America experiences the highest levels of prisoner reentry and the lowest levels of crime in a generation, the portion of the nation's crime (as reflected in arrests) that can be attributed to recently released prisoners is arguably greater than ever before. This new reality creates a powerful incentive for policymakers to focus their efforts on strategies that could reduce returning prisoners' rate of reoffending. In other words, if public officials want to keep crime rates low, they should focus resources and attention on developing successful strategies for reducing the crime rates of returning prisoners. If nearly 30 percent of the nation's arrests for violent crime can be attributed to an identifiable group of individuals, most of whom are under criminal justice supervision, then policymakers who seek to enhance public safety must find ways to promote successful prisoner reentry.

New Measures Needed

These different analyses of the BJS recidivism data suggest that we should think about prisoner reentry and public safety in a much more sophisticated way. A simple measure of recidivism—whether a former prisoner is rearrested within a specified period—is highly inadequate. At a minimum, in constructing a recidivism measure, we must know how many arrests can be attributed to the reentry cohort and the severity of the crimes for which former prisoners were arrested. For example, a measure of recidivism that does not distinguish between a single property crime committed by Prisoner A within three years following his release and three violent crimes committed by Prisoner B during the same period has little value. Clearly, Prisoner B poses a greater safety risk. Similarly, it is important to know the time elapsed between release and arrest. A measure that does not differentiate between crimes committed the day following release and crimes committed two years after release provides a weak foundation for policymaking.

From a policy perspective, the most important shift in current thinking would be to move from a recidivism measure to a safety measure. Rather than viewing the public safety risks of returning prisoners simply in terms of their rearrest rates, policymakers should assess those risks by determining the percentage of a jurisdiction's arrests that can be attributed to those prisoners. This measure—which could be called a "rearrest ratio"—would yield varying answers, depending on the type of crime, the jurisdiction, and the jurisdiction's level of overall arrest activity. Using a rearrest ratio, policymakers could focus their efforts and allocate public resources more strategically. Today, when crime rates are low and reentry rates are high, arguments for strategies that reduce recidivism rates of returning prisoners are more persuasive than ever.

These new measures of the safety risk posed by returning prisoners would also change the dynamics of public accountability. If the criminal justice system were required to publish an annual report on the relationship between the arrest rates of returning prisoners and overall arrest rates at the national, state, and local level, then criminal justice agencies could more easily be held accountable for providing programs, transitional services, supervision, and other interventions that would reduce recidivism rates. If the public received periodic reports indicating high rearrest rates during the weeks and months after prisoners are released, then corrections agencies, supervision agencies, and the larger network of public and private entities working on prisoner reentry initiatives could be evaluated on their success in reducing returning prisoners' criminal behavior during those periods. However, if the criminal justice system were held accountable in these ways, how would it respond?

Safety and Supervision

Our policies for responding to the public safety risks posed by returning prisoners are disturbingly haphazard and illogical. Sometimes, we turn a blind eye to these risks. As we discussed in chapter 4, about 20 percent of the individuals leaving the nation's prisons each year—more than 100,00 people—are not under criminal justice supervision when they get out. They are not on parole. They report to no one. They have no conditions placed on their release. They simply step off the bus and are on their own.

Lack of Supervision

Why are some prisoners unsupervised after release from prison? For one group, this reality reflects state sentencing statutes. These prisoners had been sentenced to "flat time," which means that their sentences simply did not include a postprison supervision period. A second group may have been incarcerated on a parole violation, and have returned to prison to serve the remainder of their term. Like those sentenced to flat time, these prisoners are released when their term is up, and they do not face a supervision period after they leave prison. A third group of prisoners may have been sentenced under a traditional indeterminate sentencing statute, which allows for early release followed by community supervision, but were denied release by the parole board and served their entire sentence in prison. They may have been denied parole because they had severe disciplinary records in prison. Perhaps such powerful forces as the prosecutor, the victims of their crimes, the media, or the general public combined to oppose their release by the parole board. Whatever the reason for the denial of parole, these prisoners must be released after completing their sentences because they have fulfilled their legal obligation to the state. A fourth and smaller group of prisoners choose not to seek early release. They may think their chances of being released on parole are slight and decide not to request a hearing. Or they may prefer to serve out their sentence in prison rather than subject themselves to the rigors, risks, and inconvenience of parole supervision.[12]

A policy that allows more than 100,000 prisoners to be released without supervision each year seems illogical at best, dangerous at worst. We can easily imagine an extreme but plausible case that illustrates the potential for danger. A mentally ill prisoner, sentenced to prison for a violent crime and demonstrating a history of drug addiction, is repeatedly denied parole because the parole board believes he poses a great risk of reoffending. As a consequence of a string of fights and other disciplinary infractions, the prisoner is kept in solitary confinement 23 hours a day, for months on end. His sentence eventually comes to an end and he must be released—without supervision. In solitary one day, on the streets the next—with no supervision.

From a public safety perspective, it is hard to justify this transition from total isolation to total freedom. Shouldn't some government agency be responsible for helping this returning prisoner adjust to his freedom? Shouldn't some agency make sure he is connected to a mental health facility and required to take his medication? Shouldn't he be required to undergo drug treatment, subject himself to drug testing, and stay away from his drug hangouts so he can reduce the risk of relapse? If he has no place to live, shouldn't a public or private agency refer him to transitional housing for the dually diagnosed? Shouldn't he be legally obligated, at least for a while, to abide by conditions that would reduce his risk of committing new crimes? Or should we entrust responsibility for this difficult and risky transition to this prisoner, his family, and whatever network of support is ready to help him?

Certainly few returning prisoners are as dangerous as the extreme case just described. Many pose minimal risk to public safety. Each year, however, more than 100,000 prisoners walk out of our prisons with no supervision. Within this group, our sentencing policies now make no distinctions between those who are at high risk and those who are at low risk for recidivism. Ironically, some of the highest-risk prisoners will have escaped the reach of criminal justice supervision because parole boards decided they were too dangerous to release early. Furthermore, when any of these returning prisoners commits a crime, their victims cannot claim that the government failed to protect them. And criminal justice officials can claim, with considerable justification, that prisoners like these were no longer their responsibility. So, in designing policies to reduce the safety risks posed by returning prisoners, we should start by asking why so many are released unsupervised, with no governmental responsibility for their transition. As was discussed at greater length in chapter 4, a strong policy argument can be made that all released prisoners should be supervised, at least for a while.

Yet there is another perspective on the nexus between prisoner reentry and public safety. Just as we sometimes fail to acknowledge the government's responsibility to supervise returning high-risk prisoners, we also subject other former prisoners to excessive state control, exaggerating the public safety risks they pose. For example, as crime rates started to increase in some cities early in this decade, some law enforcement officials placed the blame, in part, on the large numbers of returning prisoners. Probation Officer Billy Stewart, when asked to explain the rise in homicides in Boston, said it well: "You want my quick and dirty analysis for the jump in numbers? Simple: They're b-a-c-k! . . . and they're smarter. They're embittered. And that seasoned bitterness makes them extremely dangerous."[13]

Too Much Supervision

When crime rates start to increase, it is tempting to focus attention on former prisoners who are still under criminal supervision. They are identifiable, have already demonstrated criminal tendencies, and their parole conditions are ready-made targets of enforcement activities. Yet, as illustrated by a story from Los Angeles, severe enforcement of parole conditions may seem disproportionate to the safety risk reentering prisoners pose. Like most other cities in America, Los Angeles saw a dramatic decline in violence during the 1990s—from 1,094 homicides in 1992 to 426 in 1998. Beginning in 1999, however, this downward trend came to a halt. The rate of homicide stabilized, then started climbing again, rising from 425 in 1999 to 588 in 2001, and it continued to increase in 2002. During a four-day period in late November 2002, 13 homicides occurred, a level of killing never before seen in Los Angeles (Garrison and Hernandez 2002).

The Los Angeles police responded in some predictable ways. They claimed that the spate of violence was partly attributable to the increase in the number of returning prisoners. This analysis elicited an enforcement response, "Operation Enough" (Los Angeles Police Department 2002), that was swift, focused, and deliberate. Carrying photographs of suspected parole violators, 250 police officers, working together with parole agents, descended upon the city's skid row area, a homeless encampment just east of downtown. This part of the city was home to about 2,000 parolees, the highest concentration of parolees in the state. On the first day of the sweep, 108 arrests were made, about 50 percent of them for parole violations.

Similar sweeps occurred a month later in Oakland, a city where the homicide rates had reached a 30-year low in 1999, only to rise 16 percent by 2001. City officials launched massive sweeps throughout the city, netting 60 parolees who were charged with various parole violations—principally for violating their release conditions and possessing drugs (Martinez 2002). Parolees, according to the *Oakland Tribune,* were "prone to violence, the 'baddest of the bad'." Lt. Ben Fairow of the Oakland Police Department claimed a public safety success: "These people we got off the street, we're potentially keeping these people from being the next suspects or victims of homicides"[14] (Martinez 2002).

As these stories illustrate, parolees are convenient targets when the public wants something done about crime. Parolees are an identifiable group of individuals who, in the aggregate, present a high risk of criminal behavior. Because their liberty is contingent upon meeting certain conditions of supervision, they can be returned to prison for violating these conditions. This loss of liberty requires neither a criminal conviction nor proof that the parolee posed a public safety risk. When it comes time in America to "round up the usual suspects," it is relatively easy to round up large numbers of people on parole, charge them with violating the conditions of their supervision, and send them back to prison.

In summary, our policies cover both extremes of the spectrum of responses to the public safety risks posed by returning prisoners. From a public safety perspective, we sometimes provide too much or too little state oversight of those who leave prison. We pay too much or too little attention to the public safety risks returning prisoners pose. Ideally, our policies should strike the right balance between reducing the crime risks posed by returning prisoners and promoting their successful reintegration. To develop such policies, we need to better understand how effective our current strategies really are.

Meeting the Public Safety Challenge

When considering how best to respond to the significant public safety risks posed by returning prisoners, the debate typically focuses on the effectiveness of three traditional strategies: keep prisoners in prison longer; provide them with more in-prison programs that will reduce their reoffending rates when they leave prison; and provide more intensive supervision and supportive services when prisoners return to the community. As we will see, each of these strategies has significant limitations. If the policy goal is to significantly change the odds of success—to substantially reduce the high recidivism rates of the reentry cohort—then the investment options should be expanded to include new ideas. After examining the limitations of the three traditional strategies, we will propose a new idea that matches resources to the period when returning prisoners pose the greatest risk to public safety.

Longer Prison Sentences

For many Americans, there is a straightforward way to reduce the crime rates among former prisoners: keep them in prison longer. Proponents of this view make a simple and unassailable argument: as long as prisoners are behind bars, they cannot harm the community. More sophisticated advocates for longer prison terms argue that America's crime rate has been reduced in part because we have put so many people in prison.

There is some truth to the assertion that more prisons have meant less crime. The fourfold increase in the imprisonment rate over the past generation has undeniably impacted America's crime rate. Two leading criminologists, William Spelman from the Lyndon B. Johnson School of Public Affairs at the University of Texas, Austin, and Richard Rosenfeld from the University of Missouri, St. Louis, have documented the effect of increased incarceration on our crime rates. Using a variety of data sources and statistical models, they have independently arrived at similar estimates: About one-quarter of the reduction in violent crime during the 1990s can be attributed to more lawbreakers off the streets and in prison (Rosenfeld 2000; Spelman 2000).

Yet prison expansion is an expensive and blunt crime control instrument. We spend over $56 billion per year on corrections to incarcerate 1.3 million people, up from $9 billion in 1982 (Bauer 2004). Our prisons are home to an aging prison population; approximately 25 percent of all prisoners are over age 40, far past the crime-producing time of their lives (Harrison and Beck 2003). In addition, our prison growth may have reached the point of diminishing returns in generating added safety. With so many violent offenders already incarcerated, according to Spelman (2000), the marginal value of incarcerating one more person, in terms of crime reduction, has declined significantly. In this analysis, the yield in violence reduction by adding a prison bed today is one-third the yield of adding a prison bed in the early 1970s.

Therefore, yes, we could respond to the crime risks posed by returning prisoners by keeping them in prison longer. However, this strategy faces a number of significant limitations. First, we should not assume that crimes now committed by released prisoners within the first month of freedom could simply be avoided by extending their prison stay by a month. Both BJS recidivism studies (Beck and Shipley 1989; Langan and Levin 2002), which followed prisoners released in 1983 and those released in 1994, observed high crime rates in the months immediately following release even though the average length of stay increased over this period. In 1991, the average sentence length was 22 months; in 1997, it was 28 months (Lynch and Sabol 2001). Furthermore, Rosenfeld et al. (forthcoming) found that, controlling for other contributors to recidivism, the length of time served in prison has no effect on the probability of rearrest (see also Langan and Levin 2002). So longer prison stays might only postpone, not prevent, the crimes returning prisoners commit.

Perhaps we could be more discerning and lengthen the prison terms of only those at highest risk of reoffending. Implementing this idea, however, requires a sentencing system with more discretion at the sentencing and release stages and more reliable information about individualized risk assessments. Unfortunately, the movement away from indeterminate sentencing has made it less likely that individual risk could be a substantial factor in determining the length of a prison stay. Finally, a public safety policy promoting longer prison terms would add to the already substantial fiscal and social costs of incarceration in America. Given the condition of most state budgets, a substantial new wave of prison expansion is currently unlikely. In short, we cannot solve the problem of returning prisoners' significant crime risks by simply imposing longer prison terms.

More Programs in Prison

Many Americans propose a different strategy for reducing the crime risks posed by returning prisoners: Provide in-prison programs that will reduce prisoners' recidivism rates—e.g., improve their literacy, help them earn a high school or college degree, provide treatment for their addictions, teach them concrete job skills, and coach them in anger management. With these improvements in skills, capabilities, and attitudes, the argument goes, prisoners will be less likely to engage in crime when they return home.

There are solid reasons for embracing this strategy. As we will discuss in other chapters in this section, a growing body of research demonstrates that many of these interventions can reduce recidivism. Over the past decade, four comprehensive reviews of dozens of individual program evaluations have been conducted, all pointing to the same conclusion: Correctional programs can reduce recidivism, improve employment outcomes, and reduce relapse to drug use (Cullen and Gendreau 2000; Gates et al. 1999; Gerber and Fritsch 1994; Wilson, Gallagher, and Mackenzie 2000). Compared with a generation ago, when a prominent review of program evaluations concluded that "nothing works" to rehabilitate offenders (Martinson 1974), this more optimistic assessment represents a significant shift. Now, researchers and practitioners are focusing their inquiries and innovations on the more nuanced questions of which intervention, or combination of interventions, works best for various offender categories.

The question, however, is not whether prison-based programs effectively reduce the recidivism rates of returning prisoners. The broader policy question is whether a strategy of investing significant resources in these programs could garner political support and yield substantial reductions in rearrest rates. Clearly, political support for prison-based programs is quite weak. During the 1990s, at a time when state coffers were overflowing and state corrections budgets were growing rapidly, investments were made in facilities and personnel, not programs. According to national data, the percentage of prisoners participating in vocational, educational, and drug treatment programs from 1991 to 1997 actually declined (Lynch and Sabol 2001). More recently, in an era of unprecedented fiscal constraints, states have cut prison programs even further. Realistically, it is difficult to envision substantial new political and financial support for prison programs as a crime-reduction strategy.

These political and fiscal realities, however, should not deter advocacy on behalf of effective prison programs. Like the United Kingdom has, the United States should launch a robust national initiative to identify, through rigorous research, the prison-based programs that most effectively reduce recidivism; certify those programs that meet evidence-based standards; and fund programs in all state and federal prisons (Colledge, Collier, and Brand 1999). As defined, this initiative would undoubtedly result in certified measurable reductions in rearrest rates among returning prisoners. Yet, for three reasons, this strategy's potential to yield *significant* reductions in crime rates among returning prisoners is quite limited. First, even successful prison-based programs show modest results in well-designed evaluations. In their review of the crime-reduction effects of prison-based adult offender programs, Aos et al. (2001) estimate that the average future crime-reduction effects (effect size) range from 8 to 17 percent at best. Second, a large-scale expansion of in-prison interventions would likely draw prisoners who were less motivated to succeed, thereby reducing success rates (Bushway and Reuter 2001). Finally, a focus on in-prison programs does not directly confront the realities of reentry—particularly the high rearrest rates in the weeks and months immediately following release from prison. In short, an investment in more prison programs should be viewed as a necessary but not sufficient ingredient in a comprehensive strategy to substantially reduce crime rates among returning prisoners.

More Intensive Supervision

Supervision has been the dominant policy strategy for managing the crime risks posed by returning prisoners. Thus, faced with the challenge to reduce crime rates in a community by reducing the rearrest rates of newly released prisoners, a public official might logically demand more supervision. This policy platform might include initiatives to supervise more former prisoners, supervise them longer and more intensively, attach new conditions to the terms of their supervision, and take more punitive actions when these former prisoners fail to abide by these conditions. Before jumping on the supervision bandwagon, we should first pause to consider why we think that more supervision would result in less crime.

The dark secret of our dominant approach to reentry management is that we cannot say *definitively* that postprison supervision, as currently implemented, reduces crime. In fact, to date there is only one study comparing the outcomes of prisoners released to supervision with those released without supervision, and it indicates that supervision has little impact on recidivism rates (Solomon, Bhati, and Kachowski 2005). Using data from the BJS recidivism study (Langan and Levin 2002), researchers from the Urban Institute concluded that supervision had modest—at best—effects on rearrest rates (Solomon et al. 2005). In fact, among the largest groups of prison releasees (male drug, violent, and property offenders), the study found that expanding supervision would only improve recidivism outcomes for property offenders released by discretionary parole boards. The study also found that supervision matters most in the first months after release. In light of these findings, the need to reexamine the core operations of our system of supervision and to focus squarely on the first months after release is compelling.

INTENSIVE SUPERVISION—THE RAND FINDINGS

The most ambitious research on the effectiveness of supervision was carried out in the late 1980s by a team from the RAND Corporation headed up by Joan Petersilia and Susan Turner. With funding from the National Institute of Justice, they examined the effectiveness of intensive supervision programs (ISPs) involving 2,000 offenders in 14 programs in 9 states. Regarded by many "as the most promising criminal justice innovation in decades," ISPs were seen as an effective way to reduce recidivism rates among offenders under supervision (Petersilia and Turner 1993, 2). ISP proponents argued that offenders should be supervised closely, with smaller caseloads for each parole or probation officer, an emphasis on tight surveillance, close monitoring of conditions of release, and swift attention to parole or probation violations. The expectation was that fewer crimes would be committed, participation in services would increase, and returns to prison would go down.

The RAND evaluation was the largest, most rigorous study ever conducted on the effectiveness of community supervision. In this study, offenders were randomly assigned to intensive supervision in each site. Offenders in the control group, however, received routine probation or parole. The vast majority of the offenders in the study were men in their late 20s and early 30s, most of whom had long criminal records. The researchers tracked these offenders for a year. While the results disappointed ISP advocates, they illuminated well our examination of effective strategies for reducing the public safety risks of returning prisoners. The RAND study found that offenders in the ISPs were not rearrested less frequently and were not rearrested for less serious offenses when compared with offenders in the control group. In some of the sites, rearrest rates actually went up slightly, which raises the question as to whether increased surveillance is more effective at detecting new crimes and apprehending suspects than it is at deterring them from committing those crimes (Petersilia and Turner 1993, 5).

Yet a closer examination of the RAND findings sheds light on the relationship among the nature of supervision, the kind of program, and recidivism. Offenders who had at least two contacts a week with their probation or parole officer and participated in such prosocial activities as education, work, or community service displayed recidivism rates 10 to

20 percent lower than other offenders in the study. Merely increasing the intensity of supervision with such strategies as house arrest or electronic monitoring was ineffective. In reflecting years later on the lessons of the ISP experiment, Petersilia concluded that, to be effective, "the supervision of high-risk probationers and parolees must be structured, [be] intensive, maintain firm accountability for program participation, and connect the offender with prosocial networks and activities" (Gendreau and Little 1993, quoted in Petersilia 1998, 6).

Although these findings undermine the argument that closer supervision alone reduces crime, other results from the ISP experiment point out both the pitfalls and potential of this approach to reentry management. The level of technical violations in the ISP group was almost double that of the control group (65 percent versus 38 percent). Similarly, the offenders in the ISP program were much more likely to be sent back to prison (24 percent versus 15 percent). Thus intensive supervision may not reduce rearrest rates, but is very effective at detecting parole and probation violations and returning violators to custody. A large proportion of the technical violations were for failed drug tests, which were routinely administered under the ISP protocols. As the research team noted, "If stringent conditions are imposed and people's behavior is monitored, they have more opportunities for violations and for being found out than if there are few conditions and few contacts" (Petersilia and Turner 1993, 5).

The RAND evaluation also contained provocative findings regarding offender participation in programs designed to promote reintegration. Offenders in the ISP group were more likely than those in the control group to participate in drug and alcohol counseling programs (45 percent versus 22 percent). More than half of ISP participants were employed, compared with 43 percent in the control group. Twelve percent paid restitution, compared with 3 percent in the control group. Indeed, the largest reductions in recidivism were received when ISP participants received *both* surveillance (drug testing) and programming, not just one or the other.

Three conclusions emerge from this ambitious and rigorous study. As compared with regular supervision, intensive supervision alone (1) does not reduce rearrest rates (and may increase them); (2) significantly increases rates for violation of supervision conditions and returns to prison; and (3) is effective at increasing program participation. We need to find ways to connect returning prisoners to prosocial networks and activities; supervision can play a role in making those connections to reduce recidivism rates. Viewed from a public safety perspective, these findings suggest that we will not reduce crime much, if at all, simply by increasing the intensity of supervision. Viewed from a corrections management perspective, more supervision sends more people back to prison, mostly for technical violations. Viewed from a reintegration perspective, more supervision increases participation in programs that place offenders in jobs, helps offenders with addictions to alcohol and drugs, and facilitates restitution to victims.

Reinventing Supervision

Yet the RAND study tells only half of the public safety story. How should we understand the increased rates of return to prison for technical violations? Nearly a quarter of those subjected to intensive supervision were sent back to prison for parole or probation violations, compared with 15 percent in the comparison group. Is there no public safety benefit from supervision practices that take many more ex-offenders off the streets? Is there no incapacitation effect from policies that place so many high-risk individuals in prison? As we discussed in chapter 4, the rates of parole revocation in America have increased significantly over the past two decades. By 2000, nearly one-third of all prison admissions were parole violators, compared with 18 percent in 1980 (Blumstein and Beck 1999). At the national level, we now send as many people to prison on parole violations—nearly 200,000 per year—as we sent to prison for any reason in 1980 (Hughes et al. 2001; Rice and Harrison 2000). Certainly, a policy that results in such widespread incarceration must have a public safety payoff.

Remarkably, researchers have not evaluated the crime-reduction effects of imprisonment resulting from parole violations. Yet, given the high rates of recidivism among parolees, we can reasonably expect that this secondary imprisonment prevents many offenders from committing new crimes simply because they are behind bars. Our ability to develop sound reentry management policies is significantly hampered by the absence of rigorous research that quantifies the crime reductions attributable to this regime of imprisonment.

It would be disconcerting if the research demonstrated that the greatest crime-reduction impact of supervision occurs when supervision fails and former prisoners are sent back to custody, not when it succeeds and returning prisoners are kept in the community, struggling with but overcoming the challenges of reintegration. If we take this conclusion to its logical extension and significantly increase parole revocation rates, we will have simply created a new system of imprisonment, under the guise of parole violations, and legitimized its existence by pointing to its putative short-term effectiveness at reducing crime. Simply proving that this form of incapacitation is effective at reducing crime misses a larger point. The parole violators who are returned to prison will soon be released again after serving sentences averaging months, not years. They will be released with virtually the same risk of recidivism as they demonstrated when they were sent back to prison. Those who complete their original sentences during their second stint in prison will likely be released with no supervision because they will have "maxed out." Crimes they commit after release will not be counted as parole or corrections failures because these crimes were not committed under criminal justice supervision. Nevertheless, these crimes are no less damaging to the public. How is public safety protected under this result?

As a public safety strategy, postprison supervision, like incarceration and prison-based programs, has significant shortcomings. We should not abandon supervision, however. We should instead reinvent supervision along the lines proposed in chapter 4 to test new models that demonstrate the promise of enhancing public safety. A new model of supervision would reflect an overlooked finding in the BJS recidivism study—rearrest rates are highest in the months immediately following release from prison. Nearly 30 percent of the released prisoners were arrested within the first six months, 44 percent within the first year, and almost 60 percent within the first two years. Clearly, there is a strong relationship between the moment of release and return to crime. If the policy goal is crime reduction, then policies should be aligned to reflect this relationship. Stated differently, our public safety investment strategy should make investments proportionate to risk. If public officials want to reduce the safety risks posed by returning prisoners, then public policies should focus on these early months of freedom.

Given the high crime rates in the first months after prison, we might reasonably expect that the resources provided for supervision, support, and transitional services would be front-loaded, investing money in a time frame with the greatest need and risk. But, inexplicably, reentry resources are not allocated this way. Rather, supervision resources are generally spread equally over the supervision period. If supervision budgets were allocated according to risk of rearrest, then nearly a third of these funds would be spent in the first six months on services and supports designed to reduce the risks of failure. With additional resources, drug testing and treatment would be provided to former prisoners with addictions so that the risk of relapse can be avoided. The mentally ill would be connected with community clinics to receive counseling and necessary medications. Prisoners would be provided transitional housing so that fewer of them would wind up in homeless shelters. Resources would be provided for positive peer supports, particularly those involving former prisoners who have "gone straight," to keep the next wave of prisoners from returning to their criminal networks.

In summary, the traditional policy options do not hold much promise for significant reductions in rearrest rates among returning prisoners. Keeping prisoners incarcerated longer would prevent some crimes, at a very high cost, but would only postpone the inevitable moment of release. Providing more programs in prison would also prevent some crimes, at a lower cost, but would make only a small dent in the reality of recidivism. Implementing more intensive supervision alone would not reduce recidivism, but would improve access to services and significantly increase the rate of returns to prison for parole violations. This chapter has outlined the arguments for a new strategy in reducing the crime risk posed by returning prisoners—one not yet rigorously tested— a strategy based on the principle that crime control is best achieved by plans that intervene where and when the crimes occur. For returning prisoners, most crime occurs right after they get out of prison; therefore, the days, weeks, and months following release present the best opportunity for significant reductions in their rates of return to crime.

Looking Forward

From one perspective, the picture painted here is quite bleak. Returning prisoners are rearrested at very high rates. With the declining crime rates over the past decade, and the substantial increase in the reentry population, their contribution to the nation's overall crime rate has only increased. Furthermore, because the nation has greatly expanded the number of individuals under parole supervision, the statistical probability that a recently released prisoner will commit a horrific crime has increased. This in turn increases the pressure on public officials to be risk averse, to revoke parole when the first sign of failure appears, and to supervise parolees even more intensely. Finally, when the public demands a response to crime, people under criminal justice supervision are often the targets of enforcement that is more symbolic than it is effective.

And we have another fundamental reason for pessimism. We know surprisingly little about the phenomenon of recidivism following release from prison and interventions that could significantly reduce the level of reoffending. The descriptive data published by the Bureau of Justice Statistics tell us that rearrest rates are high, particularly so in the months following release from prison, but do not shed light on the reasons for that reality. We have little research on the effectiveness of postrelease supervision, the dominant policy response to the challenges of prisoner reentry. The evaluation literature is limited, rarely focuses on programs that span the time in prison and the return to the community, and too often assesses interventions that address only one dimension of the reentry risk (such as employment, drug treatment, or mental illness). In short, when we consider the nexus between prisoner reentry and public safety, the policy environment is characterized by enormous risk, heightened public sensitivity, and a weak empirical understanding of the policy options. It is little wonder that elected officials shy away from embracing new ideas on these topics.

Yet, from another perspective, this chapter portrays an intriguing policy challenge. If, at the turn of this century, about one-quarter of the nation's arrests for violent crime can be attributed to individuals recently released from prison, any significant reduction in their recidivism rate would result in noticeable reductions in overall crime. Furthermore, because we can identify categories of returning prisoners who pose the highest risk and the time period when the risk is highest, we should be able to focus resources—including both services and surveillance—on those individuals over those time periods in order to achieve measurable reductions in crime.

Seizing this policy opportunity requires a fundamental rethinking of the relationship between prisoner reentry and public safety. For every prisoner returning home, we should ask this question, "What will it take to keep this prisoner from committing another crime or being the victim of a crime?" In essence, we should create a safety plan for each prisoner to provide a safe transition over the first few months following release. If this strategy were fully realized, there would be drug testing and treatment for every returning prisoner with a history of addiction; transitional housing for those headed for homeless shelters; continuity of medication and care for the mentally ill; supportive networks, including former prisoners and mentors from the faith community, to work with returning prisoners, providing guidance and encouragement; notification to potential victims so that precautions can be taken; systems of electronic monitoring to keep returning prisoners away from identified individuals or places where crime risks are demonstrably high; transitional jobs for those able to work; and relocation services for individuals who believe that returning to the old neighborhood will result in a return to crime. In short, to carry out this strategy, we would do everything we could to ensure a transition from prison that reduces the chances of rearrest and victimization, and enhances the chances of success.

Implementing this safety plan would involve families, community organizations, service providers (including housing, health, drug treatment, and employment), support networks of former prisoners, and religious institutions. Government agencies would play a central role in organizing the disparate activities to achieve the crime-reduction goal. Departments of corrections would ensure that safety plans are developed before each prisoner is released. The police would identify risks, such as gang activity, that the prisoner would be required to avoid. Parole agencies would supervise the conditions of release, such as drug testing, electronic surveillance, or orders of protection, that are related to reducing the risk of reoffending. All these entities would have the same goal—to reduce the rate of reoffending, particularly in the first few months after release from prison.

In one scenario, a community could attempt to implement this strategy by realigning existing resources. Expenditures of these resources, and implementation of the safety strategy, would be the responsibility of a new entity, a "justice intermediary" like the Community Justice Corporation proposed in chapter 4. Money now spent on parole supervision in the later years when rearrest rates are low would be reallocated to the first months when those rates are high. Funding streams that now support drug treatment, transitional housing, HIV/AIDS interventions, mental health counseling, and other social services could be redirected to provide support at the time a prisoner is released. A more ambitious scenario would attempt to generate public support for additional resources, a significant challenge in an era of fiscal austerity. Perhaps the creation of a "rearrest ratio" at the community level would persuade the pubic and its elected officials that addressing a community's crime problems requires attention to the safety risks posed by returning prisoners. This new measure of public accountability might well justify additional resources for the execution of safety plans, including such services as drug testing and treatment, supportive housing, medical care, transitional employment, family counseling, community-based support networks, electronic monitoring, victim support, and more parole officers. Assuming the goal of crime reduction is realized, these additional resources would be well spent.

NOTES

This chapter was written while some colleagues and I, supported by the Harry I. Guggenheim Foundation, were exploring the nexus between prisoner reentry and public safety. That project resulted in a separate volume edited by myself and Christy Visher, *Prisoner Reentry and Crime in America*, which will be published in 2005 by the Cambridge University Press. I am indebted to those colleagues for stimulating thinking on this topic and to the Cambridge University Press for permission to reuse certain figures.

1. *Tracy v. Salmack,* 572 F.2d 393, 396 (2d Cir. 1978).

2. Department of Corrections annual reports did not provide data on participation in temporary release programs. *A Review of Temporary Release Programs in New York State* (1978) reported that participation in work/education release decreased from 766 in September 1977 to 386 in December 1977 (review period was limited to four months). The number of furloughs granted did not decrease over that period—301 granted in September and 386 in December. The Census of State Adult Correctional Facilities reported that the number of inmates regularly permitted to depart the institution decreased from 1.6 percent in 1979 to .02 percent in 1984. This made a huge impact on crowding/prison expansion. The number of inmates increased from 19,456 in 1979 to 31,266 in 1984. However, the number of inmates permitted to participate actually increased (from 321 in 1979 to 504 in 1984). For more information, see BJS (1979, 1984).

3. Martin F. Horn, personal communication with the author, January 27, 2004.

4. This chapter uses a narrow definition of recidivism, as rearrest for a new crime. Some state departments of corrections use a broader definition of the term, including both rearrests and returns to prison for parole violations. Including the latter events within a definition of recidivism dilutes the utility of the term for two main reasons. First, as was discussed in chapter 3 on parole supervision, the rate of return to prison for parole violations is highly dependent upon policy choices regarding scope and nature of parole supervision. Second, because parolees can be returned to prison for technical violations that do not require a crime in itself as a predicate, these measures will reflect system responses to behavior that is not criminal.

5. The 272,111 are an estimated two-thirds of the nation's "releases with sentences greater than one year" in 1994. The findings of the BJS report are based on a weighted sample of 33,796 of the 272,111 prisoners released in the study's 15 states in 1994. These states are Arizona, California, Delaware, Florida, Illinois, Maryland, Michigan, Minnesota, New Jersey, New York, North Carolina, Ohio, Oregon, Texas, and Virginia. See Langan and Levin (2002) for a detailed description of the research methodology.

6. BJS conducted a similar study using a 1983 release cohort. A comparison between the two cohorts is intriguing. Examining 108,580 state prisoners released in 1983 from 11 states, Beck and Shipley (1989) report that 62.5 percent were rearrested over a three-year period, very close to 67.5 percent for the 1994 cohort. Comparing the two release cohorts, the rearrest rate for property offenders rose from 68.1 percent to 73.8 percent, drug offenders from 50.4 percent to 66.7 percent, and public order offenders from 54.6 percent to 62.2 percent. The rearrest rates for violent offenders, however, remained stable. The reconviction rates varied little from the 1983 to the 1994 cohorts, with the exception of an increase in the reconviction rate for drug offenders (35.3 percent vs. 47.0 percent). The return to prison rate was 41.4 percent for the 1983 cohort compared to 51.8 percent for the 1994 cohort.

7. These percentages do not total 100 percent because some released prisoners were rearrested for more than one type of offense.

8. Arrests are a highly imperfect measure of criminal activity. Arrests are a reflection of decisions by police officers to charge an individual with a crime. These decisions are often influenced by extraneous factors such as resource availability, enforcement priorities, and community pressure. These limitations are particularly evident in the case of arrests for drug sales where police policies, not citizens' calls for service, determine the allocation of enforcement services.

9. Two states, Florida and Illinois, were dropped from this analysis because of missing data (Langan and Levin 2002).

10. The BJS study of the 1983 release cohort reached a different result. This group of released prisoners was responsible for 2.8 percent of all serious crimes between 1983 and 1987. This difference is principally accounted for by the much larger reentry cohort in 1994 (108,580 in 1983 and 272,111 in 1994) (Beck and Shipley 1989; Langan and Levin 2002).

11. The contribution of exit cohorts to future years' arrests is based on the contribution rates of the 1994 exit cohort (followed through to 1997) and does not include public order crimes. Findings based on analyses conducted by Rosenfeld et al. (forthcoming). Memorandum on file with author. I am indebted to Rosenfeld, Willman, and Fornango for their willingness to share their analysis with me prior to publication of their research.

12. Piehl (2002) documented this phenomenon in Massachusetts, where the percent of inmates eligible for parole who waived their right to a parole hearing rose from 15 percent in 1990 to 32 percent in 1999. As a result, in 1999, 4,744 inmates chose to be released without supervision. As Piehl aptly commented, "it is an unusual law enforcement policy to give inmates the responsibility for making the determination of how to serve their sentences" (Piehl 2002, 31).

13. Personal communication with the author on July 15, 2004.

14. On April 14, 2003, U.S. District Judge Nore Manella issued a preliminary injunction prohibiting the police from randomly sweeping the city in search of parole and probation violators, finding that these sweeps constituted unwarranted searches and seizures (English 2003).

6

Families and Children

As the nation debates the wisdom of a fourfold increase in our incarceration rate over the past generation, one fact is clear: Prisons separate prisoners from their families. Every individual sent to prison leaves behind a network of family relationships. Prisoners are the children, parents, siblings, and kin to untold numbers of relatives who are each affected differently by a family member's arrest, incarceration, and ultimate homecoming.

Little is known about imprisonment's impact on these family networks. Descriptive data about the children of incarcerated parents only begin to tell the story. During the 1990s, as the nation's prison population increased by half, the number of children who had a parent in prison also increased by half—from 1 million to 1.5 million. By the end of 2002, 1 in 45 minor children had a parent in prison (Mumola 2004).[1] These children represent 2 percent of all minor children in America, and a sobering 7 percent of all African-American children (Mumola 2000). With little if any public debate, we have extended prison's reach to include hundreds of thousands of young people who were not the prime target of the criminal justice policies that put their parents behind bars.

In the simplest human terms, prison places an indescribable burden on the relationships between these parents and their children. Incarcerated fathers and mothers must learn to cope with the loss of normal contact with their children, infrequent visits in inhospitable surroundings, and lost opportunities to contribute to their children's development. Their children must come to terms with the reality of an absent parent, the stigma of parental imprisonment, and an altered support system that may include grandparents, foster care, or a new adult in the home. In addition, in those communities where incarceration rates are high, the experience of having a mother or father in prison is now quite commonplace, with untold consequences for foster care systems, multigenerational households, social services delivery, community norms, childhood development, and parenting patterns.

Imprisonment profoundly affects families in another, less tangible way. When young men and women are sent to prison, they are removed from the traditional rhythms of dating, courtship, marriage, and family formation. Because far more men than women are sent to prison each year, our criminal justice policies have created a "gender imbalance" (Braman 2002), a disparity in the number of available single men and women in many communities. In neighborhoods where incarceration and reentry have hit hardest, the gender imbalance is particularly striking. Young women complain about the shortage of men who are suitable marriage prospects because so many of the young men cycle in and out of the criminal justice system. The results are an increase in female-headed households and narrowed roles for fathers in the lives of their children and men in the lives of women and families in general. As more young men grow up with fewer stable attachments to girlfriends, spouses, and intimate partners, the masculine identity is redefined.

The family is often depicted as the bedrock of American society. Over the years, we have witnessed wave after wave of social policy initiatives designed to strengthen, reunite, or simply create families. Liberals and conservatives have accused each other of espousing policies that undermine "family values." In recent years, policymakers, foundation officers, and opinion leaders have also decried the absence of fathers from the lives of their children. These concerns have translated into a variety of programs, governmental initiatives, and foundation strategies that constitute a "fatherhood movement." Given the iconic stature of the family in our vision of American life and the widespread consensus that the absence of father figures harms future generations, our national experiment with mass incarceration seems, at the very least, incongruent with the rhetoric behind prevailing social policies. At worst, the imprisonment of millions of individuals and the disruption of their family relationships has significantly undermined the role that families could play in promoting our social well-being.

The institution of family plays a particularly important role in the crime policy arena. Families are an integral part of the mechanisms of informal social control that constrain antisocial behavior. The quality of family life (e.g., the presence of supportive parent-child relationships) is significant in predicting criminal delinquency (Loeber and Farrington 1998, 2001). Thus, if families suffer adverse effects from our incarceration policies, we would expect these harmful effects to be felt in the next generation, as children grow up at greater risk of engaging in delinquent and criminal behavior. The institution of marriage is another important link in the mechanism of informal social control. Marriage reduces the likelihood that ex-offenders will associate with peers involved in crime, and generally inhibits a return to crime (Laub, Nagin, and Sampson 1998). In fact, marriage is a stronger predictor of desistance from criminal activity than simple cohabitation, and a "quality" marriage—one based on a strong mutual commitment—is an even stronger predictor (Horney, Osgood, and Marshall 1995). Thus, criminal justice policies that weaken marriage and inhibit spousal commitments are likely to undermine the natural processes of desistance, thereby causing more crime. In short, in developing crime policies, families matter. If our crime policies have harmful consequences for families, we risk undermining the role families can play in controlling criminal behavior.

This chapter examines the impact of incarceration and reentry on families. We begin by viewing the antecedents to the creation of families—the relationships between young men and young women—in communities where the rates of arrest, removal, incarceration, and reentry are particularly high. Then we discuss imprisonment's impact on relationships between an incarcerated parent and his or her children. Next we examine the effects of parental incarceration on the early childhood and adolescent development of children left behind. We then observe the family's role in reentry. We close with reflections on the impact of imprisonment on prisoners' family life, ways to mitigate incarceration's harmful effects, and ways to promote constructive connections between prisoners and their families.

The "Gender Imbalance"

To understand the magnitude of the criminal justice system's impact on the establishment of intimate partner relationships, we draw upon the work of Donald Braman (2002, 2004), an anthropologist who conducted a three-year ethnographic study of incarceration's impact on communities in Washington, D.C. In the District of Columbia, 7 percent of the adult African-American male population returns to the community from jail or prison each year. According to Braman's estimates, more than 75 percent of African-American men in the District of Columbia can expect to be incarcerated at some point during their lifetime. One consequence of these high rates of incarceration is what Braman calls a "gender imbalance," meaning simply that there are fewer men than women in the hardest hit communities. Half of the women in the nation's capital live in communities with low incarceration rates. In these communities, there are about 94 men for every 100 women. For the rest of the women in D.C.—whose neighborhoods have higher incarceration rates—the ratio is about 80 men for every 100 women. Furthermore, 10 percent of the District's women live in neighborhoods with the highest incarceration rates, where more than 12 percent of men are behind bars. In these neighborhoods, there are fewer than 62 men for every 100 women.

This gender imbalance translates into large numbers of fatherless families in communities with high rates of incarceration. In neighborhoods with a 2 percent male incarceration rate, Braman (2002) found that fathers were absent from more than one-half of the families. But in the communities with the highest male incarceration rates—about 12 percent—more than three-quarters of the families had a father absent. This phenomenon is not unique to Washington, D.C., however. In a national study, Sabol and Lynch (1998) also found larger numbers of female-headed families in counties receiving large numbers of returning prisoners.

Clearly, mass incarceration results in the substantial depletion in the sheer numbers of men in communities with high rates of imprisonment. For those men who are arrested, removed, and sent to prison, life in prison has profound and long-lasting consequences for their roles as intimate partners, spouses, and fathers. In the following sections, we will document those effects. Viewing this issue from a community perspective, however, reminds us that incarceration also alters the relationships between the men and women who are not incarcerated. In her research on the marriage patterns of low-income mothers, Edin (2000) found that the decision to marry (or remarry) depends, in part, on the economic prospects, social respectability, and reliability of potential husbands—attributes that are adversely affected by imprisonment. Low marriage rates, in turn, affect the life courses of men who have been imprisoned, reducing their likelihood of desistance from criminal activity. Thus, the communities with the highest rates of incarceration are caught in what Western, Lopoo, and McLanahan (2004, 21) call the "high-crime/low-marriage equilibrium." In these communities, women "will be understandably averse to marriage because their potential partners bring few social or economic benefits to the table. Men, who remain unmarried or unattached to stable households, are likely to continue their criminal involvement."

Braman quotes two of his community informants to illustrate these ripple effects of the gender imbalance. "David" described how the shortage of men affected dating patterns:

> Oh, yeah, everybody is aware of [the male shortage]. . . . And the fact that [men] know the ratio, and they feel that the ratio allows them to take advantage of just that statistic. 'Well, this woman I don't want to deal with, really because there are six to seven women to every man.' (2002, 166)

The former wife of a prisoner commented that women were less discerning in their choices of partners because there were so few men:

> Women will settle for whatever it is that their man [wants], even though you know that man probably has about two or three women. Just to be wanted, or just to be held, or just to go out and have a date makes her feel good, so she's willing to accept. I think now women accept a lot of things—the fact that he might have another woman or the fact that they can't clearly get as much time as they want to. The person doesn't spend as much time as you would [like] him to spend. The little bit of time that you get you cherish. (2002, 167)

The reach of our incarceration policies thus extends deep into community life. Even those men and women who are never arrested pay a price. As they are looking for potential partners in marriage and parenting, they find that the simple rituals of dating are darkened by the long shadow of imprisonment.

The Impact of Incarceration on Parent-Child Relationships

The Family Profile of the Prisoner Population

Before turning to a closer examination of the effects of imprisonment on the relationships between incarcerated parents and their children, we should first describe the family circumstances of the nation's prisoners. In 1997, about half (47 percent) of state prisoners reported they had never been married. Only 23 percent reported they were married at the time of their incarceration, while 28 percent said they were divorced or

Figure 6.1. *Marital Status of Parents in State Prison, 1997*

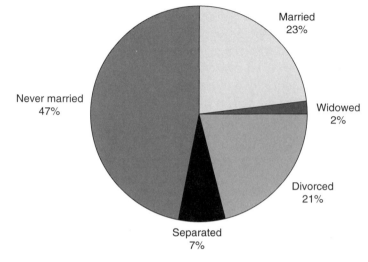

Source: Mumola (2000).

separated (figure 6.1). Yet most prisoners are parents. More than half (55 percent) of all state prisoners reported having at least one minor child. Because the overwhelming majority of state prisoners are men, incarcerated parents are predominantly male (93 percent). The number of incarcerated mothers, however, has grown dramatically in the past decade. Between 1991 and 2000, the number of incarcerated mothers increased by 87 percent, compared with a 60 percent increase in the number of incarcerated fathers. Of the men in state prison, 55 percent have children—a total of about 1.2 million—under the age of 18. About 65 percent of women in state prison are mothers to children younger than 18; their children number about 115,500 (Mumola 2000).

A mother's incarceration has a different impact on living arrangements than does that of a father. Close to two-thirds (64 percent) of mothers reported living with their children before incarceration, compared with slightly less than half (44 percent) of fathers in 1997. Therefore, as the percentage of women in prison increases, more children experience a more substantial disruption. We should not conclude, however, that the imprisonment of a nonresident father has little impact on his children. Research has shown that nonresident fathers can make considerable contributions to the development and well-being of their children

(Amato and Rivera 1999; Furstenberg 1993). They contribute to their children's financial support, care, and social support even when they are not living in the children's home (Edin and Lein 1997; Hairston 1998; Western and McLanahan 2000). Therefore, a depiction of families' living arrangements only begins to describe the nature of the parenting roles played by fathers before they were sent to prison.

The national data on incarcerated parents also fail to capture the diversity of parent-child relationships. According to research conducted by Denise Johnston (2001) at the Center for Children of Incarcerated Parents, it is not uncommon for both incarcerated fathers and mothers to have children by more than one partner. Furthermore, these parents may have lived with some but not all of their children prior to their incarceration. This perspective leads to another conclusion: Individuals who are incarcerated may also have served as parent figures to children not their own—as stepparents or surrogate parents in families that blend children into one household.

We know little about the nature of these parent-child relationships. As was noted above, even absent fathers can provide emotional and financial support prior to their incarceration. However, the profiles of incarcerated parents also point to indicia of stress and dysfunction within these families. More than three-quarters of parents in state prison reported a prior conviction and, of those, more than half had been previously incarcerated. During the time leading up to their most current arrest and incarceration, nearly half were out of prison on some type of conditional release, such as probation or parole, in 1997. Nearly half (46 percent) of incarcerated fathers were imprisoned for a violent crime, as were one-quarter (26 percent) of the mothers. Mothers in prison were much more likely than fathers to be serving time for drug offenses (35 percent versus 23 percent). Nearly one-third of the mothers reported committing their crime to get either drugs or money for drugs, compared with 19 percent of fathers. More than half of all parents in prison reported using drugs in the month before they were arrested, and more than a third were under the influence of alcohol when they committed the crime. Nearly a quarter of incarcerated mothers (23 percent) and about a tenth (13 percent) of incarcerated fathers reported a history of mental illness (Mumola 2000). Clearly, these individuals were struggling with multiple stressors that, at a minimum, complicated their role as parents.

The portrait of prisoners' extended family networks is also sobering. According to findings from the Urban Institute's *Returning Home* (Visher,

La Vigne, and Travis 2004) study in Maryland, these networks exhibit high rates of criminal involvement, substance abuse, and family violence (La Vigne, Kachnowski, et al. 2003). In interviews conducted with a sample of men and women just prior to their release from prison and return to homes in Baltimore, the Institute's researchers found that about 40 percent of the prisoners reported having at least one relative currently serving a prison sentence. Nine percent of the women said they had been threatened, harassed, or physically hurt by their husband, and 65 percent of those who reported domestic violence also reported being victimized by a nonspouse intimate partner. No male respondents reported this kind of abuse. The women reported that, other than their partners, the highest level of abuse came from other women in their families—their mothers, stepmothers, or aunts. Nearly two-thirds of inmates (62 percent) reported at least one family member with a substance abuse or alcohol problem and more than 16 percent listed four or more family members with histories of substance abuse. These characteristics highlight the high levels of risks and challenges in the families prisoners leave behind.

The Strain of Incarceration on Families

We turn next to a discussion of the impact of parental incarceration on the families left behind. One obvious consequence is that the families have fewer financial resources. According to the Bureau of Justice Statistics, in 1997 most parents in state prison (71 percent) reported either full-time or part-time employment in the month preceding their current arrest (Mumola 2002). Wages or salary was the most common source of income among incarcerated fathers before imprisonment, 60 percent of whom reported having a full-time job. Mothers, on the other hand, were less likely to have a full-time job (39 percent). For them, the most common sources of income were wages (44 percent) or public assistance (42 percent). Very few mothers reported receiving formal child support payments (6 percent) (Mumola 2000). During incarceration, the flow of financial support from the incarcerated parent's job stops, leaving the family to either make do with less or make up the difference, thereby placing added strains on the new caregivers. Eligibility for welfare payments under the TANF (Temporary Assistance for Needy Families) program ceases as soon as an individual is no longer a custodial parent—i.e., upon incarceration. In some cases, a caregiver may continue to receive TANF payments when the incarcerated parent loses eligibility, but because these benefits are now "child-only," they are lower than full TANF benefits. Food stamps are also unavailable to incarcerated individuals.

New caregivers often struggle to make ends meet during the period of parental incarceration. Bloom and Steinhart (1993) found that in 1992 nearly half (44 percent) of families caring for the children of an incarcerated parent were receiving welfare payments under TANF's predecessor program, AFDC (Aid to Families with Dependent Children). Under the recent welfare reform laws, however, TANF support is more limited than in the past, as lifetime eligibility has been capped at 60 months, work requirements have been implemented, and restrictions have been placed on TANF funds for those who have violated probation or parole, or have been convicted of certain drug crimes (Phillips and Bloom 1998). Even under the old AFDC program, most caregivers reported that they did not have sufficient resources to meet basic needs (Bloom and Steinhart 1993). Moreover, these economic strains affect more than the family's budget. According to several studies, financial stress can produce negative consequences for caretakers' behavior, including harsh and inconsistent parenting patterns, which, in turn, cause emotional and behavioral problems for the children (McLoyd 1998).

Other adjustments are required as well. Because most prisoners are men, and 55 percent of them are fathers, the first wave of impact is felt by the mothers of their children. Some mothers struggle to maintain contact with the absent father, on behalf of their children as well as themselves. Others decide that the incarceration of their children's father is a turning point, enabling them to start a new life and cut off ties with the father. More fundamentally, Furstenberg (1995) found that a partner left behind often becomes more independent and self-sufficient during the period of incarceration, changes that may ultimately benefit the family unit or lead to the dissolution of the relationship. At a minimum, however, these changes augur a significant adjustment in roles when the incarcerated partner eventually returns home.

In some cases, the incarceration period can have another, longer-lasting effect on the legal relationships between parents and children. In 1997, Congress enacted the Adoption and Safe Families Act (ASFA) to improve the safety and well-being of children in the foster care system as well as to remove barriers to the permanent placement, particularly adoption, of these children.[2] The ASFA stipulates that "permanency" decisions (determinations about a child's ultimate placement) should be made within 12 months of the initial removal of the child from the home. With limited exceptions, foster care placements can last no longer than 15 months, and if a child has been in foster care for 15 out of the previous 22 months, petitions must be filed in court to terminate parental rights. At least half the states now include incarceration as a reason to terminate parental rights (Genty 2001).

This new legislation has far-reaching consequences for the children of incarcerated parents. According to BJS, 10 percent of mothers in prison, and 2 percent of fathers, have at least one child in foster care (Mumola 2000). Because the average length of time served for prisoners released in 1997 was 28 months (Sabol and Lynch 2001), the short timelines set forth in ASFA establish a legal predicate that could lead to increases in the termination of parental rights for parents in prison (Lynch and Sabol 2001). Philip Genty (2001), a professor at Columbia University Law School, made some rough calculations of ASFA's impact. Looking only at reported cases discoverable through a Lexis search, he found, in the five years following ASFA's enactment, a 250 percent increase in cases terminating parental rights due to parental incarceration, from 260 to 909 cases.

In addition to those legal burdens placed on incarcerated parents, the new family caregivers face challenges in forging relationships with the children left behind. Some of these new caregivers may not have had much contact with the children before the parent's incarceration, so they must establish themselves as de facto parents and develop relationships with the children. Contributing to the trauma of this changing family structure, prisoners' children are sometimes separated from their siblings during incarceration because the new network of caregivers cannot care for the entire sibling group (Hairston 1995).

In short, when the prison gates close and parents are separated from their children, the network of care undergoes a profound realignment. Even two-parent families experience the strain of lost income, feel the remaining parent's sudden sole responsibility for the children and the household, and suffer the stigma associated with imprisonment. However, prisoners' family structures rarely conform to the two-parent model and are more often characterized by nonresident fathers, children living with different parents, and female-headed households. In these circumstances, the ripple effects of a mother or father going to prison reach much farther, and grandparents, aunts and uncles, and the foster care system must step into the breach. In addition, these extended networks feel the financial, emotional, and familial weight of their new responsibilities.

Incarceration has yet one more effect on the structure of prisoners' families. One of the important functions that families perform is to create assets that are passed along to the next generation. These assets are sometimes quite tangible: Money is saved, real estate appreciates in value, and businesses are built. These tangible assets can typically be transferred to one's children. Sometimes the assets are intangible: Social status is achieved, professional networks are cultivated, and educational milestones are reached. These intangible assets can also translate into economic advantage by opening doors for the next generation. Braman asks whether the minimal intergenerational transfer of wealth in black families is related to the high rates of incarceration among black men. Taking a historical view, he concludes:

> The disproportionate incarceration of black men . . . helps to explain why black families are less able to save money and why each successive generation inherits less wealth than their white counterparts. Incarceration acts like a hidden tax, one that is visited disproportionately on poor and minority families; and while its costs are most directly felt by the adults closest to the incarcerated family member, the full effect is eventually felt by the next generation as well. (2004, 156)

The ripple effects of incarceration on the family are far-reaching. The gender imbalance disturbs the development of intimate relationships that might support healthy families. Families' financial resources and relationship capabilities are strained at the same time they are scrambling for more assets to support their incarcerated loved one. Yet, despite the hardships of incarceration, families can play an important role in improving outcomes for prisoners and prisoners' children. Several studies have shown that the "quality of care children receive following separation and their ongoing relationships with parents" are "instrumental forces in shaping outcomes for children" (Hairston 1999, 205). According to one study (Sack 1977), the behavioral problems displayed by children of incarcerated fathers diminished once the children got to spend time with their fathers.

On the other hand, in a small percentage of cases, continued parental involvement may not be in the child's best interests. For example, BJS (Greenfeld et al. 1998) reports that 7 percent of prisoners convicted of violent crimes were convicted of intimate partner violence. Even more disturbing are those cases involving child abuse and neglect, where the child's best interests argue against parental involvement. According to

BJS, among inmates who were in prison for a sex crime against a child, the child was the prisoner's own child or stepchild in a third of the cases (Langan, Schmitt, and Durose 2003). Yet there has been very little research on the nexus between this form of family violence, incarceration, and reentry.

Discussion of prisoners convicted of violence within the family only raises larger questions—questions not answered by current research—about whether some parent-child relationships are so troubled and so characterized by the patterns of parental substance abuse, criminal involvement, mental illness, and the intrusions of criminal justice supervision that parental removal is a net benefit for the child. It is undoubtedly true that removing a parent involved in certain types of child abuse is better for the child. But we know little about the critical characteristics of the preprison relationships between children and their incarcerated parents, especially as to what kind of parents they were, and how their removal affects their children.

Even without a deeper understanding of the parenting roles played by America's prisoners, we still must face several incontrovertible, troubling facts. First, expanding the use of prison to respond to crime has put more parents in prison. Between 1991 and 1999, a short eight-year period, the number of parents in state and federal prisons increased by 60 percent, from 452,500 to 721,500 (Mumola 2000). By the end of 2002, 3.7 million parents were under some form of correctional supervision (Mumola 2004). Second, many children are left behind when parents are incarcerated. By 1999, 2 percent of all minor children in the United States—about 1.5 million—had a parent in state or federal prison. (If we include parents who are in jail, on probation or parole, or recently released from prison, the estimate of children with a parent involved in the criminal justice system reaches 7 million, or nearly 10 percent of all minor children in America [Mumola 2000].) Third, the racial disparities in America's prison population translate into substantial, disturbing racial inequities in the population of children affected by our current levels of imprisonment. About 7 percent of all African-American minor children and nearly 3 percent of all Hispanic minor children in America have a parent in prison. In comparison, barely 1 percent of all Caucasian minor children have a parent in prison (Mumola 2000). Finally, most of the children left behind are quite young. Sixty percent are under age 10, while the average child left behind is 8 years old.

In this era of mass incarceration, our criminal justice system casts a wide net that has altered the lives of millions of children, disrupting their relationships with their parents, altering the networks of familial support, and placing new burdens on such governmental services as schools, foster care, adoption agencies, and youth-serving organizations. As Phillips and Bloom succinctly concluded, "by getting tough on crime, the United States has gotten tough on children" (1998, 539). These costs are rarely included in our calculations of the costs of justice.

Parent-Child Relationships during Imprisonment

When a parent is arrested and later incarcerated, the child's world undergoes significant, sometimes traumatic, disruption. Most children are not present at the time of their parent's arrest, and arrested parents typically do not tell the police that they have minor children (ABA 1993). Family members are often reluctant to tell the children that their parent has been incarcerated because of social stigma (Braman 2003). There-fore, the immediate impact of an arrest can be quite traumatizing—a child is abruptly separated from his or her parent, with little information about what happened, why it happened, or what to expect.

The arrest and subsequent imprisonment of a parent frequently results in a significant realignment of the family's arrangements for caring for the

Figure 6.2. *Living Arrangements of Minor Children of State Inmates prior to Incarceration*

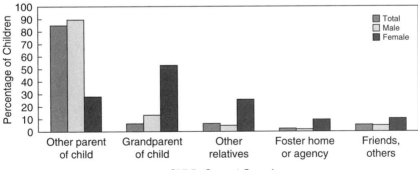

Source: Mumola (2000).
Note: Figures do not total 100 percent because some prisoners had children living with multiple caregivers.

child, depicted in figure 6.2. Not surprisingly, the nature of the new living arrangements depends heavily on which parent is sent to prison. Recall that about two-thirds of incarcerated mothers in state prison lived with their children before they were imprisoned. Following the mother's incarceration, about a quarter (28 percent) of their children remain with their fathers. Most children of incarcerated mothers, however, are cared for by an extended family that is suddenly responsible for another mouth to feed and child to raise. More than half of these children (53 percent) will live with a grandparent, adding burdens to a generation that supposedly has already completed its child-rearing responsibilities. Another quarter of these children (26 percent) will live with another relative, placing new duties on the extended family. Some children have no familial safety net: almost 10 percent of incarcerated mothers reported that their child was placed in foster care (Mumola 2000).[3]

The story for incarcerated fathers is quite different. Less than half (44 percent) lived with their children before prison; once they are sent to prison, most of their children (85 percent) will live with the children's mother. Grandparents (16 percent) and other relatives (6 percent) play a much smaller role in assuming child care responsibilities when a father in incarcerated. Only 2 percent of the children of incarcerated men enter the foster care system. In sum, a child whose father is sent to prison is significantly less likely to experience a life disruption, such as moving in with another family member or placement in a foster home.

The nation's foster care system has become a child care system of last resort for many children with parents in prison. Research by the Center for Children of Incarcerated Parents (Johnston 1999) found that, at any given time, 10 percent of children in foster care currently have a mother—and 33 percent have a father—behind bars. Even more striking, 70 percent of foster children have had a parent incarcerated at one time or another during their time in foster care.

When a parent goes to prison, the separation between parent and child is experienced at many levels. First, there is the simple fact of distance. The majority of state prisoners (62 percent) are held in facilities located more than 100 miles from their homes (Mumola 2000). Because prison facilities for women are scarce, mothers are incarcerated an average of 160 miles away from their children (Hagan and Coleman 2001). The distance between prisoners and their families is most pronounced for District of Columbia residents. As a result of the federal takeover of the District's prison system, defendants sentenced to serve felony time are now housed in facilities that are part of the far-flung network of federal prisons. In 2000, 12 percent of the District's inmates were held in federal prisons more than 500 miles from Washington. By 2002, that proportion had risen to 30 percent. Nineteen percent are in prisons as far away as Texas and California (Santana 2003). Not surprisingly, in an analysis of BJS data, Hairston and Rollin (2003, 68) found a relationship between this distance and family visits: "The distance prisoners were from their homes influenced the extent to which they saw families and friends. The farther prisoners were from their homes, the higher the percentage of prisoners who had no visitors in the month preceding the survey. . . . Those whose homes were closest to the prison had the most visits."

Geographic distance inhibits families from making visits and, for those who make the effort, imposes an additional financial burden on already strained family budgets. Donald Braman tells the story of Lilly, a District resident whose son Anthony is incarcerated in Ohio (Braman 2002). When Anthony was held in Lorton, a prison in Virginia that formerly housed prisoners from the District, she visited him once a week. Since the federal takeover, she manages to make only monthly visits, bringing her daughter, Anthony's sister. For each two-day trip, she spends between $150 and $200 for car rental, food, and a motel. Added to these costs are her money orders to supplement his inmate account and the care packages that she is allowed to send twice a year. She also pays about $100 a month for the collect calls he places. She lives on a fixed income of $530 a month.

Given these realities, the extent of parent-child contact during incarceration is noteworthy. Mothers in prison stay in closer contact with their children than do fathers. According to BJS, nearly 80 percent of mothers have monthly contact and 60 percent have at least weekly contact. Roughly 60 percent of fathers, by contrast, have monthly contact, and 40 percent have weekly contact with their children (Mumola 2000). These contacts take the form of letters, phone calls, and prison visits. Yet, a large percentage of prisoners serve their entire prison sentence without ever seeing their children. More than half of all mothers, and 57 percent of all fathers, never receive a personal visit from their children while in prison.

Particularly disturbing is Lynch and Sabol's finding (2001) that the frequency of contact decreases as prison terms get longer. Between 1991 and

1997, as the length of prison sentences increased, the level of contact of all kinds—calls, letters, and visits—decreased (figure 6.3). This is especially troubling in light of research showing that the average length of prison sentences is increasing in America, reflecting more stringent sentencing policies. Thus, prisoners coming home in the future are likely to have had fewer interactions with their children, a situation that further weakens family ties and makes family reunification even more difficult.

In addition to the significant burden imposed by the great distances between prisoners and their families, corrections policies often hamper efforts to maintain family ties across the prison walls. The Women's Prison Association (1996) has identified several obstacles to constructive family contacts, some of which could easily be solved. The association found that it is difficult to get simple information on visiting procedures, and correctional administrators provide little help in making visiting arrangements. The visiting procedures themselves are often uncomfortable or humiliating. Furthermore, little attention is paid to mitigating the impact on the children of visiting a parent in prison.

Figure 6.3. *Level of Prisoners' Weekly Contact with Children, by Method and Length of Stay, 1991 and 1997*

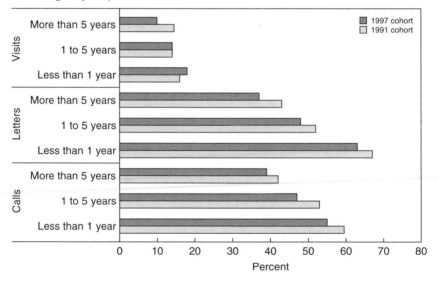

Source: Lynch and Sabol (2001).
Note: Prisoners to be released in the next 12 months.

Elizabeth Gaynes, director of the Osborne Association in New York City, tells a story that captures the emotional and psychological impact of a particular correctional policy upon a young girl who had come to visit her father. Because inmates were not allowed to handle money, the prison had drawn a yellow line three feet in front of the soda vending machines. Only visitors could cross that line. The father could not perform the simple act of getting his daughter a soda. If he wanted one, he had to ask his daughter to get it. According to Ms. Gaynes, this interaction represented an unnecessary and damaging role transformation; the child had become the provider, the parent had become the child.[4]

Family Contact during Imprisonment: Obstacles and Opportunities

For a number of reasons, it is difficult to maintain parent-child contact during a period of incarceration. For one thing, many prisons narrowly define the family members who are granted visiting privileges. The State of Michigan's corrections department, for example, promulgated regulations in 1995 restricting the categories of individuals who are allowed to visit a prisoner. The approved visiting list may include minor children under the age of 18, but only if they are the prisoner's children, stepchildren, grandchildren, or siblings. Prisoners who are neither the biological parents nor legal stepparents of the children they were raising do not have this privilege. Finally, a child authorized to visit must be accompanied by either an adult who is an immediate family member of the child or of the inmate, or who is the child's legal guardian.[5] Many prisoners' extended family networks, including girlfriends and boyfriends who are raising prisoners' children, are not recognized in these narrow definitions of "family."[6] Limitations on visiting privileges are commonly justified on security or management grounds, but fail to recognize the complexity of the prisoner's familial networks. Rather than allowing the prisoner to define the "family" relationships that matter most, the arbitrary distinctions of biology or legal status are superimposed on the reality of familial networks, limiting meaningful contact that could make a difference to both prisoner and child.

Telephone contact is also burdened by prison regulations and by controversial relationships between phone companies and corrections departments. Prisoners are typically limited in the number of calls they can make. Their calls can also be monitored. The California Department of Corrections interrupts each call every 20 seconds with a recorded message: "This is a call from a California prison inmate." Most prisons allow prisoners to make only collect calls, and those calls typically cost between $1 and $3 per minute, even though most phone companies now charge less than 10 cents per minute for phone calls in the free society (Petersilia 2003). Telephone companies also charge between $1.50 and $4 just to place the collect call, while a fee is not charged for collect calls outside of prison.

The high price of collect calls reflects sweetheart arrangements between the phone companies and corrections agencies, under which the prisons receive kickbacks for every collect call, about 40 to 60 cents of every dollar. This arrangement translates into a substantial revenue source for corrections budgets. In 2001, for example, California garnered $35 million, based on $85 million of total revenue generated from prison calls. Some states require, by statute or policy, that these revenues pay for programs for inmates. Most states simply deposit this money into the general budget for their department of corrections.

Yet who bears these additional costs for maintaining phone contact with prisoners? The families of prisoners do, of course. In a study conducted by the Florida House of Representatives Corrections Committee (1998), family members reported spending an average amount of $69.19 per month accepting collect phone calls. According to this report, "Several family members surveyed stated that, although they wanted to continue to maintain contact with the inmate, they were forced to remove their names from the inmate's approved calling list because they simply could not afford to accept the calls" (1998, 23).

This monopolistic arrangement between phone companies and prisons makes families the unwitting funders of the prisons holding their loved ones. In essence, the states have off-loaded upwards of hundreds of millions of dollars of prison costs on to prisoners' families. Subsequently, families are placed in the unacceptable position of either agreeing to accept the calls, thereby making contributions to prison budgets, or ceasing phone contact with their loved ones. Of course, there are other, deeper costs attached to this practice. If a family chooses to limit (or stop) these phone calls, then familial ties are weakened and the support system that could sustain the prisoner's reintegration is damaged. If the family chooses to pay the phone charges, then those financial resources are not available for other purposes, thereby adding to the strain the household experiences. In recent years, efforts to reform prison telephone policies have been successful in several states.[7] Yet, while these reform efforts are under way, tens of thousands of families are setting aside large portions of their budgets to pay inflated phone bills to stay in touch with their imprisoned family members.

Fortunately, a number of communities have implemented programs designed to overcome the barriers of distance, cost, and correctional practices that reduce contact between prisoners and their families. For example, Hope House, an organization in Washington, D.C., that connects incarcerated fathers with their children in the District, hosts summer camps at federal prisons in North Carolina and Maryland where children spend several hours a day for a week visiting with their fathers in prison. Hope House has also created a teleconference hookup with federal prisons in North Carolina, Ohio, and New Mexico so that children can go to a neighborhood site to talk to their fathers in prison. In another instance, a Florida program called "Reading and Family Ties— Face to Face" also uses technology to overcome distance. Incarcerated mothers and their children transmit live video recordings via the Internet. These sessions occur each week, last an hour, and are available at no cost to the families. In addition, the U.S. Department of Justice in 1992 initiated the Girl Scouts Beyond Bars program, the first mother-daughter visitation program of its kind. Twice a month, more than 500 girls across the country, much like other girls their age, participate in Girl Scout programs, but in this program these Girl Scouts meet their mothers in prison. Finally, in Washington State, the McNeil Island Correction Center has launched a program that teaches incarcerated fathers the skills of active and involved parenting, encourages them to provide financial support for their children, and facilitates events to bring prisoners together with their families.

These programs—and many others like them—demonstrate that, with a little creativity and a fair amount of commitment, corrections agencies can find ways to foster ongoing, constructive relationships between incarcerated parents and their children. It seems particularly appropriate, in an era when technology has overcome geographical boundaries, to harness the Internet to bridge the divide between prisons and families. Yet the precondition for undertaking such initiatives is the recognition that corrections agencies must acknowledge responsibility for maintaining their prisoners' familial relationships. If these agencies embraced this challenge for all inmates—and were held accountable to the public and elected officials for the results of these efforts—the quality of family life for prisoners and their extended family networks would be demonstrably improved.

Impact of Parental Incarceration on Childhood Development

Limits of Existing Research

Having examined the impact of incarceration on the institution of family and the relationships of incarcerated parents with their children, we turn next to an assessment of incarceration's impact on the children involved. Given the current state of research, it is very difficult to measure the consequences for children when a mother or father is arrested, convicted, sent to prison, and returned home. Very few studies have been conducted that directly examine the lives of the children of incarcerated parents. Most of these studies suffer from methodological limitations in that they examine only a small sample of children or fail to use appropriate comparison groups. Few studies use standardized assessment tools to measure the emotional and psychological well-being of these children. Few researchers talk to the children themselves, relying instead on parental or caregiver opinions to construct a picture of the child's changing world. Ideally, we could draw upon one or more longitudinal studies that assessed the children's well-being, the nature of the parent-child relationships, and the changing family environment beginning at the parent's arrest and continuing through the trial (when the parent may be in jail or may be released on bond), to the point of sentencing, throughout the period of incarceration (including the moment of the parent's release from prison), ending with the dynamics of post-prison adjustment. Unfortunately, no such study exists.

The extant sparse research literature only underscores the importance of more research in this area. These studies suggest that children of incarcerated parents are more likely to exhibit low self-esteem, depression, emotional withdrawal from friends and family, and inappropriate or disruptive behavior at home and in school. Two studies, each with a very small sample size, suggested that children of incarcerated parents may be more likely than their counterparts to enter the criminal justice system (Johnston 1991, 1993).[8]

One way of assessing the impact of incarceration on children is to draw connections between other research and our general understanding of the collateral costs of imprisonment. For example, several studies have found that children of young and unmarried parents experience behavioral problems, unstable family relationships, and diminished economic support (Amato and Rivera 1999; Hagan and Dinovitzer 1999; Kandel, Rosenbaum, and Chen 1994; McLanahan and Sandefur 1994; Michael and Tuma 1985; Thornberry, Smith, and Howard 1997; Wu and Martinson 1993). Similarly, economic strain can lead to harsh and inconsistent parenting, which can lead to behavioral problems in the children in the household (McLoyd 1998). Reduced financial resources can also lead to increased exposure to abuse in the family (International Society for Traumatic Stress Studies 2003).[9] Finally, children in single-parent households, particularly those born to single mothers, have higher rates of incarceration as they grow up. Indeed, as Harper and McLanahan (1999) have found, children growing up with stepparents have still higher rates of incarceration. So, to the extent that incarceration increases economic strain, the number of single-parent households, and absent fathers, then our imprisonment policies are likely to result in more developmental challenges and criminal justice involvement for the children left behind.

Understanding Parental Loss

We can also draw upon the general literature exploring how parental loss affects child development to create some hypotheses about the impact of parental incarceration. According to this literature, children always experience the loss of a parent as a traumatic event. Whether the loss is due to death, divorce, moving away, or incarceration, this event has negative consequences, including attachment difficulties, anger, depression, regression, and other antisocial behaviors. Similarly, a traumatic event in a child's life diverts energy from the developmental work that child is normally performing. When life becomes overwhelming for a child, emotional survival may take precedence over developmental tasks, resulting in delayed development, regression, or other maladaptive coping strategies (Wright and Seymour 2000). Given these general principles of child development, parental incarceration should be viewed as a traumatic event, limiting the child's emotional growth, producing stress and anger, and isolating the child from needed social supports.

It is also well documented in the child development literature that children have difficulty coping with uncertainty. The criminal justice process is filled with uncertainty. A child might have to live with such questions as, "Will Mom be arrested again?" "Will Dad be convicted and, if so, sent to prison? If so, how long will he be there?" "Will Mom get released on parole? If so, will she be sent back to prison if she uses drugs again, or if she is in the wrong place at the wrong time?" This uncertainty, which is inherent in the workings of our criminal justice system, is often compounded by the family's reluctance to tell children exactly what is happening to their parents. In his ethnographic study in Washington, D.C., Braman (2002) found that most family members rarely discuss their relative's incarceration at all outside the immediate family, even in neighborhoods where incarceration rates are high. Most family members explained that their silence stemmed from concerns about the stigma associated with incarceration. Although well-intentioned as a protective response, withholding basic information about a parent's status may only heighten children's feelings of stress and uncertainty.

Finally, the children themselves must deal with the issue of stigma. When a mother or father is imprisoned, a child may experience the disapproval of his or her peers, teachers, or other family members, resulting in feelings of shame and low self-esteem. Perhaps in neighborhoods of a high concentration of incarceration among the adults, losing one's parent to prison is so common that the social stigma is diminished, but the experience still requires the child to work through a complex set of feelings about the actions of the parent in prison. In addition, even those children who are coping well with parental incarceration may have the added challenge of overcoming the stereotype that they are destined for a life of behavioral problems and failure.

Impact by Children's Age Group

The child development literature also provides a framework for assessing the differential impact of parental incarceration on children of various ages. The chart developed by Gabel and Johnston (1995) clarifies the intersection between developmental markers and the removal of a parent to prison (table 6.1). For example, among infants (0–2 years), parental incarceration's major effect is likely a disruption of parental bonding, with the potential for later attachment difficulties. Research on this age group also shows, however, that infants can recover quickly from the loss of a parent if they experience a new, nurturing, caregiving relationship (Shonkoff and Phillips 2000). During the early childhood years (2–6 years), children have a greater ability to perceive events

Table 6.1. *Possible Effects of Parental Arrest and Incarceration on Young Children's Development*

Developmental state	Developmental characteristics	Developmental tasks	Influencing factors	Effects of separation
Infancy (0–2 years)	■ Limited perception, mobility ■ Total dependency	■ Development of trust and attachment	■ Parent-child separation	■ Impaired parent-child bonding
Early childhood (2–6 years)	■ Increased perception, mobility, and improved memory ■ Greater exposure to environment. Ability to imagine	■ Development of sense of autonomy, independence, and initiative	■ Parent-child separation ■ Trauma	■ Inappropriate separation anxiety ■ Impaired socioemotional development ■ Acute traumatic stress reactions and survivor guilt
Middle childhood (7–10 years)	■ Increased independence from caregivers and ability to reason ■ Peers become important	■ Sense of industry ■ Ability to work productively	■ Parent-child separation ■ Trauma	■ Developmental regressions ■ Poor self-concept ■ Acute traumatic stress reactions ■ Impaired ability to overcome future trauma
Early adolescence (11–14 years)	■ Organization of behavior in pursuit of goals ■ Increased abstract thinking ■ Puberty ■ Increased aggression	■ Ability to work productively with others ■ Controlled expression of emotions	■ Parent-child separation ■ Enduring trauma	■ Rejection of limits on behavior ■ Trauma-reactive behaviors
Late adolescence (15–18 years)	■ Emotional crisis and confusion ■ Adult sexual development and sexuality ■ Formal abstract thinking ■ Increased independence	■ Development of cohesive identity ■ Resolution of conflicts with family and society ■ Ability to engage in adult work and relationships	■ Parent-child separation ■ Enduring trauma	■ Premature termination of dependency relationship with parent ■ Intergenerational crime and incarceration

Source: Gabel and Johnston (1995). Reprinted with permission.

around them, but have not yet developed the skills to process traumatic occurrences. Children at this age have not yet completely separated themselves from their parents, so they tend to perceive threats or harm to their parents or caregivers as directed at themselves. Several studies suggest that traumatic stress at this age may have profound long-term effects, particularly if there is no intervention to help the child sort through those experiences (Furman 1983).

In the middle childhood years (7–10 years), when children are developing their social skills and a sense of independence, separation from a parent creates a sense of loss because a role model is taken away. If a child has poor coping skills to begin with, and particularly if he or she moves from home to home following the parent's departure, such disruptions may accelerate a spiral of strain in the child's life. Johnston and Carlin (1996) use the term "enduring trauma" to describe a situation where a child experiences several traumatic events with no time to recover and where the cumulative effect may overwhelm the child's ability to cope. A child experiencing this level of trauma may display aggression, hypervigilance, anxiety, concentration problems, and withdrawal.

The impact of incarceration on adolescents (11 to 18 years) is likely quite different. Adolescence is a time when young people test boundaries, begin to navigate the world of romantic relationships, exercise more independence, explore the adult world of work, and develop a sense of self. The arrest and incarceration of an adolescent's parent can derail those transitions to adulthood. These children may question the authority of the incarcerated parent and doubt the parent's concern for them. They may take on new roles as parent figures to fill the void left by the incarcerated parent. Some studies have shown an increase in dependence and developmental regression among adolescents of incarcerated parents (Johnston 1992).

About 1.5 million minor children have a parent in prison, most frequently a father. In many ways, these children are no different from others of their age group, but they are experiencing a distinctive disruption in their lives. They have the same emotional needs to bond with a parent or other caregiver, to establish themselves as unique individuals in a social context, and to test their independence from the adults in their lives. All these development processes are made more complicated by the loss of a parent to prison, and more complicated still if the parent was arrested for behavior involving harm to the family or child.

Reconnecting with Family at the Time of Reentry

In this section, we shift our focus from an inquiry into the impact of incarceration on parent-child relationships and child development to ask what role prisoners expect their families to play in the reentry process, what role families actually play, and what consequences befall families during this critical period.

When prisoners return home, they face multiple hurdles, many of which relate directly to the functioning of their families. They need to find housing, which may be with their relatives or immediate families. They need to find employment, which could add income to family budgets. Some have health concerns and may need to receive care for an HIV infection, secure medication for mental illness, or find substance abuse treatment to reduce the risk of relapse, all of which, if successful, would avert additional burdens and risks for their families. Many will owe the state child support payments, which, according to an extensive analysis in Colorado and Massachusetts, averaged more than $16,000 (Thoennes 2003).[10] Most prisoners will be under legal supervision, bringing a state parole agency into their homes and lives.

The Returning Home Study

In its *Returning Home* study in Maryland, the Urban Institute provides the first empirical look at the complex issues of family support for returning prisoners (La Vigne, Kachnowski, et al. 2003). The research team constructed a "Family Relationship Quality Scale" to assess the quality of familial connections.[11] This scale was repeated four times over the continuum of the project—twice in the prerelease interview (first regarding family relationships before prison and again regarding prisoners' expectations for these relationships after release) and once in each of the two postrelease interviews conducted about one and four months after release.

The *Returning Home* study reveals interesting dynamics in the prisoners' perceptions, expectations, and experiences of family support. Prisoners characterized their family relationships as more close than distant. This conclusion is based on respondents' scores on the scale, with mean values that range from one to four, one representing distant family relationships and four representing close family relationships (Visher et al. 2004, 110). During every stage of data collection, respondents provided mean scores that exceeded three, indicating that these family relationships were considered close. They were also optimistic about renewing those relationships after their release; more than three-quarters expected this would be "very easy" or "pretty easy" to do. Interestingly, the prisoners expected their families to be more supportive after their release from prison than they had been before their incarceration. This finding is subject to a number of possible interpretations. Perhaps these families were undergoing strain at the time of the arrest. Perhaps there had been an improvement in family support during the prison sentence. More likely, the prisoners—all of whom were near release at the time of the interview—were projecting their hopes that their families would be supportive during the reentry phase.

The returning prisoners had very concrete expectations of the kinds of support their families would provide. Half of the women and 39 percent of the men expected their families would provide financial support. Well over half of the women (61 percent) and about half of the men (52 percent) planned on talking to a relative about getting a job. At least two-thirds of them (75 percent of women, 63 percent of men) expected to live with family members after their release from prison, including about one-third with their mothers or stepmothers, and less than a quarter with an intimate partner. Importantly, they viewed family support as more than just providing money, jobs, or housing: Half of the inmates surveyed said that this support would be an important factor in keeping them out of prison.

These expectations were generally realized. Nearly half of the released prisoners slept at a family member's home the first night they were back in the community. Nearly half sought assistance from relatives in finding a job. As a general matter, more than 80 percent of the sample interviewed about a month after release "strongly agreed" or "agreed" that their families had been supportive. In fact, when these ex-prisoners were interviewed again a few months later, these percentages increased to about 90 percent. Furthermore, the share that believed family support was important to staying out of prison also increased. It seems plausible that, as other challenges to successful reentry proved more difficult to overcome, the relative value of family support was enhanced.

These findings from *Returning Home* underscore the importance of family in the reentry process. When facing the prospects of succeeding in the outside world, prisoners place a high value on the support that their families will provide. Moreover, families generally keep their end of the bargain, becoming even more important with the passage of time.

Future analysis of the *Returning Home* project will shed even more light on the dynamics of these familial relationships.

La Bodega de la Familia

Other research suggests that, as critical as family support may be to successful reentry, it often comes with a price. The most insightful research on this issue comes from La Bodega de la Familia, a demonstration project launched on New York City's Lower East Side in 1996 by the Vera Institute of Justice (Sullivan et al. 2002). La Bodega's mission was to test the proposition that support provided to families of offenders with histories of drug abuse could reduce their drug use and their criminal activity. The intervention was called "family case management," a novel approach to the problems of drug use and crime that utilizes the strengths of families to influence the behavior of a family member who is under criminal justice supervision. Although the overarching goal was to reduce the drug use and criminal activity of the family member under supervision, the immediate goal was to strengthen families so they could, in turn, support the drug user during treatment (Sullivan et al. 2002).

In La Bodega, the case manager spends considerable time with the offender's family. Together, they construct an "ecomap," which illustrates the public and community agencies on which the family relies, in order to find ways to coordinate existing services in the family's best interest. They construct a "genogram," a map of the family network that allows the drug offender to identify potential sources of support within the family. With these two analyses in hand, the family case manager, the offender, and the probation or parole officer construct a "family action plan," which might include drug treatment for the offender, a support group for the family members, or counseling for a child in the family who faces difficulties in school. Based on this plan, La Bodega staff members become advocates for the family in approaching social service agencies and provide 24-hour crisis interventions when an arrest, relapse, or potential eviction occurs.

An evaluation of La Bodega found that the program did result in improvements in family members' lives: they were receiving more medical and social services and their health had improved. The evaluation also found that drug use in the target population declined, just as the program designers had hoped. While 86 percent of the participants had used at least one substance during the month prior to joining the program, this proportion declined to 50 percent after six months in the program—a statistically significant reduction greater than that found in a comparison group. The participants' overall physical health also improved. Finally, program participants were also about half as likely to be arrested and convicted for a new offense than members of the comparison group, but the numbers were too small to draw statistically sound conclusions.

There were two surprises in the evaluation, however. First, there had been no increase in the proportion of La Bodega participants who received drug treatment, nor in the amount of time spent in treatment. So, these impressive declines in drug use came about without greater reliance on traditional treatment programs. Family support apparently can make a difference in and of itself. But the research also found that, notwithstanding improvements in their services, support networks, and health status, the families participating in the La Bodega program reported higher rates of emotional problems and stress than at the beginning of the program, and higher than in the comparison group. The evaluator suggested a possible explanation: "Perhaps as a consequence of having the issues surrounding drug abuse out on the table and having to deal with them openly, the La Bodega users and their family members experienced increased conflict in their relationships" (Sullivan 1993, 51). For program participants, the average overall "support index"—the measure of family support as experienced by the drug-using member—actually dropped during the six-month study, while it increased in the comparison group. As the evaluation concluded, "These unexpected results may point to the emotional burdens that La Bodega placed on the families and drug users with whom it worked" (Sullivan 1993, 51).

The story of La Bodega carries two important lessons pertaining to families' role at the point of reentry. First, families matter. They provide the innermost concentric circle of support for returning prisoners.[12] Providing support for families can translate into behavioral changes for the individual coming out of prison. Drug use can be reduced without increased reliance on traditional treatment, an important reminder in these times of fiscal constraints. Second, this is hard work for families. Even with a dedicated family case manager, a crisis intervention team available around the clock, and improvements in service coordination and health care, the family still feels the stress of helping a family member in need. If we are to design policies that support families, we must remember to pay attention to the family's emotional needs. The experience of La Bodega, now incorporated into the work of a new national nonprofit called Family Justice, points the way toward a new form of service delivery for returning prisoners that strengthens the ability of families to provide support.

In sum, this recent research from Maryland and New York City underscores the centrality of family in the reentry process. Prisoners have high expectations of family support that are often met. However, when families play a more active role in supporting the ex-offender's transformation toward prosocial behavior—particularly moving away from substance abuse—they pay a price. Our challenge is to work with prisoners and their families to maximize the support they can provide to each other, giving families the tools necessary for the hard work of family interventions, and providing the family network with external sources of emotional and other sustenance. This research suggests that, if done properly, this form of intervention might effectively ease the transition from prison, reduce substance abuse, and reduce crime.

Looking Forward

Imprisonment causes ripple effects that are felt throughout a prisoner's family network. The policies that have resulted in the imprisonment of well over a million people have magnified those effects in a strong undercurrent that is eroding the familial infrastructure of America's poorest communities. Virtually every social institution that deals with children— including families, schools, child welfare agencies, foster care, and kinship care systems—is touched by the high rates of parental imprisonment. At the center of these community institutions are children—1.5 million of them—who are buffeted about between prison visits, time with foster parents, and life with grandparents and other new adults in their lives. These children are likely to grow up in families that have been weakened, increasing the challenges they face in staying out of the criminal justice system and leading productive lives. As they reach early adulthood, they will find that their choices of life partners are more limited than a generation ago, and their family structures will be quite different.

In view of the negative effects stemming from current imprisonment policies, we must ask whether society has an obligation to mitigate these harms. The research literature provides some limited guidance as we consider the efficacy of policies that would reflect such a social commitment. Keeping families strong would reduce future criminality, enhance child development, reduce child and family trauma and stress, and increase the likelihood that the children left behind would lead productive lives. Beyond these calculations of preventable harm, the next question pertains to who would be responsible for carrying out policies that would produce these results. Certainly there is much more that corrections agencies could do, but they would first have to see family strengthening as part of their mission. This, in turn, would require governors and state legislatures to lead efforts to expand both the mission statements and the financial support of state departments of corrections. With this support, corrections agencies could improve their visitation policies, encourage rather than discourage phone calls, provide video links between prisons and community centers, find secure means for Internet communications between prisoners and families, bring families to their prisons, create family advocate positions within their organizations, eliminate the imposition of child support payments during the incarceration period, offer classes in parenting skills, and assist prisoners in asserting their rights in custody proceedings. We have no shortage of ideas, just a lack of mandate and the needed resources to carry out the new mandate.

Yet even if corrections agencies were provided adequate resources to implement a new mission to support families, they would need substantial assistance from the community. The existing network of agencies that serve children would need to recognize that these children need special attention when their parents go to prison. If communities embraced a mandate to support the families of incarcerated community members, a broad consortium of agencies would be called upon to meet the mandate. Schools would need to offer counseling to children at critical stages in the criminal justice process. Foster care agencies would have to ascertain whether a parent in prison would serve as a suitable parent upon release before moving for the termination of parental rights. Youth-serving organizations would need to help young people with family members in the justice system work through their feelings of shame, anger, confusion, and denial. Government would have to fund a network of nonprofit agencies, such as Hope House, to provide the supportive environment where children could talk to their parents over video links or Internet connections. In addition, at the point of reentry, organizations similar to La Bodega de la Familia would need to be deployed to support the family networks that struggle to absorb the reality of a family member's return. Organizing this effort would require a communitywide coalition, with strong support from local government, and partnerships with a state corrections agency committed to the same goals—to recognize the important role that families can play in successful reintegration, to minimize harm experienced by the children of incarcerated parents, and to promote strong and healthy families for each prisoner.

NOTES

An earlier version of sections of this chapter appeared in the introductory essay of Travis and Waul (2003).

1. This is a single-day prevalence and does not take into account minor children whose parents were previously incarcerated; it accounts only for those who are currently incarcerated in state and federal prisons in 2002.

2. Public Law 105-89.

3. Figures do not total 100 percent because some prisoners had children living with multiple caregivers.

4. Elizabeth Gaynes, conversation with the author, June 22, 2004. Cited with permission.

5. The Michigan restrictions were challenged in court as unconstitutional because they violated the Fourteenth Amendment's guarantee of due process, the First Amendment's guarantee of free association, and the Eighth Amendment's prohibition against cruel and unusual punishment. The Supreme Court upheld the regulations, finding that the restrictions "bear a rational relation to the [department of correction's] valid interests in maintaining internal security and protecting child visitors from exposure to sexual or other misconduct or from accidental injury. . . . To reduce the number of child visitors, a line must be drawn, and the categories set out by these regulations are reasonable" (*Overton v. Bazzetta*, 539 U.S. 94 [2003]).

6. The definition of who can visit or take children to visit is an even bigger problem in light of cultural traditions, i.e., the extended family network and fictive kin arrangements that exist in many African-American families. Family duties and responsibilities are shared among a group of individuals; e.g., a young uncle may be expected to take on the father's role and do things such as take the child to a game or on a prison visit while the grandmother provides day-to-day care and an aunt with a "good" job provides financial subsidies. Apparently this perspective was either not presented or ignored as unimportant in the Michigan case (Personal communication with Creasie Finney Hairston, January 6, 2004).

7. Missouri has announced that its next contract with prison telephone systems will not include a commission for the state. The Ohio prison system entered into a contract that will reduce the cost of prison phone calls by 15 percent. California will reduce most prisoner phone calls by 25 percent. In 2001, the Georgia Public Service Commission ordered telephone providers to reduce the rates for prisoner calls from a $3.95 con-

nection fee and a rate of $0.69 per minute to a $2.20 connection fee and a rate of $0.35 per minute. The new telephone contract for the Pennsylvania Department of Corrections will reduce the average cost of a 15-minute telephone call by 30 percent. And litigation has been initiated in a number of states—including Illinois, Indiana, Kentucky, Ohio, New Hampshire, New Mexico, New York, South Dakota, Washington, Wisconsin, and the District of Columbia—to reduce the cost of prison phone calls and kickbacks to the state (eTc Campaign 2003).

8. The Children of Offenders study and the Jailed Mothers study both had small sample sizes and were not randomized, making it difficult to conclude a causal link between parental incarceration and children's involvement in the criminal justice system. In the Children of Offenders study (Johnston 1992, 1993), the sample (N=56, N=202) targeted children of offenders who already demonstrated disciplinary problems in school or delinquent behaviors, presenting the highest likelihood of second-generation incarceration (Johnston 1995). In the Jailed Mothers study, Johnston (1991) relied on self-reported data from the surveys of 100 jailed mothers on their children's living arrangements, risk factors, and problem behaviors.

9. The report indicates that "generally, persons with fewer economic, tangible, social, physical and other personal resources may be more vulnerable to the threat of violence or abuse posed by an intimate partner."

10. This figure represents both pre-prison and during-prison nonpayment. Depending on the law of the state, prisoners may continue to accrue child supports arrears while incarcerated. According to Thoennes (2003), Massachusetts prisoners accrued on average $5,000 in arrears while behind bars.

11. The study defined "family member" as "a blood or legal relative, someone with whom the prisoner has a child in common, or a significant other or guardian our respondent lived with prior to his or her incarceration or plans to live with after he or she is released from prison" (Visher et al. 2004, 31).

12. See chapter 10 for a discussion of the concept of concentric circles of support.

7
Work

The relationship between prisons and work is kaleidoscopic. With the slightest turn of perspective, the pieces fall into place differently and a new pattern emerges. Consider these three very different ways of viewing the patterns that connect prisons and work. First, prisons are places where some people work. Sometimes prisoners work under conditions that have rightly been described as cruel and inhumane, such as chain gangs. Prisoners can also work in more positive settings, such as computer repair shops. Prisoners often do the work that keeps prisons running, like preparing the food, washing the linens, raising the crops, and sorting the mail. Second, prisons can also prepare people for work after prison. While incarcerated, prisoners can develop specific work skills that can be useful in securing work after release. Additionally, prisoners can participate in programs that increase their individual capabilities, or human capital, so they can improve their postprison job prospects. Prisoners can develop constructive work habits by participating in prison industries, thereby preparing themselves for the work world on the outside. In recent times, some prisons have even served as recruitment centers for businesses seeking to employ prisoners after their release. Third, however, prisons interrupt a pattern of work. Time in prison is time out of the rhythms of the work world of free society. A prison sentence cuts short a constructive work experience, as when someone loses a job upon arrest. Prisons also disrupt a pattern of illegal "work," such as drug selling, burglary, or extortion. Overall, the artificial world of the prison community does not test one's ability to find and hold a job, or offer the same satisfaction of providing financial support for one's self and others as does life on the outside.

In this chapter, we view the relationship between prison and work through the lens of prisoner reentry. This perspective requires us to ask this question: "In our modern era of mass incarceration, with more than 630,000 individuals entering and leaving our prisons each year, how does imprisonment affect our national economy and the labor markets in the communities from which these prisoners come?" We will analyze these labor market consequences by examining the employment profiles of prisoners, first at the front door when they arrive, then while they are in prison, and finally in the months and years after they leave. We will then aggregate those individual experiences to a national assessment of imprisonment's impact on the overall economy.

After exploring these issues, we will examine the role of prisons in promoting improvements in prisoners' employment prospects once they return home. A second question will act as a springboard for this part of our discussion: "As a matter of public policy, why should we use prisons to improve employment outcomes for prisoners?" This inquiry will require us to assess the relationship between our efforts to improve prisoners' job prospects and our goal of reducing the recidivism rates among reentering prisoners.

Finally, we will consider the public policy benefits that might be achieved by a different approach to the links among imprisonment, reentry, and the world of work. We propose two goals: First, every prisoner who can work should work while in prison and, second, every prisoner should be expected to work when released from prison. Meeting these goals will require rethinking the role of prisons in preparing prisoners for work after release as well as the role of private and public employers in supporting prisoners' transitions to productive employment. Achieving these goals would be expensive, but would certainly help alleviate the economic harms that flow from our current imprisonment policies.

Before laying the foundation for this policy proposal, a review of the history of inmate labor in America is vital. This history provides a sobering reminder that since prisons were first built in America, prisoners have been required to work, for reasons ranging from the benign belief that work is reformative to racist Jim Crow policies designed to repress former slaves. This history also demonstrates that modern American correctional practice—hindered by painful memories of exploitative inmate labor and hampered by a unique coalescence of business interests, labor advocacy, and timid political activity—has lost sight of the importance of work, and the preparation for work, as socially valuable activities that can benefit individual prisoners and the larger society. To develop a new strategy for linking work in prison with work in the community, this historical legacy must be overcome.

Prisons and Work in American History

From the Work House to Contract Labor

Throughout American history, penal reformers and prison administrators have viewed the prison experience as an opportunity to promote (and often compel) work. In the early colonial era, punishment took the form of fines, public humiliation in the pillory, or death by hanging. With the advent of the penitentiary—the great American contribution to penal policy—work and punishment became closely intertwined goals. When William Penn received his land grant from Charles II in 1682, he established a penal code that substituted imprisonment at hard labor for the death penalty and other corporal punishments. The 1682 Frame of Government of Pennsylvania declared that "all prisons shall be work-houses, for felons, vagrants, and loose and idle persons" (Garvey 1998, 347). This notion was embodied in the Pennsylvania Constitution of 1776, which called for the construction of "houses" that would punish "by hard labour, those . . . convicted of crimes not capital" (Friedman 1993, 77). For a short time, prisoners were required to work in public, as a form of shaming. In 1790, however, the Pennsylvania legislature declared this experiment a failure and required that work in prison be performed in "unremitted solitude" (78 n.70). Under the new policy, prisoners were expected to work alone in their cells, making shoes or operating small looms. In the view of the Quakers who created the American penitentiary, work and silence were integral to the reformative process.

In the 19th century, as the use of prisons expanded across the country, prison administrators came to see convict labor as cheap labor that could be bid out to private businesses. As early as 1807, Massachusetts began contracting its prisoners' labor. Under this system, the state could sell inmate labor to private firms that, in turn, sold the finished goods on the open market. Over the next two decades, New York, Connecticut, Ohio, Indiana, and Illinois followed suit. By the time of the Civil War, "the contract system had become the dominant organizational form of prison labor throughout the North" (Garvey 1998, 352).

In the South, prison labor was also bid out to private businesses, but with an important distinction. The Southern states *leased* their prison labor; in other words, private firms receiving contracts were responsible for both the production of goods with inmate labor *and* the custody and discipline of the inmates themselves. After the Civil War, many Southern states, in dire financial straits and facing rising prison populations, leased out their entire prison populations to private contractors to offset prison costs (American Correctional Association 1983, 88). During this era, the system of leased convict labor was more than a financial arrangement; it was deeply intertwined with the efforts to maintain white supremacy in the South. Before the slaves were emancipated, punishment for virtually all offenses committed by the black population was administered on plantations, under a form of "plantation justice." Following emancipation, the locus of punishment for blacks moved into overcrowded and rundown correctional facilities. As historian Lawrence Friedman observes, "the 'ultimate sanction,' the really heavy structure that propped up the labor system of the South, was the penal system" (Friedman 1993, 95). Convict labor mined coal, drained swamps, made bricks, and built railroads throughout the South. These were brutal, racist systems with deadly consequences. For example, between 1877 and 1880, 285 convicts were shipped out to build the Greenwood and August Railroad. Nearly half of them died (Friedman 1993). More evidence suggests that this event was not an isolated incident. One doctor from Alabama, writing in 1883, observed that most convicts working under these conditions died within three years (Adamson 1983, 566; Garvey 1998, n.115).

Not all convict laborers in the South worked for private businesses, however. Some were forced to work on the prison grounds, raising agricultural products. In a cruel twist of history, prisons came to resemble plantations. Under the watchful eye of white overseers, large numbers of black men worked in the fields growing cotton, sugar cane, or vegetables, knowing that to escape would invite punishment of a worse kind. These "plantation" models were the South's version of the state use system; that is, prison-plantations were set up by the state itself when it could no longer lease prisoners. These were massive operations, earning significant revenues for the states. In 1921, South Carolina had 4,168 acres under cultivation by convicts; Louisiana, 15,600 acres; Florida, 17,000 acres; Mississippi, 28,750 acres; and Texas, 73,461 acres (American Correctional Association 1983, 124).

Reform Movements and State-Use Industries

At the end of the 19th century, the contract labor system came under attack from a rare coalition of labor, business, and criminal justice reformers. Leaders of the nascent labor movement pressured Congress and the state legislatures to prohibit the use of convict labor in most public-sector markets, which significantly curtailed leasing arrangements with correctional facilities. Labor unions also had a narrow reason for supporting these laws—prisoners were often used to break strikes, as in the labor dispute at the Tennessee Coal Company in 1891. At the same time, manufacturers came to view prison labor as a form of unfair competition. In 1886, they formed the National Anti-Convict Contract Association, a group that pledged to promote prison work programs that were "least oppressive to manufacturing interests" (Garvey 1998, 359). Added to this unusual alliance between business and labor interests were pressures from reform groups and the broader public, which was incensed by journalistic accounts of maltreatment, disease, and death among convict workers.

Under attack from all sides, the 19th century experiments in private uses for prisoner labor faded from use. In the North, the New York legislature took the lead in the 1830s and 1840s by prohibiting prisoners "from being trained in or performing any mechanical trade" (Garvey 1998, 362). In 1881, the New Jersey legislature limited the number of convicts that could be employed in any one industry in its penitentiary (362, n.174). In the South, the leasing system was gradually eliminated, beginning with Mississippi in 1894. Tennessee, Louisiana, South Carolina, and Georgia soon followed suit. By 1933, leasing was prohibited in all Southern states (365).

This is not to say that prisoners stopped working. On the contrary, private contractors for inmate labor were replaced by a single public contractor—the state. By the time of the Great Depression, work in prisons was conducted mostly for "state use," and goods produced in prison were limited to government markets, principally state agencies. Prisoners manufactured license plates for state residents, furniture for state offices, linen for state institutions, and food for prison meals. Certainly this focus on state uses is understandable in fiscal terms—state governments can use prison labor to offset government expenses. However, the domination of state-use prison industries, rather than industries that could offer products for sale on the outside, can also be traced to a series of federal enactments that effectively cut off access to private markets. Under the Hawes-Cooper Act of 1929, Congress declared that prison-made goods would no longer be considered part of interstate commerce. Then, under the Ashurst-Sumners Act of 1940, Congress made the interstate transportation and sale of these goods a federal crime (Garvey 1998, 366–67). Through these measures, prison labor was relegated to producing goods for state use. Prisoners became, in many respects, workers for the state.

Partnering Attempts

Four decades later, however, Congress opened up a small sliver of access to the private markets for prison labor. In 1979, Congress passed the Justice System Improvement Act, designed to encourage states to partner with private businesses to employ prison inmates. This legislation created the Prison Industry Enhancement (PIE) Certification Program, under which states could receive an exemption from the ban on interstate commerce in prison-made goods. Specifically, the PIE Certification Program allows prisons to establish partnerships with private businesses, enabling inmates to work at prison jobs provided by private-sector companies. Prisoners in PIE programs are paid wages comparable to civilian wages for the same job, but they do not actually receive this income in full. The legislation provides that wages can be reduced up to 80 percent to cover state and federal taxes, room and board, family support, payments to a crime victims' fund, and contributions to an interest-accruing account that inmates may receive upon release (Atkinson and Rostad 2003).

Notwithstanding two expansions to the PIE program stemming from the Justice Assistance Act of 1984 and the Crime Control Act of 1990, this effort has been a spectacular failure. In 2002, there were only 188 partnerships with private firms, employing only 3,734 inmates (less than 0.3 percent of the prison population) (National Correctional Industries Association 2002; Rostad 2002). This failure should not be a surprise. Few private firms find it economically viable to establish a production capacity behind prison walls, especially considering the attendant costs of doing business in a prison environment and the need to pay a low-skill workforce the prevailing wage. The business logic behind the PIE program is inherently flawed. Therefore, the promise that private markets might employ a large portion of America's prisoners in productive activities remains a hollow one.

No Common Rationale

As we have seen, prisoner labor has been justified on numerous grounds throughout American history—as part of public shaming, as income producing, as rehabilitative, as deterrence, as well as a form of punishment. These disparate objectives can still be seen in today's discussions about the relationship between prison and work and in various correctional practices. At one extreme, Alabama reinstated the chain gang in 1995, reviving the debate over one of America's most notorious correctional practices. At the other extreme, voters in Oregon, by a 72 percent margin, amended their constitution in 1994 to require that all able-bodied prison inmates work or be engaged in work-related activities 40 hours a week as part of an ambitious plan to involve the private sector in providing prison jobs.[1] In 2002, two unlikely allies, former Attorney General Edwin Meese and the American Civil Liberties Union, joined forces to urge Congress to reform federal legislation thereby allowing more prisoners to work in prison (National Center for Policy Analysis 2002). Yet these widely disparate efforts lacked a coherent rationale, a sense of purpose that links prisoners' work to society's expectations of prisoners when they are released. Our failure to pursue a common goal for the link between prisons and work has significantly diminished the economic contributions of the millions of individuals who pass through our nation's prisons. Before articulating a common goal, we must first understand the impact of imprisonment on labor markets in America. We begin this analysis by documenting the employment profiles of these prisoners— before they come to prison, while they are in prison, and after they leave.

Prisoners' Employment Profiles

Before Entering Prison

Most prisoners are working when they are arrested. According to a 1997 survey conducted by the Bureau of Justice Statistics, 56 percent of prisoners reported that they had full-time jobs in the month before their arrest. Another 12.5 percent had part-time jobs or were occasionally employed (BJS 2000a). Incarceration thus has simple, direct, and sometimes dire consequences for these prisoners' families and others who are dependent on this income—they have lost a source of financial support.

At first glance, the high employment levels among this population are quite striking. However, we must recognize that the glass is more empty than full. Even though most prisoners were working when arrested, 31.5 percent were not employed—some actively looking for work and some not. According to the Bureau of Labor Statistics (2001), individuals are classified as unemployed if they do not have a job and/or if they have actively looked for work in the previous 4 weeks. This high unemployment rate must be placed in context. In 1997, when the BJS survey was conducted, the nation was in the midst of an economic boom, resulting in historically low unemployment rates. In that year, the overall unemployment rate was 4.9 percent. African-American men age 20 and older exhibited an 8.5 percent unemployment rate (U.S. Department of Labor 2002). By comparison, the unemployment rate for the incoming prison population that year was 17.8 percent. So before drawing hopeful conclusions from the BJS findings, we must still acknowledge the glass as half-empty—the unemployment level in this population is clearly very high.

The Urban Institute's *Returning Home* study in Maryland adds rich detail to our understanding of the work profile of the prisoner population. Much like the BJS findings, the Urban Institute study found that 65 percent of the prisoners had worked during the six months prior to incarceration. Yet, for half of the respondents (46 percent), the longest they had ever held a job was two years or less. In addition, nearly half (45 percent) had been fired from a job at least once before (Visher et al. 2004). The picture that emerges is of a population with high levels of unemployment, little continuity in work experiences, and a high level of job dismissals.

Of course, many prisoners were engaged in the illegal labor market when they were arrested. Twenty-two percent of male inmates in state prisons in 1997 reported illegal sources of income in the month before their arrest (Mumola 1999). Indeed, those activities may have been the reason for their arrest. Moreover, many incoming prisoners were engaged in both legal and illegal employment at the same time. The economic rationale for illegal work is straightforward. In a review of the research on illegal earnings, Richard Freeman (1999) found that, with one exception, all studies on the topic come to the same conclusion: Crime pays more per hour than legal work pays.

One other perspective on this employment profile is informative, and sobering. Comparing prisoners' educational levels with those of low-wage workers of similar ages reveals striking differences. According to Bernstein and Houston (2000), prisoners are more than twice as likely as low-wage[2] male workers to be high school dropouts (nearly 60 percent vs. 30 percent). The comparison is even more pronounced among low-wage African Americans (nearly 60 percent vs. 23 percent). Where nearly a third of low-wage male workers have either a college degree or some college or vocational education (31.6 percent), only 7 percent of prisoners have pursued these avenues of self-improvement. Stated differently, over a third of African-American male high school dropouts have been incarcerated (Tyler and Kling forthcoming; Western and Pettit 2000). In sum, former prisoners are a class apart, a "disadvantaged subset of the low-wage workforce" (Bernstein and Houston 2000, 7).

We can also view imprisonment's impact on the workforce from a national perspective. From this vantage point, we count the more than 1.1 million work-ready individuals in prison as potential workers taken out of our traditional labor markets. At current incarceration levels, about 1 percent of the American labor force is held in prison or jail on any given day. Harry Holzer, former chief economist for the Department of Labor, has made a rudimentary assessment of how this level of incarceration affects the nation's economy. In this calculation, the annual flow to prison of about 630,000 individuals—half of whom are engaged in full-time employment and another eighth in part-time employment—reduces America's gross domestic product (GDP) by the extent of prisoners' lost earnings while they are incarcerated. According to Holzer, incarceration reduces America's overall employment rate by about 1 percent, and the nation's GDP by 1 to 2 percent,[3] or $100 to $200 billion a year.[4]

These costs are rarely included in calculations of the financial impact of our criminal justice policies. One could argue that these costs are mitigated, to some extent, by prisoner productivity during incarceration. However, as we shall see in the following section, the value of goods and services produced by prison labor does not come close to compensating for the productivity lost due to incarceration. More importantly, this argument misses a critical point. The economic productivity of prisoners who work in prison does not benefit their families and others who depended on their income before they were incarcerated. Since most prison industries produce goods for the state, the beneficiaries of prison labor are no longer prisoners' families and communities, but the general taxpayers who realize savings from the goods and services prisoners produce.

In summary, imprisonment has its costs beyond facilities, staffing, and maintenance expenses. Our era of mass incarceration has resulted in significant losses in earnings for those sent to prison, and lost productivity while they are in prison. In addition, as we shall see in the following sections, imprisonment effectively diminishes prisoners' lifetime earnings after they leave prison. These economic losses are borne not only by the millions of Americans who pass through our prisons, but also by their families, their communities, and the national economy.

While in Prison

In examining the world of work in America's prisons, we need to address the issues of "unemployment" in prison and prisoners' work experience during their incarceration. Obviously, the concept of "unemployment" takes on a different meaning in the prison setting. Prisoners are not seeking and securing work in the traditional sense. Whatever work is available in prison is provided by prison administrators. Theoretically, a prison could be a full-employment economy—anyone who wanted and was capable of performing a job could work, if prison management embraced this goal. The available data, however, paint a picture of high unemployment rates in prison. Of the nearly 1.1 million state and federal prisoners deemed eligible for work in 2000, only 53 percent had a current work assignment. (Slightly more than 100,000 prisoners were classified as on "restricted status" and could not work.) Most eligible prisoners (43 percent) performed "general work" assignments, the kinds of institutional maintenance jobs that keep the prisons running. A small share (2.5 percent) worked on farms. Only 7 percent were employed by prison industries, making goods available for general consumption. Sales of those products, however, generated income of $1.185 billion, and the prison industries in four states—California, Florida, New York, and Texas— accounted for more than $402 million of the sales. Only 3,531 prisoners— or 0.3 percent of the eligible population—worked in the federally approved PIE program (Atkinson and Rostad 2003; Camp and Camp 2002; National Correctional Industries Association 2002).

One answer to the high levels of unemployment in prison might be to require that prisoners engage in activities other than work while they are in prison. In this view, prisoners should be working to overcome deficits in their human capital. They should be attending school, getting counseling to help them overcome their addictions, learning specific skills that will help them find jobs on the outside, or taking classes in anger management. Most prisons offer these kinds of programs, but they are provided to only a small percentage of prisoners. According to an Urban Institute study examining prison programs in seven states, fewer than 10 percent of inmates in those states participated in vocational, educational, or employment programs (Lawrence et al. 2002). Therefore, if about half of America's prisoners are working, and 10 percent are involved in prison programs, our prisons still fall far short of fully engaging the prison population in productive activity. In short, the level of idleness in America's prisons is very high, resulting in substantial lost productivity.

More important, the lost opportunity is immeasurable. The disparity between the current situation and full employment represents lost opportunities for prisoners themselves to develop a work ethic, learn skills, and create a track record of job experience, all of which are valuable to potential employers. An incarceration period could, with a different policy emphasis, be viewed as an opportunity to improve the human capital of those imprisoned, with the modest goal of ensuring that prisoners do not lose ground in terms of employability compared with their counterparts on the outside. However, our prison systems have in fact reduced their investments in the kinds of programs designed to prepare prisoners for work in the community. In 1991, 31 percent of soon-to-be-released prisoners reported they had participated in vocational programs while in prison. By 1997, that share had dropped to 27 percent. In 1991, 43 percent of this group said they had participated in educational programs. By 1997, that proportion had declined to 35 percent (Lynch and Sabol 2001). The recent fiscal crisis facing the states has forced even deeper cuts in these investments in the future employability of returning prisoners.

All in all, America's prisons fall far short of a full-employment economy and exhibit a high level of idleness. To the extent prisoners do work, the goods and services they produce are overwhelmingly consumed by the prison community or by state governments. Most important, our prisons represent a massive failure to prepare prisoners for their return to the world of work. By failing to achieve full employment and failing to prepare prisoners for a return to work, our current prison policies damage the American economy, one prisoner at a time. Moreover, these negative effects are not evenly distributed. They are concentrated in impoverished communities that already experience high rates of unemployment and social disadvantage.

After Reentering the Community

Finding work is a critical need for returning prisoners. According to an exploratory study by the Vera Institute of Justice, which documented the experiences of 49 individuals leaving prison in New York State, "the number-one concern for most of the people in the study was landing a job. Throughout the first month after release from prison, people consistently were more preoccupied with finding work than avoiding drugs and other illegal activity or staying in good health" (Nelson, Deess, and Allen 1999). Some of this pressure to find work comes from the criminal justice system. According to a 1991 survey of state parole agencies, 40 of the 51 jurisdictions surveyed (the 50 states and the District of Columbia) required parolees to "maintain gainful employment" (Rhine, Smith, and Jackson 1991). In fact, the need to find work is even more basic than meeting supervision requirements. Finding a job is a way of securing income for one's self and others, establishing a positive role in the community, and keeping a distance from negative influences and opportunities for illegal behavior.

Given the centrality of work for the period following release, it is surprising how little is known about the employment experiences of former prisoners. How many of them have jobs lined up when they leave prison? How many of those jobs are still there when the release date comes? For those seeking work, how do they look for work? What roles do family members, former employers, or employment programs geared to ex-offenders play? What assistance is given by parole agencies?

Ideally, we should know the level of unemployment for returning prisoners, just as we know that 56 percent were employed full-time and another 12.5 percent worked part-time at the time of their arrest. Recent research in fact offers some provocative findings that suggest the nexus between work and reentry is quite dynamic. The Maryland *Returning Home* study found that, among former prisoners interviewed between four and six months after their release, 76 percent had worked at least a month, and of those, 72 percent were employed at the time of the interview. Most of those employed (55 percent) held full-time jobs (Visher et al. 2004). These employment levels are strikingly similar to those found prior to incarceration—65 percent of the Maryland respondents had worked during the six months before they went to prison. Other studies show high levels of employment immediately after release from prison with a sharp decline in employment levels in the following months. A University of Washington study found that prisoners exhibited employment rates of about 30 percent before incarceration and 44 percent in the quarter immediately following incarceration. Yet, within two years those rates dropped sharply to 26 percent (Pettit and Lyons 2003). Using administrative data from Ohio during 1999 and 2000, Sabol (2003) documented a similar drop off; in the second quarter after release, the employment rate was 50 percent, but by the sixth quarter this had declined to 40 percent.

These findings underscore the importance of research documenting the job-seeking and job-retention activities of former prisoners. The Vera Institute of Justice study sheds some light on these phenomena. By the end of the first month following their release, more than a third (18 of 49) of the returning prisoners surveyed had found full- or part-time jobs in the mainstream labor market. Of those returning prisoners who found work, most were either rehired by former employers or had help from family or friends. Relatively few (3 of 18) found jobs on their own. Only 3 found jobs through employment programs that specialize in helping ex-offenders (Nelson et al. 1999). Data from the Maryland *Returning Home* study confirm these findings. The largest share (39 percent) of former prisoners who secured employment in the four to six months after prison found their jobs through friends (39 percent) or relatives (12 percent). Some had success with newspaper ads (9 percent) or temp agencies (9 percent) (Visher et al. 2004). Clearly, the informal networks of friends and family are most helpful in securing employment. However, we need to better understand the successful strategies that connect released prisoners to jobs and the dynamics that apparently reduce employment levels over time.

Collecting data such as these on a large scale would shed light on the pathways between prison and work and could reorient our thinking about the respective roles that families, jobs programs, former employers, and other private-sector employers play in linking returning prisoners to the world of work. Future large-scale studies might test two provocative hypotheses generated from these exploratory studies. First, the level of employment before and after prison may be similar. Granted, as we shall discuss later, looking for a job is difficult and the barriers to good jobs are formidable, but jobs *are* found—not necessarily good jobs, nor jobs with desirable wages, but jobs nonetheless. Therefore, when criminal justice and social service agencies focus on whether a former prisoner simply has a job, they are asking only one right question. A parallel question, which is just as important, is whether the job has a future. Second, friends and families are key partners in finding work. Parole agencies' strategy of simply referring former prisoners to traditional employment agencies may be misplaced. Perhaps the resources of family, friends, and community networks should be mobilized more systematically. Yet even as we focus on these two insights, we should not lose sight of the over-riding conclusion, namely that this population is experiencing high rates of unemployment. Furthermore, the employment prospects of this population do not improve with the passage of time.

Prison's Impact on Employment Prospects

If we look beyond the experiences of individual prisoners and examine the large-scale effects of imprisonment (and of a felony conviction generally) on participation in the workforce, a very sobering picture emerges. We see that our criminal justice policies have penetrated deeply into the world of work, with severe consequences for those who pass through our prison system.

About 13 million Americans—7 percent of the adult population and 12 percent of the male population—have felony convictions. An estimated 3 million Americans are former prisoners (Uggen, Thompson, and Manza 2000). Under state and federal laws, a felony conviction explicitly bars these individuals from a long list of jobs (Legal Action Center 2004). Their criminal record also serves as a de facto barrier to employment. According to recent surveys, American employers are unsurprisingly far more reluctant to hire ex-offenders than comparable groups of disadvantaged workers. Fewer than 40 percent of all employers said they would "definitely" or "probably" hire someone with a criminal record for an unskilled, noncollege position. These findings should be compared with distinctly different employer attitudes regarding other groups that are frequently stigmatized in our society. Many more employers would "definitely" or "probably" hire someone on welfare (92 percent), with a general equivalency diploma (GED) credential (96 percent), with a spotty work history (59 percent), or who had been unemployed for a year (83 percent) (figure 7.1; Holzer, Raphael, and Stoll 2002). Ex-offenders find themselves at the bottom of the employability hierarchy.

Figure 7.1. *Employers' Willingness to Hire Workers from Various Stigmatized Groups*

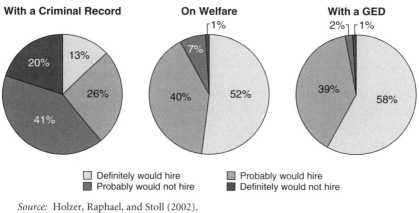

With a Criminal Record   **On Welfare**   **With a GED**

☐ Definitely would hire   ■ Probably would hire
■ Probably would not hire   ■ Definitely would not hire

Source: Holzer, Raphael, and Stoll (2002).
Note: GED = general equivalency diploma.

Today, it is remarkably easy to determine whether a job applicant actually has a criminal record. Several states post criminal history records on the Internet (Petersilia 2003). For certain positions, such as child care workers or health care providers, employers are required by law to conduct background investigations to make sure they screen out ex-convicts. According to an employer survey in the early 1990s, about a third of employers said they "always" checked criminal history records before hiring an applicant; half said they checked "sometimes" (Holzer et al. 2002).

The impact of a felony conviction on employment can also be understood from the job applicant's perspective. Sociologist Devah Pager (2002) sent pairs of individuals to apply for the same entry-level job. One applicant had a criminal record; the other did not. She found that applicants with criminal records received 50 percent fewer job offers than applicants without a criminal past. For African-American applicants, the impact was even greater; African-American applicants with criminal records experienced a 64 percent reduction in job offers. We should not conclude, however, that the rejected applicants never found work. Rather, for them, the job search was more prolonged, the barriers more numerous, and the universe of potential jobs more restricted.

The poor employment prospects of returning prisoners can be partially attributed to incarceration's effects. According to some theorists, imprisonment tends to weaken a prisoner's "social capital," his or her access to social networks, and information sources that could be helpful in finding jobs. Prisons may simultaneously strengthen the prisoner's ties to antisocial and criminogenic networks, such as gangs and criminal associations, which facilitate continued criminal activity upon release. As a result, returning prisoners pull away from access to legitimate work opportunities and push toward the secondary labor market of day labor and part-time jobs and toward illegal income (Wolff and Draine 2003). Research showing that the likelihood of securing legitimate employment decreases as time in prison increases confirms this notion that prison weakens social capital (Hagan and Dinovitzer 1999). Thus, because the average length of prison sentences has increased over the past decade (Lynch and Sabol 2001), we can expect that future cohorts of released prisoners will experience even greater difficulty finding and keeping jobs.

The combined effect of these forces—the explicit and actual barriers to employment, the lost opportunities to improve human capital, and the loss of social capital—is a decrease in the employment prospects of released prisoners. In the language of labor economists, imprisonment imposes a "wage penalty" on the lifetime earnings of former prisoners. In this calculation, individuals who have been in prison experience a lifetime reduction in earnings of between 10 and 30 percent (Western and Pettit 2000). For the 3 million former prisoners who live in America, this wage penalty is a continuing consequence of their incarceration, a consequence borne by them and their families. For a national economy supporting about 142 million workers (Executive Office of the President 2003, table B-35), this wage penalty may be dismissed as having little consequence. For the local economies of communities with high concentrations of former prisoners, however, this wage penalty becomes, in effect, a penalty suffered by an entire neighborhood.

Finally, the buildup of the prison population must be viewed against the backdrop of changes in the national economy. During the 1990s, the country experienced an unprecedented, rapid economic expansion. Unemployment rates declined, job vacancy rates increased, and average earnings rose. Yet that decade's rising tide did not lift all boats. Low-skilled men, the labor category that describes most prisoners, did not fare well. The average wages of low-skilled men remained stable, while average wages for low-skilled women and those individuals with greater skills improved (Holzer and Offner 2002).

The short-term future does not hold the promise of better times. The kinds of jobs for which former prisoners are most likely to get hired—

blue-collar and manufacturing jobs—are decreasing as a share of the workforce. On the other hand, the jobs for which former prisoners are least likely to get hired—jobs involving contact with children and the elderly, the health care sector, and direct customer services—are increasing as a share of the workforce (Rubenstein 2001). A longer view promises a more positive economic future, however. According to a study by the Hudson Institute, labor markets will likely tighten significantly as the "baby boomers" exit the workforce over the next 25 years. These tight labor market conditions will not just affect jobs requiring high-level education and training skills (Judy and D'Amico 1997). The low-wage sector will experience these tight market conditions as well. If this is true, then employers will be compelled to turn to new sources of labor, including the ex-offender population. Should this occur, the policy challenge before us will be to develop mechanisms to support former prisoners, whose workforce participation has been marginal, and to create productive work relationships with employers, who have little experience with this population. The nation's experience with welfare reform, during which large numbers of new workers with little job experience entered the labor market, should provide useful lessons in meeting this challenge.

Whether we predict bad economic times in the short term, or better times decades from now, a troubling conclusion seems inescapable—prisons diminish labor market productivity for individuals, their communities, and our country. This damage to the national economy is substantial. The labor market group that is now falling behind all others—low-skilled men, particularly African-American men—is struggling to succeed against enormous odds. A substantial number of men in this group have spent time in prison, and this experience has hurt their ability to find work. Their ex-con status makes employers less interested in hiring them. Their legal status as felons bars them from a long list of jobs. Every year, hundreds of thousands of individuals leave prison struggling to overcome these obstacles.

Prisons as a Place to Improve Work Prospects

Why should we be concerned about the job prospects of former prisoners? In a harsh world, we could imagine a criminal justice policy that took no affirmative steps to improve those prospects and simply let prisoners fend for themselves in the job market. This world could be justified on pure retributivist grounds. After all, the person in prison committed a crime and must suffer the consequences, even those consequences that make it more difficult to work and earn a living. Yet for decades, we have aspired to a different goal—to improve the employment outcomes of prisoners when they return to the community. Why?

The primary reason that we have invested time, money, and hope in improving the work prospects of former prisoners is to reduce crime. The rationale behind this policy goal is straightforward—unemployment and crime go hand in hand. According to this logic, if prisons offer programs that improve inmates' chances of getting a job on the outside, the employment levels of returning prisoners will be increased, and their recidivism rates will go down.

There is common sense behind this logic. A number of studies have found that an individual's likelihood to commit a crime is affected by his or her work status. In other words, when someone is working, he or she is less likely to be involved in criminal behavior (Bushway and Reuter 2001). Different studies have made even more refined conclusions. One study found that crime went down as wages went up (Needels 1996). Another study concluded that job instability was associated with higher arrest rates (Sampson and Laub 1993). A third inquiry found that earning money in the legitimate labor market tended to reduce illegal earnings (Uggen and Thompson 2003). The fundamental point is the same, however: If someone has a legitimate job, he or she is less likely to be involved in criminal activity.

Prison, then, could be viewed as a promising point of intervention— a place to improve public safety by enhancing the future employment levels of returning prisoners. The superficial appeal of the argument is clear: With more than 630,000 individuals going into and coming out of prison each year—most with very low educational levels and poor work records—why not take advantage of the time in prison to improve their human capital so that they can face the work world better prepared? The logic is clear, but could we deliver on this promise? In the following section, we answer this question by examining three categories of correctional programs designed to prepare prisoners for work: prison-based programs, work release programs, and postrelease programs.

Prison-Based Programs

Virtually every prison in the United States offers a variety of programs designed to help prisoners improve their ability to function in the world outside. (This is not to say that programs are available to all who need them. Most prisons face waiting lists for their programs.) Many programs aim to enhance the prisoners' work skills, or to improve their academic standing. Some prisons offer opportunities for inmates to work in a prison industry, such as making license plates, linens for prison beds, or furniture for state agencies. Even if the skills learned are not directly transferable to a job on the outside, the work habits learned in prison industries are thought to be helpful in finding and retaining a job after release.

Prison administrators devote money to these programs for a number of reasons. For example, prison administrators may be legally required to provide in-prison schooling to young inmates. Providing programs can also be viewed as a sound management decision, because programs occupy prisoners' time and help maintain order in the institutions. Yet the primary rationale for these programs is that they reduce the recidivism rates of prisoners once they return home. However, two major studies published a generation ago disputed this rationale. In 1973, a comprehensive review of the evaluations of prison-based vocational programs (commissioned by the Department of Labor) concluded that only a few programs resulted in reductions in recidivism (Rovner-Pieczenik 1973). In addition, Robert Martinson's review (1974) of 231 rehabilitative (including employment-focused) programs concluded that "with few and isolated exceptions, the rehabilitative efforts that have been reported so far have had no appreciable effect on recidivism" (25). The conclusion of that article—captured in the shorthand phrase "nothing works"—played an important role in undermining popular support for interventions designed to improve outcomes for offenders.

Weighed against this earlier research, more recent examinations of program effectiveness are more encouraging. Within the past several years, three teams of researchers have conducted comprehensive reviews of individual program evaluations to determine whether these programs are effective at reducing recidivism among program participants. One team, headed up by Gerber and Fritsch, found "a fair amount of support for the hypothesis that adult academic and vocational programs lead to . . . reductions in recidivism and increases in employment opportunities" (Gerber and Fritsch 1994, 11). Another team, headed by Gerald Gates, then director of research for the Federal Bureau of Prisons, found that, "despite methodological shortcomings and challenges, the evidence suggests that carefully designed and administered education and work programs can . . . reduce recidivism and promote involvement in prosocial activities after release." This report concluded that "when considered as a body of developing scientific work on the impact of prison programs, education and work programs appear able to contribute significantly to increasing offenders' prospects for success" (Gates et al. 1999). Wilson, Gallagher, and Mackenzie (2000) came to similar conclusions. After reviewing 33 independent evaluations of education, vocation, and work programs, they found that "program participants recidivate at a lower rate than nonparticipants."

The evaluation literature also identifies program characteristics that are associated with successful outcomes. These "principles of effective intervention" include focusing on developing skills that can be used in the job market; matching the inmate's needs with program offerings; timing the program participation to be close to the inmate's release date; providing programs that focus on the prisoner's attitudes regarding prosocial behavior; and ensuring that prison-based programs are linked to community-based programs upon release from prison (Cullen and Gendreau 2000).

Compared with studies that concluded "nothing works," this body of research yields a more optimistic assessment of program effectiveness. We now have a relatively strong empirical basis for concluding that we can reduce the risk of recidivism with well-designed, well-administered, well-timed programs, particularly those that link prison-based services with community-based support systems. This optimistic view should be tempered by an important caution, however. The prisoners who participate in these programs do so voluntarily, so the programs attract the most motivated prisoners. This fact limits the broad application of these findings to the general prison population. Would nonmotivated prisoners benefit in the same way as those who seek out these relatively scarce programs? Probably not. At some point, difficult to determine abstractly, even widely available programs would yield diminishing returns. Several researchers have asked if there are ways to foster and support a prisoner's motivation to improve himself and take advantage of these programs. According to Bushway and Reuter (2001), "The overwhelming evidence from 30 years and billions of dollars of government spending is that it is very difficult to change an individual's employment status and earnings level. We believe the primary reason is that they themselves need to be motivated to work before things like job skills can make a difference" (221). In this view, the key to success is to understand the internal process that results in a moment of resolve to change one's life. Understanding this internal process should be at the top of our future research priorities.

In conclusion, there are reasons to be encouraged about prisons' ability to improve the job prospects of returning prisoners. As was noted above, these programs now serve only a small fraction of the prison population—approximately 10 percent at any given time—so there is ample room for expansion. Yet, even if sufficient resources were available to offer effective programs to every prisoner, we might soon reach a level of diminishing returns as programs dipped deeper into the prison population, enrolling more prisoners with less motivation. Our policy challenge, then, is to view these programs as more than isolated instructional courses and connect them to larger initiatives that support prisoners' efforts to create a prosocial identity that includes work as a central component.

Work Release Programs

Prison-based programs face an obvious and significant limitation—they are administered in the corrections institution itself, and do not typically link the prisoner to a job following his or her release from prison. For more than a century, prison reformers have attempted to overcome this limitation by offering prisoners opportunities to work in the outside world as their release date approaches. Alexander Maconochie, the 19th century reformer credited with developing the early parole system in the English penal colony at Norfolk Island (off the coast of Australia), developed the "ticket of leave" concept (resembling today's work furlough program) to establish links between prison work and the world outside (Morris 2002). Beginning in the 1920s, American prison administrators formalized this concept by developing structured work release programs. These programs were designed to allow eligible prisoners near the end of their prison terms to work in the community during the day and return to prison or a halfway house at night. Work release programs expanded significantly during the 1970s, with substantial funding support from the federal government (Turner and Petersilia 1996a). When the federal funding dried up, however, much of the enthusiasm for work release programs shriveled up as well.

The research on work release programs is very enlightening. The most comprehensive study is an evaluation of Washington State's program, conducted between 1991 and 1994. Countering the national movement away from work release programs, Washington policymakers targeted more than a third of the state's community corrections funds to a large-scale work release initiative. Selected inmates were allowed to serve the final four to six months of their prison sentence in a community-based facility, operated by a private entity. They were required to work, submit to drug testing, observe curfews, and return to the facility at night. In an evaluation using random assignment, Susan Turner and Joan Petersilia (1996a, 1996b) of the RAND Corporation found some surprising results, surely disappointing to program administrators. First, the program did not save money. The costs of keeping people in prison or supervising them in a work release facility were about the same. Second, contrary to expectations, the recidivism rates for the two groups were about the same. However, the "return to prison" rates for the two groups were strikingly different. Because of the heightened supervision of the work release cohort (particularly the frequent drug testing and monitoring of the numerous conditions of supervision), a quarter of the work release participants were returned to prison, compared with 1 percent of the control group. This rigorous evaluation of an ambitious program provides little support for work release programs on the basis of their potential to save money, cut crime, or reduce the rate of returns to prison resulting from supervision violations.

For various reasons—the withdrawal of federal support, weak research results, and the risk of a released prisoner committing a high-profile crime—work release programs have lost their popularity. Although 43 states have laws authorizing such programs, only a third of the prisons operate them, and fewer than 3 percent of the prisoners in America participate in them (BJS 1993). Work release is an idea still struggling for its rightful place in the array of policies supporting successful reentry.

Postrelease Work Programs

Virtually every jurisdiction in the country has employment programs that provide services to former prisoners. This is the inevitable result of the overlap of two populations in America—those with a criminal past, and those seeking work. Programs that seek to improve employment outcomes for hard-to-employ populations will invariably find former prisoners among their clientele. Few jurisdictions, however, operate employment programs specifically designed to target individuals as they leave prison. Because these programs focus squarely on improving job prospects of returning prisoners, they are more relevant to our discussion than the more generic programs that serve ex-offenders as part of a broader client base. Three programs provide a typology of these kinds of postrelease work programs.

Project RIO (for "reintegration of offenders") in Texas is an example of a program that is closely linked to the prison system. Project RIO provides job-preparation services to inmates while they are still in prison. Specifically, the program offers a weeklong job search workshop, one-on-one assistance with job placement, a resource room, and postrelease follow-up. It provides job placement services for almost 16,000 individuals a year and has a statewide pool of 12,000 employers that have hired parolees. Based on a one-year follow-up study, a 1992 independent evaluation reported that 69 percent of RIO participants found jobs, compared with 36 percent of non-RIO parolees. Only 23 percent of high-risk RIO participants returned to prison, compared with 38 percent of a control group (Menon et al. 1992).

Other programs, like the Center for Employment Opportunities (CEO) in New York, follow a "supported-work" model. CEO offers parolees day-labor assignments, four days a week. These jobs are intended to provide immediate income, structure in the parolees' lives, and opportunities to develop good work habits. Many of these jobs are community service jobs, such as graffiti removal, roadside clean-up, upkeep of city-owned housing, and painting dormitories and classrooms in the New York City University system. Simultaneously, CEO participants receive job development and job counseling. CEO reports that they are able to place about 60 percent of their participants in full-time employment within two to three months. Approximately two-thirds of CEO participants are still employed at the same job after one month, and of those, half are still there after six months.[5]

The Opportunity to Succeed Program (OPTS) represents yet a third approach. OPTS is based on a case-management strategy for helping ex-offenders move toward self-sufficiency. Working with former prisoners who have significant alcohol or drug histories, OPTS provides services that deal with substance abuse, housing, family strengthening, and health and mental health issues. Services are also available to assist clients in finding and maintaining employment. According to an Urban Institute evaluation, OPTS had a statistically significant positive effect on full-time employment during the first year post-incarceration. In other words, OPTS clients demonstrated significantly longer periods of full-time employment during this year (in terms of number of months of employment and percentage of months with employment) than did the control group (Rossman et al. 1999). Furthermore, the evaluation found statistically significant relationships between employment and criminal behavior. Increased employment levels (both full-time and part-time) were linked to reductions in drug dealing, crimes against persons, and crimes against property (Rossman et al. 1999).

These three models of postrelease programs are very encouraging, but those who argue for expansion of these models must contend with the pessimism of an earlier era. In the 1960s, the Department of Labor sponsored a number of supported-work programs for ex-offenders and other disadvantaged groups. A variety of programs were started under the Economic Opportunity Act;[6] however, these experiments were unsuccessful in showing that supported-work programs improved participants' employment or earnings, and the weight of the research evidence demonstrates that these programs were not successful at reducing recidivism (Piliavin and Masters 1981). According to a 1973 report sponsored by the Department of Labor's Manpower Administration (Rovner-Pieczenik 1973), the disappointing results were partly attributable to implementation issues where there were "problems in persuading correctional institutions to focus on education and postrelease objectives" (Bushway and Reuter 1997).

Another major experiment in transitional employment in the 1970s yielded mixed results. Under the Transitional Aid Research Project, income support and job assistance were provided to several thousand randomly selected prisoners who were released over a six-month period from Texas and Georgia state prisons. The results were disappointing: recidivism rates immediately after release from prison did not decrease (Needels 1996). A long-term follow-up showed "the absence of any large or statistically significant treatment effects on either recidivism or earnings" (Berk, Lenihan, and Rossi 1980). One exception to these discouraging conclusions is the more recent finding that transitional employment programs are effective for older ex-offenders. In a reanalysis of the data from the supported work experiments of the 1970s, Christopher Uggen (2000) found that these programs in fact had significant crime reduction and work placement effects for male ex-offenders over the age of 26.

Why, in the face of this evidence, should we continue to be optimistic about transitional work programs? Seen from today's perspective, these studies offer only limited guidance to discussions about whether a comprehensive program could improve employment outcomes and reduce crime. The realities of prisoner reentry require more than a job, or income support, and job referrals. Lessons from the modern programs highlighted above—Project RIO, CEO, and OPTS—help structure the outline of a new effective strategy, one quite different from the programs of the 1970s.

This new strategy would respond to three realities of prisoner reentry. First, employment needs do not first arise when someone leaves prison. If we expect a prisoner to make a smooth transition from prison life to a job in a competitive private labor market, that process should start in prison, with training programs, actual work experience, and assistance securing a job on the outside before leaving prison, as does Project RIO. Second, if the need for work is an immediate challenge for many returning prisoners, then creating work opportunities immediately upon release also makes intuitive sense. If prisoners work in prison industries providing goods and services for the prison community, the government, and the broader community, we could provide similar opportunities for released prisoners beginning with their first day out of prison. Recently released prisoners could also perform community service and make goods that benefit the community, as they do in CEO programs. Third, the reality of reentry is complicated by a number of challenges. Prisoners who are placed on parole must report to a parole officer and abide by numerous conditions of supervision. Those with a history of substance abuse confront the risk of relapse. Prisoners with families face the complex realities of reunion and possible estrangement. Those without housing stay with friends, gravitate toward single-room occupancy hotels, end up in homeless shelters, or sleep on the streets. These realities can make finding and holding a job difficult. For some returning prisoners, trying to find and hold a job may in fact be the wrong priority upon release, because other needs should be addressed first. The OPTS model, which employs a case manager to serve as overall troubleshooter, helping the former prisoner navigate work, drug treatment, health care, housing, and family issues, squares nicely with the complicated pathways of transition from prison to community.

If we combine the ingredients of the three programs discussed above, we arrive at a program model quite different from those tested in the 1970s. Outside the criminal justice context, supported-work experience like Job Corps has proven to be one of the most effective employment and training interventions for other disadvantaged populations (Schochet, Brughardt, and Glazerman 2001). However, that model is not tailored to the unique circumstances of the returning prisoner population. No other population in America faces the same combination of challenges—

criminal justice supervision, limited work experience, low human and social capital, and the transition from a controlled environment to one full of risk and need. What is needed is an intervention that begins in prison, offers flexible work opportunities immediately after release, and provides case-management support for returning prisoners as they deal with the complex demands and risks of the reentry period. The disappointing research findings from the 1970s should lead not to pessimism, but to a new generation of demonstration programs that reflect the reality of reentry.[7] These programs would link the world of work, job training, and skill-building programs in prison with the world of work and programs in the community. These demonstration programs would provide a bridge between these two worlds with a simple goal—to significantly improve the employment prospects of returning prisoners.

Looking Forward

Throughout our history, Americans have used a number of justifications to support the idea that prisoners should work while in prison and should be prepared to work when they are released from prison. Work has been viewed as integral to the rehabilitation process—as a way to reduce prison costs, as a form of racial domination, and as an essential component of prison management. However, we have only approached the full employment standard typical of the late 19th century, an era where prison work was synonymous with leased labor, chain gangs, prison farms, and inhumane treatment. Furthermore, our efforts to incorporate job training, education, and skills-building programs in prison have fallen prey to fiscal and political constraints. In addition, disappointing research results, the withdrawal of federal support, and harsh political realities have weakened our plans to use work release programs as a way of improving employment outcomes and reducing recidivism. Postrelease employment programs, though promising, lack the rigorous research needed to support a call for their expansion. Absent that, they remain hopeful models that serve a small number of clients.

In today's era of mass incarceration, we should simultaneously pursue two distinct rationales for putting prisoners to work while incarcerated, preparing them for work after prison, and actually linking them to work in their communities. First, we should continue to embrace the traditional goal of reducing recidivism by increasing the employment levels of returning prisoners. The second rationale—one that exists independent of the recidivism reductions goal but has received insufficient attention—can be understood as a "labor market rationale." As we have seen in this chapter, our prison policies depress the earnings of many individuals, mostly men, who live primarily in hard-pressed inner cities, where, in the words of William Julius Wilson (1996), "work has disappeared." To reverse these harsh effects, we should set a new goal for the prison system—to increase, not diminish, the employability of prisoners as they leave prison.

Setting this new goal requires rethinking the policy justification for work programs for prisoners and former prisoners. Historically, work programs have been evaluated primarily on their effectiveness in decreasing crime rates. This goal is hard to quarrel with, but it cannot be the sole justification. The crime-reduction effects resulting from work programs are likely to be small, so programs will always have difficulty justifying their existence on this basis. Moreover, the employment needs of the reentry population are large, requiring a broad and costly series of interventions. A labor market rationale, by contrast, argues for a broad application of work programs and a different measure of success. Under this rationale, the work programs, whether inside or outside prison, may or may not decrease recidivism, but they should be deemed successful if they improve returning prisoners' employment outcomes.

Employment in Prison

What would this labor market strategy look like? It would have two components: making prisons places where prisoners work (and are prepared for work) and making work available to prisoners returning home. The first building block is a commitment to make prisoners work—to make work in prison available for all prisoners and to require able prisoners to work. This is, in essence, what the voters of Oregon imposed on their prison system. Through a voter referendum, Measure 17 (enacted in 1994 with 72 percent of the vote), Oregon required that prisoners work as hard as taxpayers do—40 hours a week, either in a job or in activities that prepare them for jobs (e.g., education, drug treatment, or on-the-job training).

The changes in the Oregon prison system have been dramatic. Now, when an individual comes through the front door of the prison, he or she undergoes a battery of tests to identify possible barriers to employment. A plan is then designed to help the inmate surmount these barriers, a plan that includes literacy, job-training, or educational programs. Private companies have been invited into Oregon prisons to create jobs for inmates, including Manufacturing Country (a firm that produces custom-cut wood products), Trussbilt (a producer of doors and window frames for correctional facilities), Pan-Tec (a production machinery supplier), and PSC, Inc. (a company that builds products, such as retail scanners, that collect, process, and transmit bar code data). Perhaps the best-known items produced in Oregon prisons are Prison Blues blue jeans, manufactured and marketed by the Portland-based Array Corporation with the slogan "made on the inside to be worn on the outside." Because Measure 17 also required prison administrators to reduce state expenditures, prisoners build customized computers for state agencies, run a telephone answering service for the Department of Motor Vehicles and the Secretary of State, and create computer-generated maps for water and tax districts from aerial photographs (Butterfield 2001).

A sophisticated computer system tracks all inmate activities to determine whether Measure 17 goals have been met. Prisoners are awarded points for successful participation in work, education, and treatment activities. Earned points are then translated into monetary awards and noncash awards. Poor performance, misconduct, and idleness result in the loss of points. Because the more desirable jobs require a high school diploma, Oregon inmates are now taking more education courses and completing their GED requirements more quickly than before. There has been a 60 percent reduction in major disciplinary reports since 1995, likely because a disciplinary report can result in expulsion from popular work assignments. A prisoner who leaves the Oregon prison system now leaves with a résumé based on his work experience, recommendations from his supervisors, and a modest nest egg reflecting accumulated monetary awards. According to Steven J. Ickes, assistant director of the Oregon Department of Corrections, "The bottom line here is, we want inmates practicing on the inside what works on the outside, to try to undo all the bad crime-inducing habits they learned in the years before they got here" (Butterfield 2001).

According to Oregon prison officials, the implementation of Measure 17 has been highly successful. In June 2002, there were 11,490 inmates in the Oregon correctional system, over three-quarters of whom (8,924, or 78 percent) were considered eligible for work. Of these, 6,982 (78 percent) were fully compliant with the 40-hour work requirement, while only 650 (7 percent) were classified as "idle," and 1,292 (15 percent) participated in work or program activity less than 40 hours a week. Unfortunately, there has been no formal evaluation of Oregon's efforts to achieve full-employment prisons. Over the long term, these policies should be assessed for their effectiveness at improving employment rates and wages for released prisoners. In the near term, research should examine the effects of the drive to full employment on life inside the prisons. For example, critics of Measure 17 assert that many of the jobs are "make work" that do nothing to improve inmates' skills.[8] Inmate complaints of poor treatment, partly related to the implementation of Measure 17, culminated in a series of disturbances and boycotts in the Oregon prisons.[9] Ideally, implementation of full employment policies within the nation's prisons would maximize opportunities for meaningful work and training opportunities for prisoners, not serve as another opportunity for the exercise of control over inmates' lives.

The Oregon story teaches another lesson. This reform did not occur because prison administrators saw it in their best interest or because prison reformers convinced the Oregon legislature to put more money into prison programs. This reform came about because the public demanded it. Oregon made this important shift without changing federal law and without bowing to opposition from the business community or labor organizations, but rather as a matter of political will.

If Oregon could make this transformation, other states could do so as well. Certainly, reforms at the federal level could encourage more states to pursue this course. For example, Congress could significantly reduce the limitations on the transportation of inmate-produced goods in interstate commerce. But the history of reform efforts at the federal level provides little basis for optimism for sweeping changes. The Oregon example shows that states need not wait for Congress to act.

Transitional Employment

The second building block of this new approach to prisons and work would be to develop a full-employment policy to address the short transitional period prisoners face after they are released from prison. It seems odd that an individual who is gainfully employed in prison one day is the next day dropped off in a neighborhood where he may or may not have access to social networks but is expected, as a condition of his supervision, to find gainful employment. How is the job supposed to materialize? Who is supposed to help him find work?

For many returning prisoners, perhaps most, these questions do not come up—they find work. However, finding work is difficult, and sometimes impossible. We could attempt to meet the employment needs of returning prisoners by strengthening job placement services and inviting more private businesses to offer jobs. Yet the available evidence indicates that these programs serve only a small percentage of all returning prisoners and are not linked to work and employment programs in prison. If one of our goals is to minimize incarceration's negative impact on the earnings of former prisoners, then the intervention must be systematic (linking prison and community programs) and widespread (including as many returning prisoners as possible). This logic leads to an ambitious idea: If work (or participation in work preparation programs) is required while in prison, and work opportunities are provided in prison, then why not continue to encourage work and provide work where needed for a transitional period after prison? In this new framework, a primary goal of the transition from prison to community would be to increase the long-term employment prospects of returning prisoners; a primary strategy would be to provide intensive short-term assistance with securing work, even if that requires providing government-subsidized jobs.

The first step in implementing this strategy would be to create a "justice intermediary," an organization that would be measured on its effectiveness at improving the employment profile of returning prisoners. The operations of this intermediary would borrow the successful ingredients of Project RIO, CEO, and OPTS. Following the OPTS model, each returning prisoner would also be assigned a case manager responsible for helping the ex-prisoner navigate the tricky waters of housing, drug treatment, criminal justice supervision, and family adjustments, while keeping a clear focus on the goal of improving employment rates. As with Project RIO, employment specialists would begin working with a prisoner a few months before his or her release date. Private employers would be encouraged to come into prison to interview prospective applicants. For those without a job waiting for them upon release, work would be made available, as in the CEO model.

With the services of a justice intermediary in place, we should then articulate an expectation that all prisoners should work—or participate in programs designed to improve their chances of successful reentry—during the period of supervision. Some private employers will hire this population without additional supports or incentives. As the research has demonstrated, however, the resistance to hiring ex-offenders runs deep. The availability of incentives, including government-sponsored benefits and protections, may make a difference to some employers. Federal bonding programs insure employers against any losses arising from theft, forgery, larceny, and embezzlement perpetrated by high-risk employees. Such programs are available for employment arrangements expected to last six months or longer. Other employers may be influenced by Work Opportunity Tax Credits, which can be awarded for up to 35 percent of the first $6,000 of an individual's wages, provided he or she has been employed for at least 180 days (Holzer et al. 2002). But the work of Holzer et al. (2002) suggests private employers react most positively to the prospect of another agency screening potential job candidates, providing job counseling to new employees, and offering support in such areas as child care, transportation, health care, and housing—issues that could, if left unattended, interfere with job success. This is precisely the role the justice intermediary should play to increase private-sector employment during a period of supervision.

For those not working in the private sector, however, temporary public-sector jobs should be made available, paying market wages and providing health benefits. The jobs would be community service jobs, such as renovating abandoned housing, performing groundskeeping services for local parks, painting city-owned buildings, and removing graffiti, all of which provide visible, needed services to the community. This new form of transitional employment need not be expensive. The CEO model of community service work is largely self-funded. Because the work crews perform tasks on a contract basis, 90 percent of the program costs are covered by payments for their work (Finn 1998). Other costs—such as vocational training and job placement—are supported through government grants. The total cost per client is about $3,000 a year.[10] The goal of this justice intermediary would be to move clients into private-sector employment wherever possible by the end of the supervision period.

This strategy would also serve important justice purposes. Performing work that is valued by the community could help former prisoners reestablish a positive civic identity and overcome the stigma associated with their criminal past. Several years ago, Dennis Maloney, director of Community Justice for Deschutes County, Oregon, decided to organize the probationers and parolees under his supervision as a workforce available for public purposes. He made the following offer to the business and government leaders of the county: If this workforce were mobilized for public purposes, which community projects would provide the greatest benefit? Providing affordable housing was the answer. Therefore, the Community Justice Department launched a program of renovating old buildings and constructing new ones. Whenever a new housing unit was opened, the ex-offenders who had built it would form a line, passing the key from one to the next, finally handing the key to the new owner. In this case, the transitional work not only taught useful skills and kept the ex-offenders busy, but it also provided a very visible, public example of ex-offenders' contributions to their community.

This strategy would also require active participation by the private sector. As we discussed above, Congress should fundamentally restructure the PIE program to make prison industries an attractive business proposition. Tax incentives should be granted to those businesses that both employ prisoners while they are incarcerated and offer jobs to prisoners when they return home. To open up the private sector to returning prisoners, Congress should expand the reach of the Earned Income Tax Credit (EITC)[11] to include childless adults, a move that would benefit returning prisoners.

Our nation has experience with a similar effort to increase employment rates in a population long accustomed to low levels of employment. In many ways, the model for the proposal advanced here is based on our national experiment with welfare reform. Although the analogy is not perfect, welfare reform provides many relevant lessons. Most important is the fact that the transition from a state of dependency, in which basic needs are provided for by the state, to independence, where one is self-sufficient, requires a full-court commitment of the government, the private sector, and the individual. Progress is not simple; two steps forward are often followed by one step back. Nevertheless, with the right mix of incentives, supports, and sanctions, we learned that millions of poor people could be removed from the welfare rolls. The welfare reform movement rallied to the challenge of moving people "from welfare to work." The justice reform suggested here would have a similar rallying cry—moving people "from prison to work." Both reform efforts have similar goals—to bring into the mainstream a large number of individuals who are increasingly marginalized and unproductive.

Public Support

The proposal developed here would certainly face significant hurdles in the arenas of public opinion and state and federal legislatures. Yet there are a number of encouraging signs that the public may be willing to support policies that improve employment prospects for returning prisoners. The 72 percent vote for Measure 17 in Oregon signals broad support for full-employment prisons. Backed by that popular mandate, Oregon found a way to overcome whatever labor and business opposition may have blocked other efforts to put prisoners to work. The deep fiscal crisis facing many states today provides a strong rationale for identifying public services that citizens behind bars can perform.

Recent public opinion surveys suggest a "prison-to-work" strategy would find popular support. Public Agenda, a nonprofit public opinion firm, conducted focus groups in Philadelphia in March 2002 to ascertain, in a more general sense, the public's mood on prisoner reentry. Three focus groups were convened—one each from a high-income urban neighborhood, a low-income urban neighborhood, and a suburban community—and a striking finding emerged. Nearly all of the participants thought that helping ex-offenders find stable work was the most important step in helping them reintegrate into their communities. According to the group participants, getting jobs for ex-offenders would help protect neighborhoods from crime. Even though they supported substance abuse treatment and counseling programs, these Philadelphia residents viewed employment as a higher priority (Immerwahr and Johnson 2002).

The ground may be shifting. With public support, the strategy of putting prisoners to work in prison and transitioning them to work after their release may have a chance of overcoming our neglect of this dimension of prisoner reentry. After examining America's prisons in 1833, Beaumont and Tocqueville (1964, 67) wrote that "the interest of the prisoner requires that he should never be idle; that of society demands that he should labor in the most useful way." The same imperatives exist today.

NOTES

1. Ore. Const. art. I, sec. 41.
2. Bernstein and Houston (2000, 6) define low wage as "the poverty-level wage for a family of four and excludes those whose main activity is school."
3. Harry Holzer, personal communication with the author, May 16, 2002.
4. According to a January 2005 Bureau of Economic Analysis news release, the current-dollar GDP is $11,967 billion.
5. Mindy Tarlow, personal communication with the author, February 12, 2003.

6. As part of the "Great Society" legislative agenda of the Johnson administration, Congress passed the Economic Opportunity Act of 1964 (EOA). By providing training and services to disadvantaged populations, the EOA was created to address the roots of poverty in the United States.

7. A recent research demonstration initiative of the federal government presents an opportunity to test these new models. The Enhanced Services for Hard-to-Employ Demonstration and Evaluation Project, sponsored by the U.S. Department of Health and Human Services and the U.S. Department of Labor, is a multisite, multiyear evaluation of job placement programs. The project's purpose is to rigorously test employment services for low-income parents who face serious obstacles to stable employment. CEO has agreed to participate in the evaluation using a random assignment evaluation design (Manpower Demonstration Research Corporation 2002).

8. Interview with Brigette Sarabi, Western Prison Project, January 12, 2005.

9. Interview with Brigette Sarabi, Western Prison Project, January 12, 2005.

10. Mindy Tarlow, personal communication with the author, February 12, 2003.

11. Initiated by President Gerald Ford, the EITC has been a powerful mechanism for lifting people out of poverty and placing them on the work rolls. Under EITC, a low-income worker can receive a tax credit that is the equivalent of a 40 percent wage increase. For example, a $5-an-hour job becomes a $7-an-hour job. The EITC is now a $30-billion-a-year program, larger than TANF, and indeed the largest antipoverty program in America. However, childless adults are not eligible for the full range of benefits under the EITC. (Childless adults [age 25 and above] are currently eligible for a very small EITC. The maximum credit is about $340, less than one-tenth of what parents with two or more children get.) Although most prisoners have children, 54 percent of them (56 percent of men and 36 percent of women) were not living with their children at the time of their arrest. Therefore, they are considered "childless" and are ineligible for EITC.

8

Public Health

Compared with the overall U.S. population, prisoners are in extremely poor health. They exhibit markedly higher rates of HIV and AIDS, tuberculosis, Hepatitis C, and mental illness. They have histories of significant alcohol and substance abuse, with addiction levels that far exceed those found in the general population. Yet, unlike most Americans, prisoners have access to a free health care system (paid for by state and federal taxpayers) that attends to a wide range of their health needs. Within the first few weeks of their admission to prison, inmates typically undergo a detailed health evaluation that includes a review of their health history and a physical exam. In some states, but far from all, they are screened for communicable diseases. Prisoners are usually checked for mental illness, substance abuse, acute dental needs, and chronic disease. While in prison, they can call upon this health care system to respond to health needs ranging from routine illnesses to kidney dialysis and even heart transplants.

There is, nevertheless, considerable debate over the adequacy of our nation's prison health system. For some prisoners, prison health care may represent the best health care they have ever received. However, in a number of instances, American prisons have failed to provide health care that meets the minimal standards of the medical profession. Even so, there is no question that prison health care has improved significantly over the past three decades. Gone are the days when medical services were provided by unlicensed military corpsmen assisted by untrained inmate "nurses" and by a few doctors who were impaired or had restricted institutional licenses (Anno 2002).

A number of national organizations are working energetically and with considerable success to improve the quality of health care in America's prisons. The National Commission on Correctional Health Care (NCCHC) has promulgated standards for prison health care and offers voluntary accreditation to prisons (and jails and juvenile facilities) that wish to comply with those standards. The American Correctional Association and the Joint Commission on Accreditation of Healthcare Organizations also offer accreditation to prison health systems. In some states, such as Massachusetts and Texas, prison health care is augmented through collaborations with state-sponsored medical schools. In 2001, the states spent roughly $3.3 billion a year on prison medical care, or about $2,600 per inmate per year, up from $2.5 billion, or about $2,400 per inmate per year, in 1996 (Stephan 1999, 2004).

Even as we note this progress, advocacy groups, prisoners' rights litigators, investigative journalists, and individual prisoners frequently remind us of egregious examples of inadequate prison health care. They argue, with substantial evidence, that the significant advances in prison health care have resulted from litigation, judicial oversight, and consent decrees, not from a public desire to treat prisoners humanely. Securing adequate health care for this underserved and stigmatized population, they assert, will always require external pressure and vigilant oversight. Perhaps the most salient lesson we can draw from the history of prison health care in America is that most reforms are made possible by a combination of professional pressure from within the system and advocacy from outside forces (Nathan 1985).

In this chapter, we view the system of prison health care from the perspectives of the returning prisoner, his or her family, and the community. Rather than simply assessing the adequacy of the prison health care system, we will ask whether the period of imprisonment and the reentry process are viewed as opportunities to improve the health status of returning prisoners, connect them to ongoing health care in the community, and reduce the health risks they pose to the broader society.

These questions take on particular urgency when considering the high level of communicable diseases within the prisoner population. For example, more than 200 prisoners with active tuberculosis are released from state and federal prisons each year. Similarly, upwards of 15,000 HIV-positive prisoners, 2,500 inmates with AIDS, and an estimated 200,000 prisoners with Hepatitis C (HCV) leave our nation's prisons annually. These individuals are of intense interest to public health officials as communities struggle to contain these communicable diseases. Our reentry perspective compels us to ask whether prison officials—in particular, prison health officials—are adequately working with local health departments and community health care practitioners to inform community service providers that these prisoners are scheduled for release, to develop discharge plans to ensure continuity of any treatment being provided in prison, and to provide counseling to prisoners' family members. The reentry framework thus requires us to examine not only the response to these diseases in prison, but also the policies governing the management of the public health risk posed by reentering prisoners.

This analytical framework is equally valuable in considering other health conditions that pose different risks. Many mentally ill prisoners take psychotropic medicines to treat their illness, thereby regulating their behavior while in prison. From both a health and a safety perspective, society has an interest in knowing whether these prisoners continue to receive their medications following release. For prisoners with a substantial history of drug use, who during their incarceration were forcibly abstinent and were perhaps even participating in programs treating their addictions, the period immediately following incarceration poses a high risk of relapse. A reentry perspective requires us to ask what provisions are being made to reduce the chances that prisoners will return to drug use following their release.

As these examples demonstrate, our inquiry seeks to link the issue of prison health care with the health concerns of returning prisoners, their families and communities, and the well-being of the broader society. This chapter develops the argument that, for three reasons, special efforts should be made to link returning prisoners to public health and community health care systems. First, as a matter of equal treatment, returning prisoners who have been receiving health care while in prison should be considered the same as any other patients discharged from any other health service facility. The fact that the patient is also a prisoner should have no bearing on our ethical and medical obligations to establish a postrelease plan for that individual's continuing health care. Correctional health care providers should be required to develop discharge plans for returning prisoners that include specific links with local hospitals, clinics, and doctors, just as if these were patients being discharged from a traditional medical facility.

Second, because the rate of communicable diseases is so high within the prison population, health professionals (including prison health officials) have an obligation to society as a whole to make special efforts to reduce the transmission rates of these diseases. These efforts should include strategies to reduce transmission in the prisons themselves, but should also extend to encompass policies that reduce transmission within the communities to which the prisoners return. The fact that this population is imprisoned only underscores this obligation. In essence, our prisons present opportunities to diagnose diseases and health problems within this high-risk population, prescribe medications to treat these diseases, and engage prisoners in sustained prevention efforts to reduce the health risks they experience and pose to others.

Third, because prisoners present health conditions, particularly mental illness and addiction, that are strongly correlated to the risk of recidivism, corrections professionals and local government officials have an obligation to link returning prisoners to health services and treatment programs, as this may reduce the likelihood that these prisoners will commit new crimes. Crimes committed by mentally ill prisoners who are released without continuing medication and thereby lose control of their behavior are crimes that might have been prevented. Similarly, crimes committed by released prisoners whose addiction was not treated, either in prison or upon release, are also crimes that might have been avoided. Of course, there is no guarantee that a public health strategy will prevent these crimes, but a strong body of research shows that the overall level of criminal behavior among released prisoners who are mentally ill or addicts can be reduced with appropriate interventions.

To build this argument, we begin by briefly describing the current state of prison health care and then depict the health profile of the prison population. We will specifically examine three categories of health conditions—communicable diseases (including HIV/AIDS, hepatitis, and tuberculosis), mental illness, and alcohol and drug abuse. We then describe the state of transition planning, focusing on the links between health care in prison and in the community and highlighting innovative efforts to improve these connections. The chapter concludes with thoughts on how the reentry framework requires new approaches to health care for those sent to and released from prison.

The State of Prison Health Care

As with so many other criminal justice reform efforts, the movement to improve health care in America's prisons gathered momentum in the early 1970s, just as America's prison population began its 30-year period of relentless growth. The federal judiciary played a critical role in exposing the deplorable state of health care in some American prisons. In *Newman v. Alabama,*[1] one of the first federal cases to review the constitutionality of prison health care, the Eleventh Circuit Court of Appeals found shocking conditions. In Alabama prisons in the early 1970s, inmates—not medical personnel—provided medical treatment, dispensed medicine, and performed minor surgery. The court documented unnecessary amputations, deaths attributable to medical neglect, and maggot-infested wounds. Emergency care patients were left unattended for extended periods.

Conditions such as these spurred a wave of reforms from various sectors of American society. In 1973, the National Advisory Commission on Criminal Justice Standards and Goals issued a report recommending standards for medical care in correctional settings. A year later, the National Sheriffs' Association (NSA) adopted similar recommendations. The American Correctional Association (ACA) revised its *Manual of Correctional Standards* in 1977 and again in 1981 to include extensive standards for correctional health care. The health professions joined the reform movement, with standards promulgated by the American Public Health Association in 1976 and the American Medical Association (AMA) in 1977 (for jails) and 1979 (for prisons).

These activities by criminal justice and health professionals were augmented by funding from the Law Enforcement Assistance Administration (LEAA), a newly established agency of the federal government devoted to improving state and local criminal justice operations. Beginning in the mid-1970s, LEAA awarded grants to a small number of states and other entities to upgrade correctional health care programs. For example, in 1975, LEAA provided the AMA a grant to develop model health care delivery systems. Then in 1977, the Michigan Department of Corrections received LEAA funding to provide technical assistance to 10 other states to improve their prison health systems (Anno 2002).

As valuable as these professional and governmental initiatives were, they lacked teeth. In the 1976 landmark case of *Estelle v. Gamble,*[2] the Supreme Court provided the leverage needed to significantly accelerate the pace of improvements in prisoner health care delivery. In this case, the Supreme Court ruled that the Eighth Amendment's prohibition against "cruel and unusual punishment" required a minimum standard of health care for incarcerated persons. The Court held that "deliberate indifference" by corrections officials toward the serious medical needs of inmates was unconstitutional:

> This is true whether the indifference is manifested by prison doctors in their response to the prisoner's needs or by prison guards in intentionally denying or delaying access to medical care or intentionally interfering with the treatment once prescribed. Regardless of how evidenced, deliberate indifference to a prisoner's serious illness or injury states a cause of action. (*Estelle v. Gamble*, 104–5)

The *Estelle* decision does not guarantee prisoners the best possible health care for all health conditions. Indeed, the decision's reach is limited in significant respects. The *Estelle* ruling only prohibits "deliberate indifference" to a prisoner's "serious medical needs," which has been interpreted to mean those conditions that "cause pain, discomfort, or threat to good health."[3] Yet, this ruling's reach cannot be underestimated. In essence, the Supreme Court held that prisoners have a constitutional right to a certain minimum standard of health care, making them the only group in America that can claim such a right.

This Supreme Court ruling has provided the foundation for a series of constitutional challenges to prison health care systems. Hundreds of class action suits challenging prison conditions have since been filed, and most of these lawsuits have listed poor health care among the constitutional violations. Virtually every state in the nation has been a defendant in these actions, many of which were settled by consent decrees or, in a few cases, by appointing a special master to oversee the upgrade of prison health systems to meet constitutional standards.

This combination of professional standards and federal court oversight has profoundly changed health care in our prisons. According to one court-appointed special master, Vincent Nathan (1985), who oversaw efforts to achieve compliance with court decrees in Georgia, New Mexico, Ohio, Puerto Rico, and Texas,

> No serious student of American correctional history can deny that litigation has provided the impetus for reform of medical practice in prisons and jails; likewise, no one who has been a judge, litigating attorney, or a special master in a case involving correctional medical care can argue that meaningful reform is possible in the absence of the human and scientific resources of medicine. Indeed, the standards of medical care in jails and prisons adopted by the American Medical Association and the American Public Health Association have, to a large extent, translated the vague legal rulings of the courts into practical and

viable tests for measuring the legal adequacy of institutional health care programs. (3–41)

We may have passed the high water mark of federal judicial involvement in improving prison health care. In the years to come, the federal courts' oversight role will be significantly constrained by the Prison Litigation Reform Act (PLRA) of 1996. This federal legislation limits the scope of federal court involvement in lawsuits challenging prison conditions (including health care) and restricts individual prisoners' ability to seek relief in the courts. For example, the PLRA requires federal courts to order remedies to constitutional violations only when the remedy is "narrowly drawn, extends no further than necessary to correct the violation of the Federal right, and is the least intrusive means necessary to correct the violation of the Federal right."[4] Even existing judicial decrees governing prison conditions must be terminated unless the remedy imposed is found "necessary to correct a current and ongoing violation of the Federal right."[5] The PLRA also prohibits inmates from instituting legal actions challenging prison conditions "until such administrative remedies as are available are exhausted."[6] These congressionally imposed restrictions on federal courts' jurisdiction are certain to be challenged, but the conservative tenor of today's federal judiciary virtually guarantees that the PLRA will withstand constitutional scrutiny. Federal courts, the engine for much of the improvement in prison health care, will play a restricted role in the future—a reality that we will confront later when considering a role for the judiciary in promoting new policies to reduce health risks posed by prisoners following their release.

In most American prisons today, the provision of prison health care begins when a prisoner arrives. Physicians or other health care workers first conduct a diagnostic work-up. Many prisons screen for tuberculosis or other communicable diseases, evaluate the need for medication, and screen for mental illness, substance abuse, or developmental disorders. They often administer eye exams and identify dental needs. Once admitted to the general population, a prisoner can request medical attention by submitting a "sick call" request to the health services unit, seeking permission to visit the prison clinic. According to NCCHC standards (2002), these nonemergency requests should be reviewed within 24 hours and the prisoner should be seen by a health professional within the following 24 hours, or within 72 hours on a weekend. In cases of medical emergency, the prisoner need not submit a written request.

Most prisons provide on-site ambulatory health care in trauma, examination, and pharmacy or medication rooms, in addition to specimen labs and dental and X-ray facilities. For more specialized medical services, most prisons use local hospitals and service providers. With rare exceptions, prisons do not operate their own acute care hospitals (Anno 2002). Most prison health care workers are state employees, although a number of states have also entered into contracts with private health care professionals. Many states have, in fact, completely privatized their health care delivery system. The nation's largest private provider is Correctional Medical Services, which provides health care in every prison in 10 states, and a portion of health care in another 17 states (Hylton 2003).

This health care system is almost entirely funded directly out of state budgets. Private medical insurance will not cover these costs, although many prisoners are insured before their incarceration. A study by the Minnesota Department of Corrections (2001) found that 43 percent of prisoners had health insurance in the year before going to prison—half of them through their employers, 30 percent through public programs, and 17 percent through individual policies. Employer-sponsored insurance obviously ends when employment ceases, and most insurance policies are automatically cancelled when the policyholder goes to prison. States have found another way, however, to procure nongovernmental contributions to offset health care costs. According to a 1995 survey of state corrections departments, one-quarter (24 percent) charged inmates a fee for individual health care, and another third had received legislative approval to initiate an inmate user fee (NCCHC 1996; Weiland 1996). Medicaid and Medicare coverage is not available, as those programs also stipulate that eligibility ceases when the individual is incarcerated. As a result of these restrictions on benefits, virtually all prison health care—health care for a population with expensive health care needs and a constitutional guarantee of health care for their "serious medical needs"—is paid for by a direct appropriation from state budgets. Prison health services are thus analogous in some ways to health care for military personnel, veterans, and Native Americans, in that the costs are borne by the government. But in the case of prison health care, state governments—not the federal government—bear the financial burden.

The states spent $3.3 billion on prison health care in 2001 (Stephan 2004). In some states, the cost of this system is staggering—California's annual prison health care budget is nearly half a billion dollars. State spending varies significantly; on average, states set aside 11.7 percent of their state prison budgets for health care, ranging from 3.6 percent in Oregon to 18.4 percent in Nevada. The average expenditure was $70 million per state, while the median was slightly more than $32 million (Anno 2002). In a survey of prison health care costs, the National Institute of Corrections found that corrections agencies spent an average of $2,610 per inmate per year for medical services (Lamb-Mechanick and Nelson 2000). Massachusetts spent the most ($4,365 per inmate per year) and Alabama spent the least ($1,004 per inmate per year).

In summary, the past three decades have witnessed a revolution in prison health care, from a highly inadequate, primitive system to a complex network of public and private service providers, subject to extensive litigation and judicial oversight and costing billions of dollars. We now examine the health profile of the men and women who pass through our prisons, focusing specifically on three categories of health concerns—communicable diseases, mental illness, and alcohol and drug abuse. For each condition, we will briefly describe the prison health care system's current response to assess whether, from a reentry perspective, that response is adequate.

The Health Profile of Prisoners—Prevalence and Response

Perhaps it is not surprising that prisoners are, relative to the general population, in poor health. After all, the prisoner population reflects the communities from which inmates came—typically low-income with limited access to high-quality health care and substantially greater heath concerns than the general population. Many prisoners enter prison with a history of intravenous drug use, unprotected sex, and alcohol abuse, behaviors that are associated with a variety of diseases. Yet, notwithstanding this common sense observation, the health profile of the country's prison population is still quite shocking. We find extraordinarily high levels of communicable diseases, chronic diseases, mental illness, and addiction among prisoners. This profile is even more striking when we place it in the broader social context and calculate the percentage of all Americans with these health conditions who pass through a prison or jail each year. Seen from this perspective, the data lead to a simple conclusion: If the public health community is committed to tackling America's top-priority health challenges, it must develop

Table 8.1. *Major Infectious Diseases among the U.S. Population and Released Prisoners, 1997*

Condition	Estimated number of releasees with condition, 1997	Total number in U.S. population with condition	Releasees with condition as percentage of total population with condition
AIDS	39,000	247,000	16
HIV infection	112,000–158,000	503,000	22–31
Total HIV/ AIDS infection	151,000–197,000	750,000	20–26
Hepatitis B infection	155,000	1–1.25 million	12–16
Hepatitis C infection	1.3–1.4 million	4.5 million	29–32
Tuberculosis	12,000	32,000	38

Source: Hammett, Roberts, and Kennedy (2001).

effective partnerships with correctional facilities, as these facilities hold a high percentage of Americans burdened by these health conditions.

In reaching this conclusion, we rely extensively on a report commissioned by the U.S. Congress and carried out by the NCCHC that investigates the health status of inmates in American correctional facilities, with particular emphasis on those nearing their release date. Published in 2002, the NCCHC report paints the first detailed picture of the health profile of prisoners coming home. The picture is sobering. As shown in table 8.1, 20 to 26 percent of the nation's individuals living with HIV or AIDS, 29 to 32 percent of the people with HCV, and 38 percent of those with tuberculosis were released from a prison or jail in 1997.[7]

Communicable Diseases

In taking a closer look at the health status of prisoners, we start by examining the prevalence of communicable diseases, including HIV/AIDS, HCV, and tuberculosis.[8] These diseases pose a distinctive health risk, both to the prison community and to free society. By definition, such diseases can endanger both the person infected and others with whom he or she may come into contact. In addition, they may be transmitted, perhaps without the carrier's knowledge, to family members, friends, and the broader community upon the carrier's release. For these reasons, we might assume that prison health officials place a high priority on the detection, treatment, and postrelease care of these health conditions. Unfortunately, such a continuum of care is often the exception rather than the rule.

HIV/AIDS

HIV/AIDS is a virus transmitted through blood and other bodily fluids. When HIV (human immunodeficiency virus) attacks the body's immune system, AIDS (acquired immunodeficiency syndrome) can result, weakening the body's ability to resist a number of infections. HIV infection also attacks the central nervous system, causing progressive dementia.

America's correctional institutions reflect the ravages of the nation's AIDS epidemic. According to the Bureau of Justice Statistics, 22,627 state prison inmates (2.0 percent of the men, 3.2 percent of the women) were reported HIV-positive at the end of 2001. These HIV-positive inmates were concentrated in a small number of states; New York (5,500), Florida (2,602), and Texas (2,388) housed the largest number. On a percentage basis, New York also had the highest level of HIV-positive inmates (8.1 percent), followed by Florida (3.6 percent) and Georgia (2.5 percent). The regional differences are also striking. In the Northeast, 4.9 percent of the prison population was HIV-positive, in marked contrast to the South (2.2 percent), the Midwest (1.0 percent), and the West (0.8 percent). Nationally, the level of HIV-positive inmates in state prisons remained fairly constant between 1995 and 2000, and has steadily decreased since 2000. The incidence of AIDS among prisoners is a similar story. In 2001, 5,754 inmates in state prisons had confirmed cases of AIDS, making up 0.5 percent of inmates in state prison and 0.4 percent of those in federal prison. Again, these cases were concentrated in a small number of states. New York (1,160), Texas (859), and Florida (677) held more than half of all state prisoners with AIDS in America. Seventeen states had fewer than 10 confirmed AIDS cases in their prisons; four had none (Maruschak 2004).

These data do not fully reflect, however, the extent of the epidemic in America's prison population. To put the incidence of HIV/AIDS in our prisons in a broader perspective, the NCCHC study (2002) compared the prevalence of HIV/AIDS in prison with its incidence in the general population. In 1997, the HIV rate in the prison population was five to seven times greater than that of the general population, while the rate of confirmed AIDS cases was five times greater (NCCHC 2002). In 2001, the overall rate of confirmed AIDS among the prison population (0.49 percent) was still more than three times that of the U.S. general population (0.14 percent). The BJS study used another index to assess the HIV/AIDS burden among prisoners. In 2001, nearly 9 percent of deaths among state prisoners were attributable to AIDS-related causes. By comparison, only 3.9 percent of deaths among Americans between the ages of 15 and 54 in 2000 were designated AIDS-related (Maruschak 2004). America's incarcerated population clearly illustrates the penetration of the AIDS epidemic into our poorest communities—communities from which most of the prison population is drawn. These neighborhoods carry the burdens of crime and incarceration as well as the ravages of AIDS.

So what do these data mean from a reentry perspective? We know that hundreds of thousands of people go in and come out of our prisons regularly. According to the NCCHC, an estimated 11,600 to 15,000 HIV-positive inmates were released from prison in 1997. In that same year, 2,500 inmates with AIDS were released from prison. The public health implications of these findings are clear: Prisons and jails present unique opportunities for interventions that could significantly impact the course of the AIDS epidemic.

What are state prisons doing to meet the challenges posed by large numbers of prisoners with HIV/AIDS who are being discharged each year? Many prisons use the incarceration period as an opportunity for interventions with prisoners presenting higher risks of contracting HIV/AIDS. According to a report by the National Institute of Justice (1995), 75 percent of state and federal prison systems offered HIV/AIDS education and prevention programs in their facilities in 1994. In Bedford Hills, New York, for example, outreach workers and educators of the AIDS Counseling and Education (ACE) Program currently counsel female inmates on prevention and treatment, and these inmates later serve as peer counselors in the program. In addition, the program provides discharge planning, support groups, and other services (Stockett and Fields n.d.).

Testing is another method correctional facilities use to respond to the incidence of HIV. However, only 20 states administer HIV tests to all inmates upon admission. All of the remaining states test inmates only under certain conditions: (1) if the inmate is in a high-risk group; (2) if he or she requests a test; (3) if there are clinical indications that a test is warranted; or (4) upon court order (Maruschak 2002). But more is required than testing at admission or on a case-by-case basis. HIV can be contracted in prison as well. Consensual sex provides another avenue for transmission and, unlike prisons in Europe, Australia, and New Zealand, American prisons do not generally make condoms available to their inmates (Rafter and Stanley 1999). Only two state prison systems (Vermont and Mississippi) and five jails (New York City, San Francisco, Philadelphia, Washington, D.C., and Los Angeles) provide condoms to male inmates (Hammett et al. 1995). Forced sex is yet another transmission route. According to one estimate, one out of five prisoners is raped one or more times during his prison stay (Struckman-Johnson and Struckman-Johnson 2000).[9] Given these dynamics of prison life, it would be logical to test inmates for HIV both upon admission and release; however, only three states—Missouri, Alabama, and Nevada—and the Federal Bureau of Prisons test at both points (Maruschak 2002). It would also make sense to use the time in prison to educate prisoners about ways to avoid infection; however, only 10 percent of America's prisons provide comprehensive HIV/AIDS education and prevention services (Hammett, Harmon, and Maruschak 1999). Given the magnitude of the AIDS crisis in America and the clear opportunity given to prison health care systems to detect and treat the disease, the failure to develop a national program of prison-based health policies that addresses this epidemic is simply irresponsible.

Notwithstanding this rather anemic response to the AIDS epidemic, recent data on HIV/AIDS prevalence in prison are quite encouraging. In 2000, the number of reported AIDS cases in prisons declined for the first time. Even more noteworthy is the fact that the number of AIDS-related deaths among state prisoners has dropped significantly. Between 1995 and 2001, the number of prisoners who died of AIDS-related diseases plummeted from 1,010 to 256, a 75 percent drop. In 1995, these diseases accounted for 32 percent of all deaths among state prisoners; in 2001, they accounted for nearly 9 percent. According to the BJS report, these impressive results can be attributed principally to the availability of new drugs: "The introduction of protease inhibitors and combination anti-retroviral therapies produced a vast improvement in the effectiveness of HIV/AIDS care" (Maruschak 2004, 6). These improvements are particularly significant because they occurred at a time when the level of confirmed cases in the general population increased. We can only imagine the lives that might have been saved had the nation's prisons been more aggressive in combating HIV/AIDS earlier.

HEPATITIS B AND C

Hepatitis is an infection of the liver, caused by viruses acquired through exposure to contaminated blood products, particularly during intravenous drug use and sexual activity. Hepatitis B can develop into a chronic liver disease that results in about 5,000 deaths in America each year. There is, however, a vaccine to prevent hepatitis B. Hepatitis C (HCV) is a blood-borne virus that, if undetected, can linger for years before manifesting. About 50 percent of persons with HCV are unaware of their infection. The disease can cause fatigue, jaundice, and vomiting. It gradually affects the liver, killing one in five of its victims from thrash cirrhosis or liver cancer. HCV is the leading cause for liver transplants in America; an estimated 8,000 are attributed to HCV each year. There is no vaccine for HCV (Weinbaum, Lyerla, and Margolis 2003).

According to the NCCHC study, approximately 2 percent of the prison population had current or chronic hepatitis B in 1997. HCV is far more prevalent, infecting about 18 percent of all prisoners. Other estimates place HCV levels even higher. Random sero-prevalence studies conducted in California, Virginia, Maryland, Connecticut, and Texas have found infection rates for HCV ranging from 29 to 42 percent of the prison population (Positive Populations 2000, 1, cited in Anno 2002, 10), whereas the infection rate in the general American population is only 2 percent. According to the Centers for Disease Control and Prevention (CDC), of the 4 million Americans with chronic HCV infection, 39 percent were once in prison (CDC 2001).

The extent of HCV within the prison population is staggering. According to BJS analysis of the 2000 Census of State and Federal Adult Correctional Facilities, 57,018 HCV tests were completed in state prisons between July 1, 1999, and June 30, 2000. Roughly 31 percent (17,911) of these tests were positive, confirming HCV infection. Among those facilities that tested only a targeted group of inmates, a third (33 percent) of all hepatitis C tests were confirmed positive. By contrast, among facilities that tested more broadly, slightly more than a quarter (27 percent) of all tests were confirmed HCV positive (Beck and Maruschak 2004). Dr. David Smith, chancellor of Texas Technical University (which manages health care in Texas state prisons jointly with the University of Texas) aptly captured the magnitude of this HCV challenge. After leading a successful fight to make hepatitis screening mandatory in the Texas prisons, he commented, "It's just the smart thing to do. We have almost 30 percent of our prison population in Texas infected with hepatitis. That's not so different from the numbers you see in the Dark Ages with the plague" (Hylton 2003).

The hepatitis "plague" presents prison health administrators with a real dilemma. Unlike hepatitis B, there is no vaccine to prevent HCV, and current treatment regimes are often inadequate and very expensive. In contrast to HIV treatment, which costs $10,000 to $15,000 *per year,* HCV treatment costs between $10,000 and $15,000 per patient *per treatment session,* is effective in only about 50 percent of cases, and has serious side effects. In patients with liver failure resulting from the disease, treatment costs range from $50,000 to $250,000. To be effective, the treatment must be continued for up to 12 months, which is why the National Institutes of Health (NIH) recommends treatment only for people who will be available for a full year of intensive care. For these reasons, most prisons do not screen for HCV (Anno 2002). Furthermore, most prisons will not even treat an inmate infected with HCV unless he or she will be incarcerated for at least 15 months (Positive Populations 2000).

However, there are some encouraging signs that the corrections profession is coming to grips with the magnitude of the hepatitis crisis. In 2003, the CDC recommended that all prison inmates with a history of injection drug use be screened for HCV infection (Voelker 2004). Texas, Pennsylvania, and New Jersey have already instituted screening and treatment programs. These states were willing to bear the considerable cost of these programs, increasing prison health budgets by millions of dollars. At the national level, an initiative to test all new prison admissions would cost upwards of $120 million, at the rate of $25 to $158 for each test.[10] But even a targeted hepatitis-screening program would produce results. A study in Wisconsin found that if prison administrators screened only those inmates with a history of intravenous drug use, 60 percent of hepatitis infections would be detected. If a history of liver disease were added to the selection criteria, 83 percent would be detected. Under this protocol, testing costs would be reduced by two-thirds (Allen 2003; Burnett 2003).

The larger budgetary concern, however, is that once hepatitis is detected, prison health officials have to provide treatment, which is expensive. However, a decision *not* to screen inmates because the screening might detect HCV and thereby commit the correctional facility to provide costly treatment is very shortsighted. Every year, tens of thousands of individuals with undetected hepatitis leave the nation's prisons. These former prisoners may be unaware of their condition and oblivious to the risk they pose to others. At a minimum, the failure to screen for hepatitis poses a legal risk. Take the case of Randy Vallad. The Michigan Department of Corrections knew he had HCV, but did not tell him, and his longtime girlfriend was infected upon his return home (Butterfield 2003a). Mr. Vallad and his girlfriend have now filed suit against the Michigan Department of Corrections for negligence. However, the costs of inaction are even greater than the settlement of one lawsuit. Ultimately, society bears the costs of treating individual prisoners, prisoners' intimate partners, and others for a disease that, in many cases, could have been prevented.

TUBERCULOSIS (TB)

Millions of Americans have TB infection. A person is infected with TB if the TB bacteria have entered the body, but the infection is inactive. An infected person is not sick, and may not even know of the infection. Active TB disease, by contrast, is a serious, progressive illness caused by TB bacteria. If the body's defenses are weak, one can contract the TB disease soon after the bacteria enter the body, or even many years later, when the body's defenses are weakened due to aging, drug or alcohol abuse, HIV infection, or a serious illness. TB infection can be detected by a skin test. Active TB is detected by clinical signs, X-rays, and sputum tests. Most patients with active TB can be cured, assuming they have proper medical treatment and take their prescribed medications over a 6- to 12-month period. Unfortunately, the appearance of drug-resistant TB now poses a new challenge to public health officials. Drug-resistant TB results from inadequate treatment and may be transmitted to others.

TB presents a particular challenge to prison administrators. Because the disease is airborne, overcrowded prisons with poor air circulation are particularly conducive environments for its transmission. For example, the early 1990s witnessed a TB outbreak in several U.S. jails and prisons. In New York State, 36 prisoners and one corrections officer died from multidrug-resistant TB. Responding to the crisis, New York State prison health administrators instituted a comprehensive TB control program, including TB screening for staff, prisoners, and parolees. Health records of persons with TB were matched to prison records. The crisis subsided, but it was a frightening reminder that mixing the prison environment and TB can be particularly lethal.

According to the NCCHC, an estimated 90,000 prisoners tested positive for latent TB infection in 1997. About 37,000 of these prisoners will leave prison *each year.* An estimated 500 prisoners had active cases of TB and were undergoing treatment; about 200 are released from prison annually. Compared with the HIV/AIDS and hepatitis situations, the prison health care response to tuberculosis has been quite impressive. According to a 1997 survey conducted by the National Institute of Justice and the CDC, more than 90 percent of state prisons routinely screen for TB as part of their health intake procedures (CDC 1998a). Virtually all of these prisons (98 percent) report that they isolate prisoners with confirmed TB disease. Nine out of ten (91 percent) directly observe patients to make sure that they swallow their medications (NCCHC 2002). This commendable organizational response, standing in stark contrast to the minimal screening and treatment offered for other communicable diseases, demonstrates that prisons *can* mobilize effectively to address a serious communicable disease, particularly one like TB that spreads quickly in the prison environment and can infect prisoner and officer alike.

The prevalence of and response to three communicable diseases in the prison population tell an important and disturbing story. America's prisons are populated by large numbers of individuals with communicable diseases, but efforts to detect and treat these diseases range from commendable (for TB) to inconsistent (for HIV/AIDS) to unsatisfactory (for hepatitis). In some respects, this conclusion could apply to all aspects of prison health care; some diseases are treated well, others not so well. Yet, we are viewing the prison health care system through the distinctive lens of prisoner reentry. Seen from this perspective, the failure of prisons to adequately respond to communicable diseases among inmates has far-reaching consequences. Some consequences are borne by the prisoner, whose medical condition may not be diagnosed as early as possible and who will likely suffer adverse health outcomes after returning home. Some of these consequences are suffered by those who come into contact with the prisoner following release, such as an intimate partner who may then contract HIV or HCV. Other consequences are borne by a close circle of acquaintances and contacts, such as peers who share dirty needles, coworkers exposed to TB, or strangers who might come into contact with the former prisoner's blood. Finally, the broader society bears the costs of the prisons' failure to detect and treat communicable diseases, and the public health care system is burdened by responding to diseases that could have been prevented by timely interventions in prison.

Seen this way, the failure of our nation's prison systems (and the legislatures that fund them) to come to grips with the reality and consequences of communicable diseases among prisoners is a gross display of social negligence. Disregarding the immediate and long-term impact of releasing prisoners into the community without appropriate screening and treatment procedures in place jeopardizes community health and well-being. A more enlightened policy would implement a systematic, professional program of detection and treatment for communicable diseases in American prisons. Moreover, because the benefits of this policy would be shared by the society at large, the taxpaying public would likely be willing to pay its price.

Mental Illness

Using self-reports, the Bureau of Justice Statistics estimated that in 2000, 16 percent of state inmates—or about 191,000 prisoners—had a mental condition, or had spent at least one night in a mental hospital or a mental health facility (Beck and Maruschak 2001). Other researchers have calculated higher levels of mental illness; Human Rights Watch (2003) estimates that between 200,000 and 300,000 prisoners are mentally ill. Some of these mental conditions are quite severe. In a paper prepared in conjunction with the NCCHC study, Veysey and Bichler-Robertson (2002, 64) estimated the lifetime occurrence of seven disorders among state prison inmates: Schizophrenia/psychosis (2.3 to 3.9 percent), major depression (13.1 to 18.6 percent), bipolar (manic) disorder (2.1 to 4.3 percent), dysthymia (8.4 to 13.4 percent), posttraumatic stress disorder (6.2 to 11.7 percent), anxiety (22.0 to 30.1 percent), and anti-social personality disorder (26.0 to 44.5 percent).

Prisons do not universally screen to determine whether a newly admitted prisoner suffers from mental illness. Only 70 percent of prisons reported that they screen for mental disorders at intake, while two-thirds (65 percent) conduct psychiatric assessments (Beck and Maruschak 2001). And the record of mental health treatment in prison is equally unimpressive—only 60 percent of the prisoners suffering from major mental illnesses, such as schizophrenia, major depression, and bipolar disorder, receive mental health treatment while in prison (Ditton 1999).

The current state of practice regarding discharge planning and post-release supervision for mentally ill prisoners is also quite disappointing. Only two-thirds (66 percent) of prisons help released prisoners obtain community mental health services (Beck and Maruschak 2001). According to a National Institute of Corrections survey of corrections departments,[11] only 19 of the 43 responding agencies reported partnerships with public health agencies designed to provide health services to mentally ill inmates once they return to the community (NIC 2003). In addition, a survey of parole administrators found that only one-quarter provided any special programs for parolees with mental illness (Watson et al. 2001).

Clearly, much more can be done to provide continuity of care for mentally ill prisoners. The TAPP (Transition and Aftercare for Probationers and Parolees) program in Georgia shows what can be done. TAPP is a joint initiative of Georgia's Department of Corrections and the Department of Human Resources, Mental Health Division. The Mental Health Division provides case managers to assist returning prisoners and probationers with mental illness. These case managers offer assistance with housing, employment, and medical and mental health care (NIC 2003). Unfortunately, too few states recognize, as did Georgia, the importance of collaboration between the criminal justice system and mental health fields in meeting the needs of the tens of thousands of mentally ill prisoners returning home.

Histories of Alcohol and Drug Abuse

A remarkably high portion of the state prison population (about 80 percent in 1997) report a history of drug and/or alcohol use (Mumola 1999). In fact, according to this survey, more than half the state prisoners reported using drugs and/or alcohol when they committed the offense that led to their arrest and incarceration. The level of addiction is also substantial. One-quarter of state prison inmates fit the CAGE profile of alcohol dependence.[12] Yet most prisoners who need addiction treatment do not get it. In fact, over the past decade, the level of treatment has fallen. In 1997, only 10 percent of state inmates reported receiving formal substance abuse treatment, down from 25 percent in 1991 (Mumola 1999). According to a 1997 survey conducted by the Department of Health and Human Services, 45 percent of state prisons offered no substance abuse treatment at all (GAO 2001).

The low level of treatment for prisoners with drug and alcohol addictions represents a particularly acute policy failure. A growing body of research shows that prison-based drug treatment, especially when coupled with treatment in the community, can reduce the levels of drug use and criminal behavior among program participants (Hiller, Knight, and Simpson 1999). The magnitude of these reductions can be quite impressive. According to research conducted in Delaware, in-prison treatment for drug-addicted inmates combined with postrelease treatment reduced the probability of rearrest by 57 percent and the likelihood of a return to drug use by 37 percent (Inciardi et al. 1997). Failing to address these addictions while prisoners are incarcerated and under criminal justice supervision simply translates into lost opportunities for crime and drug use reduction in the community.

These stark statistics paint a portrait of a population with significant health problems and a corrections system that has yet to meet the challenge of screening for these health conditions and treating those who are ill. We are particularly concerned about the implications of this health profile for the cohort of individuals leaving our prisons each year. The analysis conducted for the NCCHC helps frame this reentry challenge in concrete terms. How should the public health and corrections professions deal with the more than 6,000 prisoners released each year with AIDS? The approximately 20,000 released each year with HIV? The 200 released with active TB? The nearly 100,000 (using conservative estimates) who are mentally ill? Or the approximately 450,000 with histories of drug and alcohol abuse prior to their incarceration? Or, to further complicate the task, how should those professions respond to the unique challenges of those returning prisoners who are dually and triply diagnosed, suffering from, for example, AIDS, drug addiction, and mental illness?

To meet these challenges will require a different vision of the role of prison health care. This vision was articulated by Jordan Glaser and Robert Greifinger (1993, 143) when they argued that the prison system presents a "public health opportunity" to meet "broad public health imperatives through treatment and prevention of highly prevalent diseases. Without such attention, these diseases will pose a risk to the communities to which the inmates return." In this view, prisons and jails can serve as a vital link in the network of public health interventions. Public health practitioners now devote enormous time, money, and ingenuity to identifying, tracking, and engaging individuals with HIV/AIDS, tuberculosis, hepatitis, sexually transmitted diseases, mental illness, and addiction. Yet Glaser and Greifinger argue that health professionals need not look very far to find their clients: A large percentage of seriously ill individuals pass through correctional institutions each year. But society does not view those institutions opportunistically, as presenting a low-cost locus for a public health intervention that could save lives, save money, and improve the health of numerous individuals, many of whom come from impoverished communities poorly served by the current system of health care.

Following is a framework for developing this new view of correctional institutions. Here, these institutions present a "public health opportunity," and we will look at case studies of communities that have provided national leadership by seizing this opportunity and providing new models demonstrating ways that public health professionals—working both inside the correctional institution and in the community—can collaborate across the prison walls.

Health Care and Reentry—Seizing the "Public Health Opportunity"

If we challenged prisons to address some of the health burdens facing prisoners, their families, and the broader society, how would we ideally expect these institutions to meet that challenge? Most profoundly, prisons would embrace responsibility for the health of prisoners during and after incarceration, and the health of those with whom ex-prisoners come in contact after they leave prison. The organization of health care *inside* the prison walls would be fundamentally realigned to meet health goals that can only be measured *outside* the prison walls. The clearest examples of this realignment would be seen in policies regarding communicable diseases. Prisons would establish universal prevention programs that would educate inmates about the consequences of certain high-risk behaviors. Prisons embracing this public health opportunity would also provide universal screening for such communicable diseases as HIV, tuberculosis, hepatitis, syphilis, and gonorrhea. In this way, our prisons would serve as sentinels for the larger society, detecting at their front door those communicable diseases among incoming prisoners, providing appropriate treatment while these individuals are in prison, and increasing the chances that when they leave, as all but a few will, they will be healthy and will not transmit these diseases to others.

Education

To improve the health of prisoners following release, prison administrators should place a high priority on educating prisoners on the consequences of high-risk behaviors. Recent research has suggested that prisoners are likely to engage in high-risk behaviors, including unprotected sex, after release from prison. In a longitudinal study of sexual behaviors of young releasees, more than 100 male inmates were interviewed at three intervals—just prior to release, one week after release, and six months after release (Mac-Gowan et al. 2003). Among the sample population, 37 percent had reported a previous diagnosis of a sexually transmitted disease (STD). In the 30 days before incarceration, 33 percent had engaged in sex with a risky partner, while 59 percent had had sex with multiple female partners. These behaviors continued following release from prison: 34 percent reported engaging in unprotected sex with multiple partners within six months after release, 13 percent within the first week.

To reduce the probabilities of recurrent risky behavior following the release from prison, some states have formed partnerships with community-based groups and health organizations to provide preventive education. In California, for example, the collaborative partnership among San Quentin State Prison, the University of California at San Francisco, the Center for AIDS Prevention Studies, the Marin AIDS Project, and Centerforce has resulted in mandatory HIV/AIDS education for all men entering San Quentin prison. This program offers a health orientation class for all incoming inmates, provides individual counseling for newly diagnosed inmates, and helps soon-to-be-released inmates develop personalized risk-reduction plans. The program is largely supported through the volunteer assistance of peer educators, prisoners who take part in a comprehensive peer-training program. A randomized experimental evaluation of the program showed that subjects who received the intervention were significantly more likely to use a condom the first time they had sex after release from prison, and were less likely to use drugs, inject drugs, or share needles in the first two weeks after release (Grinstead et al. 1999).

Screening

Universal screening would also be a priority for corrections departments that embrace a public health mission. As part of its report to Congress, the NCCHC estimated the impact of a prison-based system implementing universal screening for communicable diseases. The commission concluded that a program of screening, testing, and counseling for HIV, tuberculosis, syphilis, gonorrhea, and chlamydia would be *cost effective* for all diseases; in other words, the benefits of the intervention, including averted illnesses and death, would outweigh the costs of providing services. In some circumstances, the intervention would also be *cost saving,* and society would actually save more money in averted medical costs than it would spend for the program.

Some highlights of the NCCHC analysis illustrate the far-reaching consequences—and significant savings and health impact—of universal screening in our prisons. Commission researchers examined the prevalence of certain diseases in the prison population; calculated the costs of implementing screening protocols, health awareness programs, treatment and other interventions; and then, using relevant health research, made estimates as to the effects of those programs on detecting and preventing the designated diseases. For example, the commission estimated that if correctional health providers implemented a program of testing and HIV education for 10,000 inmates, this intervention would prevent three future cases of HIV. This program would cost only $117,000, an expenditure far lower than the cost of treating three cases of HIV over a patient's lifetime. Similarly, if a correctional institution screened 10,000 inmates for TB, and provided treatment for those with latent TB, the commission estimated this program would prevent 989 cases of active TB each year. Detecting these 989 cases, and providing preventive therapy of known effectiveness, would save more than $7 million per 100,000 inmates, or about $7,250 per prevented case of TB.[13] In addition, cost-benefit analyses of HCV treatment show potentially significant cost savings. One analysis of six months of HCV therapy (with interferon alpha) demonstrated a net savings of $400 to $3,500 over the lifetime of each patient (Wong 1999).

Transition Planning

In this realignment of the correctional heath care mission, prisons would also connect returning prisoners to the health services they need after release. For some diseases and medical conditions, transition planning is a medical imperative. For prisoners with HIV, TB, and HCV, a break in treatment can result in increased morbidity and mortality, increased risk of disease transmission, and the development of resistance to medications. For example, one study in North Carolina found that prisoners with HIV who were released without access to medications and care in the community were much more likely to experience viral rebound than their counterparts who remained under care in prison (Stephenson et al. 2000). Providing for these life-saving services need not be the exclusive domain of corrections agencies: A recent ruling by the Health Resources and Services Administration allows "Ryan White" funds (the federal program that funds health services for HIV/AIDS patients) to cover transitional services for returning prisoners (primarily linkage with community-based services) as long as these services are not otherwise funded by the correctional system.

Embracing this new mission would also require prison administrations to ensure that prisoners who were eligible for federal benefits, such as Medicaid, Medicare, the AIDS Drug Assistance Program (ADAP), or Supplemental Security Income (SSI), were in fact registered for those programs upon their release. For example, Medicaid, which pays for prescription drugs, can be a critical factor in ensuring health care continuity. A break in coverage can interrupt antiretroviral medications, which can lead to the development of drug-resistant strains of the treated disease, and can interrupt antipsychotic medications, which can lead to the recurrence of antisocial behavior. Yet ensuring continuity of coverage is not standard practice.[14] On the contrary, federal Medicaid regulations prohibit payment for health services and suspend a prisoner's eligibility during incarceration. When a prisoner is released, the process of determining eligibility must start all over again, and states are allowed up to 45 days to make this determination. This is a critical time for the returning prisoner—a time when health services, such as medication and drug treatment, are vital as he or she navigates the risks and hazards of life on the outside. Some states, such as Maine, have found a simple way to solve this problem. Maine state law grants the Department of Health Services 45 days to determine eligibility for Medicaid; the Department of Corrections submits applications for its prisoners at least 45 days before their scheduled release, so eligibility determinations are made before the transition from prison begins (Boober 2004).[15]

In summary, prisons could play an important role in reducing the burdens of disease and addiction that prisoners and the community experience through more effective screening and treatment, health education, and discharge planning. Granted, implementation of this new mission would encounter numerous obstacles, principally the additional costs. Treatment costs for the large number of prisoners identified with these diseases could be prohibitive within the constraints of current prison health budgets. However, savings from these interventions would be realized in the budgets of the larger public health care system. What we need is a broader definition of our system of public health—and public health financing: a definition that recognizes the central role of correctional health care in advancing the general public's health interests.

Health Care Partnerships

In arguing for this redefinition of correctional health care's mission, the commission's report to Congress noted that "a number of jurisdictions have found ways to overcome some of these barriers, often through collaborations with public health departments and national or community-based organizations" (NCCHC 2002, iii). The obstacles are not insurmountable. Instead, what is lacking is a national recognition that correctional institutions "offer a unique opportunity to establish better disease control in the community by providing improved health care and disease prevention to inmates before they are released" (NCCHC 2002, iii). We turn next to a discussion of some partnerships between the health care systems on both sides of the prison walls to understand the potential—and the challenges—inherent in a new approach to health services for returning prisoners.

The past several years have witnessed a number of notable efforts to link the health care systems on both sides of the prison wall, many sponsored by the CDC. As part of its response to the AIDS epidemic in America, the CDC commissioned a study of discharge planning for HIV-infected inmates in 10 large state correctional systems between 1999 and 2001.[16] The study, carried out by Abt Associates, concluded that "discharge planning services for inmates with HIV were seriously deficient" (Roberts et al. 2001). In order to test new models for discharge planning and continuity of care, the CDC formed a partnership with the Health Resources and Services Administration (HRSA) to create a multisite demonstration project in six states and one city to help prisoners with HIV make better transitions to the community.

Even though the evaluation of the program's impact is not yet complete, the demonstration project is already pointing the way toward a new framework for providing health care services for the released prisoner population. According to an interim evaluation, the most effective approach to discharge planning includes three components. First, each inmate's needs for continuing health care following release should be assessed. Second, the plan should identify, prior to the release date, a community-based medical or case-management provider for each inmate. Third, the prisoner should be scheduled for a specific appointment with the health service provider, rather than merely be referred (Roberts et al. 2002).

This plan, however, covers only the minimum requirements for effective discharge planning. A more robust vision of in-prison and post-prison medical care would fully realize its potential benefit to public health. Such a vision requires comprehensive networks among health care providers on both sides of the prison walls, criminal justice professionals in prisons and in parole agencies, and community-based social service providers (Roberts et al. 2002). Two new programs illustrate the potential of these partnerships. In Rhode Island, the department of corrections has formed a partnership with the state department of health, an academic medical center affiliated with Brown University, and about 40 community-based organizations to develop health strategies that span the prison walls. This partnership has developed a systematic approach to disease surveillance in the prison population, implemented disease-prevention programs, coordinated discharge planning, and worked through complicated legislative barriers and union issues related to the implementation of these new policies. Specifically, the partners have developed protocols providing that the same physician who treats HIV-infected inmates in prison will treat them in the community. Furthermore, to ensure continuity of care, the department of corrections notifies the state health department's TB unit whenever a prisoner with active or suspected TB is scheduled for release. Finally, the partner agencies have organized community-level services for released prisoners with and at risk for HIV infection so that these former prisoners have access to appropriate housing, drug treatment, support networks, and case management.

The early results are impressive. According to independent evaluations, participants in the Rhode Island programs were much more likely to keep their medical appointments after they got out of prison, maintain medical services in the community, and experience lower rates of recidivism. Participants in the Women's HIV/Prison Prevention Program who were at the highest risk of reincarceration and HIV infection had lower recidivism rates than those in the control group, both at 3 months after release (5 percent vs. 18.5 percent) and at 12 months after release (33 percent vs. 45 percent) (Vigilante et al. 1999). Participants in Project Bridge who were HIV-positive and soon to be released from the Rhode Island state prison received intensive case management and were tracked for 18 months. During this time, 75 percent of those who needed health services were linked to medical care and, of those, 100 percent received HIV-related medical services. Sixty-seven percent of participants who were receiving substance abuse treatment successfully attended all of their appointments (Rich et al. 2001).

A second model program operates in Hampden County, Massachusetts, where the local jail is testing a public health model of correctional health care with far-reaching implications. Unlike the Rhode Island project, which focused initially on HIV/AIDS cases, the Hampden County initiative covers inmates with any serious medical condition (Flanigan et al. 1996). The jail population is divided into groups based on the ZIP Code of the inmate's residence. Within each ZIP Code, inmates with serious medical and mental health conditions are assigned to health teams that span the institution's boundaries, working both inside and outside the prison in the community health centers. Case managers in these teams develop discharge plans for all inmates with HIV/AIDS and serious mental health problems. Nurses assigned to the correctional facility also develop discharge plans for inmates with chronic diseases.

The Hampden County model has also shown notable successes in its early stages of development. According to an evaluation by Abt Associates, inmates participating in the program were substantially more likely to access medical care in the community (Roberts et al. 2002, 13). Some of the simplest interventions were most effective; ensuring that an inmate had a specific appointment with a health care provider soon after release was significantly associated with the inmate's receipt of health care back in the community (14).

These partnerships, though in the early stages of development and testing, highlight the promise of a public health approach to prisoner reentry. At a minimum, policies that coordinate the delivery of health care across prison walls increase the continuity in services. For some medical conditions, simply maintaining treatment during a major life transition (such as leaving prison) can have positive health outcomes. Early results from these partnerships and similar efforts also indicate that recidivism rates can be reduced. However, the definitive word on the value of a partnership strategy to meeting the health challenges of prisoner reentry must await large-scale testing of system-wide demonstrations. The field is now ready for a demonstration project that would determine the benefits and the costs of a comprehensive program of screening, treatment, and transitional care for prisoners, particularly those with communicable diseases, mental illness, and addictions. Based on fragments of suggestive research and NCCHC projections, there is reason to believe the benefits would far outweigh the costs, and the gains would extend far beyond the individual prisoners to include improved health and safety for the wider community.

Looking Forward

Over the past 30 years, the quality of prison health care in America has improved significantly, spurred by federal court rulings and guided by professional associations. However, these reforms have focused primarily on the quality of health care in the prisons, not the broader health implications stemming from the annual flow of hundreds of thousands of individuals with substantial health burdens exiting our prisons. This chapter has argued that the next generation of reforms should embrace this broader public health mission. The dimensions of this expanded mission would reflect lessons learned from the HIV/AIDS demonstration projects funded by the CDC and HRSA, drug treatment initiatives that provide continuity across the prison walls, and the innovative efforts of jurisdictions such as Rhode Island and Hampden County, Massachusetts. Following are three recommendations that serve as the foundation for the next generation of reforms:

1. *Prisons should provide immunizations, screening, treatment, and prevention programs for communicable diseases.* First, we should view prisons as institutions uniquely positioned to reduce communicable diseases. Every prison system should provide immunizations that can prevent Hepatitis B and influenza. Every prison system should institute a policy of routine screening for HIV/AIDS, TB, HCV, and sexually transmitted diseases on intake. These diseases are readily detected at low cost. A policy of routine screening and treatment would discover large numbers of infected individuals who should then receive treatment while in prison. Prisons should also implement a comprehensive education program for all prisoners on the risks and transmission methods associated with these diseases, and steps that can be taken to prevent transmission.

2. *Prisons should provide comprehensive treatment programs for addiction and mental illness.* Second, prisons should institute drug and alcohol treatment for all inmates with histories of substance abuse. Similarly, prisons should adopt universal screening protocols to detect mental illness, and provide mentally ill prisoners with appropriate medications and treatments while in prison. These in-prison programs should then be linked to residential or outpatient drug treatment and mental health programs in the community.

3. *Prisons should implement universal health discharge planning.* Third, every prison should create a health-related discharge plan for every released prisoner. At a minimum, this discharge plan should provide continuity of care and medication so there is no break in medical treatment following release. A key ingredient in these plans is establishing immediate eligibility for Medicaid and other benefits upon release. Beyond this minimum, prison health officials should create alliances with their colleagues in community health care to view the entire period of criminal justice involvement—from the moment of incarceration to the end of community supervision—as an opportunity to improve the health status of the prisoner, his extended familial network, and his community.

Over the years, many of these ideas have received support from health organizations such as the CDC or the NCCHC. Implementing this expanded mission will undoubtedly require a significant organizational realignment of the nation's prisons. Screening protocols and clinical guidelines, drug treatment, care for the mentally ill, and comprehensive discharge planning will require staff, supplies, space, and added security. Yet at a time when state budgets are tight, corrections agencies are cutting core services, and the federal courts are less likely to support prison reforms, the prognosis for substantial new investments in prison health care is admittedly poor. But a shift in focus, from simply providing quality prison health care to viewing prisons as a public health opportunity, also reframes the threshold questions of who should pay for prison health services, and why. If the next generation of prison health reform embraces an expanded mission to improve health outcomes for released prisoners, then the benefits will be observed not only in the prisoners themselves, but also in their families and the broader society. These benefits will include cost savings but, because these savings will be realized outside the prison system, there is no incentive for corrections administrators to make the needed investments. So, we face a structural problem in allocating budgetary responsibility for the costs of this new public health mission. States, and perhaps the federal government, would be required to view investments in prison health care as part of society's investments in public health. Even though the immediate recipient of the health intervention would be a prisoner, the beneficiaries of that intervention would extend far beyond the prisoner to include family members and society at large.

The argument advanced here is not based on a notion that returning prisoners are entitled to better health care than their neighbors. On one level, these new policies would simply level the playing field by restoring eligibility for benefits, for example, or continuing prisoners' medical treatment following their release. This step would constitute what Wolff (2003) calls "treatment parity," not preferential treatment. Yet, on another level, this chapter argues for treatment that is clearly preferential—immunizations and screening for communicable diseases, assessment and treatment for mental illness, and treatment for drug and alcohol addiction. These health services are not readily available, at public expense, to ordinary citizens. This dimension of our policy recommendations is based on the straightforward proposition that our prisons provide, ironically, a low-cost, high-yield opportunity to detect and treat diseases that pose a serious public health risk and to deal with addictions and mental illness that, left untreated, increase crime and drug use—and thereby an opportunity to improve the health and safety of the larger community. These added investments reflect sound public health policy that will yield improved community health, reduced crime, and budgetary savings.

The impetus for these reforms will necessarily come from outside the corrections profession. As has been true throughout the history of correctional health care, litigation will play a key role in creating systemic changes. A new category of legal challenges can be based on the recognition that prisoners are not the only individuals harmed by the failure of prison health care. For example, as in the case of Randy Vallad and his girlfriend, the plaintiffs will be those whose illnesses could have been prevented by timely screening, treatment, and education. Prisoners will experience the harms after they return home, and the allegations of negligence will challenge the system's failure to provide continuity of medical treatment between prison and community. Whether the federal and state courts are hospitable forums for such claims is unclear. Certainly the conservative tenor of the federal judiciary and the dampening effect of the Prison Litigation Reform Act on prisoners' rights litigation do not bode well for a robust judicial role in promoting this reform agenda.

Another lesson from the early history of correctional health care reform bears repeating, namely that professional organizations played an important role in defining standards of care. In this next phase of professional maturation, it will be important to identify the stakeholders in a prison health system as extending beyond those who live and work in our nation's prisons. Areas with an interest in these reforms are not limited to the corrections field, but include the public health profession, advocacy groups for the mentally ill, service providers working with HIV and AIDS patients, and community crime-prevention coalitions that experience the harms caused by the release of mentally ill prisoners without medications and drug addicts without treatment. In this next era of reform, the ethical and social obligations of health care providers and corrections professionals should be expanded to include obligations to the prisoners' families, neighborhoods, and the broader society. If those obligations can be articulated clearly, and the potential for saving money and lives can be documented, then the face of prison health care will change in dramatic ways. Prisons will become public health centers, places where society takes advantage of the opportunity presented by the incarceration of large numbers of men and women with significant health burdens to provide interventions that improve prisoner as well as public health.

NOTES

1. *Newman v. Alabama,* 503 F.2d 1320, 1330 n. 14 (5th Cir. Ct. App. 1974), cert. denied, 421 U.S. 948 (1975).

2. *Estelle v. Gamble,* 429 S. Ct. 97 (1976).

3. *Dean v. Coughlin,* F. Supp. 392, 404 (S.D.N.Y. 1985).

4. *U.S. Code* 18, sec. 3626(a)(I)(A).

5. *U.S. Code* 18, sec. 3626(b)(3).

6. *U.S. Code* 42, sec. 1997e(a).

7. The NCCHC study includes jails and prisons. From a public health perspective, the jail population represents both greater opportunities and greater challenges. Because far more people pass through the nation's jails, programs that make screening and treatment available will reach a larger number of the target population. Because jail inmates have shorter detention periods, however, screening and treatment programs are more difficult to implement. Jail inmates are also detained under different legal auspices (many are pretrial detainees) and their release dates are less predictable, making coordination

with community health providers more difficult. This book focuses on the reentry challenges posed by the population leaving state prisons, but the argument for improving reentry planning for health reasons can also be applied to the jail population.

8. This analytical framework could be applied to another category of communicable diseases: sexually transmitted diseases (STDs), including syphilis, gonorrhea, and chlamydia. The NCCHC estimated that between 2.6 and 4.3 percent of the correctional population in 1997 had syphilis, 1 percent had gonorrhea, and 2.4 percent had chlamydia. All three of these STDs can be easily screened for and treated in the early stages. All three accelerate the transmission of HIV (CDC 1998b). The NCCHC report (2002, 29) states: "Very few correctional systems routinely screen inmates for syphilis. Despite the availability of fairly inexpensive diagnostic and treatment modalities for syphilis, a national survey conducted by the Centers for Disease Control and Prevention (CDC) found that fewer than one-half of all jails (46 to 47 percent) offer routine laboratory testing for the disease as a matter of policy." Because there is little information on the prison (as opposed to jail) health care response to STDs, they will not be covered in this chapter.

9. A recent study of prisons in four Midwestern states found that approximately 1 in 5 male inmates reported a pressured or forced sex incident while incarcerated. About 1 in 10 male inmates reported that that they had been raped. Rates for women, who are most likely to be abused by male staff, reach as high as 1 in 4 in some facilities (Struckman-Johnson and Struckman-Johnson 2000).

10. The price varies depending on the test used. Currently, there are several testing methods employed to detect HCV. For further details, see Lin and Fazlollah (2003).

11. The responding agencies included state departments of corrections, the Federal Bureau of Prisons, and local jails in Chicago, Philadelphia, New York, and Washington, D.C.

12. Developed by Demmie Mayfield, Gail McLeod, and Patricia Hall, the CAGE instrument is used to screen for alcohol abuse. The following four questions, which lead to the mnemonic CAGE, are used in the screening process: (1) Have you ever felt you should Cut down on your drinking? (2) Have people Annoyed you by criticizing your drinking? (3) Have you ever felt bad or Guilty about your drinking? (4) Have you ever had a drink first thing in the morning to steady your nerves or to get rid of a hangover (Eye opener)? (Adams, Barry, and Fleming 1996).

13. The NCCHC analysis reached similar conclusions regarding sexually transmitted diseases. Routine screening and treatment of prisoners for syphilis would save nearly $1.6 million for every 10,000 prisoners screened. Screening 10,000 male inmates for gonorrhea would identify the 6 percent who are likely to be infected. Treating them would detect 296 cases and thereby prevent 5 new cases. This intervention would cost a net of $267 for each detected or prevented case. Similarly, screening men for chlamydia would detect a substantial number of cases and decrease transmission from men to women. This screening program would cost only $198 per detection. Screening women for this disease would also substantially reduce the number of untreated or undiagnosed cases, and would reduce the number of pelvic inflammatory diseases.

14. In the states participating in the CDC/HRSA demonstration program, "eight of the nine department of corrections discharge planners who completed the survey worked on SSI applications, seven worked on Medicaid, four worked on ADAP, and four worked on Medicare. Eight DOC discharge planners provided the client with the

information and applications forms, and five of these reported actually filling out the applications" (Wolff and Draine 2003).

15. Maine state law allows inmates to apply for public benefits using the inmate's community address 45 days prior to release. Eligibility, if restored, becomes effective on the date of release.

16. These systems were in California, Connecticut, Florida, Georgia, Maryland, Massachusetts, New Jersey, New York, Pennsylvania, and Texas.

9

Housing

Of the many challenges facing returning prisoners, none is as immediate as the challenge of finding shelter. Work can wait. Drug treatment can wait. Most connections to community-based health care can wait. Reestablishing relationships with families may take a while. On the first day after prison, however, the released prisoner's immediate concern is, "Where will I sleep tonight?" Most returning prisoners have an answer to that question before leaving prison—they have made housing arrangements, typically with family members. Others remain uncertain, usually awaiting decisions by others to see if they will be welcomed home. Many start out with one housing solution and wind up shuttling between family, friends, shelters, and the street. Some live in homeless shelters or mental institutions. Some return quickly to prison. Housing, therefore, has been appropriately characterized as the "lynchpin that holds the reintegration process together" (Bradley et al. 2001, 1).

This chapter explores the housing dimensions of prisoner reentry. We will first examine the housing status of returning prisoners in the months following their release. In particular, we will document the barriers they face in securing housing, their access to private and public housing options, and the impact of today's large-scale reentry phenomenon on the nation's efforts to reduce homelessness. The chapter will end with some reflections on ways to improve the connections between those housing options and returning prisoners so that fewer of them face undesirable answers to the question, "Where will I sleep tonight?"

Housing after Prison

Most prisoners return to live with their families. When researchers at the Vera Institute of Justice followed 49 individuals released from New York State prisons, they found that 40 of them were living with a relative, their spouse, or their partner in the month immediately following their release (Nelson, Deess, and Allen 1999). In the Maryland *Returning Home* study, 153 respondents were interviewed approximately two months after their release. When asked where they went after getting out of prison, nearly half (49 percent) said they slept at a family member's home their first night. More than 80 percent reported they were living with a family member at the time of the interview. Over a third of the respondents were living with their mother or stepmother; 20 percent were living with a spouse or an intimate partner (Visher, La Vigne, and Travis 2004). Clearly, for most returning prisoners, home is where the family lives.

Yet, the family dynamics surrounding prisoner reentry can be very complicated. The story of Jean Sanders, chronicled by *Time* magazine, captures the dilemma many families face. After nearly seven years in prison for stealing a car, Jean tried to reunite with his mother, Ophelia, but was told he was not allowed to stay at her home. Remembering that things had not worked out the last three times he came home from prison, the family did not trust Jean's promises that things would be different this time around. Prior to Jean's release from prison, his mother and two brothers had held a family meeting and decided that Jean was not welcome. Therefore, after a brief reunion with his mother, Jean went to the local homeless shelter two and one-half miles away to spend the night. He lived there for the next six months, getting up every morning, putting on a suit and tie to go on job interviews, and returning at night to sleep in the shelter (Ripley 2002).

Even if the family is willing to take in the returning prisoner, that arrangement might not be in his or her best interest. A middle-aged prisoner participating in the Enterprise Foundation's Reentry Partnership program in Baltimore, Maryland, articulated the conflict clearly. (In that program, prisoners returning to three Baltimore communities are offered transitional housing for up to 30 days following their release.) In the "exit orientation," a meeting between prisoners returning to the community (which occurs about a month before their release) and the coalition of community organizations that make up the partnership, he said, in essence, "I understand the offer of transitional housing. But am I still eligible? My family wants me to live with them. They are not my blood relatives, but they are the 'family' that was always there for me during my struggle with heroin addiction. However, I know if I go live with them now, before I can be a productive member of the household, paying my share of rent, I will feel dependent on them. And I will fail. I know I can only cope if I am a full member of the family, making my own contribution to the household, rather than being dependent. Can I take the offer of transitional housing for a few months, until I have a job, so I can join the family as a contributing member?"[1]

When their family homes are not available, many returning prisoners choose to live with their extended network of friends and relatives. In the Maryland *Returning Home* study, 7 percent of the respondents slept at a friend's house the first night out of prison (Visher, La Vigne, and Travis 2004). Returning to live with family or friends may pose legal risks to both parties, however. According to a 1988 survey regarding conditions placed on former prisoners under parole supervision, 31 of the 51 responding parole agencies reported that they prohibited parolees from associating with anyone who had a criminal record (Rhine, Smith, and Jackson 1991). For many ex-prisoners, this restriction places significant portions of their social network off limits. Underlying this legal risk is the more fundamental risk that reconnecting with family and friends who are involved in crime enhances the likelihood that former prisoners will return to crime. Conversely, the prisoners' families may also assume legal risks following reunification. At the most basic level, the returning family member may resume criminal activity that harms the family. Furthermore, as will be discussed later in this chapter, for families that live in public housing, the return of a family member with a criminal record may even jeopardize the family's tenancy.

Some newly released prisoners end up in homeless shelters. According to a study in New York State, 11.4 percent of prisoners released to New York City between 1995 and 1998 entered a homeless shelter within two years of their release (Metraux and Culhane 2004). This finding is consistent with the results of a Bureau of Justice Statistics survey documenting that, in 1997, approximately 13 percent of prisoners scheduled to be released in the next year had been homeless at some time during the year prior to their arrest, living either in a homeless shelter or on the street (Mumola 2002). As we will discuss in greater depth later in this chapter, there is significant overlap between the prison population and the homeless population in America—as many individuals down on their luck move back and forth between these two forms of public shelter.

In summary, most prisoners return to live with their families or friends. So, in a literal sense, their housing needs are met. However, these relationships are complicated and made more complicated by the prisoners' return. Some families have been victimized, abused, or otherwise harmed by these prisoners, and understandably fear a recurrence of that dynamic. Some fear their decision to accept a returning family member back from prison may subject them to profound legal consequences. These living situations are often temporary, with former prisoners moving back and forth between family and friends. A significant proportion—perhaps one in nine—ends up in a homeless shelter at some point after leaving prison.

We now turn to a closer examination of some of the hurdles returning prisoners must face as they attempt to access different housing options. We look first at the private housing market, and then focus on the barriers individuals convicted of sex offenses face. We then examine public housing, a unique housing sector populated by large numbers of families whose members are in and out of prison. Finally, we explore the overlap between the population of individuals involved in the criminal justice system and those accessing the nation's homeless shelters. The chapter ends with some thoughts on ways to improve the housing prospects for returning prisoners.

The Private Housing Market

Availability

The private housing market represents 97 percent of the total housing stock in the United States, but returning prisoners have a very difficult time accessing this source of shelter (Bradley et al. 2001). While the number of individuals coming out of prison has increased, the number of units available in the private housing market has declined. The number of rental units affordable to poor families declined from 85 units for every 100 poor families in 1987 to 75 units for every 100 poor families in 1999.[2] The number of available units is even lower. In 1999, there were 39 affordable and available units for every 100 poor renters (Sard and Waller 2002).

The problem is compounded as housing prices in many urban areas, such as the District of Columbia, San Diego, Baltimore, Boston, Chicago, and Los Angeles, have skyrocketed. The strong market has generated housing prices that are out of reach for many individuals and households, even those in moderate- and middle-income brackets.

Barriers

Former prisoners seeking to access the private rental market face a number of barriers over and above this general lack of availability, the first of which is money. Most prisoners leave prison without enough money for a security deposit on an apartment. Most states provide a token amount of "gate money," ranging from a low of $25 to a high of $200 and hardly enough for a deposit in most cases. One-third of all states provide no gate money at all (Petersilia 2003). Beyond money, returning prisoners face a number of obstacles directly connected to their status as ex-convicts. For good reasons, landlords typically require prospective tenants to provide credit references, details on current and prior jobs, and a payment history from a prior rental. A former prisoner who answers these questions truthfully gives the landlord reason to rent to another applicant. However, answering untruthfully means potentially being disqualified for lying. Some private landowners also ask directly, "Have you ever been arrested or convicted?" The former prisoner's dilemma is the same: Tell the truth, and risk losing the apartment; lie, and risk losing the apartment; or don't answer and look elsewhere. A study in Seattle, Washington, documented the extent of private landlords' exclusionary practices. A survey of 196 property managers and owners found that 67 percent inquired about criminal history on rental applications. Forty-three percent said they would be inclined to reject an applicant with a criminal conviction (Helfgott 1997).

Community Opposition

Perhaps the most extreme example of exclusionary practices can be found in the community of Lancaster, California (Los Angeles County). In response to a high level of crime, specifically drug-related crime, city officials designated a 20-block area of north downtown a "drug-free zone." Known as the Lancaster Community Appreciation Project, the plan's goal is to keep parolees and probationers out of the zone. The plan's sponsors expect that judges will order probationers and parolees to stay out of the area as a condition of their supervision. The law also prohibits anyone on parole or probation from renting or owning property in the area. Violators of this law face a warning and then arrest.

Sometimes community opposition can also block a returning prisoner's efforts to find stable housing. The story of Thomas Trantino vividly illustrates this dilemma. Trantino served 38 years in prison for the 1963 murders of a police officer and a probation officer. After being denied parole nine times, he was finally released from prison in February 2001 and sent to live in a halfway house in Camden, New Jersey (Sullivan 2002c). Trantino then planned to move directly to a group home in Collingswood, New Jersey. Four days after he arrived at the new group home, the state parole board sent him back to Camden, responding to the public uproar against moving the convicted murderer of a police officer in that neighborhood. Mayor Jim Maley was particularly upset that Trantino's group home was located across the street from a school (Sullivan 2002b). After he was forced to leave the group home, Trantino lived in a homeless shelter in Camden (Sullivan 2002a).

The private housing market has become increasingly inhospitable to returning prisoners. Landlords are reluctant to lease to ex-offenders. Community resistance, particularly to group homes, can constrain housing options. Moreover, the demand for affordable housing outstrips the supply, even for those with more assets and fewer liabilities than former prisoners have.

The Unique Housing Challenge Facing Sex Offenders

The pressures to exclude ex-convicts from public and private housing markets are particularly acute in the case of sex offenders. Sex offenders who are required to register with the local authorities are explicitly barred from public housing.[3] While there is no legal ban on housing for sex offenders in the private housing sector, new statutes requiring community notification often effectively keep sex offenders out of neighborhoods where they are not welcome.

Community Notification Policies

Responding to a number of highly publicized sex crimes and a growing public concern over convicted sex offenders returning to communities, the federal government and 47 states have enacted sex offender registration statutes called "Megan's laws," so named in memory of a 7-year-old girl who was sexually assaulted and murdered by a neighbor who—unbeknownst to her family—was a convicted sex offender. These sex offender laws fall into two categories, each with different implications for sex offenders' ability to find housing. Registration laws simply mandate that convicted sex offenders tell the local law enforcement authorities where they are living. Notification laws, by contrast, invest law enforcement agencies with the authority to provide the community with details about sex offenders, including where they plan to live (CSOM 2001). Thus, these laws can potentially unleash community opposition to a sex offender's plan to establish residence in a particular neighborhood.

As of 2001, 19 states provide "broad community notification," meaning that law enforcement agencies are authorized to release information about sex offenders to the general public. Fourteen states have adopted narrower policies, only requiring "notification to those at risk," such as specific individuals or institutions that provide services to children or vulnerable populations. Seventeen states follow a "passive notification" policy, making information on sex offenders available to the general public, but not requiring the government to notify anyone. States use a variety of methods to inform a community about a sex offender's return—including media release, door-to-door flyers, mailed flyers, or Internet distribution. All of these methods can potentially interfere with the search for decent housing (CSOM 2001).[4]

There is very little research on how and if these community notification policies reduce the rearrest and recidivism rates among sex offenders. Research so far indicates that notification programs are not associated with lower recidivism rates (Leib 1996). In terms of impact on returning prisoners' housing prospects, however, evidence suggests that these laws are making it more difficult for these particular ex-offenders to find housing. According to a 1998 evaluation of Wisconsin's community notification law in which 30 convicted offenders who were subjects of community notification were interviewed, 83 percent reported they were excluded from specific residences due to the community notification policies (Zevitz and Farkas 2000).

This finding is supported by anecdotal evidence. In Kentucky, for example, a convicted rapist left prison and returned to Danville where, within days of his arrival, his picture appeared in the local newspaper with the warning that he was "high risk" and a "sex offender" (Breed 1999). The ex-prisoner soon lost his job at a packaging plant, lost his housing, and ended up living in his car. In Waukesha County, Wisconsin, two convicted child sex offenders voluntarily agreed to remain in prison past their release dates because officials could not find housing in the community (Sink 2002). In Canterbury, Connecticut, town officials filed a lawsuit to force a sex offender whose home was located near the town's two schools to relocate (Associated Press 2003b). Another sex offender in Boulder, Colorado, voluntarily revoked his parole because he was homeless and unemployed (Associated Press 2003a). Concerned that operators of group homes were opening their doors to sex offenders, a number of communities in Colorado passed local ordinances prohibiting unrelated sex offenders from living together in single-family residences.[5]

Perhaps the story of Pioneer Square, a neighborhood in Seattle, Washington, best illustrates the intersection between community notification policies for sex offenders and the challenge of finding housing. A small community of almost 1,500 residents, Pioneer Square is full of disparities. On the one hand, the historic area hosts more than 500 businesses, including upscale stores and restaurants. At the same time, Pioneer Square contains many homeless shelters that house about 500 men and women, including the highest concentration of homeless sex offenders in the state. Victoria Roberts of the Washington State Department of Corrections, in commenting on the situation in Pioneer Square, explained in a radio interview the lengths to which communities go to keep sex offenders out of their neighborhoods: "I've been in communities where people have literally bought property in order to keep the offender from moving in. They've built a day care next door. They built a park. They actually buy the house the offender was going to live in, in order to keep the offender out, not realizing that offender has to go somewhere" (Roberts 2003). In her view, these exclusionary practices have created a new social problem, vividly on display in Pioneer Square—a sex offender population that is very transient, frequently homeless, and concentrated in areas where they can find shelter and do not face organized community opposition.

New Solutions

These extreme examples highlight the housing dilemma facing sex offenders, a unique category of returning prisoners. A number of states have embarked on programs to mitigate the harsh effects of these community notification laws, trying to find ways to involve the community in a more constructive dialogue about the issues posed by sex offenders. In Washington State, for example, local law enforcement and corrections officials convene a community meeting whenever a sex offender is scheduled to move into a particular neighborhood. Participants at the meeting discuss the offender's profile, including the crimes he was convicted of, his treatment program, and the conditions of his supervision. They also discuss the general risks of sexual assault, best practices on sex offender management, and the role of the community in minimizing those risks (CSOM 2001). In Tampa, Florida, the police department has created a program called Sexual Predator Identification and Notification (SPIN). Moving beyond the minimum requirements of Florida's notification laws, the SPIN program assigns a community-policing officer to contact sex offenders every month in order to verify their addresses and compliance with state laws. Police officers team up with probation officers to make sure that offenders are following their probation conditions. The SPIN coordinator also meets with community members to explain the program, discuss offenders' rights, and engage the community (CSOM 2001).

These two programs attempt to involve the community in constructive approaches to a complex problem: Sex offenders have to live somewhere, but community notification laws have increased the chances that the community will not accept them as neighbors. Rather than allow community reactions to run unchecked, these programs attempt to harness those reactions and move toward a more thoughtful and pragmatic resolution to the conundrum of finding housing for sex offenders in an environment made more inhospitable by community notification.

Public Housing

Over the past 20 years, the federal government has adopted a number of policies that have effectively restricted access to public housing for significant numbers of ex-offenders. A substantial portion of the nation's prisoners lived in public housing before their arrest. According to a recent study, almost 10 percent of the prisoners in Maryland, Minnesota, and Ohio reported they were living in public housing prior to their incarceration. Another 15 percent reported that their families were living in Section 8 housing (recently renamed the Housing Choice Voucher Program), the second major federal program for publicly supported housing (Steurer, Smith, and Tracy 2001).

We do not have good national data on the exact number of released prisoners who return to public housing. Nor should we automatically assume that those who lived in public housing before prison will return to public housing—the family might have moved away, or the returning prisoner might have outgrown the family setting. Nevertheless, the fact that, in the three states studied, nearly a quarter of the individuals leaving prison each year formerly lived in publicly supported housing underscores the importance of federal policies regarding ex-offender access to these facilities. Significant restrictions on prisoners' ability to return to public housing could have profound consequences for the housing profile of the reentry population.

Availability

Before discussing these new restrictions, we should first understand the centrality of public housing to poor and working-class communities in America. About 1.2 million families live in public housing developments and scattered-site homes in the United States. These facilities are managed by more than 3,400 local public housing authorities (PHAs) (Hirsch et al. 2002). The available stock of public housing has never been large enough to meet demand, but in recent years the shortage has become more acute (Joint Center for Housing Studies of Harvard University 2001). Waiting lists for public housing have grown to include nearly a million families. In large cities, a family's average time on a waiting list rose from 22 months to 33 months between 1996 and 1998, a 50 percent increase. In New York City, the average wait is 8 years; in Oakland, California, families wait an average of 6 years, while in Washington, D.C., and Cleveland, Ohio, the average wait is 5 years (HUD 1999).

Another 2.8 million families participate in the Housing Choice Voucher (HCV) program, formerly called the Section 8 program. In one HCV program, families rent from private landlords, but their rent is subsidized by the Department of Housing and Urban Development (HUD). Under a second provision, families also rent from private landlords, but the housing units, not the tenants, are subsidized. The waiting period for HCV vouchers is also substantial—10 years in Los Angeles and Newark, 7 years in Houston, and 5 years in Memphis and Chicago (HUD 1999). Another 800,000 families live in housing made possible through other miscellaneous HUD programs (Hirsch et al. 2002).

Admissions Criteria

These long waiting periods alone mean that, as a practical matter, few returning prisoners can be admitted to public housing as new tenants soon after their release from prison. However, the larger reality is that ex-offenders generally stand a poor chance of meeting the admissions criteria. According to federal regulations, a PHA may deny admission to "applicants whose habits and practices reasonably may be expected to have a detrimental effect on the residents or the project environment."[6] In selecting families for admission, the PHA may consider "a history of criminal activity including crimes of physical violence to persons or property and other criminal acts which would adversely affect the health, safety or welfare of other tenants."[7] These criteria, however, are not automatic bans on applicants with criminal histories. In fact, regulations also authorize the PHA to consider "evidence of rehabilitation," or, for applicants with histories of drug or alcohol use, whether the applicant "is participating in or has successfully completed a supervised drug or alcohol rehabilitation program, or has otherwise been rehabilitated successfully."[8] However, given the high demand for this scarce public commodity, and eligibility criteria that disfavor those with criminal histories, a former prisoner seeking admission to public housing as a new tenant stands little chance of success.

These barriers to public housing seem particularly harsh in instances where substantial time has passed since the prisoner left prison and his or her reintegration seems successful. Consider the story of Frank, as told in "Every Door Closed: Barriers Facing Parents with Criminal Records":

> In 1961, Frank was caught shoplifting and pled guilty to a charge of grand theft. He served jail time. He had no further brushes with the law in the years that followed and was a productive member of society. Many years later, Frank, now a senior citizen, applied for admission to public housing. His application was rejected because of his four-decade-old criminal record. (Hirsch et al. 2002, 45)

Frank's case, although quite unjust, does not describe the typical intersection between public housing policies and the housing needs of returning prisoners. The more salient example is the case of the prisoner who lived with his family in public housing before going to prison and wishes to return to live with his family in public housing following his release. Although there is no research documenting the portion of prisoners who return to live in public housing, studies of public housing communities support the notion that many residents of these communities move in and out of prison.

Reentry–Public Housing Nexus

Research conducted in Chicago's Robert Taylor Homes by Sudhir Venkatesh (2002), a Columbia University sociologist, paints a graphic picture of our criminal justice policy's deep penetration into the fabric of this particular community. The Robert Taylor Homes development is one of America's most notorious public housing developments, long depicted in the popular media as a crime-ridden, gang-dominated community. When it was constructed in the early 1960s, this development occupied a 95-acre site that was a quarter of a mile wide and two miles long. The complex initially housed 27,000 residents, and at its height it consisted of more than 4,000 units in 28 16-story buildings (Bowly 1978). All the residents were poor, and most were African-American.

The picture of life in the Robert Taylor Homes that emerges from Venkatesh's research is quite sobering. One striking finding is the absence of men as legally recognized tenants. Women and children accounted for 98 percent (26 percent and 72 percent, respectively) of all tenants. About a third (29 percent) of these families had a family member (or a household member) in jail or prison and expected that person to return to live with them within the next nine months. An additional 12 percent expected that at least one person, currently incarcerated, would return to live with them within the next two years. Although we should not consider Robert Taylor Homes representative of all public housing—in fact, this particular housing project better illustrates one of America's most troubled facilities—it is nonetheless striking to realize that 4 in 10 families living there expected that, within the next two years, a household member would leave prison to come live with them again. In addition, since few men were listed as tenants on the leases, most of the returning prisoners were returning not as legal tenants, but in a very attenuated legal status.

The Venkatesh study also underscores the residents' ambivalence about accepting returning prisoners back into the household. Nearly half (43 percent) of the families expecting a household member to come out of prison in the next nine months reported they did not want the individual to live in their household again. On the other hand, these families did not plan to prevent the prisoner's return. They took this view fully realizing the risks posed by the returning family member. More than half (56 percent) predicted that the released inmate would once again be involved in some form of illegal activity. Drug dealing was most frequently cited, but the families also foresaw property theft, loan-sharking, extortion, and racketeering. In this particularly crime-ridden public housing development, family reunification meant heightened risk—risk of crime and, as we shall see, risk of eviction.

Eviction Policies

Recent federal legislation has made the reunification of families living in public housing more difficult. In the late 1980s, at a time when the national homicide rate was soaring and the onset of crack cocaine touched off a national scare about drug dealing and urban violence, Congress enacted the Anti-Drug Abuse Act of 1988, declaring that drug dealers were "increasingly imposing a reign of terror on public and other federally assisted low-income housing tenants."[9] This legislation gave PHAs (including providers of Section 8 housing) a number of tools for responding to this "reign of terror." In particular, it authorized criminal background checks on adult applicants. It gave PHAs, for the first time, explicit authority to terminate the leases of public housing tenants and their families for criminal behavior carried out by a household member, guest, or "other person under the tenant's control."[10] It also authorized PHAs to evict a tenant when any household member's use of illegal drugs or alcohol affects the rights of other tenants.[11] Furthermore, the Act mandated that PHAs implement local policies to deny public housing to individuals engaged in proscribed criminal behavior, and outlined in detail the screening, lease, and eviction procedures that PHAs were required to adopt. Over the next decade, Congress gave public housing managers even greater latitude to evict residents. In 1990, Congress expanded the language to include not just "criminal activity," but also "any drug-related activity."[12] In addition, in 1996, Congress gave PHAs the power to evict tenants for conduct performed "on or off the premises," not just "on or near the premises."[13]

These new powers to evict individuals from public housing are remarkably broad. A conviction is not required.[14] There need not even be an arrest. The criminal incident need not be recent. The incident can occur on or off the public housing premises. The housing authority must simply prove to a judge, by a preponderance of the evidence, that the criminal activity occurred.[15] In addition, an entire household can be evicted when a family member, a family guest, or someone "under the tenant's control" is engaged in criminal activity.[16]

Although broad, these statutory provisions are not self-executing. To be effective, they must be implemented by housing authority managers around the country. Therefore, under President Clinton's leadership, the federal government embarked on an intensive campaign to encourage housing authorities and Section 8 providers to aggressively use their statutory powers. Drawing on the political popularity of the "three strikes and you're out" movement that swept the country in the mid-1990s (in which several states and the federal government embraced legislation requiring lifetime imprisonment for certain persistent felony offenders), President Clinton in his 1996 State of the Union address urged local housing authorities and tenant associations to get rid of drug dealers and other criminals with the rallying cry, "One strike and you're out" (HUD 1996).

The Department of Housing and Urban Development soon rolled out a "one strike" program to carry out the presidential mandate. An ambitious national training program was launched. Under HUD's Public Housing Assessment System, housing authorities were given financial incentives to adopt strict admission and eviction standards by which they could screen out individuals engaging in criminal behavior.[17] Then in 1997, HUD surveyed the nation's PHAs to see whether the "one strike" program had been successful. Slightly more than half (56.9 percent) of the nation's 3,190 PHAs responded to the survey. About 75 percent said they were using the "one strike" initiatives in their communities. The results were dramatic. In the six-month period before the "one strike" policy took effect, these PHAs denied admission to 9,835 people because of their criminal or drug-related activities. In the six months after implementation, the rejection level nearly doubled, as 19,405 people were denied admission on those grounds. That year, PHAs denied admission to a total of 45,079 individuals, meaning that the "one strike" ban provided the basis for 43 percent of all rejections (HUD 1997).

The number of evictions from public housing also increased. In the six-month period before the "one strike" policy took effect, the responding PHAs carried out 2,698 evictions for criminal or drug-related activities. During the following six months, 3,794 tenants were evicted on those grounds, a 40 percent increase. Several PHAs took advantage of the HUD survey to register their objections to the "one strike" policy, reporting that many law-abiding residents were being evicted because of the criminal behavior of their children or grandchildren. Notwithstanding these qualms about the new policy, the bottom line of HUD's assessment was clear. The combination of legislative mandate, presidential leadership, and aggressive administrative implementation was having the desired effect: Fewer individuals with criminal histories—and their families—were living in public housing (HUD 1997).

Court Challenges

Not surprisingly, HUD eviction policies have since been subjected to numerous court challenges. The language of the statute and regulations is hardly crystal clear. Can innocent family members be evicted, even if they have severed relationships with the person engaged in criminal activity? Who qualifies as a guest of the family? Does criminal activity far removed from the housing development fall within the meaning of "on or off the premises"? If tenants may be evicted for criminal activity committed by someone "under the tenant's control," what does it mean to be "under the tenant's control"?

The core legal issue to be resolved in the courts has been the issue of "innocent tenants." Can public housing managers evict a tenant for the criminal activity of someone else, someone not on the lease, who has engaged in criminal activity that the tenant knew nothing about? This issue was brought to the Supreme Court in the case of *Department of Housing and Urban Development v. Rucker et al.,*[18] decided in 2002. The *Rucker* case involved four tenants who challenged their evictions by the Oakland Housing Authority. Pearline Rucker was a 63-year-old woman who lived in public housing with her daughter, two grandchildren, and a great-grandchild. The housing authority went to court to evict her because her daughter had been found with cocaine and a crack cocaine pipe three blocks from the apartment. Willie Lee and Barbara Hill were also long-time residents of public housing—Mr. Lee for 25 years and Ms. Hill for 30 years. Their grandsons, who lived with them and were listed as residents on their leases, were arrested for smoking marijuana in the parking lot. Herman Walker, 75 years old, was disabled and had lived in public housing for many years. He required the assistance of a caregiver. The caregiver and two guests were found with cocaine in Mr. Walker's apartment on three instances within a two-month period. Even though Mr. Walker fired the caregiver, the Oakland Housing Authority moved to evict Mr. Walker.

The Supreme Court's decision hinged on a matter of statutory interpretation: Did Congress intend for PHA managers to be allowed to evict tenants because of the criminal activity of others, no matter how "innocent" the tenant was? In the Supreme Court's eyes, the answer is clearly yes—the statute's language is unambiguous. In an 8-0 decision (with Justice Breyer abstaining), the Court held that PHAs could indeed evict tenants "for the drug-related criminal activity of household members and guests whether or not the tenant knew, or should have known, about the activity."[19] Ironically, following the Supreme Court decision, the Oakland Housing Authority decided to allow three of the four *Rucker* plaintiffs to stay in their apartments (Associated Press 2002).

PHA Interpretation

Whether the powers granted to PHAs by Congress and upheld by the Supreme Court in *Rucker* are exercised depends, in large measure, on the policies of individual housing authorities. According to an article in the *Journal of Housing and Community Development* (Shafer 2002), public housing managers were generally gratified by the *Rucker* decision—they appreciated having a tool to evict disruptive tenants. But the same article found tremendous variation in PHAs' willingness to use the powers granted them by Congress. Some, such as the Minneapolis Public Housing Authority, have adopted a policy of strict enforcement. If residents, family members, or guests are involved in drug-related or criminal activity, residents are routinely given a seven-day notice of termination. If they do not move out, an eviction action is filed in court. Others, such as the Housing Authority of the City of Santa Barbara, are more flexible. Robert Pearson, the executive director, expressed concern about the potential for overreach: "Consider your own situation should your child or a guest of yours be caught using drugs away from your home . . . your landlord could use that incident to evict you from your home" (Shafer 2002, 16). Santa Barbara has established a Rental Mediation Task Force, made up of residents and landlords, to try to resolve difficult cases. According to Pearson, "It's our last straw to evict. We mediate whenever we can first" (Shafer 2002, 16).

Given the high-level attention to this national initiative to protect public housing tenants against a "reign of terror," one might expect to find a body of research evaluating the impact of these restrictions on the level of crime and drug-related activity in and around public housing. This research does not exist. One notable exception is a preliminary study examining the effect of the "one strike" program on evictions and perceptions of public safety. According to these experts, "To the extent that we have isolated the effects of the one strike policy, it is, if anything, associated with a decrease in perceived neighborhood safety for public housing residents" (Heintze and Berger 2004, 20). From a public safety perspective, then, even though public housing managers consider these powers as valuable tools in their crime control toolkit, the benefits of the "one strike" policy have not been proven.

The Dilemma

From a reentry perspective, however, the "one strike" policy is far too sweeping. For some individuals such as Frank, our senior citizen, the results seem simply unjust. Certainly an individual whose only criminal conviction occurred 40 years ago should not be denied access to public housing solely for that reason. The effects are felt far beyond individual cases, however. In a public housing project such as the Robert Taylor Homes, where 40 percent of households expect a family member home from prison, the intersection between public housing policy and the prisoner reentry process is significant. Blocking the return home of large percentages of public housing residents who have been imprisoned also seems unjust. What we need is a system that makes individualized determinations to exclude those ex-offenders who pose a demonstrable risk to their families' safety or the well-being of the broader public housing community.

Ironically, the tenuous status of ex-offenders who may legally be excluded from their family's leases is further exacerbated by the recent HOPE VI initiative, designed to improve public housing in America. Under the HOPE VI program, large housing projects in many American cities are being torn down and replaced with new, smaller housing developments.[20] To implement this large-scale relocation, housing managers are implementing de novo screening procedures to assess potential tenants' eligibility. As a result, "ineligible" tenants, including those convicted of crimes, are being screened out, forcing their families to choose between subsidized public housing and family unity (Popkin et al. 2002). In short, as a consequence of an unprecedented national commitment to public housing reform, ex-offenders are finding their housing options restricted even further.

Public housing in America was created as a form of transitional housing for the working poor. Yet, over the past 15 years, this public resource has been placed beyond the reach of a particular segment of America's working poor—those with criminal records, those arrested for crimes, and those found "engaged" in criminal activity. These individuals can be rejected at the front door, no matter how distant their criminal past. They can be evicted, no matter how long they have lived in the apartment, no matter how trivial the crime. Perhaps most troubling is recent legislation, upheld by the Supreme Court, that places the families of these individuals at risk of losing their public housing, even if they had no connection to the criminal activity and even if they tried to stop it. It hardly seems fair that, in order to fight crime in America's public housing projects, we have created a system in which many law-abiding residents live under the constant threat that the activities of a relative, friend, or guest can result in eviction.

One could argue that there is little reason to be concerned about returning prisoners' limited access to public housing. After all, few of them will make it to the top of waiting lists for new units, and housing managers have ample discretion to overlook old criminal convictions. Furthermore, those prisoners who do return to public housing often meld back into the rhythms of life in public housing. Those returning prisoners not on the family's lease will enter the shadowy world of illegal tenancies, a reality that many tenants accept. But one must recognize that these policies place enormous burdens on returning prisoners' families. The families, already ambivalent about the return of a loved one from prison, will now face new risks posed by public housing rules. If strong family support is associated with successful reentry, then these regulations place a high price on that support, to the detriment of the reintegration process facing thousands of returning prisoners.

Homelessness and the Criminal Justice System

There is a significant overlap between two groups of Americans—those who are homeless and those who have been involved in the criminal justice system. Both groups are disfavored by policymakers and shunned by the public. Both groups use large-scale social service systems—the homeless, a vast array of homeless shelters; the criminal justice population, an expansive system of community supervision. Neither system claims to be adequate in meeting the needs of the population it serves and both have been criticized as uncaring and punitive. Yet only rarely do practitioners operating in these systems fully grasp the connection between homelessness and involvement with the criminal justice system. Criminal justice agencies, particularly state parole agencies, understand only superficially the extent to which parolees are homeless or use public shelters. The agencies serving the homeless are only indirectly aware of the connection between their clients and the reentry process. The following discussion explores the overlap between these two populations from the perspective of policies designed to reduce homelessness and of those intended to promote successful prisoner reentry.

Homelessness Policies

We begin our exploration by looking at a profile of the shelter population to determine how many homeless shelter residents have been in prison. In the absence of national data, we turn to a number of local studies that have addressed this question. According to a 1997 profile of the residents of Boston's homeless shelters, 57 percent had lived in at least one institutional setting within the prior year, including hospitals, mental health facilities, jails, detoxification centers, or halfway houses. Almost a quarter of them (22 percent) had lived in a prison or jail (Friedman et al. 1997).

A broader view is even more informative. The Boston survey is limited to those homeless people living in shelters. But what about those living on the streets? The National Survey of Homeless Assistance Providers and Clients, conducted by the Urban Institute between October 1995 and November 1996, includes interviews with homeless individuals wherever they are found—in shelters, on the streets, or in abandoned tenements. According to this survey, an estimated 49 percent of homeless individuals had spent five or more days during their entire lifetime in a city or county jail, 4 percent had spent time in a military lock-up, and 18 percent had been incarcerated in a state or federal prison (Burt et al. 1999). An Urban Institute study conducted in 1987 arrived at a similar conclusion—nearly a quarter of all homeless people had served time in prison (Burt and Cohen 1989). Using these studies, we can project the overlap between these two populations: Of the 350,000 to 600,000 individuals estimated to be homeless in America, about a quarter, or between 87,500 and 150,000 individuals, have served time in prison.

America has committed substantial energy and resources to reduce homelessness and provide shelter to the homeless. One particularly promising strategy involves developing "supportive housing," a program that links affordable housing with such social services as drug treatment, counseling, or health services. The Corporation for Supportive Housing (2002) describes this intervention as a permanent, affordable option "designed to help the tenants stay housed and build the necessary skills to live as independently as possible." This mix of services, shelter, and community support would seem an ideal mix for returning prisoners who face the prospects of homelessness. Yet housing providers interested in offering supportive housing to returning prisoners face a significant hurdle: the federal government excludes from the definition of "homeless" anyone "imprisoned or otherwise detained pursuant to an Act of Congress or a State law."[21] In some states, this language has been interpreted to mean that former prisoners are forever ineligible. In other jurisdictions, only people currently detained are declared ineligible; once ex-prisoners are out of prison for a while, they become eligible. At a minimum, this language makes it difficult, perhaps impossible, for supportive housing providers to work with corrections officials and make their services available to those prisoners who otherwise would be released directly to the homeless shelters or the streets.

Yet, by scraping together funding from a variety of public and private sources, a number of housing providers have found creative ways to make supportive and transitional housing available for ex-offenders and returning prisoners. A particularly dramatic and symbolic new housing facility for ex-offenders, for example, is Fortune Academy in New York City. For 20 years, anyone driving down the West Side Highway would have noticed a beautiful but abandoned gothic building perched majestically on Riverside Drive at 140th Street. In 2002, the Fortune Society, an advocacy organization that provides services to former prisoners, combined government funding from at least seven different sources at the city, state, and federal levels and transformed that abandoned building into the Fortune Academy, a residential facility for prisoners transitioning back into society.[22] This innovative program now provides clients with emergency and longer-term beds as well as access to the Fortune Academy's range of support services (Solomon et al. 2004). Successes such as this, however, must be placed in context. The Fortune Academy has just 59 beds. It would take dozens of Fortune Academies to meet all the needs for transitional and supportive housing in New York City.

Research suggests, however, that supportive housing for homeless former prisoners could be very effective at reducing crime and saving money. In a large-scale evaluation of a supportive housing program for homeless individuals with severe mental illness developed by New York State and New York City (called "NY/NY"), researchers at the University of Pennsylvania examined supportive housing's impact on reducing participants' use of public shelters, public and private hospitals, and correctional facilities. They analyzed data on the experiences of program participants and compared them with a matched sample. These researchers found that placing ex-prisoners in supportive housing resulted in 7.9 fewer days in prison and 3.8 fewer days in jail per person in the program. These positive results translated into an estimated savings of more than $2.5 million in incarceration costs annually (Culhane, Metraux, and Hadley 2002). Granted, these findings do not directly test the proposition that supportive housing for returning prisoners who are homeless, or are at risk of becoming homeless, could reduce rearrest rates, reduce the number of returns to prison, and save money. However, they do offer hope that a well-developed demonstration program could achieve positive results.

In summary, when developing policies to reduce homelessness, we must come to terms with the substantial overlap between the homeless population and the population of former prisoners. President George W. Bush has recognized the importance of this connection in his administration's plan to end chronic homelessness within the next decade. The Bush administration has committed $35 million as an "inducement . . . to get prisons, hospitals and treatment centers to plan for long-term housing for inmates from the day they first enter their systems" (*New York Times* 2002a, A24). According to Philip Mangano, executive director of the Bush administration's Interagency Council on Homelessness, one of the Council's top priorities will be to ensure that people leaving these institutions and programs have somewhere to live other than the street (*New York Times* 2002a). This federal leadership is long overdue.

Criminal Justice Policies

When we examine homelessness from the criminal justice policy perspective, the available research evidence points to a conclusion with important implications for reentry management: many returning prisoners are soon homeless. In a groundbreaking study of the overlap between reentry and homelessness in New York, Metraux and Culhane (2004) found that, within a cohort of 48,424 persons released from New York State prisons to New York City in 1995–98, 11.4 percent entered a homeless shelter within two years of release. Similarly, a 1997 survey by the California Department of Corrections found that 10 percent of the state's parolees were homeless (California Department of Corrections 1997). Within the state, the rate of homelessness was significantly higher in major urban areas, such as San Francisco, San Diego, and Los Angeles, where as many as 30 to 50 percent of parolees were estimated to be homeless. In a three-state evaluation of the effectiveness of prison-based education programs, Steurer et al. (2001) found that approximately 15 percent of prisoners released in Maryland,

Minnesota, and Ohio were "released homeless," mostly in urban areas. A study in Massachusetts reported that nearly a quarter of all released prisoners were homeless at some point during their first year after release (Bradley et al. 2001). Finally, in its study entitled "The First Month Out," the Vera Institute of Justice found that 15 percent of the prisoners interviewed (13 of 88) said they expected to live in a shelter after they got out (Nelson et al. 1999).

These studies indicate, therefore, that 10 to 25 percent of released prisoners will be homeless within a year following their release. Available research does not, however, provide a response to the intriguing, and disturbing, possibility that imprisonment actually contributes to the size of the homeless population in America. One could hypothesize that imprisonment's disruption of housing arrangements, coupled with the legal and practical barriers that returning prisoners face in their search for housing, forces large numbers of former prisoners, who had been adequately housed prior to prison, into the ranks of those who wander the streets in urban America and live in our homeless shelters. We have seen similar results in other contexts. As we discussed in chapter 7, research has now demonstrated that time in prison is associated with a 10 to 30 percent reduction in earnings over the former prisoner's lifetime. Could it be that time in prison has the same effect on returning prisoners' housing status? No research on this question exists, but all the variables are present for an equation that produces greater homelessness—diminished social ties, significant legal barriers, and social stigma.

Although this hypothesis still needs to be tested, we do have another indication of the interactive effects of homelessness and incarceration. The Metraux and Culhane (2004) study found that 45.1 percent of returning prisoners who entered homeless shelters had been homeless before they were incarcerated. Moreover, of those who entered homeless shelters, 42 percent returned to prison within two years. This research has identified a subpopulation that experiences two revolving doors—one that leads in and out of prison, and one that leads in and out of homeless shelters.

Housing and Reentry Management

We could imagine a criminal justice system that pays no attention to the housing needs of released prisoners. In this world, ex-prisoners would have to fend for themselves, navigating the tricky waters of family support, the private real estate market, public housing, and homeless shelters. For decades, however, our nation's criminal justice system *has* made some efforts to connect prisoners to housing. In addition, housing providers in local communities have made some efforts to include former prisoners in their programs. On closer examination, however, these efforts seem highly inadequate to the task at hand, particularly in light of the large numbers of prisoners returning home each year.

The American criminal justice system attempts to address returning prisoners' housing needs in a number of ways. The dominant strategy is to require parolees to live at approved addresses as a condition of their release. In the classic model of indeterminate sentencing, a prisoner applying for parole release lists the address where he plans to reside. A community-based parole officer then verifies that address and submits a report back to the parole board considering the application. For reasons discussed in chapter 3, however, only one-quarter of the more than 630,000 prisoners now released each year are released by parole boards, so this mechanism for ensuring a residence after release is not used in three-quarters of all cases (Harrison and Karberg 2004). Yet most community supervision agencies still require that a parolee reside at an approved address. In a 1988 survey of parole conditions in 51 jurisdictions, Rhine et al. (1991) found that almost all of them (46) required the parolee to maintain a verifiable address and notify the parole officer of any change in residence. Almost as many (42) stipulated that the parolee must permit the parole officer to visit him or her at home, or elsewhere, whenever a visit was deemed appropriate. This strategy reflects the common-sense notion that having a residence improves a parolee's chances of successful reintegration. However, it also reflects a very middle-class notion of residential stability, a notion quite at odds with the transient lifestyle of many former prisoners.

The criminal justice system also has other ways to improve the chances that a returning prisoner will have a place to live. Corrections agencies sometimes provide housing in the community as a buffer between prison life and life in the free world. Typically called "halfway houses," these facilities offer prisoners who are near the end of their sentences a structured and regulated environment as they adjust to life in the community. During the residency period, prisoners are allowed to work, visit with family members, and engage in a limited range of activities, but they must return to the halfway house each night, observing a tight curfew. Failure to follow house rules can result in return to prison or rearrest for absconding.

This strategy would appear to be a reasonable way to facilitate a successful reentry from prison. The notion of a transition period between prison and community life seems quite logical. From a housing perspective, time spent in a halfway house allows the returning prisoner to resolve any family issues that might hinder a return to the family residence. It also enables the returning prisoner to search for an apartment, a boarding house, or a friend's house, so that the transition from prison to a residence is smooth. Halfway houses have been shown effective at reducing recidivism. An evaluation of the Ohio halfway house program found that prisoners released through halfway houses committed fewer and less severe offenses during the year following their release than prisoners released directly into the community (Seiter 1975). However, despite their effectiveness, halfway houses face stiff community opposition. According to a public opinion poll, 77 percent of Americans approve of the concept of halfway houses, but 50 percent do not want one in their neighborhood, and only 22 percent thought their neighbors would approve the location of a halfway house in their community (Abadinsky 1997). The NIMBY ("not in my backyard") syndrome, which undermines public support for the transitional and supportive housing important to a wide variety of needy groups, is particularly effective at blocking the siting of facilities designed to assist prisoners in their transition back home.

In part because of public opposition, very few correctional systems use halfway houses as a substantial part of the reentry process. According to a survey conducted by the Criminal Justice Institute, there were 564 halfway houses in America in 2001.[23] Only 25 states, the District of Columbia, and the federal government used these halfway houses (also called "adult correctional community centers"), which serviced just 22,832 prisoners.[24] Of that total, the Federal Bureau of Prisons housed by far the largest number of prisoners, 7,688, in halfway houses (Camp and Camp 2002). The remaining 15,144 prisoners came from 25 state prison systems (and the District of Columbia). The remaining 25 state systems did not use halfway houses at all. Thus, although halfway houses are inherently logical, have proven successful in reducing crime rates, and help returning prisoners connect with needed support systems, they now play a very limited role in facilitating the transition from prison.

Looking Forward

Housing is a fundamental need among all returning prisoners. In most cases, prisoners return to live with family and friends. In a fraction of cases, between 10 and 25 percent, the returning prisoner fails to find stable housing and ends up in the nation's homeless shelters or on the street for a period of time. In our review of the intersection between prisoner reentry and housing policy, we identified three distinct policy challenges that warrant attention. First, can we reduce the high level of homelessness within the ranks of former prisoners? Second, can we smooth the rough edges of current policies that exclude former prisoners, and sometimes their families, from public housing? Third, can we reduce the anxiety that returning prisoners, their families, and their communities experience as a result of the reentry process? This concluding section examines each of these policy challenges.

Reducing Homelessness among Former Prisoners

In 2001, the Council of State Governments created the national Reentry Policy Council, which brought together researchers, legislators, community leaders, crime victims, law enforcement officials, and service providers to develop principles that policymakers should consider when tackling issues relating to prisoner reentry. In its final report, the Council articulated a principle that equates to a simple, yet powerful, mandate: no prisoner should be released homeless (Council of State Governments 2005). An ambitious goal, certainly, but how should this goal be met?

We can take our first clue from former prisoners themselves. Researchers at Community Resources for Justice in Massachusetts interviewed prisoners caught in the revolving doors of homeless shelters and prison. The prisoners were asked what strategy would have helped them most to secure housing when they were released from prison last time. The top choice of 69 percent was a prison counselor who could help them understand and exercise their housing options (Bradley et al. 2001). This is an important finding: More than money for rent or a deposit (60 percent) or free transportation (51 percent), these prisoners wanted someone to be their guide to the housing world. Unfortunately, corrections departments do not typically assign staff to help prisoners secure housing after release. Perhaps, consistent with the Reentry Policy Council's aspiration, these agencies could embrace the goal that no prisoner be released homeless.

To see how this new approach might work, we look more closely at Project Greenlight, a demonstration project of the Vera Institute of Justice designed to assist prisoners in their transition back home. Over a six-month period between September 2002 and March 2003, Project

Greenlight worked with 225 men who were close to release from prison. Of these, about a quarter (66) requested assistance in finding housing. Fifteen of them found housing with friends or relatives during the Greenlight program, leaving a hard-core group of 51 who had no housing awaiting them. The project embraced the challenge of finding housing for all of them. A specially trained community coordinator interviewed the prisoners, creating profiles of their criminal history, job skills, family ties, and experiences with substance abuse. The coordinator then determined whether the prisoners would be able to adapt to group home requirements. Could they abide by a curfew? Could they contribute to the household maintenance? Did they have special health needs? Simultaneously, the coordinator connected and built relationships with the network of group homes and transitional facilities in New York City. As time came for each inmate to be released from prison, the coordinator tried to make a match between the prisoner and the housing facility. The project was quite successful at finding homes for these men; 32 of the 51 men (63 percent) moved from a prison setting to a transitional housing facility. As for the rest, most declined the offer of assistance, preferring to search for housing on their own (Rodriguez and Brown 2003).

The Greenlight experience teaches several important lessons that should inform efforts to ensure that "no prisoner is released homeless." First, we must ask prisoners about their housing plans, verify the plans that look promising, and work hard with those prisoners who have none. Second, the system needs a boundary-spanning advocate like the community coordinator in Greenlight. The process of locating housing begins in prison, but requires intimate knowledge of available housing in the community. Third, we must pay attention to the special needs of special populations. A prisoner with HIV/AIDS, a long history of drug addiction, or mental illness requires a different housing plan.

Of critical importance in the Greenlight success story is the network of community-based housing facilities. These were not criminal justice facilities, but mostly group homes located in residential areas and operated by private housing organizations. Greenlight spent no new money to fund beds for the Greenlight participants, but worked with the housing managers and prospective tenants to build a package of benefits, income, and community service that would cover the monthly rent. The key lesson here is that these community resources were made available to returning prisoners at the time of greatest need, the moment of release. Because Greenlight was able to redirect these resources to meet the unique risks of returning prisoners, many more of them had a satisfactory answer to the question, "Where will I sleep tonight?"

Few communities have enough affordable and adequate housing to meet this need, however. Even Greenlight had participants turned away because of waiting lists. Therefore, a parallel task to creating a community coordinator function following the Greenlight model is to build this kind of housing capacity. In 2003, Rep. Danny Davis (D-IL) introduced a bill that would stimulate the development of temporary low-income housing and supportive services for ex-offenders through tax credits.[25] This bill, still before the House Ways and Means Committee at press time, represents a creative effort to encourage housing developers to meet this critical social need.

So, in looking forward, our first goal is to ensure that no one is released from prison homeless. This will require careful assessments of all returning prisoners' housing plans, in-depth work with those who have no housing arrangements, and the creation of a network of community-based residential facilities offering transitional or supportive housing for this population.

Reconsidering Returning Prisoners' Access to Public Housing

According to one estimate (Steurer et al. 2001), up to a quarter of America's prisoners lived in public or Section 8 housing prior to their incarceration. We do not know how many wish to return to public housing, nor how many actually do return. However, as this chapter has documented, the laws and regulations governing public housing have made it much more difficult for prisoners to return, and have also placed prisoners' families at risk of eviction. Significant modifications to these laws, therefore, seem appropriate. Strong arguments can be made that the core principle should be retained—that PHAs should be able to evict leaseholders engaged in criminal activity—while dispensing with the provisions that create unjust results, such as allowing evictions for the criminal behavior of guests or others off the premises. Perhaps Congress will enact legislation to allow for an "innocent tenant" defense, although the political reality is that these reforms are unlikely. In the meantime, our challenge is to create mechanisms allowing PHAs to use their discretion, evicting (or not admitting) those who pose a risk to the safety of the housing community while retaining (or admitting) those who do not.

To better understand the dynamics of this challenge, we turn again to La Bodega de la Familia, an award-winning program designed to assist families in supporting family members returning from prison (see also chapter 6). La Bodega de la Familia is located on New York's Lower East Side, a community dominated by several large public housing projects. Since 1996, La Bodega has offered a range of support services to participants, including family case management, referral and prevention services, and 24-hour crisis support for drug-related emergencies (Council of State Governments 2005). A critical dimension of the La Bodega intervention, one not originally envisioned, is helping families of returning prisoners deal with the rules of the PHA. The project's family case managers encourage public housing administrators to be flexible in applying the lease provisions so that drug offenders can live with their families as legally recognized tenants if families prefer it (Sullivan et al. 2002). This kind of family-focused advocacy can help secure housing and support that could make a difference in the reentry experience.

Working through the Conflicts of Reentry

As we have seen, most prisoners return home to their families. Yet we have also seen, particularly in the research by Venkatesh (2002), that many families are deeply ambivalent about the prospect of a son, daughter, mother, father, or other relative is returning home. Similarly, all prisoners return to a community, but many community members, particularly in the case of sex offenders, are ambivalent about this prospect. These conflicts have consequences as we consider the nexus between prisoner reentry and housing policy. Conflict within the family often means that the former prisoner is forced to live elsewhere. As a result of conflict within the community, ex-offenders are kept out of certain neighborhoods and concentrated in others.

Few communities currently have the capacity to address these issues, but some noteworthy innovations illustrate the potential. In the Baltimore Reentry Partnership program, the Community Conference Center (a member of the reentry coalition) facilitated meetings of family members with a formerly incarcerated relative to work out issues that had arisen during or that predated incarceration. New York City's Project Greenlight arranged for family meetings behind the prison walls to discuss potential problems and construct the new relationships that would exist after reentry. The Washington State program mentioned above, which helps communities work through difficult issues regarding sex offenders moving into their neighborhoods, is another example of efforts to resolve conflicts that ultimately relate directly to returning prisoners' housing prospects.

Meeting these three challenges—reducing homelessness in the reentry population, improving access to public housing, and mediating family and community conflicts—will require a combination of financial resources and organizational creativity. The financial resources required are not overwhelming. In many communities, the first step would be to redirect existing resources that pay for homeless shelters, drug treatment, HIV/AIDS, or mental health services into a network of independent group homes that can provide transitional and supportive housing. Nevertheless, additional resources will certainly be required. As the NY/NY demonstration project suggested, however, creating this network may result in reduced incarceration costs. The public housing initiative described here, modeled on the successful work of La Bodega de la Familia, requires modest additional investments, but more so requires housing managers to commit time and energy to working through these difficult cases. Finally, the mediation services provided in Baltimore also represent a new social investment, but this, too, is likely to produce savings in criminal justice and social service expenditures.

The most important new resource needed is a public commitment to helping returning prisoners secure housing and recognizing that housing is a key ingredient in successful reintegration. This commitment needs to start with the corrections departments—both prisons and parole agencies. They should first embrace the goal that no prisoner is released homeless. Once they attempt to meet this objective, they will find community resources they never knew existed. And once they advocate for decent and affordable housing as critical to the eventual reintegration of former prisoners, they will create alliances with a broader community of policy advocates, elected officials, and community leaders who share the ambitious goal of improving housing for all Americans.

NOTES

1. Personal observation at the "exit orientation" meeting of the Enterprise Foundation's Reentry Partnership program in Baltimore, Maryland, October 19, 2001.

2. Affordable housing is defined as housing in which the family pays less than 30 percent of its income for housing costs.

3. 24 CFR 960.204.

4. Some states have been more creative. In Louisiana, for example, the offender is required to place an ad in a local newspaper and mail the notification to neighbors and the superintendent of the school district in which he or she intends to reside. In Texas, judges can order the posting of signs on an ex-offender's home, warning neighbors that a sex offender resides within. California, Florida, New York, and Wisconsin maintain "800" or "900" telephone lines that the public may call to inquire whether individuals are registered sex offenders. In California, a CD-ROM containing a list of all registered sex offenders is available for public viewing at local law enforcement offices throughout the state (CSOM 2001).

5. Kim English, Director, Office of Research and Statistics, Colorado Department of Public Safety, personal communication with the author, June 19, 2003.

6. 24 CFR 960.202.

7. 24 CFR 960.203.

8. 24 CFR 960.203.

9. *U.S. Code* 42, sec. 11901(3).

10. *U.S. Code* 42, sec. 1437d (l)(6).

11. *U.S. Code* 42, sec. 1437d (l)(6).

12. *U.S. Code* 42, sec. 1437d (l)(6).

13. *Housing Opportunity Program Extension Act of 1996,* Public Law 104-120.

14. *U.S. Code* 42, sec. 1437d (l)(7).

15. 24 CFR 966.4 (l)(5)(iii).

16. *U.S. Code* 42, sec. 1437d (l)(6).

17. 24 CFR 966.203(b) and 966.4(l)(5)(vii).

18. 535 U.S. 125 (2002).

19. 535 U.S. 125 (2002).

20. Robert Taylor Homes are slated for demolition under HOPE VI.

21. *U.S. Code* 42, sec. 11302.

22. Sherry Goldstein, Executive Assistant to the Executive Director, The Fortune Society, personal communication with the author, March 29, 2004.

23. Private contractors operated the vast majority of these halfway houses. In fact, only 57 were operated by corrections agencies in 10 states (Camp and Camp 2002).

24. A total of 19,322 prisoners resided in privately contracted halfway houses, and 3,510 lived in agency-administered facilities (Camp and Camp 2002).

25. *Public Safety Ex-Offender Self-Sufficiency Act of 2003,* HR 2166, 108th Cong., 1st sess.

10
Civic Identity

Ned Rollo is a big, burly Texan with a criminal past. He has served time for manslaughter, narcotics possession, and two federal firearms violations. Having spent more than five years in federal and state prisons, he knows life behind bars firsthand. He also knows the realities of leaving prison. Rollo's reentry experience is described on the back cover of his book *99 Days and a Get Up: A Guide to Success Following Release for Inmates and Their Loved Ones:* "After release he ended up at a Chicago YMCA with nothing but a bad attitude, a 1946 Harley, and a drug habit. Not surprisingly, he put himself back behind bars a few years later as a 'habitual criminal.' "

During his second term of incarceration, Ned Rollo's father died. Rollo was allowed to attend the funeral, but in shackles. That day, Rollo decided to devote his life to helping prisoners make the transition to the free world and to challenging society's assumptions about the ex-felons who live among us. So in 1979, he founded an organization called OPEN, INC. (Offender Preparation and Education Network, Inc.), a nonprofit agency in Dallas, Texas, that has published dozens of books, pamphlets, and training materials offering concrete advice to returning prisoners. His books have been distributed in dozens of prisons across the country. The strength of Rollo's work rests in its no-nonsense directness and its ability to translate the experiences and accumulated wisdom of hundreds of returning prisoners into self-help guidebooks for others who are making a similar journey.

249

For returning prisoners and their families, Ned Rollo (2002, 5) offers these words of advice:

> Too often inmates and their loved ones buy into the false idea that only one problem stands between them and happiness—attaining release. But this isn't true: release is only the midpoint of a much larger experience that begins the day the gavel falls and follows you to the grave!

Earlier chapters have explored some of the obvious challenges prisoners face when they return home: where to live, how to find a job, and how to secure health care when the prison gates have closed. But these are only a part of the larger struggle former prisoners face as they try to find their place in a free society. This struggle has external and internal dimensions. From an external perspective, mainstream society does not welcome prisoners home; society does not readily set a place at the communal table for those who have violated the law. We deny ex-felons access to jobs, housing, health care, welfare benefits, voting rights, and other privileges and rights of citizenship through a vast network of invisible punishments. On a more fundamental level, we create a symbolic distance between mainstream society and ex-felons by attaching a powerful, seemingly indelible stigma to those who have violated society's laws. Society shuns ex-felons, while simultaneously expecting them to work, support their children, respect the law, and observe their release conditions.

At the same time, returning prisoners face the internal challenge of reestablishing their identity in an unwelcoming society. Many former prisoners have lived their lives with deeply embedded patterns of antisocial behavior. Their identity as criminals may have been solidified during their imprisonment. While behind bars, they may have strengthened their attachments to gangs, hardened their resistance to authority, or developed new criminal networks that are ready for activation once they return home. Upon release, they must make decisions about which identity they will embrace—that of a criminal, or that of a former prisoner who is determined to make it in the "straight" world.

This chapter will explore the "civic identity" of formerly incarcerated individuals. There are, of course, numerous dimensions to this identity; as with most people, the identities of returning prisoners incorporate their distinct qualities as employees, as parents, and as members of the community (Uggen, Manza, and Behrens 2004). By using the phrase "civic identity," this chapter focuses on dimensions that are shaped by the interaction of external and internal forces: the societal pressures to maintain a distance between "us" and "them," and the individual struggle to decide between continuing to identify as an outlaw or identifying as a reformed felon.

We begin by examining the historical antecedents to this interaction, realizing that the instinct to create distance between criminals and the mainstream is deeply rooted in our society. We then take a closer look at two specific issues pertinent to former felons' reintegration, namely their right to vote (a primary mechanism of citizenship), and their legal ability to put their criminal history behind them. The chapter then shifts to the individual dimension of the identity challenge, exploring desistance, or the critical process by which a former criminal decides to "make good" (Maruna 2001). In this context, we discuss Maruna's theories about the role of "self-narratives" in creating mechanisms for ex-offenders to establish new, prosocial civic identities. Finally, in looking forward to ways by which these reintegration challenges can be met, we will discuss new strategies for overcoming the distance between "us" and "them."

The Tradition of Social Exclusion

Treating convicted offenders as lesser members of society is nothing new. In early Roman history and among some Germanic tribes, offenders were subject to the penalty of "outlawry." The outlaw's wife was deemed a widow, his children considered orphans. He lost his possessions and was deprived of all his rights. In ancient Athens, the penalty of "infamy" was imposed, which means the offender was denied the right to attend public assemblies, hold office, make speeches, and serve in the army. Later in the Roman Empire, offenders were barred from certain trades. In the medieval era, life imprisonment resulted in "civil death"; the prisoner essentially lost the right to inherit or bequeath property, enter into contracts, and vote (Marshall 1964).

Enlightenment philosophers saw little room in the social contract for those who had violated the laws that bind society together. Writing in 1762, Jean-Jacques Rousseau argued that criminals should be separated from their fellow citizens, both metaphysically and physically:

> Every malefactor, by attacking the social right, becomes by his crimes a rebel and a traitor to his country; by violating its laws, he ceases to be a member of it and, in fact, makes war upon it. The existence of the State then becomes incompatible with him; one of the two must therefore perish; and when the criminal is executed, he suffers less as a citizen than as an enemy. The proceedings and the judgment pronounced in consequence, are the proofs and the declaration that he has broken

the social treaty, and, consequently, that he is no longer a member of the State. But as he is still considered as such at least while he sojourns there, he must be either removed by exile, as a violator of the pact, or by death, as a public enemy. (32–33)

When Rousseau wrote these words, exiling criminals was in fact a common practice. England had enacted the Vagrancy Act long before (1597), a law that authorized the deportation of convicts overseas to British colonies facing severe labor shortages. Felons were sent to work on plantations or at sea as galley slaves. As the colonies developed and African slave importation increased, transportation of convicts to America waned, finally ending when the last convict ship, the *Swift,* arrived in Maryland in 1783. After that, the newly formed United States of America refused to accept convict ships, which were then rerouted to Central and South America and Australia. England continued the practice of criminal exile for another century; in fact, between 1787 and 1875, more than 135,000 prisoners were transported from England to Australia (Bateson 1974).

The American colonies, and later the United States, followed in the European practice of excluding "malefactors" from many rights and privileges of citizenship. Legislatures of the American colonies passed laws denying convicted offenders the right to enter into contracts, automatically dissolving their marriages, and barring them from a wide variety of jobs and benefits (Olivares, Burton, and Cullen 1996). Following the Civil War, the nation ratified the Fourteenth Amendment to the U.S. Constitution, which explicitly recognizes states' power to deny voting rights to individuals guilty of "participation in rebellion or other crimes." In the latter years of the 20th century, the network of statutes that deprived American citizens of rights and privileges following a felony conviction was significantly extended (see chapter 4). States extended the reach of "invisible punishments" by declaring more jobs off limits to ex-felons, requiring criminal registration of sex offenders, and generally diminishing the opportunities available to those who violate the law. Congress also got into the act. As part of the reform to the welfare system, the federal government disqualified large numbers of former felons from critical elements of the social safety net, such as public assistance, food stamps, and public housing. In these laws, the age-old practice of declaring the "civil death" of society's felons found modern expression. In reviewing this history, we discern a social impulse with formidable staying power.

In today's discourse on crime, which is dominated by conservative voices, we can detect modern variants of Rousseau's dictum that society must cast out those who have "attack[ed] the social right." We hear criminal offenders referred to as sociopaths, social misfits, incorrigibles, career criminals, and super-predators (Maruna 2001). John Irwin (1985), an ex-felon who is a professor emeritus of sociology at San Francisco State University, calls this widespread public attitude the "myth of the bogey-man"—the belief that there exists a population of inherently bad people who are immutably different from the rest of society. So, before promoting the inclusion of former criminals in our society, we must first recognize the existence, throughout the history of Western civilization, of a profoundly deep, culturally embedded impulse to demonize those who have violated the law. Efforts to curb this impulse face an uphill battle.

Two Legal Perspectives on the Diminished Status of Ex-felons

Reformers seeking to promote ex-felons' full participation in society have challenged the tradition of diminished status for these individuals in two particular policy domains. Case studies for each domain carry lessons that should inform modern reform efforts. The first case study examines the effect of laws that deny ex-felons the right to vote and describes recent efforts to restore the franchise to these individuals. In today's era of widespread criminal convictions, the political impact of these laws is significant. The cautionary lesson here is that those who would lose power if ex-felons voted would likely resist any systematic campaign to restore their right to vote. In other words, the American tradition of social exclusion has significant political consequences. The second case study recounts efforts to create legal vehicles for restoring the rights lost at the time of a felony conviction. These reform efforts have also met stiff resistance; the deeper lesson from this narrative is that creating a new civic identity is not a simple legal process. Legislative reforms must confront a deep philosophical problem—does the adoption of a new identity require that the old identity be discarded? The chapter's concluding section examines this issue at the individual level, exploring the process by which people with a criminal past construct new identities.

Citizenship, Ex-felons, and the Right to Vote

THE EVOLUTION OF DISENFRANCHISEMENT

In his classic work on citizenship and social class, T. H. Marshall (1950, 28) offered this definition of citizenship: "A status bestowed on those who are full members of a community. All who possess the status are equal with respect to the rights and duties to which the status is endowed." By this definition, former offenders are not "full members" of our society. Their separate status is clearly defined by laws denying them the right to vote, the right to hold elective office, and the right to serve on juries. In short, former offenders are excluded from some of the basic activities of our democracy. Moreover, these laws have been legitimized on a number of grounds. The principal justification is that the felon has breached the social contract.[1] Judge Friendly summarized the rationale in *Green v. Board of Elections:* "A man who breaks the laws he has authorized his agent to make for his own governance could fairly have been thought to have abandoned the right to participate in further administering the compact."[2]

The right to vote has been called fundamental to a democracy, for this is the dimension of citizenship that "makes all other political rights significant" (Piven and Cloward 2000). Over the centuries of America's experiment with democracy, this fundamental right has been extended to previously excluded groups—those without property, former slaves, women, and young adults between 18 and 21 years of age. During the civil rights movement, a national campaign successfully knocked down barriers to the right to vote, including the poll tax, literacy tests, grandfather clauses, and other restrictions that had effectively kept African Americans from fully participating in our democracy. Today, however, one group of citizens is still explicitly and systematically excluded from participation in our democracy—those with felony convictions.

Interestingly, unlike other restrictions that have been abandoned over our nation's history, the practice of excluding felons from the voting booth is not rooted in our early history as a nation (Keyssar 2000). In 1800, in fact, no state in the Union prohibited felons from voting. Yet by 1860, about 80 percent of the states had passed laws restricting felons from exercising the franchise. Once established, this prohibition remained remarkably durable. Despite the franchise expansion to former slaves, women, and young adults, ex-felons were not extended the right to vote (Mauer 2002; Uggen and Manza 2002). On the contrary, as the nation's criminal justice policies became more punitive in the 1980s, the laws disqualifying ex-felons from voting became even more extensive (Harrison 1999). It is only in recent years that the states have rolled back some of their most egregious voting bans (Kalogeras 2003).

Voter eligibility is principally governed by state law, and state laws on this matter vary enormously, ranging from highly permissive to highly restrictive (see table 10.1). Two states—Vermont and Maine—allow

Table 10.1. *Felon Disenfranchisement Laws in the 50 States and the District of Columbia, 2004*

State	Prison	Probation	Parole	Ex-felons All	Ex-felons Partial
Alabama	x	x	x	x	
Alaska	x	x	x		
Arizona	x	x	x		x
Arkansas	x	x	x		
California	x		x		
Colorado	x		x		
Connecticut	x		x		
Delaware	x	x	x		
District of Columbia	x				x
Florida	x	x	x	x	
Georgia	x	x	x		
Hawaii	x				
Idaho	x	x	x		
Illinois	x				
Indiana	x				
Iowa	x	x	x	x	
Kansas	x	x	x		
Kentucky	x	x	x	x	
Louisiana	x	x	x		
Maine					
Maryland	x	x	x		x
Massachusetts	x				
Michigan	x				
Minnesota	x	x	x		
Mississippi	x	x	x	x	
Missouri	x	x	x		
Montana	x				
Nebraska	x	x	x	x	
Nevada	x	x	x		x
New Hampshire	x				
New Jersey	x	x	x		
New Mexico	x	x	x		
New York	x		x		
North Carolina	x	x	x		
North Dakota	x				

(*continued*)

Table 10.1. *Continued*

State	Prison	Probation	Parole	Ex-felons	
				All	Partial
Ohio	x				
Oklahoma	x	x	x		
Oregon	x				
Pennsylvania	x				
Rhode Island	x	x	x		
South Carolina	x	x	x		
South Dakota	x				
Tennessee	x	x	x		x
Texas	x	x	x		
Utah	x				
Vermont					
Virginia	x	x	x	x	
Washington	x	x	x		x
West Virginia	x	x	x		
Wisconsin	x	x	x		
Wyoming	x	x	x		x
U.S. Total	49	31	35	7	7

Source: King and Mauer (2004).

Notes: X = felons or ex-felons banned from voting. States appearing in the "all" column do not provide an automatic process for ex-felons to restore their right to vote. Arizona denies the right to vote after a person has committed two felonies. Delaware denies the right to vote to ex-felons for five years. Maryland denies the right to vote to ex-felons for three years after conviction for two felonies. Nevada does not deny the right to vote to first-time nonviolent offenders. Tennessee disenfranchises ex-felons convicted before 1986, and Washington disenfranchises ex-felons convicted before 1984. Wisconsin denies the right to vote to ex-felons for five years.

prisoners to vote while incarcerated.[3] (Two other states, Utah and Massachusetts, had previously granted prisoners the right to vote but passed referenda in 1998 and 2000, respectively, eliminating that right.) Some states deny the vote to inmates, but do allow ex-felons to vote once they leave prison or are on probation or parole. Four states allow people on probation to vote, but deny the vote to those in prison or on parole. Thirty-one states disenfranchise prisoners, probationers, and parolees. And in 11 states, many ex-felons face a lifetime voting ban. In these states, the rule is, once a felon, never a voter.[4]

Consequences of Voting Bans

The consequences of these restrictions on full citizenship are profound. According to one estimate (Uggen and Manza 2002), more than 4 million Americans—one in 50 adults—are either currently or permanently prohibited from voting because of a felony conviction. Because African Americans and Hispanics are disproportionately represented in the population of convicted felons, the laws on felon disenfranchisement disproportionately affect African-American and Hispanic communities, thereby diluting their influence in American policy. Nationwide, 1.4 million African Americans are denied the right to vote, accounting for 13 percent of the adult black male population in America. There are as yet no national estimates of disenfranchisement of Hispanic ex-felons (Demeo and Ochoa 2003).[5] In states that impose lifetime voting bans on convicted felons, the aggregate consequences for African-American communities are far-reaching: in Alabama, Florida, Iowa, Mississippi, New Mexico, Virginia, and Wyoming, one in every four African-American men has lost the right to vote for life.[6] It is not surprising that the increase in felon disenfranchisement has naturally tracked the increase in rates of imprisonment and felony convictions generally in the United States. Uggen and Manza (2002, 782) estimate that the total disenfranchised population rose from slightly less than 1 percent of the electorate in 1976 to 2.3 percent in 2000.

Because the effects of the American experiment with mass incarceration are concentrated in a small number of urban communities, the affected neighborhoods also experience the highest rates of felon disenfranchisement. A recent study found that the mean disenfranchisement rate of Atlanta neighborhoods was 3.7 percent (King and Mauer 2004). Yet in the neighborhood with the highest level of disenfranchisement, 11.6 percent of the voting population could not vote. In this same neighborhood, more than a quarter (27.1 percent) of African-American men were ineligible to vote as a result of their felony convictions.

Not surprisingly, high disenfranchisement rates in such neighborhoods have likely restricted the residents' political voice. If it is true that politicians go where the votes are, then the political process is less responsive to the needs of residents in communities with high concentrations of disenfranchised former felons. This loss of political power is particularly acute in one area of public policy: political leaders who have enacted our nation's criminal justice policies are less accountable to those who are most affected by those policies.

Beyond the community-level impact is the issue of how restrictions on voting rights affect election outcomes. In other words, would different policies regarding voting rights for felons make a difference in any contested elections? Given that less than 3 percent of the electorate is barred from voting due to felony convictions, we might reasonably surmise that the effect of voting policies is minimal and have little impact on electoral outcomes. Furthermore, we might assume that voting turnout rates within this population are so low that these votes would make little difference. Indeed, one analyst stated that ex-felons' votes would be "electorally insignificant" (*Harvard Law Review* 1989, 1303).

Christopher Uggen and Jeff Manza (of the University of Minnesota and Northwestern University, respectively), however, have produced a substantial body of empirical evidence refuting these arguments. To estimate the impact of current voting bans, they extrapolated from the voting patterns of citizens whose demographic profile resembles that of the ex-felon population in every respect except for the felony conviction.[7] With these statistical models in hand, Uggen and Manza (2002) estimated that, if felons had the right to vote, their turnout rate would range from a low of 20.5 percent (for the 1974 congressional election) to a high of 39 percent (for the 1992 presidential election), with an average predicted turnout rate of 35 percent for presidential elections and 24 percent for Senate elections in nonpresidential years. These votes, had they been cast, would have overwhelmingly favored (about 7 out of 10) Democratic candidates, reflecting the historical alignment between poor and minority voters and the Democratic Party.

The obvious next question is whether these votes would have made a difference in any election outcomes. The results of the Uggen-Manza analysis are quite provocative. Uggen and Manza found that, in the more than 400 Senate elections that have been held since 1978, 7 would have resulted in different outcomes if the level of felon disenfranchisement had not increased. Even more startling is their conclusion that the Democrats might well have retained control of the Senate in the 1990s. Presidential elections would have been affected as well. John F. Kennedy won the presidency by the thin margin of 118,550 popular votes and won in the Electoral College by a vote of 303 to 219. If our present rate of disenfranchisement had existed in 1960, then Kennedy would have received approximately 225,000 fewer votes, making Nixon the victor in the popular vote, although Kennedy would have still prevailed in the Electoral College.[8] In 2000, Al Gore won the popular vote but lost the critical state of Florida by a few hundred votes, thereby losing to George W. Bush in the Electoral College. If disenfranchised felons in Florida had been allowed to vote, Gore would have prevailed and become the 43rd president of the United States. This analysis leads to a thought-provoking conclusion: the exclusion of ex-felons from the voting booth has had profound consequences for our country's political direction.

Exclusion from the voting booth also affects the ex-felons themselves. We might be inclined to think that, with all the other barriers and hurdles ex-felons face, the ban on voting might make little difference. While the research on this topic is scarce, the Urban Institute's *Returning Home* study in Illinois sheds some light on this topic. Of the 389 prisoners who responded to the survey, 58 percent reported voting at some point prior to incarceration, and 82 percent responded that they would vote after their release if they could.[9] Certainly amid the daily struggles to reconnect with family, get a job, find housing, adjust to supervision, and avoid antisocial behaviors, wondering about voting in some future election is probably low on a list of concerns. However, the results of 33 semi-structured interviews conducted by Uggen and Manza suggest that the loss of the right to vote, on top of other losses, may carry a uniquely symbolic importance to many ex-offenders. The words of Pamela, a female prisoner, convey the sting that comes from this particular "salt in the wound":

> I think that just getting back in the community and being a contributing member is difficult enough. . . . And saying, "Yeah, we don't value your vote either because you're a convicted felon from how many years back," okay? . . . But I, hopefully, have learned, have paid for that and would like to someday feel like a, quote, "normal citizen," a contributing member of society, and you know that's hard when every election you're constantly being reminded, "Oh yeah, that's right, I'm ashamed." . . . It's just like a little salt in the wound. . . . It's like, haven't I paid enough yet? . . . You can't really feel like a part of your government because they're still going like this, "Oh, you're bad. Remember what you did way back then? Nope, you can't vote." (Uggen and Manza 2004, 183)

NEW LEGISLATION AND PUBLIC OPINION

Recent years have witnessed a flurry of national and state activity to roll back some of the restrictions on voting rights for ex-felons. In August 2001, the National Commission on Federal Election Reform, a bipartisan group created in the wake of the 2000 presidential election controversies and cochaired by former presidents Carter and Ford, recommended that all states restore voting rights to citizens who have fully completed their criminal sentences. If this recommendation is followed, tens of thousands of citizens in the 14 states with lifetime voting bans for some ex-felons will once again have a meaningful role in the electoral process. In 2002, a consortium of foundations led by the JEHT Foundation launched the Right to Vote Campaign, whose stated mission it is to "remove barriers to voting faced by people with felony convictions." Using media, litigation, and research activities, this campaign has targeted Alabama, Florida, Maryland, New York, and Texas for its reform efforts. These reform efforts have shown modest results. According to an analysis conducted by Christopher Uggen and Jeff Manza (with Thompson and Wakefield) (2002),[10] changes in felon disenfranchisement legislation in five states (Connecticut, Delaware, Maryland, New Mexico, and Texas) between 1997 and 2003 resulted in voting rights restoration for 471,000 felons.

Contrary to the supposition that the general public supports felon disenfranchisement, these legislative reforms appear to reflect the current public mood. According to a July 2002 Harris Interactive poll, 80 percent of Americans believe that ex-felons who have completed their sentences should have the right to vote. More than 60 percent of those polled thought citizens on probation or parole should be allowed to vote (Manza, Brooks, and Uggen 2004). In 2003, the American Bar Association (ABA) added its voice to the debate. The ABA Standards on Collateral Sanctions and Discretionary Disqualification of Convicted Persons recommended that the voting ban on ex-felons be lifted, except for the ban on voting during incarceration. The movement to restore voting rights to ex-felons was given a strong boost from an important quarter when the *New York Times* (2002b) published an editorial arguing that "disenfranchising felons is an archaic practice, at odds with basic American values about both punishment and democracy."

In summary, we have created a large class of individuals, largely minority men, who have been cut off from the most basic form of democratic participation—the right to vote. This political marginalization of ex-felons has had significant political consequences. Had these policies not existed, the balance of power between Republican and Democratic parties may well have shifted after past elections. Al Gore would almost certainly have been sworn in as president in 2001, and the Republican Party would likely not have controlled the Senate during the 1990s. The strongest argument for restoring the vote to ex-felons, however, is not that these reforms would favor one party over another. Rather, it is that the voting ban exacerbates and perpetuates the isolation of those who have broken the law. These disfranchised citizens are concentrated in communities that are already politically alienated. Our laws banning ex-felons from voting have increased that alienation, widening the distance between "us" and "them." The "salt in the wound" is a gratuitous and sometimes lifetime reminder that even though one's sentence has been served, all is not forgiven.

Restoration of Rights

When does punishment end? Recall that according to Ned Rollo, leaving prison is "only the midpoint of a much larger experience that begins the day the gavel falls and follows you to the grave." Having explored the strength and durability of society's inclination to diminish the status of law violators and examined the history and effects of disenfranchisement, we will go on to trace reformers' efforts to create statutory mechanisms designed to restore the legal status of ex-felons. This examination will shed light on a larger question, namely whether the criminal justice system can play a role in restoring ex-offenders' lost status and, if so, on what terms and with what participation by the ex-offender.

THE RATIONALE

The basis for these legal reforms is simple: in order to facilitate the reintegration of former offenders, society should offer ways by which ex-offenders can remove the stigma of their diminished legal status, what Maruna (2001, 165) calls "permission to legally move on from the past." These restorative mechanisms are important for three reasons. First, society arguably benefits from a lower rate of recidivism because former offenders, freed of the burdens of legal stigma, are better able to find work, access needed social services, and generally engage in civic life. Second, the goal of justice is better served when all parties to the criminal proceedings—defendant, victim, and state—formally recognize that the debt has been paid. Finally, by allowing for the creation of a new civic identity, the criminal justice system can support the larger goal of successful reintegration for former offenders. In the words of Maruna (2001, 165), "Without this right, ex-offenders will always be ex-offenders, hence outsiders, or the Other."

These are laudable sentiments in theory, but difficult to accomplish in practice. The history of recent reform efforts aimed at creating legal mechanisms to facilitate the restoration of ex-offenders' rights illustrates both the conceptual dilemmas and political obstacles surrounding this reform agenda.[11] In 1956, the National Conference on Parole, sponsored by the U.S. Attorney General, the U.S. Board of Parole, and the National Council on Crime and Delinquency, recommended the repeal of laws depriving convicted persons of their civil and political rights. According to the conference report, these laws were "an archaic holdover from early times" (National Probation and Parole Association 1957, 136). In particular, the report recommended enactment of legislation authorizing sentencing judges to "expunge" criminal convictions. The consequence of an order of expungement would be far-reaching: "The individual shall be deemed not to have been convicted" of the crime (137–38).

The idea of expungement had first been developed in the juvenile justice system to allow youthful offenders to mature into adulthood without the stigma of a criminal conviction. The concept was enshrined in federal law under the Federal Youth Corrections Act of 1950. According to one judicial interpretation of the provision's purposes:

> [Congress intended that] rehabilitated youth offenders be spared the far more common and pervasive social stigma and loss of economic opportunity that in this society accompany the "ex-con" label. While the legislative history offers little guidance as to the reasoning behind the drafters' choice of terminology, it is crystal-clear in one respect; they intended to give youthful ex-offenders a fresh start, free from the stain of a criminal conviction, and an opportunity to clean their slates to afford them a second chance, in terms of both jobs and standing in the community.[12]

In 1962, almost a decade after the National Conference on Parole, the drafters of the Model Penal Code (MPC) followed suit, proposing model legislation allowing for the restoration of civil and political rights to convicted citizens of all ages. Under MPC Section 306.6, a sentencing court would be authorized to enter an order relieving "any disqualification or disability imposed by law because of the conviction" once the offender had completed his sentence. Furthermore, under a second provision, if the offender had exhibited a period of good behavior, the court could issue an order "vacating" the judgment of conviction.

The Model Penal Code approach was different from that proposed by the National Conference on Parole in key respects. In her review of the history of this reform movement, Margaret Love (2003), former pardon attorney for the Department of Justice and chair of the ABA Task Force on Collateral Sanctions, found the "distinguishing feature" of the Model

Penal Code framework to be its "candor": neither the restoration order nor the vacating order would allow the offender to deny that he had a criminal conviction. More important, she concludes:

> The MPC's two-tiered process was evidently intended to accomplish the maximum by way of legal and social restoration for rehabilitated ex-offenders. But it was specifically not intended to remove the conviction from the records, or indulge the fiction that the conviction had somehow never taken place. Unlike the [National Conference] proposal, the MPC did not propose to rewrite history, but rather to confront history squarely with evidence of change. (1712–13)

LEGISLATIVE PROPOSALS

These differences, however, were outweighed by the common purpose embraced by the reformers of their era. By the 1970s, most states had enacted legislation providing that an offender's rights would be automatically restored upon completion of his or her criminal sentence. In 1984, the year Love (2003, 1715) called the "high water mark of restoration reform efforts," the House Judiciary Committee introduced a bill that could have had far-reaching consequences. The purpose of the legislation was to "restore the convicted person to the same position as before the conviction."[13] The bill would have ensured that individuals with federal convictions were not unreasonably denied eligibility for federal benefits and federal and state employment. For first-time violators of federal law, courts could set aside the criminal conviction and restore the offender's rights. According to the report accompanying the bill, this provision would allow these offenders "the right to deny the conviction."

Congress, however, did not adopt the House bill, choosing instead to enact legislation developed in the Senate that embraced a totally different approach to rights restoration. Sponsored by Senators Edward Kennedy and Strom Thurmond, two legislators representing opposite ends of the political spectrum, the Senate version of the 1984 Sentencing Reform Act led to the creation of a federal sentencing commission whose guidelines embodied a strong presumption of imprisonment for most offenders. The national schism over punishment policy—the battle between the reform movement of the fifties, sixties, and seventies that favored liberal policies toward ex-offenders and the more recent retributive philosophy embraced by "tough on crime" conservatives—played out in the differences between House and Senate reform measures. And, this time, the conservatives prevailed. In the final version of the bill, Congress not only decided against extending the "set-aside" provisions of the Federal Youth Corrections Act to first-time federal offenders, but also repealed those provisions altogether and encouraged the states to do the same. This watershed event took the steam out of the reform movement. As Love (2003, 1716) concluded: "For the next two decades, the official government position would be that criminals were to be labeled and segregated for the protection of society, not reclaimed and forgiven."

Today, most states retain scattered statutory provisions for pardons, certificates of good conduct, or case-by-case expungement orders (Legal Action Center 2004). In New York, for example, a former prisoner may receive a Certificate of Good Conduct or a Certificate of Relief from Disabilities. If a person obtains one of these certificates, then he can no longer be "automatically" barred from being considered for a job or any type of professional license. Both certificates also restore the ex-felon's rights to serve on a jury and to vote. The Certificate of Relief from Disabilities covers any number of misdemeanors, but no more than one felony conviction. A Certificate of Good Conduct covers any number of misdemeanors and two or more felonies, but the individual must demonstrate a period of crime-free living over a certain waiting period. For example, a less serious class E felony would require a person to wait a minimum of three years; the most serious class A felony would require a waiting period of five years. This Certificate of Good Conduct is mandatory for individuals who wish to work as public servants, such as law enforcement officers or firefighters.

In recent years, a new generation of reformers have supported legislation authorizing the restoration of ex-offenders' rights. Joan Petersilia (2003), a prominent scholar of corrections policy, recommended that America follow the United Kingdom's lead; in 1974, that nation adopted the Rehabilitation of Offenders Act. Under this law, an offender is deemed "rehabilitated" and his convictions "spent" if he is not convicted of a new felony within three years of his first conviction. This act also allows ex-offenders covered by its provisions to say, if asked, that they have not been convicted of a crime and that they do not have a criminal record. In New York State, former mayor Ed Koch (New York City), civil rights activist Rev. Al Sharpton, and Harvard law professor Charles Ogletree, an unlikely coalition, have proposed "second-chance" legislation that allows an ex-offender's criminal record to be sealed after five years of good behavior. Their proposal requires the ex-offender to successfully complete drug and alcohol treatment, if applicable, and obtain a GED credential if no high school diploma was earned.[14]

These reform proposals face an uphill battle. They must confront the overwhelming political reality that legislation to restore ex-offenders' rights is unpopular. To mollify this opposition, these "second-chance" proposals are often so narrowly limited to small categories of offenders or so weighted down with new hurdles to eligibility that they will benefit very few people. The United Kingdom model has the advantage of being automatic—three years with no new felony conviction entitles the ex-offender to a restoration of his rights—but this concept is highly unlikely to find support in the current American political climate.

More important, these legal mechanisms, although meritorious in their own right, do not offer much hope for overcoming the distance between the artificial constructs of "us" and "them." Nor do these proposals strike the proper balance between forgiving and forgetting. Moreover, it seems doubtful that these tensions can be resolved satisfactorily in a sterile courtroom by invoking the dry words of a statute. That is not to say, however, that the criminal justice system cannot play a role in establishing new identities for former offenders. On the contrary, courts *can* provide a valuable public forum for the construction of new relationships between ex-offenders and the broader community. What we need now is a new concept of the courts' role, a concept we will explore at the end of the following section.

The Internal Process of Developing a New Identity

These legal reform strategies are fundamentally limited because they do not build upon the natural processes of desistance, the way that some ex-offenders are able to reshape their identities. Granted, restoration of rights does carry heavy symbolic weight, but there is more to reclaiming a place in society. The desistance process requires that a person shed the identity of law violator and embrace an identity as a law-abiding member of society. Thus, having examined ex-offenders' civic identity from the perspective of laws that disqualify them from voting and laws that provide for the restoration of their rights, we step back now to explore the other side of the identity coin—the ex-offender's internal process of deciding to "go straight."

Desistance

To place this intensely personal decision in appropriate context, we should first note that most criminals ultimately "go straight." Crime is a youthful activity. In fact, the peak offending age for violent crimes is 18 years, and 16 years for property crimes (Farrington 1986; Hirschi and Gottfredson 1983). As criminals get older, however, their unlawful behavior drops off dramatically. They essentially "age out" of crime. This is not to say that there are no older criminals, just that most criminals give up the criminal life as they get older.

In the criminological literature, this process of "going straight" is called desistance. Researchers have been able to document a number of important life events that are associated with this process. For example, getting married, joining the military, and securing employment are all correlated with reductions in criminal behavior (Sampson and Laub 1993; Uggen 2000). But the deeper question, one not easily answered by empirical research, is how the individual who decides to "go straight" actually experiences the identity shift.

Shadd Maruna is a psychologist who has studied the desistance process. His groundbreaking book, *Making Good* (2001), reports the results from the Liverpool Desistance Study, which examined a sample of nonrandomly selected subjects categorized as either criminally active or actively "going straight." Using a methodology analyzing the content of his subjects' life stories, Maruna searched for clues that might explain the differences between those who "make good" and those who do not. Maruna acknowledges there are many paths to reform. Some offenders simply burn out. Others find God. Still others simply drift away from the criminal lifestyle. But according to Maruna (2001, 8), there is a "common psychosocial structure" underlying all of these different self-stories of reform.

The Transformation Process

According to Maruna's analysis of the Liverpool Desistance Study interviews, most criminals believe that, although they have committed crimes, they are not "real criminals." This analysis echoes Samenow's findings (1984, 60) almost 20 years earlier: "[Offenders] will acknowledge that, from society's point of view, they are criminals. But no one really regards himself that way. Every [offender] believes that he is basically a decent human being." Surveys of offenders have "generally confirmed this clinical observation, with only a small percentage of prison inmates identifying themselves primarily or even secondarily as 'criminal' " (Burnett 1992; Shover 1996).

So how do former offenders who do not view themselves as "criminals" see themselves as "decent human beings"? How do they accommodate the truth about their pasts as they move toward a new, law-abiding identity? According to Maruna (2001), the key to desistance is recognizing that past criminal behavior is not part of the "core self." The offender must consciously decide that his past behavior did not represent his true self and that the new self is "what was supposed to be all along" (Garfinkel 1956, 421). As Meisenhelder (1982, 140) wrote, "The plan to exit from crime is in large part founded on the sense of the self as noncriminal."

In his examination of the lives of criminals "gone straight," Maruna found they had employed a transformation process he calls a "redemption script." A redemption script is a narrative that explains the past, while creating an identity that will sustain the ex-offender in the future as he repositions his role in society. In these scripts, past criminal acts are often minimized, or responsibility for those acts is placed on the offender's circumstances. For example, an offender's crimes may be blamed on his drug use, the poverty of his upbringing, or a history of childhood neglect and abuse. Although this attitude may be at odds with the public's desire for criminals to accept full responsibility for their actions, Maruna argues that the creation of this new narrative is central to the desistance process. This process, also called "re-biography," is a way of reconceptualizing one's past in order to create a better future. When an ex-offender can come to terms with his past, albeit through the selective lens of a new narrative, he can better focus on the present and on the "real" person he is and wants to become. Desistance is only possible, according to Maruna (2001, 7), when ex-offenders "develop a coherent prosocial identity for themselves."

Maruna's work has its critics. Laub and Sampson (2003), for example, conducted life story interviews with men who had desisted from resistant patterns of serious criminal activity and did not find extensive use of Maruna's narrative style of identity creation. These researchers summarize their critique as follows: "There is no need to 'make good' if situations and structures engender a commitment to desist from crime. Indeed, for many of our men, their identity reflection changed not a whit, and, in fact, for many offenders the capacity for self-reflection was painfully absent" (229).

Recognition Ceremonies

We need not resolve this dispute over the transformation process in order to ask whether the criminal justice system could adopt a different posture toward the desistance process—looking not simply to reduce recidivism, but rather principally to bridge the gap between "us" and "them." In his research, Maruna focuses on an insight that could provide the basis for reform efforts designed to bridge the gap between "us" and "them." He observed a number of "redemption rituals" in the life stories of offenders who had "gone straight." Many of them were quite accidental. For example, in one case, a judge officially acknowledged offenders who had progressed along the path toward rehabilitation. Maruna (2001, 163) develops a provocative proposal to formalize these moments of recognition:

> Redemption rituals, especially those certified by the State, can provide a psychological turning point for ex-offenders. If police officers, judges, and wardens were to shake the hand of the desisting ex-offender, and say, 'Well done,' . . . the ex-offender would have to acknowledge some level of justice in the 'justice system.' This would take away a crucial neutralization and would pull ex-offenders more deeply into mainstream society.

Other criminologists have explored variations on this idea. Lofland (1969, 227) proposed an "elevation ceremony," a public and formal announcement to "tell and spread the fact of the actor's new kind of being." Likewise, Meisenhelder (1977) suggested that one of the keys to achieving a social identity as noncriminal is a formal or informal "certification process" declaring the offender as rehabilitated. An established member of the community "must publicly announce and certify that the offender has changed and that he is now to be considered essentially noncriminal." Meisenhelder proposed that testimony could be offered formally by the criminal justice system or informally by recognized members of the community. Similarly, Trice and Roman (1970, 539) envisioned a "delabeling process" whereby the stigma attached to criminal convictions is removed and subsequently replaced with a label that is acceptable by community standards. One way this could occur, they proposed, is for the agency that initially labeled the offender to hold a public ceremony proclaiming that the label no longer applies.[15] These would be "highly visible and explicit 'delabeling' or 'status-return' ceremonies which constitute legitimized public pronouncement that the offending deviance had ceased and the actor is eligible for reentry into the community."[16]

The proposition central to all these proposals—namely, that the attachment of the label "offender" leads to a change in status that should be reversed when the sentence has been served and the offending behavior has ceased—was stated succinctly by Kai Erikson (1962, 311):

> [The convicted offender] is ushered into the special position by a decisive and dramatic ceremony, yet is retired from it without hardly a word of public notice. As a result, the deviant often returns home with no proper license to resume a normal life in the community. From a ritual point of view, nothing has happened to cancel out the stigmas imposed upon him by earlier commitment ceremonies; the original verdict or diagnosis is still formally in effect.

The policy question, then, is whether the criminal justice system should create opportunities to recognize the ex-offender's return to full citizenship through public forums that commemorate a successful internal journey. Certainly there are numerous other opportunities presented for this commemoration, such as when a family welcomes back a loved one who has given up his involvement in criminal activity. And we are not suggesting that desistance can be recognized as occurring at a single point in time; on the contrary, desistance is properly understood as the result of a series of decisions. Rather, the question is whether it would be appropriate for the criminal justice system, having previously ratified the offender's diminished citizenship status, to later recognize a return to full citizenship.

The picture Maruna paints—where "police officers, judges, and wardens . . . shake the hand of the desisting ex-offenders, and say, 'Well done' "—would certainly inject an element of humanity into an impersonal justice system. Similarly, the criminal justice system could play a role in removing legal barriers that impede successful reintegration and officially declare the end of a period of criminal justice supervision. This step would be an improvement over the current situation where, in Erikson's words (1962, 311), the convicted offender is placed in a diminished status with a "decisive and dramatic ceremony, yet is retired from it without hardly a word of public notice." Designing this new role for the justice system would require rethinking the relationship between justice agencies and desistance processes. However, this more ambitious vision of the justice system is still too limited. The literature on desistance underscores the need for greater public involvement in the processes of redemption and "going straight." Ultimately, the creation of a new civic identity requires both a new narrative for ex-offenders and public acknowledgement of their new identities. While the justice system can provide limited opportunities for that recognition, much broader public acceptance is required.

Looking Forward

Throughout our history, Americans have expressed—by legislation, government policy, and public attitudes—a desire to separate criminal offenders from the rest of society. The prisons that now house nearly 1.4 million serious law violators are perhaps the most concrete embodiment of this drive to separate "us" from "them." Even after these offenders are released, the expanded reach of criminal supervision and the extensive network of invisible punishments continue to contribute to a diminished citizenship status for those who have violated society's laws. This chapter has explored three aspects surrounding the issue of ex-offenders' civic identity: the denial of voting rights, the most fundamental right of citizens in a democracy; the rise and fall of a reform movement intended to create avenues to restore ex-offenders' civil and political rights; and the ways that ex-offenders choose to "go straight" and embrace a new identity. From distinctly different perspectives, these three narratives have explored the same issue: How do we recognize the ex-offender's return to "citizenship," defined by Marshall (1950) as "a status bestowed on those who are full members of a community."

As we look forward, we face a challenge best articulated by Mark Moore, professor at the Kennedy School of Government: "How do we live with the ex-felons amongst us?" This challenge is certainly made more daunting by the expansive reach of criminal sanctions in America and the retributive posture evident in much of our criminal justice system. Yet, despite the sheer size of the ex-offender population and the countervailing pressures of exclusion over inclusion in mainstream society, we can be optimistic about creating new mechanisms to bridge the divide between "us" and "them." A number of reform initiatives are promising; the next step is to construct a more systematic and purposeful strategy allowing for the recognition of new civic identities.

Reform Options

On one level, we can easily restore ex-offenders to the status of full citizen simply by enacting changes in the law. As was discussed in chapter 4, the recommendations of the ABA Standards on Collateral Sanctions provide a straightforward roadmap for legislatures seeking to roll back the panoply of legal restrictions that have been enacted over the years. Congress could repeal the laws restricting access to welfare benefits, food stamps, public housing, education loans, and other federally funded programs. State legislatures could create mechanisms for expunging criminal records and certificates of relief from civil disabilities—ideas that captured reformers' imaginations 50 years ago. As advocated by a new generation of reformers, legislatures could also restore voting rights to ex-felons.[17] Indeed, in recent years, there has been some significant progress in this arena: According to estimates by Uggen and Manza (with Thompson and Wakefield, 2002) for The Sentencing Project, a criminal justice advocacy organization, recent legislative reforms have restored the right to vote to approximately 500,000 individuals with criminal records.

We must not be overly optimistic, however, about the potential for legislative reform. Enacting the ABA recommendations requires articulating a politically palatable rationale for reversing several decades' worth of legislative pronouncements about the eligibility of ex-offenders for certain benefits and privileges. Carrying out this agenda will take a rare combination of political courage and legislative acumen. Political obstacles of a more partisan variety also stand in the way of restoring voting rights to large numbers of ex-felons. As Uggen and Manza's research (2002) suggests, this single step could change the course of political history in our country, likely favoring Democratic candidates and deciding important electoral contests. For this reason alone, a call for electoral reform is likely to be vigorously opposed, despite its popular support in the electorate.

Similarly, proposals to enact legislation allowing for expungement of criminal records and certificates of relief stand little chance of passage and, if passed, little chance of widespread benefit. If the expungement statute creates the legal fiction that the offense "never occurred," broad political support is unlikely. Furthermore, given the widespread public availability of criminal records in the electronic age, granting ex-offenders the legal right to deny their criminal conviction seems like a cruel hoax. Yet, these proposals still contain the kernel of a powerful idea: the courts could serve as avenues for ex-offender reintegration. The ABA Standards on Collateral Sanctions, in fact, envision a role for the courts in determining if a particular collateral sanction applies to a particular defendant's individual circumstances. "Second-chance" legislation allows the courts to grant an ex-offender a certificate, lifting legal prohibitions connected with the original conviction. Under the Model Penal Code proposals, a court could go even further: following a period of good behavior, the original judgment could be vacated, thereby prohibiting the use of the conviction to disqualify the ex-offender from benefits or opportunities unless there were a nexus between the offense and the benefit (e.g., a pedophile could still be barred from obtaining a day care license).

The Reentry Court

If we put these pieces together, a new vision emerges for the judiciary's role in overseeing the reintegration process. This vision fits neatly with the concept of "reentry courts," an idea I first developed in 1999 (Travis 2000). Reentry courts have enormous potential for changing the way prisoners return to society and, of importance to this discussion, for altering the relationship between former prisoners and society. The basic idea is fairly straightforward, but it represents a marked departure from current practice. In a reentry court, a judge oversees the period of supervision following an offender's release from prison. The parole officer (or some other agency, perhaps a nonprofit justice intermediary, serving a similar function) serves as a case manager working for the court. When a prisoner is released, he or she is placed under court supervision. In some experimental reentry courts, the prisoner is actually released in the same courtroom where the original sentence was imposed. The former prisoner then makes regular appearances before the court, reporting on progress and setbacks on the road toward successful reentry. The idea of reentry courts borrows from lessons learned from drug courts; in these courts, a judge oversees an offender's participation in drug treatment, using both incentives and sanctions to promote desistance from drug use and, ultimately, recovery from addiction. A judge sitting in a reentry court would use a similar system of rewards and graduated sanctions to promote desistance from crime and, ultimately, successful reintegration into society.

Compared with the current system, reentry courts offer many advantages for managing prisoner reentry, advantages detailed elsewhere in this book. Perhaps their greatest contribution could be to facilitate the recognition of a new civic identity for ex-offenders and thereby reduce the distance between "us" and "them." Specifically, reentry courts could perform several critical new functions. First, they could address the issue of legal barriers to reintegration. For example, a judge presiding over a reentry court could be authorized to determine whether a returning prisoner should be barred from a particular category of employment, excluded from public housing, or suffer the termination of parental rights. Similarly, a reentry court judge could mark the end of a supervision period by granting the ex-offender a certificate of relief from disabilities and restoring his or her right to vote. Finally, the same judge could, after finding that an ex-offender had completed a period of crime-free living, grant an expungement order. In short, the legal avenues that promote restoration of civic identity could become routine proceedings in a reentry court that is charged with overseeing the process of prisoner reintegration.

Reentry courts could also play a vital role in healing the wounds caused by crime and incarceration. For example, a reentry court could oversee programs that mediate reconciliation between ex-offenders and their victims. This court could also assist families torn apart by imprisonment, create new relationships, and provide opportunities for returning prisoners to perform redemptive community service. Because reentry courts reflect a "strength-based" perspective on ex-offenders and recognize the assets they offer to their families and communities (Maruna and LeBel 2003), they could provide a needed counterweight to the forces that now stigmatize ex-offenders.

Reentry courts could also enhance the legitimacy of the criminal justice system in the eyes of the offender, the victim, and their support networks. Tyler's work (1988) on procedural justice shows that individuals have greater respect for the law and are more likely to obey the law in the future if the officers enforcing the law—in this case, a judge and, by extension, the parole officer—explain the reason for an enforcement action and offer opportunities for the subjects of the enforcement action to ask questions or provide reasons for their behavior. Research on drug courts has shown an increased respect for the justice system (Harrell, Cavanagh, and Roman 1999); reentry courts have the same potential.

Reentry courts' most important contribution would be to help our society meet the challenge of creating a civic identity for the ex-felons who live among us. Properly conceived, reentry courts could provide the "elevation ceremony" recognizing completion of the sentence. They could provide a forum for the narrative of redemption, the "re-biographing" that Maruna identified as the key ingredient in the desistance process. The literature on drug courts describes "graduation ceremonies" in which successful participants receive praise from the judge and public acknowledgment that they have completed a difficult and important journey on the road to addiction recovery. These ceremonies frequently involve family members, friends, and treatment counselors, as well as prosecutors, defense attorneys, and sometimes even arresting officers. Such events often culminate when the judge awards certificates recognizing this accomplishment. In many cases, participants thank the judge, relate the difficulties encountered during the program, and acknowledge that the drug court experience represented a singular positive interaction with the criminal justice system. Properly designed, reentry courts could offer similar opportunities for marking significant transitions and celebrating important accomplishments. Holding his certificate of graduation from the reentry court in Richland County, Ohio, a satisfied participant commented: "Yeah, I'm very proud of myself. It took three years to get here and seven months in prison. . . . [T]his is my first time in the reentry program. I'm very proud of myself, very proud. Because I see where I was and where I've come now. . . . So, yeah, this [is] gonna go on my wall."

The contours of a reform idea now come into focus, based on the importance of establishing a new legal status for the ex-offender, the power of judicial symbolism, and the centrality of the "redemption narrative" to the reintegration process. Granted, there are many obstacles facing this reform idea. Legislation would be required to create reentry courts. Funding would be necessary to support this new role for the judicial branch of government. The relationship between the reentry court and the case management functions of the parole or supervisory agency would need delineation. A key issue for careful consideration would be the relationship between the terms of supervision and the court's power to impose sanctions. (See chapter 3 for the argument that sanctions for violations of administrative conditions of supervision should be significantly restricted.) And a carefully controlled experiment could test whether a reentry court cuts recidivism rates, improves reintegration outcomes, and promotes stronger perceptions of the justice system's legitimacy. But the reentry court concept offers a unique opportunity to combine, in one institution, a legal mechanism that allows for the restoration of an ex-offender's status and a public forum that validates the redemption narrative.

An Ethos of Reintegration

If implemented systemwide and applied to all returning prisoners, these legal reforms would slowly start to change the attitudes of returning prisoners, their families, their victims, other members of their communities, and criminal justice practitioners. But, in reality, much more would be needed to lift the stigma facing returning prisoners and ex-offenders. The countervailing tradition of stigmatizing those who have violated the law is simply too strong to bend under the slight weight of reforms in the criminal justice system. To be most successful, these reforms should be implemented simultaneously with a broad-based movement to change public attitudes and to reduce the chasm between "us" and "them." We need to embrace an ethos of reintegration, recognizing that individuals who have broken the law, particularly those who have been in prison, *can* be productive members of society. We need to value their contributions, particularly the contributions of those who are likely to help others making a similar journey on the path to redemption. As President George W. Bush stated in his 2004 State of the Union address,

> In the past, we've worked together to bring mentors to children of prisoners, and provide treatment for the addicted, and help for the homeless. Tonight I ask you to consider another group of Americans in need of help. This year, some 600,000 inmates will be released from prison back into society. We know from long experience that if they can't find work, or a home, or help, they are much more likely to commit crime and return to prison. So tonight, I propose a four-year, $300 million prisoner reentry initiative to expand job training and placement services, to provide transitional housing, and to help newly released prisoners get mentoring, including from faith-based groups. America is the land of the second chance, and when the gates of the prison open, the path ahead should lead to a better life.

Coming from different life experiences, Ned Rollo and George W. Bush agree that the day the prison gates open is only a midpoint in a longer journey. Whether America becomes the land of the second chance depends on a public commitment and a legal framework to support and recognize the thousands of individual journeys of former prisoners and other ex-offenders searching for a better life.

NOTES

1. The ban on the right to vote for ex-felons is also justified as necessary to keep criminals from influencing the criminal law, to guard against election fraud, and to exclude individuals with poor moral character (*Harvard Law Review* 1989).

2. 380 F.2d 445 (2nd Cir. 1967), *cert. denied,* 389 U.S. 1048 (1968).

3. In this regard, Vermont and Maine follow the example of numerous countries, including Denmark, France, Israel, Japan, Kenya, Norway, Peru, Sweden, and Zimbabwe. In 2000, the Constitutional Court of South Africa found that a law barring prisoners from voting violated that country's constitution. (*Minister of Home Affairs v. National Institute for Crime Prevention and the Re-integration of Offenders (NICRO)* Case CCT 03/04).

4. Every state has its own process of restoring voting rights to ex-offenders. In most cases, these processes make it difficult for ex-offenders to take advantage of them. However, recently some states, including Alabama, Kentucky, and Virginia, have adopted legislation that streamlines the restoration process (King and Mauer 2004).

5. The report estimates Hispanic felony disenfranchisement rates for the 10 states participating in the Right to Vote Campaign. These estimates range from 2.58 to 36.74 percent of the population.

6. Most states have procedures for petitioning the government for reinstatement of voting rights, but these procedures can be complicated and in many cases require gubernatorial pardon (Rottman et al. 2000).

7. Uggen and Manza calculated the level of disenfranchisement by relying on the laws that were in place at the time of each election they examined.

8. In brief, the Uggen-Manza calculations proceed as follows: In 2000, there were 4.7 million potential voters disenfranchised due to felony convictions, or 2.28 percent of the voting age population. In 1960, 2.28 percent of the voting age population would be approximately 2.5 million voters. However, since the convicted felon population was lower in 1960, Uggen and Manza estimated about 1.4 million convicted felons were actually disenfranchised in 1960. So, if the disenfranchisement rate had been 2.28 percent and approximately 1 million additional people were not allowed to vote in 1960 (above and beyond the 1.4 million who already could not vote), what would have happened? Assuming 40 percent of the 1 million people that actually voted in 1960—counting 75 percent for Kennedy and 25 percent for Nixon—Kennedy would have lost 225,000 votes and Nixon would have won the popular vote by a 106,261 margin. However, the electoral votes would have still favored Kennedy.

9. Christy Visher, principal investigator, Illinois *Returning Home* study, personal communication with the author, December 7, 2004.

10. This report was published in 2002, but it examines legislation implemented through the end of 2003.

11. I am indebted to Margaret Love, whose research on this question provides the framework for this discussion.

12. *Doe v. Webster,* 606 F. 2d 1226, 1234–35 (D.C. 1979).

13. House Judiciary Committee, *Sentencing Revision Act of 1984,* 98th Cong., 2nd sess., 1984, H.R. Rep. 98-1017, 142.

14. The "second-chance" legislation also provides that the criminal record can be unsealed if the ex-offender commits a new crime or if the district attorney successfully appeals the record sealing. This law does not apply to violent offenders or sex offenders or to cases where the ex-offender applies for a job in law enforcement or applies for a gun permit.

15. Trice and Roman also envision two other "delabeling" mechanisms. First, organizations representing the "deviants" could work to change the norms of society so that

the offending behavior becomes acceptable. Second, a mutual aid organization, such as Alcoholics Anonymous, would reject the deviant behavior and promote the values of conventional society. Trice and Roman also recognize that some deviant behaviors are "too far removed from ordinary social experience for easy acceptance of the former deviant to occur," particularly in instances involving mental illness (1970, 545).

16. Membership in the "honor roll" would be granted to those who have succeeded in their work, participated constructively in their communities, succeeded in their education, or provided support to others in self-help groups. The idea advanced here is far less selective and would apply to all who had completed the terms of their sentence.

17. Litigation represents another avenue for restoring the right to vote. The most sweeping judicial decree granting prisoners the franchise was issued in October 2002 by the Supreme Court of Canada, which invalidated a law that deprived prisoners serving two or more years in a correctional institution the right to vote. The Canadian Charter of Rights guarantees the right to vote to all citizens. The same document also protects the right to equal treatment under the law. The justices felt that this law violated both of these rights. The Supreme Court of Canada's Chief Justice wrote, "*Charter* rights are not a matter of privilege or merit, but a function of membership in the Canadian polity that cannot lightly be cast aside." (*Suavé v. Canada* (Chief Electoral Officer) [2002] 3 S.C.R.) Lawsuits are now pending in Florida, New Jersey, and New York to restore voting rights to ex-felons. Because the U.S. Constitution, unlike the Canadian Charter of Rights, does not guarantee the right to vote, these lawsuits challenge felon disenfranchisement statutes on other grounds, usually as violating the equal protection clause or provisions of state constitutions.

11
Community

W e have frequently characterized the increased use of incarceration in America as a large-scale social experiment. This experiment finds its origins in the early 1970s when, through a mix of legislative enactments, shifts in criminal justice philosophy, and new priorities established by elected officials committed to getting "tough on crime," America's imprisonment rate began to increase steadily and inexorably. Over a 30-year period, the rate quadrupled. Now, a generation later, we are faced with the consequences of this profound shift in social policy.

The consequences of this social experiment are not distributed equally throughout the country, however. A small number of communities in America's urban centers have experienced most acutely the collateral damage associated with our war on crime. In these neighborhoods, our criminal justice policies have penetrated deeply into community life, rearranging the rhythms of family life and the pathways of individual development, and altering the networks and relationships that define a society.

This chapter explores the impact of the era of mass incarceration and reentry on community life. We begin by analyzing the "concentration" of reentering prisoners through documenting, in a few illustrative jurisdictions, the flow of prisoners returning to particular communities. We then explore the multiple consequences of concentrated incarceration and reentry on family life, political participation, economic viability, adolescent development, attitudes toward the criminal justice system, and community reputations. Next comes an assessment of how concentrations of incarceration and reentry affect community capacity—the community's ability to perform traditional social functions. We then explore the provocative hypothesis that our unprecedented incarceration rates have so damaged these neighborhoods that their ability to exercise the kinds of informal social control that prevent crime is diminished. The chapter next documents some communities' efforts to organize grassroots initiatives to reduce the harmful effects of incarceration, promote prisoner reintegration, and reverse the patterns of disinvestment that have drained human and financial resources from neighborhoods already struggling to overcome enormous social and economic disadvantages. The chapter ends with some thoughts on how to meet the challenge of overcoming a generation of collateral damage.

A note about language is in order first, however. The word "community" has many meanings. On one hand, "community" is often used to refer to a place, a geographic location with set boundaries that distinguish one neighborhood from adjacent neighborhoods. We will first refer to communities in this way—as places—so we can document incarceration's impact on specified neighborhoods with defined boundaries using geocoded data that facilitate a spatial analysis of the concentrations of arrest, removal, incarceration, and return cycles. When criminal justice agencies keep data on the residences of individuals arrested, prosecuted, and sentenced, this kind of analysis is possible. However, "community" has other meanings, too. Kasarda and Janowitz (1974, 329) defined "community" as a "complex system of friendship and kinship networks and formal and informal association ties rooted in family life and ongoing socialization processes." This broader definition of a community also contains some spatial elements—familial and social networks are indeed often rooted in certain locations—but the critical dimension is one of relationships. As we move beyond the discussion of the geographic concentrations of incarceration and reentry found in the next section, we will concentrate more on how our criminal justice policies influence the networks and associations that make up a community.

Communities of Concentrated Return

Uneven Distribution

Not surprisingly, the American prison population is not evenly distributed across the states. Some states have high rates of incarceration, some much lower. It follows, then, that the reentry population—the individuals released from prison each year—is also unevenly distributed across the country, with high concentrations in a small number of states. In 1998, for example, five states accounted for half of all releases, and 16 states accounted for 75 percent. California alone accounted for nearly a quarter (24 percent) of all prison releases (Lynch and Sabol 2001). Within the 50 states, however, returning prisoners are increasingly concentrated in "core counties," those counties that contain the central city of a metropolitan area. In 1984, as the prison-building boom was gathering steam, half of all returning state prisoners—about 110,000—came back to core counties. In 1996, by contrast, about two-thirds of the reentry population returned to these counties. Furthermore, over the intervening years, the size of the reentry cohort increased significantly from 220,000 to 500,000 prisoners. The net effect of the increased reentry concentration and the rising number of prison releases was profound: about 330,000 individuals left state prison in 1996 to return to America's core counties (Lynch and Sabol 2001). In a 12-year period, the number of prisoners returning to these counties had tripled.

Within these counties, a small number of communities bear the burden of reintegrating record numbers of returning prisoners. Research conducted by the Urban Institute in connection with the *Returning Home* project has documented this powerful fact in every city studied so far. Some examples will illustrate the phenomenon:

- In Illinois, one-half (51 percent) of prisoners released from the state's prisons in 2001 returned to Chicago. Of Chicago's 77 communities, 6 communities—Austin, Humboldt Park, North Lawndale, Englewood, West Englewood, and East Garfield Park—accounted for a third (34 percent) of the prisoners returning to the city. In other words, approximately 5,000 prisoners returned to these 6 communities in 2001 (La Vigne, Mamalian, et al. 2003).
- In Maryland, more than one-half (59 percent) of state prisoners released in 2001 returned to Baltimore City. Within Baltimore City, 30 percent of ex-prisoners returned to 6 of Baltimore City's 55 community areas—Southwest Baltimore, Greater Rosemont, Sandtown-Winchester/Harlem Park, Greenmount East, Clifton-Berea, and Southern Park Heights. Some of these communities received more than 200 released prisoners that year, more than the number that returned to some entire counties in Maryland (La Vigne, Kachnowski, et al. 2003).

- In Ohio, 18 percent of state prisoners released in 2001 returned to the city of Cleveland. Of Cleveland's 36 communities, 5 areas—Hough, Central, Glenville, Mount Pleasant, and Union-Miles—accounted for 28 percent of prisoners returning to that city (La Vigne and Thomson 2003).
- In Texas, approximately one in four prisoners released in 2001 returned to Houston. Within Houston, a quarter of all returning prisoners were concentrated in just 5 of the city's 185 ZIP Codes in the neighborhoods of Alief, East Houston, Third Ward and MacGregor, Kashmere Gardens, and East Little York/Homestead and Trinity/Houston Gardens (Watson et al. 2004).

Concentrated Disadvantage

These communities of concentrated return are typically also communities of concentrated disadvantage. The Urban Institute's research on prisoner reentry in Chicago illustrates this point. High rates of poverty, crime, and other measures of disadvantage characterize the six neighborhoods receiving a third of all prisoners returning to Chicago. For example, in the North Lawndale community, nearly 42 percent of all families live below the federal poverty level (FPL), a rate that is 140 percent greater than the city average. Female-headed households account for more than 46 percent of households in that community, compared with an average of just under 19 percent citywide. In Humbolt Park, 50 percent of residents are high school graduates, which is 30 percent below the city average. The unemployment rate is 13 percent in the West Englewood community, a rate 71 percent higher than the city rate. In the community of Englewood, the Part I crime rate is 142.1 per 1,000 residents, while the citywide rate is only 65.9 per 1,000 residents, a difference of over 115 percent. The population in all six communities is predominantly nonwhite, ranging from 95 percent to 99 percent of the total population, compared with a citywide nonwhite population of 68 percent (La Vigne, Mamalian, et al. 2003). In the Urban Institute's *Returning Home* study, these markers of disadvantage have been found in all communities of concentrated return.

Another way to depict the community-level concentrations of return is by using a map. The map of Brooklyn (figure 11.1) shows that former prisoners who are under parole supervision are concentrated in relatively few neighborhoods. Three percent of the block groups account

Figure 11.1. *Parolees per Block Group, Brooklyn, New York, 2000*

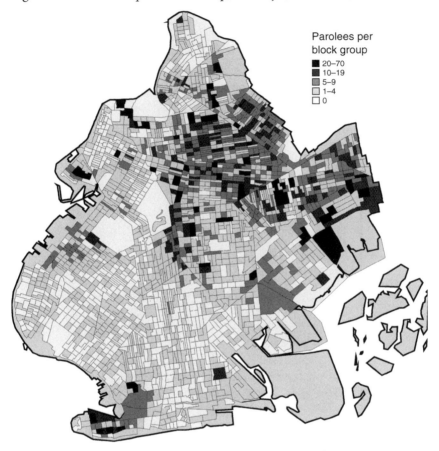

Source: New York State Division of Parole, Snapshot File, Nov. 30, 2000.
   Map produced by Charles Swartz and Eric Cadora. Community Justice Project, CASES.
Copyright © 2001 CASES.
   Printed here with permission from CASES.

for 9 percent of the population in Brooklyn, yet house 26 percent of the individuals on parole supervision. As we discussed in chapter 3, this spatial distribution of the parolee population raises important questions about the best way to organize criminal justice supervision functions. Interest in developing true neighborhood-based supervision reflects, in large part, the realities of high concentrations of incarceration and reentry in a small number of neighborhoods.

Comparative Reentry Burden

Still another analytical approach to understanding the impact of increased incarceration and return is to compare the reentry burden experienced by the communities of concentrated return against the reentry burden borne by other neighborhoods in the same city. For example, as mentioned above, the Urban Institute's examination of prisoner reentry in Texas found that most prisoners returned to Harris County, which includes Houston, and that within Houston, 25 percent of returning prisoners went back to five ZIP Codes. As shown in figure 11.2, the ratio of supervised returning prisoners to the population ranged from 6.6 to 24 prisoners for every 1,000 residents, or two to eight times the rate for the rest of the city (3.1 prisoners per 1,000 residents). In one of those ZIP Codes—77078, which includes large portions of the East Houston neighborhood—the reentry burden was eight times the citywide average.

Taxpayer Expense

A final analytical framework places the phenomenon of concentrated effects of prisoner reentry in stark fiscal terms. The Urban Institute team

Figure 11.2. *Rates of Supervised Releasees Returning to Texas, Harris County, Houston, and Houston's High-Return ZIP Codes, 2001*

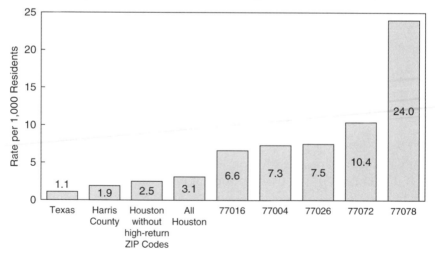

Source: Watson et al. (2004).

analyzed data from the six Chicago communities with the highest concentration of reentering prisoners to determine how long these men and women had been incarcerated, and for what crimes. The researchers then determined the total number of "inmate years" represented by the returning cohort, in other words, the total years served in prison by men and women returning to each neighborhood. Next, the team attached the cost-per-inmate-year as published by the Illinois Department of Correction, and arrived at an estimate of the costs to Illinois taxpayers of incarcerating the 2001 reentry cohort for each neighborhood (table 11.1). According to this analysis, the community-level incarceration costs for the prisoners who returned in 2001 ranged from a high of $45 million (Austin) to a low of $11 million (East Garfield Park). The analysis also shows a per capita expenditure for each resident of these neighborhoods. For example, for every resident of East Garfield Park, Illinois taxpayers spent $506 to incarcerate the residents of East Garfield Park who returned home from prison in 2001.

This fiscal analysis is another way of illustrating the reentry burden experienced by neighborhoods of concentrated return—lives of community members sent to prison are translated into incarceration costs and then recharacterized as per capita expenditures. Although not intended to replace a more sophisticated cost-benefit analysis of a state's incarceration policies, this framework certainly raises questions about possible alternative investment strategies for those public funds.

In their block-level analysis of Brooklyn, Cadora and Swartz (1999) looked at the cycle of arrest and incarceration through a slightly different lens. Rather than using a reentry cohort as a starting point, as the

Table 11.1. *Incarceration Costs for the 2001 Reentry Cohort, Six Communities in Chicago*

	Person-years in prison	Cost	Population	Cost per capita
Austin	1,961	$45 million	117,527	$380
Humboldt Park	934	$21 million	65,836	$323
North Lawndale	761	$17 million	41,768	$414
West Englewood	741	$17 million	45,282	$373
Englewood	598	$14 million	40,222	$338
East Garfield Park	464	$11 million	20,881	$506
City of Chicago	20,231	$460 million	2,949,913	$156

Source: Travis, Rossman, and Kane (2004).

Urban Institute did, these researchers used an admissions cohort. They found that on certain blocks in Brooklyn where incarceration levels were the highest, there was one admission to jail or prison for every eight men of parenting age (age 16 to 44) each year. In a subsequent study, Cadora, Swartz, and Gordon (2003) calculated the costs of detaining these men in prison and jail to arrive at a total per-block incarceration cost. In the high-incarceration blocks, they calculated that New York State taxpayers were paying up to $3 million a year per block to house the arrested men. When they combined all the blocks contained in one police precinct in this part of Brooklyn, they found that the taxpayers were spending more than $50 million a year in prison and jail costs to incarcerate the men from that precinct.

This neighborhood-level analysis of incarceration and reentry concentrations, when combined with projections of incarceration costs per neighborhood, raises an obvious public policy question: would there be better ways to spend $3 million to address the criminal behavior of the men who live on one block in Brooklyn? If the police, community groups, service providers, and faith institutions in the police precinct were given a significant portion of the annual $50 million expenditure of taxpayer funds, would they be more effective at reducing crime in that precinct and promoting the successful reintegration of ex-offenders?

We thus have a variety of perspectives on the phenomenon of concentrated return. From a national perspective, we see that most prisoners are incarcerated in, and therefore released in, a small number of states. Throughout the nation, the incidence of reentry is increasingly concentrated in "core counties," those jurisdictions with urban centers. Moreover, within those counties, the reentry phenomenon is highly concentrated in a small number of neighborhoods. Those neighborhoods bear a disproportionate reentry burden, meaning that they have to absorb large numbers of prisoners, mostly men, who have been incarcerated for more than two years, on average, and return to families, peer networks, and communities where they struggle to get back on their feet. Seen from a financial perspective, the nation's taxpayers are investing enormous sums of money to support this social experiment in mass incarceration; however, that money is not being spent on the neighborhoods where prisoners lived and to which they will return, but on the jails and prisons that house them far away from home.

Consequences of Concentration

Maps showing the concentration of incarcerated individuals and reentering prisoners at the block or community level are certainly provocative. They effectively upend traditional discussions of crime policy, and make a classic discourse on the deterrent effect of criminal law seem less relevant. On these blocks, incarceration is a frequent occurrence, so the stigma associated with a felony conviction is arguably less powerful. Knowing that taxpayers spend up to $3 million per year to house these men in prisons and jails, calculations of the costs and benefits of prison programs seem to explore a comparatively small financial territory. Our traditional frameworks for discussing sentencing policy seem inadequate to the task of understanding the new realities of mass incarceration.

Even measurable savings attributable to successful prison-based programs pale in comparison with the money spent to incarcerate community residents. We will discuss later the implications of this community perspective on incarceration's financial consequences for our nation's crime policy. Before turning to that topic, however, we should first consider the effects of high concentration on other aspects of community life. We will examine briefly the impact of mass incarceration and reentry on families and marriage, voting and political participation, economic viability, community stigma, and the legitimacy of the criminal justice system. These overviews, many of which draw upon discussions in preceding chapters, lead to a simple conclusion. In ways we are only now beginning to understand, the buildup of our prison population has significantly diminished the viability of communities burdened by high rates of incarceration and reentry.

Families and Marriage

In communities that experience high rates of imprisonment and reentry, the social experiment in mass incarceration touches most families. In their in-depth interviews of nearly 100 residents in two Tallahassee (Florida) communities, Rose, Clear, and Ryder (2002) found that nearly every one of them had experienced (or expected to experience) the return of a family member from prison. In his survey of families living in the Robert Taylor Homes in Chicago, Venkatesh (2002) found that 29 percent of residents currently had a relative in prison. Twelve percent expected a family member to return from prison within the next two years. In communities such as these, the actual prisons may be far away, but the realities of prison life are part of the family fabric.

As we discussed in chapter 6, the cycles of imprisonment and reentry have altered the patterns of relationships between young men and young women in these communities. Because about 90 percent of the individuals who go to prison and come back are men, the intersection between our criminal justice policies and the higher rate of offending among men is affecting the ratio between men and women in these high-concentration neighborhoods. In his study of shifting family patterns in Washington, D.C., Braman (2002) found that in the District's neighborhoods with the highest incarceration rates, there were only 62 men for every 100 women in the community, as compared with 94 men for every 100 women in neighborhoods characterized by low incarceration rates. This "gender imbalance" affects every aspect of male-female relationships in ways that undermine the stability of couples and families. As Braman explains (2002, 123), "Men and women in neighborhoods where incarceration rates are high described this as both encouraging men to enter into relationships with multiple women, and encouraging women to enter into relationships with men who are already attached."

The forced removal of large numbers of men from these neighborhoods, coupled with an increasing number of women, also has significant ripple effects for the children. Nationally, 2 percent of all minor children and 7 percent of all African-American children have a parent in state or federal prison (Mumola 2000). If we also include parents who are in jail or under community supervision, the rates increase significantly—to 10 percent (Travis, Cincotta, and Solomon 2003). These rates are certainly much higher in communities of concentrated return, although no researcher has yet documented the exact neighborhood rates. However, an estimate from the District of Columbia provides the rough contours of incarceration's effect on children. According to The Sentencing Project (1997), about half of all African-American men between the ages of 18 and 35 are under some form of correctional supervision in the District. Following national averages, we can project that 55 percent of these men are fathers (Mumola 2000). In the nation's capital, the criminal justice system touches the lives of a substantial share of the city's children.

From a community perspective, we know very little about the cumulative effects of the deep penetration of the criminal justice system on family life and human development. Nor do we have an empirical understanding of the impact of high incarceration and reentry rates on the social service networks, such as schools, foster care agencies, churches, mental health centers, and homeless shelters that struggle to support children and families. However, we can readily imagine that as America's incarceration rate has quadrupled over the past 25 years, the family institution and the community infrastructure of social service agencies have shouldered enormous new burdens, leaving them less capable of meeting the ordinary needs of community residents.

Voting and Political Participation

Another critical dimension of community life—the relationship between the community's citizens and their government—is clearly affected by the buildup in imprisonment rates over the past generation, although the contours of the altered relationship are still poorly understood. In communities where a high percentage of residents have felony convictions, the relationship between the government and the citizenry is fundamentally altered because ex-felons do not possess all the attributes of citizenship. Depending on state laws, ex-felons typically cannot serve on juries, often cannot hold public office, and, most important, are barred from voting, at least for some period of time.

Loss of voting rights is particularly problematic because it diminishes the political voice of high-incarceration communities on all issues of concern to that community. In those states that have enacted a lifetime voting ban for felons, the widespread diminution of citizenship among a large share of community residents, overwhelmingly men, results in particularly high levels of alienation from the political process. Furthermore, because felony convictions are found at higher levels in racial minority groups, the loss of political power is concentrated in those groups. For example, one in every four African-American men in Alabama, Florida, Iowa, Mississippi, New Mexico, Virginia, and Wyoming has permanently lost the right to vote (Fellner and Mauer 1998).

There is limited research calculating the exact level of disenfranchisement in communities experiencing high rates of felony convictions among residents. However, it is reasonable to assume that, in some communities, up to half of the men may not be eligible to vote, and those who are technically eligible after finishing their period of parole supervision may not know that their right to vote has been restored. Little research has been done to examine the effects of these policies on actual voting behavior at the local level, but clearly the communities in

America that are already most alienated from the political system have suffered, over the past generation, a steady diminution of their political power as more and more of their residents are convicted of felonies (Mauer 2002).

The political power of high-incarceration communities has been further weakened in another way over the past generation. In conducting the decennial enumeration required by the Constitution, the Census Bureau follows a policy of counting people in their place of "usual residence," which is defined as the place where a person lives and sleeps most of the time. Under this policy, state and federal prisoners are counted where they are incarcerated. Between the 1980 and 2000 census counts, the American prison population grew from 300,000 to 1.3 million, which means that 1 million people are now counted as "residents" in the counties where they are imprisoned (Lawrence and Travis 2004).

The political implications of this shift in the enumerated population are far reaching. First, because the apportionment of legislative districts is based on the census, communities that now house large numbers of prisoners gain political power. Second, because the federal government distributes over $14 billion in grant money to state and local governments using formulas based in part on census data, communities with large prison populations will receive increased funding. Ironically, such funding supports Medicaid, foster care, adoptions assistance, and social services' block grants, assistance for which prisoners generally are ineligible (GAO 2003). Third, many states also allocate funds for community services, road construction, public housing, and public libraries according to census data, which means that the communities from which prisoners are drawn are further disadvantaged in the competition for critical public resources. When added to the loss of voting power, the dilution of the "one person, one vote" principle of representative democracy and the loss of financial assistance resulting from Census Bureau policy further undermine the political standing of communities with high incarceration rates.

Economic Viability

We have little empirical understanding of how incarceration and reentry influence the economic viability of the communities under discussion in this chapter. Yet, we can develop some reasonable hypotheses of the possible damage. As we discussed in chapter 7, about half of all prisoners are working in a full-time job at the time of their arrest; another one-fifth are working part-time. As was mentioned earlier, the communities sending the highest share of men and women to prison have high rates of unemployment, so these data are hardly surprising. Yet the simple fact remains that incarceration severs the employment relationship for large numbers of individuals. From a labor market perspective, this means that the supply and demand for local labor is frequently disrupted, adding costs and inefficiencies to the local economy. On a more human level, this means that prisoners' families are not receiving their employment income, rents are not being paid, debt accumulates, and the financial resources of the extended family network are strained. The social service agencies that step in to provide foster care, unemployment checks, temporary housing, and mental health counseling are undoubtedly affected, albeit it to unknown degrees, by the substantial increase in incarceration and reentry in these neighborhoods. This competition for resources negatively affects the community's economic health.

When prisoners return to their home communities, their prospects for employment are bleak. Employers are less likely to hire them (Holzer, Raphael, and Stoll 2003), they are barred from certain jobs, and the simple step of looking for work is made more difficult by the demands of reintegration and criminal justice supervision. Furthermore, ex-felons find that more job categories have been placed off-limits (Rubenstein and Mukamal 2002) and more hurdles have been placed in their way to self-improvement. As discussed in chapter 4, welfare reform legislation enacted in 1996 stipulates that individuals with certain drug convictions are denied public assistance and food stamps, and may be ineligible for student loans. When these effects are concentrated, the dynamics of social support and employment opportunity are fundamentally altered. The combined result of these factors is that the lifetime earnings of former prisoners are significantly diminished—by 10 to 30 percent—due to their history of incarceration (Kling 2002; Western, Kling, and Weiman 2001). In communities of concentrated reentry, where a substantial portion of the residents have been incarcerated, these individual-level effects add up to a significant community-level impact. In essence, the gross domestic product of these high-concentration neighborhoods—their collective output of goods and services—has been diminished by our high rates of incarceration.

Financial assistance for ex-convicts and their families has also been reduced in recent years, largely as a result of the Personal Responsibility and Work Opportunity Reconciliation Act of 1996 (PRWORA) signed into law by President Clinton. This law led to the implementation of Temporary Assistance for Needy Families (TANF), ending individual entitlements to welfare and providing states with block grants. TANF imposes a five-year lifetime limit on benefits and requires welfare recipients to work in order to receive benefits. Although the TANF legislation affects mostly women, and returning prisoners are mostly men, the networks of familial and social support that are often critical in the reintegration process are now struggling with the new demands of welfare reform. One provision of the law requires that states permanently bar individuals with drug-related felony convictions from receiving federally funded public assistance, including food stamps, for life (Rubenstein and Mukamal 2002).[1] No one is excluded from the felony drug ban, including pregnant women, individuals in treatment or recovery, or people suffering from HIV/AIDS. The effects of the ban are particularly detrimental to individuals who cannot afford drug treatment and cannot find safe and sober housing once they have completed treatment, a dilemma that makes successful reentry even more difficult (Rubinstein and Mukamal 2002).

We have little understanding of the impact of high incarceration rates at the community level—most research focuses on individual-level effects. Nevertheless, the decrease in former prisoners' lifetime earnings, the disruption of work experiences, and the reduction in federal benefits would certainly result in a substantial cumulative effect. Determining whether the negative economic effects—and human costs—are outweighed by any economic benefits stemming from increased levels of incarceration (and resulting crime reduction) would require an extremely different calculation. However, the larger point remains: to assess the costs and benefits of our experiment in the expanded use of incarceration, we must use the community as an essential unit of analysis.

Community Stigma

Criminological literature contains numerous examinations of the stigma that someone convicted of a crime experiences. Much of this literature is rooted in labeling theory, which posits that when an individual has an encounter with the criminal justice system, he or she is thereafter classified as a criminal. This label may reinforce the offender's self-identity as a criminal and further encourage deviant behavior (Becker

1963). Thus, an individual's deviant behavior is directly affected by the labeling experience. Research evaluating labeling theory generally examines an individual's altered identity, exclusion from conventional opportunities (such as legitimate employment), and additional participation in criminal activity (Paternoster and Iovanni 1989; Laub and Sampson 2001). In other words, when an individual is labeled as a criminal, a combination of internal and external dynamics interact to increase the likelihood of criminal behavior.

When we explore the impact of the nation's increased use of imprisonment from a community perspective, we face a parallel question, one that has received little research attention: have some communities experienced such pervasive incarceration and reentry concentrations that they, too, now experience a kind of stigma that alters their life course for the worse? As documented in this chapter, there is ample evidence that the criminal justice experience has become widespread in certain communities. Rose, Clear, and Ryder (2002) found that, of 100 residents interviewed in two Tallahassee communities, nearly all had experienced or expected to experience a family member's return from prison. Case and Katz (1991) found that, in some neighborhoods, children "are more likely to know someone involved in the criminal justice system than to know someone who is employed in a profession such as law or medicine." In high-incarceration Cleveland neighborhoods studied by Lynch and Sabol (2001), 8 to 15 percent of the black men between the ages of 18 and 29 are incarcerated on any given day. It is reasonable to assume that these neighborhoods become known as communities where the prison experience is widespread, residents are frequently arrested and detained, families are struggling with the disruptions caused by incarceration, and the patterns of social intercourse are highly irregular.

To better understand incarceration's impact on a community's "self-identity," Clear, Rose, and Ryder (2001) took a close look at a high-incarceration neighborhood in Tallahassee, Florida. They investigated the processes of removing and returning offenders to assess their impact on social networks. They found that prisoners who had returned to the community were unable to overcome the stigma of "offender" and, as a result, had difficulty obtaining employment and housing and reintegrating into the community. More relevant to this discussion, they also found that this stigma extended to the ex-offender's family and friends, causing those individuals to withdraw from the community, not only during the offender's incarceration, but also upon his release. They found that the prisoner's family may encounter strained relationships with neighbors and friends, and when the prisoner returns home, neighbors and community members are often cautious, suspicious, and fearful.

Clear et al. (2001) found that as a result of this accumulated stigma, neighborhoods with high levels of incarcerated residents were themselves stigmatized. In effect, these communities were labeled and their reputations as good places to live, work, and start businesses suffered. How this stigma plays out—and how it can be reversed—will require a sustained new inquiry and further experimentation. In fact, supporting these restorative activities may in the long term be as important as overcoming the social stigma that individual ex-offenders experience.

Legitimacy of the Criminal Justice System

Our discussion of the consequences of incarceration and reentry concentrations would not be complete without looking at the attitudes of community residents toward the criminal justice system itself. In its Maryland *Returning Home* study, the Urban Institute interviewed returning prisoners to gauge their attitudes about the law, the police, and the criminal justice system. About half of the respondents reported that the police in their neighborhoods were racist (49 percent) and did not respond properly to crime victims' needs (53 percent). Most thought the police performed poorly at preventing crime (60 percent) and brutalized people in the neighborhood (62 percent). Along all of these dimensions, men's views were far more negative than women's (Visher et al. 2004). These findings point to a widespread distrust of the police among the population of former prisoners.

On one level, some distrust is not surprising—after all, this population has a history of negative contact with the police. However, the *depth* of these negative views is particularly noteworthy. According to research by Tyler (1988), a person's views of a social institution such as the police department will play a role in the success or failure of interactions with that institution. Specifically, Tyler has found that an individual's perceptions of police legitimacy will influence whether that person is likely to obey the law in the future. Thus the wide and deep distrust of the police in communities of concentrated return may adversely affect that community's overall level of law-abiding behavior. Stated differently, in these communities, the high level of imprisonment may be undermining respect for the law and law enforcement.

Community members' attitudes toward the criminal justice system are also influenced by the reentry phenomenon, although community residents voice ambivalent views regarding an appropriate response to returning prisoners' needs. Immerwahr and Johnson (2002) conducted focus groups in an inner-city neighborhood in Philadelphia and found that community members understood the challenges returning prisoners face and perceived that the community should have a role in supporting the reentry process. Yet this support was tempered by residents' concerns for fairness to law-abiding citizens, public safety, and leniency. For example, Immerwahr and Johnson noted that respondents' desire to help contrasted with their belief in punishment; their belief that people can change conflicted with their desire to limit public and personal safety risks in their community; and their awareness of the difficulties prisoners face was at odds with their low tolerance for failure. Therefore, while it appears that community members believe released prisoners should be assisted as they return to productive roles, it is clear that this assistance will find little support from community members if it comes at the expense of other social welfare programs or presents new safety risks.

This overview leads to a disturbing conclusion: In the era of mass incarceration, several building blocks of civil society have been weakened in communities of concentrated return. Families are weaker and marriage is undermined. Voting rights are restricted, political participation is diminished, and political representation is diluted. The economic viability of neighborhoods already struggling with concentrated disadvantage has been harmed. These communities suffer a new brand of stigma as places that send high percentages of residents to prison. Finally, the very legitimacy of the criminal justice system—in the agencies of government directed to enforce the policies that result in mass incarceration—has been undermined, leading to a cycle of distrust, cynicism, and further noncompliance with society's laws. We turn next to a discussion of a provocative hypothesis, first articulated by Rose and Clear (1998), proposing that the process of cycling large numbers of individuals in and out of prison might weaken a community's informal process of social control to the point where it actually increases crime rates.

Impact of Incarceration on Community Capacity

The phenomenon of mass incarceration, as concentrated in a small number of communities, leads to a series of research questions with no precedent in the American experience. Central to these questions is the impact of the cycle of removal and return on these communities' ability to perform the social functions that define communal life—in other words, supporting human networks that facilitate individual and familial development. A number of scholars are exploring these issues using the framework of "social capital," which can be defined as the ability of individuals to activate social networks to advance their own interests (Bourdieu 1986; Coleman 1990; Putnam 1993).[2] If a person can access strong social capital, then these personal ties and social networks are available to address a wide variety of problems and challenges. Within the social capital framework, these scholars are asking what impact high rates of incarceration have upon the community's "capital." The analysis starts with the understanding that the time spent in prison is typically a time of diminishing social capital (Wolff and Draine 2003). Social relationships are strained and weakened when an individual is removed from the community and incarcerated because contact with friends and family is not only infrequent, but also closely monitored. In addition, as family and community ties are weakened, the incarcerated individual develops a new set of social connections in prison, identifying more closely with the prison culture and relying on new networks for survival. In other words, the prisoner becomes more deeply "embedded" in the criminal culture (Hagan 1993).

Incarceration also results in the loss of skills associated with autonomy and independent living. Due to the highly controlled nature of prison, basic decisions regarding what to do, how to do it, and when to do it are determined by the institution and strictly enforced. As a result, the social skills needed to activate the networks found in the community atrophy. Finally, some prisoners actually undergo an identity transformation. They socialize with those who are like them and reconstruct their social relations to incorporate those who have similar experiences. They will become less like the people they were prior to incarceration, and more like the prisoners they live with. This process creates a strong social bond among prisoners. Some prisoners are able to establish relationships with individuals on the outside; however, these relationships are usually weak because imprisonment has changed both the prisoner and the outside individual. For most but certainly not all prisoners, incarceration results in a net loss of social capital, a diminution of the skills needed to access social rewards, and a shift in identity that ultimately impedes the reintegration process (see chapter 10).

Hundreds of thousands of residents each year are, as a result of criminal activity, removed from and returned to their communities with diminished social capital. Seen from a community perspective, therefore, our criminal justice policies cause more isolation and alienation. These individual effects are then compounded by the broad negative impact of our incarceration policies on the overall social capital of these communities, specifically the networks of families, businesses, churches, and social institutions.

Weakened Social Controls

Rose and Clear (1998) propose that these negative effects at the community level are so pronounced that processes of informal social control are weakened and, because these controls are instrumental in controlling criminal behavior, the net effect is increased crime rates. "Informal social control" describes social forces that produce compliance with community norms but are not derived from state power. By contrast, when state power is used to produce compliance with norms, the process is called "formal social control." In their first documentation of findings from their Tallahassee, Florida, research, Clear and Rose (1999) examined incarceration's impact on perceptions of the utility of formal and informal social control. They found that Tallahassee residents who knew someone who had been to prison had low assessments of the utility of both formal and informal social control. The residents were skeptical that either government or community could produce compliance with community norms. By contrast, those residents who had not been exposed to incarceration and had a low assessment of formal control placed a higher value on informal social control. These findings were the same for all racial groups, after controlling for exposure to incarceration. In other words, this research suggests that as the realities of incarceration have touched the lives of more and more Americans, popular support both for state agencies that enforce compliance with the law and other norms and for the informal mechanisms of community that encourage compliance has been eroded.

Isolation

The Tallahassee research also illuminates the impact of mass incarceration on the family, a critical institution in the production of informal social control. As we discussed in chapter 6, incarceration places enormous burdens on prisoners' families. When a family member goes to prison, the family's resources are often dedicated to supporting the new demands for travel to and from prison, collect phone calls, and child support. An increasing number of children have lost a parent to prison, often resulting in the need for foster or grandparent care and reducing parental supervision at critical times in children's lives. Beyond these more obvious effects on families, Rose, Clear, and Ryder (2002) have documented a more subtle effect. According to their Tallahassee study, community residents who have a family member in prison report that they find themselves more isolated from other people. Families who are thus burdened in prison are less likely to engage in relationships, particularly in civic life, and interact with friends and neighbors. Incarceration thus weakens the family's role as a mechanism of social control.

In addition to "private" social controls, such as families, researchers also point to "parochial" social controls, such as faith institutions, employers, civic associations, and other community organizations (Bursik and Grasmick 1993). With the increased burden of incarceration and reentry, these institutions are also weakened. At levels higher than ever before, church members are sent to prison and their families are struggling with the realities of imprisonment; employees are arrested and incarcerated and then eventually looking to reconnect with work on their return; and block associations and tenant organizations are challenged to handle the risks posed by returning prisoners. As community members withdraw from social contact and new strains are placed on existing networks and institutions, Rose and Clear's (1998) thesis—mass incarceration leads to weakened informal social controls and therefore to increased crime rates—becomes quite plausible.

Increased Crime?

To test this hypothesis, Clear et al. (2003) examined the impact of increasing rates of incarceration on crime rates in Tallahassee. In an article in *Justice Quarterly,* they reported that increases in the number of community residents sent to prison had the effect of reducing crime in the following year, but only when the level of prison admissions was low. As the incarceration rate increased, the community experienced a "tipping point" where incarceration was no longer associated with crime reduction, but, in fact, was associated with an increase in crime rates in the community. At this tipping point, the authors conclude, the levels of "coercive mobility"—the involuntary removal and return of community residents—were so high that the community's capacity to take collective action—to exercise informal social control—was weakened, leading to more crime (Clear et al. 2003, 57–58).

These provocative findings from Tallahassee do not definitively prove, however, the hypothesis that high rates of incarceration can result in higher crime rates. Before such a conclusion can be reached, the study should be replicated. Indeed, the original research team has now been expanded to include other investigators; together they have formed the Collaborative Project on Concentrated Incarceration, which is testing the hypothesis in 10 other cities. If the replication studies confirm the original findings, then our country will have to face a sobering reality. Not only has our national experiment in the increased use of incarceration resulted in profound harms to individual prisoners, their families, their communities, the pursuit of racial justice, and our democracy, but a primary rationale for these policies—that they would reduce crime— has turned out to be flawed.

Looking Forward

For a number of communities already struggling with concentrated disadvantage, the consequences of America's experiment in mass incarceration have been profoundly damaging. Large numbers of community residents have been harmed by the prison experience. Their children, families, and peer networks have suffered. The social institutions that hold communities together have been weakened. This is not to say, however, that imprisonment never results in a net benefit or never reduces crime. Certainly in individual cases, prison is an appropriate and socially beneficial response to crime. Furthermore, the incarceration of large numbers of individuals has indeed contributed to the nation's recent crime reduction (Blumstein and Wallman 2000). According to two separate analyses, the growth in the nation's prison population was responsible for about one-quarter of the decrease in violent crime in the 1990s (Rosenfeld 2000; Spelman 2000). Nevertheless, both the scale and concentration of prison's harms have reached unprecedented levels. While as a nation we have no single empirical compass to guide our understanding of this experiment's consequences, every indication tells us that the harms experienced by the communities bearing the incarceration burden are deep and lasting.

As we look forward, the challenge we face is to mitigate those harms so that these communities can do what communities do best—provide a safe and healthy environment in which individuals, families, economies, and social institutions can thrive. One response would be to reduce the overall level of incarceration in America by reforming our sentencing laws and enforcement policies. This would be the clearest and most obvious solution to the harms outlined in this chapter. As discussed in chapter 2, a number of states have recently begun to roll back some sentencing policies that have contributed to their high levels of incarceration. States have eliminated mandatory minimum sentencing laws, recalculated the amount of time that must be served in prison under the states' truth-in-sentencing laws, and revived the use of parole as a mechanism for releasing inmates from prison. Some states have focused on the back end of the incarceration cycle, reforming the rules regarding postrelease supervision so that fewer recently released prisoners will be returned to custody on parole violations. As that discussion highlighted, in order to have maximum impact on the level of incarceration, reformers should focus on drug cases, the category of criminal convictions that has, by an overwhelming margin, contributed most to the buildup of American prison populations.

These reforms are likely to reduce, to some extent, the burden of incarceration on poor communities. These reform initiatives are incomplete, however, unless they simultaneously attempt to repair the harm these communities have suffered. Two innovative strategies have emerged in recent years that seem particularly noteworthy in this regard: justice reinvestment and community engagement.

Justice Reinvestment

In the starkest budgetary terms, the assignment of incarceration costs to certain blocks in selected American cities represents a missed opportunity for our nation's investment strategy. Rather than investing more than $3 million to incarcerate the young men arrested on a single block in East New York (Brooklyn), we could have invested in other crime-reduction strategies that would have been less harmful to those men, their families, and their neighborhoods, and potentially more effective at reducing crime. The brainchild of Susan Tucker and Eric Cadora (2003) of the Open Society Institute, the justice reinvestment strategy recommends that the level of imprisonment be reduced and, very importantly, that the resulting savings should be shared with the communities that have been harmed by overincarceration.

Assuming that savings in prison budgets can be realized,[3] the next question in a justice reinvestment strategy would be how best to "reinvest" the savings. In tight fiscal times, state budget strategists would understandably be under pressure to use those savings to close budget gaps. An alternate investment strategy would be to use the savings to finance community-level activities that would accelerate reductions in prison populations and thereby produce cost savings in the prison budget. For example, creating a network of "halfway back" houses in the community to house parolees who would otherwise be returned to prison for technical parole violations would free up more prison beds. Funding of electronic bracelets or other monitoring systems for recently released, high-risk prisoners might reduce reoffending rates. Providing drug treatment for all who need it would likely cut drug abuse and recidivism rates. A program of family group conferencing might reduce conflicts at the point of reentry. All in all, this strategy's main goal would be to dedicate savings from prison population reductions to those activities that are demonstrably capable of further reducing the cycle of crime, arrests, and incarceration.

Versions of this concept have been implemented in Oregon and Ohio, but limited to the juvenile justice system. These states have enacted legislation allowing counties to keep the savings if they send fewer juveniles to state-level secure detention. With this incentive, local jurisdictions have created new programs as alternatives to detention, programs that have resulted in measurable reductions in the number of cases sent to the state for confinement (Executive Leadership Institute 2002). With support from the Open Society Institute, the states of Connecticut and Louisiana are now developing legislation that would flow savings from prison reductions back into those communities with high incarceration rates. In many ways, the justice reinvestment idea mirrors the successful welfare reform strategy: setting goals for reductions in caseload (or incarceration levels), sharing savings with the state (or county), and requiring that those savings be invested in programs that would further reduce the caseload (or levels of incarceration).

Community Engagement

One of the most troubling issues we have visited is the notion that the high level of incarceration and reentry in America has damaged community capacity and created greater cynicism toward the criminal justice system. A justice reinvestment strategy, standing alone, will do little to reverse these damaging effects. As important as the money is, simply providing funding for community-based services will have only a minor impact on the decades of damage our criminal justice policies have caused.

At the community level, there is deep ambivalence about society's current patterns of sentencing, incarceration and reentry. On the one hand, residents realize that these policies reflect an attempt by criminal justice agencies to "do something" about crime in their neighborhoods. Residents may, in fact, feel much more secure knowing that a particular neighbor has been arrested and sent away. On the other hand, these same residents intuitively understand the limitations and consequences of these policies. They know that prison is not forever, that nearly all who are sent there come back. They know, and may have experienced firsthand, that imprisonment can cause enormous harm to the children and families left behind. And, on some level, they know that society has other options for responding to crime, options that use prison less, cause less harm, and may even produce greater safety (Immerwahr and Johnson 2002).

These shared realizations form the basis for a new community-level conversation about prisoner reentry. Properly guided, this conversation can yield new perspectives on the reentry phenomenon, bring new assets to the table, create new partnerships between the criminal justice system and the citizenry, and mitigate some of the communal harms resulting from our current policies. Around the country, some communities have come to the opinion that the reentry problem is, in part, their problem to solve. In these communities, groups of neighbors, working with elected officials, criminal justice practitioners, church leaders, service providers, and other stakeholders, have gathered to address the communal impact of large numbers of their neighbors returning home from prison.

Winston-Salem, North Carolina

The potential for this kind of community engagement was evident in a meeting held at the Ashley Elementary School in Winston-Salem, North Carolina, on June 16, 2003.[4] The purpose of the meeting could be found in its title: "Reentry and Revitalization: A Community-Based Approach to Restoring Neighborhoods." The meeting took place in northeast Winston-Salem, a Weed and Seed community where the percentage of families living below the federal poverty level was three times the city rate, the per capita income was 56 percent below average, and the percentage of residents receiving public assistance was four times the citywide rate. Over 50 individuals participated, including community residents, former prisoners, social service providers, faith leaders, police and criminal justice agencies, and researchers.

The meeting began with a series of presentations that had been prepared by the Center for Community Safety at Winston-Salem State University. Sylvia Oberle, center director, and Alvin Atkinson, deputy director, showed community maps documenting incarceration and reentry concentrations. The maps also included community assets, such as employment programs and social services. Oberle and Atkinson presented results of a survey of residents, conducted by former prisoners, detailing the residents' perceptions of the challenges of prisoner reentry. The Center for Community Safety had also conducted focus groups for prisoners returning to this neighborhood in order to learn more about their needs and the challenges they faced, and these results were presented to the group. A police officer discussed crime rates in the neighborhood. The presentation of these various data provided the starting point for a discussion about how to improve outcomes for prisoners returning to the neighborhood.

After an uncertain start, the discussion became quite lively. Community residents complained that their neighborhood got little attention and few services. One woman commented that the area was perceived as being run-down and dangerous, with the result that businesses were hesitant to establish themselves in this community. This, she said, made it difficult for anyone to find jobs, let alone those with a criminal record. As the meeting progressed, individuals started suggesting solutions for each problem that was aired. When the local minister reported that former prisoners often told him they had problems finding a place to live, the director of the housing agency proposed some options. When someone observed that employers were more willing to hire ex-offenders once they get to know them, someone proposed an internship program in which local construction contractors could provide subsidized work for individuals with criminal records. A local elected official mentioned that a major construction project for an airport business park was about to get under way. As a member of the business park's board of directors, she promised to urge the construction firms procured for the project to hire ex-offenders. A man who had been released from prison 17 days earlier commented that he had never heard about the transitional housing that was available in the community. Another man, who was a member of the Assembly of God's ex-prisoner support group, talked about the importance of obtaining identification and connecting with a support group after leaving prison. A local church's pastor reported that his organization offered a food pantry, GED classes, mentoring, and other supportive services. Responding to the maps showing high concentrations of abandoned housing, a housing expert offered to contact the buildings' owners and propose that the owners provide the buildings rent free to former prisoners who were willing to fix up the properties. He also offered to explore funding that would provide transitional housing for this population. Another pastor said his church owned two vacant houses and would like to explore funding from public or private sources to transform these houses into homes for returning prisoners. Noting that many prisoners came from public housing and would like to be reunited with their families, the Housing Authority of Winston-Salem agreed that night to meet with the probation department to address this problem. If the Housing Authority could be certain that individual prisoners were committed to returning safely, then it would be amenable to making allowances to promote family reunification.

By the end of the meeting, the brainstorming had coalesced around a central idea—that the community should create a "resource center" or "one-stop shop" as a base of operations for returning prisoners. The participants suggested that it stay open late to meet the clientele's needs, offer bus passes for job interviews, and provide on-site job training and family support. As the meeting drew to a close, the participants were discussing possible funding sources, center locations, and the formation of a coalition of sponsoring agencies. The "Reentry and Revitalization" meeting ended with the following commitments: construction training for 12 ex-offenders, to be provided by the Office of Workforce Development; a new protocol for public housing and returning prisoners; exploration of the conversion of abandoned buildings into transitional housing, with improvements made by former prisoners; an agreement by the Urban League and the Office of Workforce Development to develop a proposal for a resource center; housing for reentering prisoners provided by several churches; and an increase in mentoring programs by the churches. All this was accomplished in about three hours.[5]

Communities have enormous untapped resources. As the ideas proposed in the Winston-Salem meeting make clear, many of those assets can address some of the immediate needs facing returning prisoners. Even without new funding programs or the reinvestment of saved prison costs, this form of community engagement can provide short- and long-term assistance to returning prisoners and thus benefit the community at large. The meeting also demonstrated that a community collaboration can address some of the less tangible needs returning prisoners face—to be valued, supported, and embraced by the community once they come home. The greatest result of this meeting was the community's realization that the issues presented by high rates of incarceration and reentry were not just individual challenges, they were community challenges. The awareness of collective responsibility becomes the antidote to the weakening of collective action that, according to Rose and Clear (1998), results from concentrations of mass incarceration.

THE JUSTICE INTERMEDIARY

We can only imagine what would happen if communities were provided adequate funding and demonstrated the appropriate infrastructure to develop a sustained campaign of community engagement. We can imagine a world in which a justice intermediary, along the lines of the community justice development corporation proposed in chapter 3, were funded to create a community coalition devoted to prisoner reintegration. We can only imagine the impact of a systematic approach to the needs and the risks of every returning prisoner, drawing up the available community assets and augmenting those assets where needed.

This book has proposed that the nation develop a new approach to prisoner reentry, centered on the creation of a new entity—the justice intermediary—that would operate at the community level to facilitate the reintegration of returning prisoners. By documenting the harms experienced in communities of high incarceration and reentry, this chapter has underscored the strongest argument for this new approach, namely that a new strategy is needed to overcome the alienation and damage caused by our experiment in mass incarceration. Merely asking the existing agencies that make up the justice system to overcome the legacy of harm will not suffice. These agencies must play a role, and indeed can make enormous positive contributions; however, we need a fresh approach. The justice intermediary proposed here would have the benefit of a new beginning, the credibility that comes from an arm's-length relationship with government, and the authority that comes from serving a public purpose at the request of government agencies.

A justice intermediary would represent a test of the justice reinvestment model by achieving reductions in prison admissions, drawing upon the surveys in corrections budgets, melding public and private funding into a single budget for prisoner reintegration, and reinvesting those resources and the human resources of returning prisoners toward the goal of community strengthening. The justice intermediary would also pursue a community engagement goal that would draw upon community assets, providing community members with a stake in reentry outcomes, and would seek to reduce the stigma associated with criminal justice involvement. Finally, the justice intermediary would serve as a justice development corporation, brokering needed services, making investments in properties needed to support the transition from prison, and building local institutional support for a new strategy for prisoner reentry.

The time is right for such an experiment. Continuing along our present course will produce another generation of social harms even deeper than those described in this chapter. Another future is possible, however. A national commitment to new approaches to prisoner reentry, organized around the justice intermediary model, could mean that, with the passage of time, the levels of incarceration in America would be significantly reduced, the savings would be passed along to communities to improve justice programs, and the communities adversely affected by our current policies would be given a meaningful role in the creation of a new system of prisoner reintegration. If this future comes to pass, then we will be able to say that our nation has emerged from this period of experimentation in mass incarceration with a valuable new experiment in community justice.

NOTES

1. States may opt out of this ban; 12 states have done so, while 21 have limited the ban in some way (Legal Action Center 2004).

2. Generally, social capital refers to the activation of actual or potential resources embodied in communities stemming from a durable network of relationships or structures of social organization (Roman and Moore 2004).

3. The realization of savings in prison budgets is particularly problematic. A prison can house a range of inmate populations, so reducing the prison population by a small number of inmates may only result in savings in the costs of meals, health care, and similar individual expenses. The fixed operational costs for the prison would be unaffected. At a certain point, however, the population may be sufficiently reduced to allow for the closing of entire wings of a prison, and prisons themselves. At this point, the budgetary savings become more significant.

4. This discussion is based on interviews with Sylvia Oberle, director of the Center for Community Safety, and Vera Kachnowski, a research associate at the Urban Institute who helped facilitate the meeting.

5. Sylvia Oberle, letter to author, May 21, 2004. About a year after the meeting in the Ashley Elementary School, Sylvia Oberle of the Center for Community Safety provided this update. Plans for the resource center were progressing under the leadership of a community reentry group with ex-offenders and a faith-based group called Faith Seeds. Using the mapping data, they were identifying the best location for the center, and were pursuing funding. The construction-training program for ex-offenders was off the ground, had graduated its first class, and was collaborating with a local community development corporation to renovate housing in the neighborhood. The City had pursued legislation to expedite the transfer of abandoned buildings for the creation of transitional housing for ex-offenders. The Faith Seeds group had created a support group for ex-offenders in the community and was conducting a survey of local churches to identify resources for this population.

Building the Policy Argument for Reentry Reform

The preceding chapters have painted a disturbing picture. Our nation's incarceration policies have indeed had profound ripple effects throughout our society. Our efforts to produce safe communities are complicated by the return of 630,000 individuals from prison each year. Our policies promoting strong families and healthy children are impeded by high rates of incarceration among parents and young men. National strategies to counter communicable diseases, mental illness, and addiction to drugs and alcohol must confront the reality that a high percentage of individuals suffering from these health burdens cycle in and out of correctional facilities. Policies designed to reduce homelessness and secure affordable housing must accommodate the significant overlap between the populations that inhabit shelters and public housing as well as prisons. At a more fundamental level, our nation's aspirations for a tolerant, diverse society are compromised as a handful of American communities grapple with the tens of thousands of individuals who cycle in and out of prison each year.

Yet the picture is not totally bleak. In every chapter, we have learned about programs that are attempting, often with documented success, to overcome the harmful effects of our incarceration policies. In communities across the country, government officials, service providers, nonprofit leaders, and foundation executives are testing new strategies for meeting reentry challenges. Each chapter has concluded on an optimistic note, suggesting ambitious new approaches that might significantly improve reentry outcomes for the 630,000 individuals who leave prison each year, the families and communities of these prisoners, and our society at large.

Put together, these new strategies would create a very different national policy regarding prisoner reentry. If these recommendations were implemented, we would, with a broad coalition of stakeholders:

- Make every effort to reduce the high incidence of rearrest among prisoners immediately following their release from prison. Create a safety plan for each returning prisoner. Frontload supervision services to match resources to the time of greatest safety risk.
- Expand the mission of corrections to include the maintenance of strong family ties for individuals in corrections custody. Mobilize community-based child welfare agencies and other service providers to minimize the harm children with parents in prison experience, with a particular focus on reuniting families (where appropriate) at reentry.
- Create full-employment prisons and provide work opportunities for every returning prisoner. In many cases, this postrelease work could repair damaged relationships by providing visible, valued services to the community.
- Expand the corrections mission to include a public health dimension, holding prisons responsible for detecting and treating communicable diseases, and creating links to community health care providers so services for addictions, mental illness, and all other health conditions are provided on both sides of the prison wall.
- Challenge corrections agencies to release no prisoners into a homeless status. Recalibrate the nation's public housing policies to allow prisoners in appropriate cases to return home openly. Provide counseling services to families and communities allowing them to work out conflicts arising from a family member's reentry.
- Provide more opportunities for former prisoners (and all ex-offenders) to be welcomed back into society, including restoring the right to vote and providing certificates of rehabilitation. Create reentry courts to oversee the reentry process.
- Create opportunities for communities to become fully and productively engaged in prisoner reintegration, relying more on families, faith organizations, and the business sector to play a constructive role in supporting reintegration. Create a justice

intermediary in communities demonstrating high rates of incarceration and reentry to facilitate successful reentry.

To these new policy strategies we must add the recommendations that emerged from chapters 2, 3, and 4 in which we described the new landscape of punishment. Those recommendations include rethinking our drug enforcement policy, because it drives so much of our current level of imprisonment; reorganizing supervision around a reentry court and a justice intermediary, with a community focus; and enacting new legislation that would limit the application of collateral sanctions to those cases deemed necessary and appropriate by a sentencing judge.

If implemented, these new strategies would represent a fundamental shift in our country's approach to prisoner reintegration. The chapters that follow recommend a framework of five principles of successful reentry that should reorient our current approach to reentry as well as create a new jurisprudence of reintegration. We must first, however, address a more practical concern: How could we justify the expenditure of funds that this realignment would require?

A student once asked me how we could justify the allocation of taxpayer funds on college education programs for prisoners when she was not eligible for any public funds for her education. Why, she asked, should people who violate the law get a public benefit that was not available to her and others who did not violate the law? The traditional answer is that these programs are effective at rehabilitating offenders, thereby reducing crime, so they represent worthwhile expenditures of public funds. This argument always engenders a number of challenges. Researchers often question the assertion that a particular intervention reduces crime. However, even if the research is clear and a program is highly effective, the thought behind the student's argument still stands: These program recipients are not "deserving" of that public service, no matter how effective it may be, because they violated the law. In this case, the contrast is more pointed because prisoners are eligible for public benefits that the student herself could not obtain.

Throughout the preceding chapters, this book has advanced a different argument for public expenditures on the population of returning prisoners (and their families and communities). Precisely because prisoners have violated the law and served time behind bars, we should be concerned about the short-term consequences of their reentry. We should, within reasonable limits, assist returning prisoners as they try to get back on their feet. We should support transitional housing as a bridge between prison and permanent self-supported housing. We should help families in working through the stress of reentry because we believe that the family is an important institution that can assist in the reintegration process. We should insist on work in prison and support work during the transition because work is associated with independence and self-sufficiency. We should create forums for elevation ceremonies to reduce the high level of social exclusion that accompanies high rates of incarceration. In other words, we have a separate rationale—a reentry rationale—that argues for investments in transitional supports for returning prisoners.

The rationale for these expenditures is not a rehabilitation rationale—these efforts may or may not reduce a prisoner's propensity to reoffend—but a risk-reduction rationale. By putting people in prison, society has created a separate reality, namely the transition from prison, and has an obligation to individuals who undergo that transition, as well as those affected by it, to mitigate the harms and promote the benefits associated with prisoner reentry. We live in an era of tight budgets, so the first imperative in a fiscally responsible reentry initiative should be to align existing resources to meet the returning prisoners' reentry needs at the time of highest risk—right when the prison gates close. Transitional housing, drug treatment, continuity in health care and medication, employment opportunities, and support networks should all be redirected to the moment of release. The testable hypothesis is that this realignment will both reduce crime and promote reintegration.

If this realignment proved successful, it might well provide a compelling argument for increased public expenditures. The student questioner might note that a public program providing college education to prisoners does not fit neatly into this rationale. If such a program reduced rearrest rates significantly, it might pass the first test for public funds, but measured against this second test—the reentry rationale—it would fall far below arguments for transitional support, such as housing, health care, or drug treatment. From a reentry perspective, providing a prisoner with a college education is a lower priority than providing for the needs that arise upon release. This reentry rationale for public expenditures may disappoint those who would prefer investing in rehabilitation programs. However, investments in a smoother transition from prison might result in reductions in rearrest rates, enhanced attachments to family, work, housing, and health care, and may, in the long run, be more beneficial both to society and to the returning prisoner.

Throughout these chapters, we have unwittingly developed a third argument for investing scarce resources in prisoners, families, and the communities to which they return. We have documented the high degree of overlap between this population and the populations that are already served by other service sectors outside the criminal justice system. For example:

- If up to 30 percent of the individuals arrested for crimes of violence in recent years had been released from prison in the preceding three years, then the police and advocates for community safety have an interest in successful reentry.
- If about 10 percent of admissions to foster care are due to parental incarceration, and 40 percent of the residents of the Robert Taylor Homes, for example, expect a family member to return from prison next year, then service providers working in the foster care system and in public housing have become stakeholders in the reentry process.
- If a high percentage of low-skilled minority male workers who are characterized as "hard to employ" have recently been in prison, then advocates for new approaches to workforce development have an interest in efforts to improve prisoners' employment prospects while they are incarcerated.
- If a high percentage of Americans with communicable diseases, mental illness, and substance abuse histories pass through correctional facilities each year, then the public health sector has an interest in maximizing the value of the incarceration period to reduce those health risks.
- If a high percentage of residents of homeless shelters cycle in and out of prison, then policymakers interested in breaking that cycle should find common purpose with their corrections counterparts.
- If the effects of felon disenfranchisement statutes are distorting the profile of eligible votes in our democracy, particularly for minority groups, then civil rights advocates have an interest in challenging the laws that create this inequality.
- If our incarceration and reentry processes adversely affect a small number of neighborhoods, then advocates of community-strengthening initiatives cannot avoid engaging issues of justice policy if they hope to reverse the trends of concentrated disadvantage.

As these examples illustrate, the high level of incarceration in America has created overlapping circles of common cause between those interested in criminal justice policy and those interested in these related policy domains. These networks of common cause create a series of new justifications for investing in policies that would promote successful reentry. To the extent that those related policy sectors justify spending public funds to achieve their own goals, their arguments can be used in debates on criminal justice policy. For example, if the public health sector has developed policy arguments for identifying and treating communicable diseases, those same arguments can be used to support health programs that begin in prison and continue into the community. Similarly, if adolescent development specialists have tested interventions involving children suffering from a traumatic separation from a parent and found that those interventions result in improved social functioning, then those arguments can be advanced to support programs for the children of incarcerated parents.

The magnitude of the overlap between the populations using these service delivery systems and the criminal justice population might actually provide efficiencies-of-scale arguments for substantial investments in the reentry population. Certainly this is true in the case of communicable diseases, where public health researchers now argue that the criminal justice system presents a "public health opportunity" to improve the health status of large segments of the population. With creative thinking, similar arguments can be made in a number of social service sectors. It is indeed ironic that the era of mass incarceration may provide the greatest opportunity in many decades to engage social service agencies in attending to the needs of prisoners, their families, and their communities.

Keeping in mind the policy dimensions of prisoner reentry and the complexities of the policy arguments favoring a new set of strategies to improve reentry outcomes, we now turn to two frameworks for moving forward to meet the challenges of prisoner reentry. In the next chapter, we will articulate five principles of effective reentry. In essence, this chapter develops a set of guideposts that could be used by practitioners, communities, policymakers, and advocates to reorganize existing criminal justice processes to improve the odds of successful reentry. Then, in the final chapter, we step back from these reentry reform principles to revisit the jurisprudential issues that framed the beginning of the book. If, as we discussed in chapter 1, the consensus over indeterminate sentencing present in 50 years of American jurisprudence has fallen apart, is there a new model that could take its place—one that would accommodate today's realities of punishment? In the final chapter, we will explore modifications to our sentencing framework that would reorient the criminal justice system to support successful reentry. To move from concept to reality, legislators and corrections officials would be required to embrace the goal of reintegration, then devise new operational philosophies and realign agency responsibilities to achieve this goal.

PART III
Facing the Challenges

Defining the
Reform Agenda

The first two parts of this book have documented the rise and fall of the American consensus on indeterminate sentencing, described the new landscape of punishment in America, and deconstructed the various overlaps between the phenomenon of incarceration and reentry and other social policy domains. Throughout those discussions, we took note of various programs and policies designed to improve reentry outcomes, explored different strategies for meeting specific policy challenges associated with today's realities of reentry, and suggested new structures, such as reentry courts and community justice corporations, that could facilitate a smoother journey from prison to community.

In this final section of the book, we step back from a discussion of specific program ideas, policy innovations, and reform strategies to take a broader view of the phenomenon of prisoner reentry. The two final chapters will propose a new architecture for our criminal justice system and our sentencing philosophy, one that reflects the modern realities of prisoner reentry. Implementing isolated programs, no matter how effective they might be in improving reentry outcomes, will make little difference in reducing the significant social harms documented throughout this book. Carrying out more ambitious reform agendas in a single policy sector, such as public health or workforce development, will have limited effect without a fundamental reorientation of criminal justice philosophy, particularly among corrections and parole agencies. New justice institutions like reentry courts and community justice corporations, even if successful on their own terms, will fail to realize their full potential without legislative reforms that promote reintegrating citizens who have violated the law.

Accordingly, the next two chapters contain recommendations for a more fundamental reform of our approach to reentry and reintegration. Chapter 12 views prisoner reentry as a process, a transition from prison to home that is shaped by a complex interaction of public policies and private decisions. This chapter proposes five principles that should guide any sustained effort to reorient the workings of the criminal justice system and related activities to promote successful reentry outcomes for the hundreds of thousands of men and women leaving prison each year, carrying with them a mix of resolve, risk, fear, and potential. Chapter 13 proposes that a modern American jurisprudence should embrace, as a goal, the social reintegration of former prisoners. Today, long after the prison doors close, the parole term ends, and the last legal debt is paid, former prisoners continue to live in communities across America and yet are not granted equal membership in American society. In an earlier era, our sentencing philosophy recognized the importance of preparing prisoners for reentry and reintegration, but that objective has largely vanished in the wake of sentencing reforms that have swept the country over the past generation. Recognizing that a return to that earlier era is unlikely, this chapter makes five recommendations for statutory reform that would infuse our current sentencing laws with a reintegration jurisprudence.

Compared with earlier chapters, chapters 12 and 13 address a different policy plane and speak in a different voice. They contain broad recommendations that cannot be carried out by a single agency. They propose guiding principles, not programmatic interventions. Implementing these recommendations will require new coalitions cutting across sectors of government, innovative partnerships with the nonprofit sector, and constructive involvement by the people most directly affected by reentry, namely the prisoners themselves and their families. Enacting the proposed legislative changes will require political will and stamina. Notwithstanding changes in public attitudes on crime and punishment over the past decade, the champions of this important work will have the added burden of educating the public about the importance of reentry and reintegration issues.

In this respect, the reforms proposed earlier in the book provide support for the more profound reforms outlined in these final chapters. For example, every police officer working on safety planning could become an advocate for removing barriers to prisoner reintegration. Every public health official treating prisoners returning home with communicable diseases could push for reentry preparation, the first principle of effective reentry. Every organization that promotes a positive civic identity for ex-offenders could support statutory reforms that promote preparation for the moment of release from prison.

In essence, the ten reform proposals presented in the next two chapters could form the foundation for a broad-based agenda for change that would unite the many voices now advocating for a new approach to prisoner reentry. Following these two chapters, the book will close with some observations about the future of the national discussion of prisoner reentry. Notwithstanding the sobering realities of mass incarceration and reentry in America, there are solid reasons for optimism. But for this optimism to be more than wishful thinking, those interested in fundamental reform will need to summon the courage, stamina, and strategic savvy necessary to launch some big ideas. The next two chapters are intended to serve as guideposts for those interested in taking up this challenge.

The Principles of
Effective Reentry

W e have already established that prisoner reentry is a process—a virtually inevitable consequence of imprisonment. With rare exceptions, everyone sent to prison returns home. Seen from one perspective, reentry is a governmental process; in other words, the institutions that define the contours of prisoner reentry are principally government agencies. Government policies determine reentry preparation, supervision realities, and integration hurdles. However, the process is also fundamentally an intensely personal process, involving prisoners, families, and extended social networks. Their actions can significantly influence the realities of reentry. The end result of the reentry process reflects decisions that are made by a variety of individuals—some of whom are government employees, many of whom are not. This chapter articulates the principles that should govern the way those decisions are made. Because many of these decisions reflect government policy, the principles developed in this chapter are directed to the leaders of those government agencies. However, these principles are also intended to guide the individual thought processes of those who leave prison and those in their familial and social networks.

In essence, we will carry out a classic "reengineering" exercise. In their book *Reengineering the Corporation: A Manifesto for Business Revolution,* Hammer and Champy (1993, 32) define reengineering as "the fundamental rethinking and radical redesign of business processes to achieve dramatic improvements in critical, contemporary measures of performance, such as cost, quality, service, and speed." This process involves "rejecting the conventional wisdom and received assumptions of the past. Reengineering is about inventing new approaches to process structure that bear little or no resemblance to those of previous eras" (49). We hope to invent some new approaches to prisoner reentry that could, if implemented, achieve dramatic improvements in important performance measures for the reentry process. Developing these new approaches will require a fundamental rethinking of the current state of practice.

I propose five principles of effective reentry, each derived from a number of sources. Some reflect lessons learned from strategic planning projects carried out by the Urban Institute, which has worked with community groups to design new approaches to prisoner reentry. Other ideas have been articulated over the past few years by various groups developing reentry reform proposals. Still others have been abstracted from research on effective reentry programs. The Transition from Prison to Community Initiative of the National Institute of Corrections has been a rich source of experience in the rewards and challenges of organizational transformation to promote successful reentry. These ideas also reflect our emphasis on the importance of prisoner reintegration. This chapter's goal is to distill these pieces of wisdom into a set of guiding principles that could be embraced by practitioners, community groups, currently or formerly incarcerated individuals, and reform advocates who undertake the challenge of improving their jurisdiction's approach to prisoner reentry.

Each of these five principles requires action:

1. prepare for reentry;
2. build bridges between prisons and communities;
3. seize the moment of release;
4. strengthen the concentric circles of support; and
5. promote successful reintegration.

In a very real sense, anyone involved in the reentry process should observe these principles. For example, prison staff, the prisoner, his or her family, and the community should all "prepare for reentry." Successful prisoner reentry demands that all stakeholders in the process—individual prisoners, their families, criminal justice agencies, and ultimately all members of society—actively participate in the process. These five principles also serve as yardsticks for assessing particular government initiatives or community activities. For example, a correctional administrator might ask whether family visitation policies strengthen the family as a circle of support or whether such policies promote successful reintegration. These principles will have the greatest impact on transforming the reentry process, however, if taken together they serve as a guide for the fundamental reengineering of the transition from prison to home.

Prepare for Reentry

Obviously, the first principle of effective reentry is to prepare for reentry. After all, except for those few prisoners who die in prison, reentry is an inevitable consequence of incarceration. This reality—however obvious—has not manifested itself in correctional agency mission statements across the nation. On the contrary, in discussions with correctional administrators over the years, I have been struck by the fact that reentry planning is not central to their departmental operations. Too often, administrators view their agency's mission as a task limited to maintaining safe and secure institutions. Embracing the added goal of preparing prisoners for reentry represents a major shift in correctional thinking.

The Ohio Plan

Dr. Reginald Wilkinson, director of Ohio's Department of Rehabilitation and Correction, has led the campaign for effective reentry preparation. In a groundbreaking article, he referred to the new national interest in prisoner reentry as a "storm overdue." According to Wilkinson, "This change will involve a shift from the historical dichotomy that has evoked fragmentation between institutional and community service divisions within the correctional system. The challenge is to achieve a more systemic approach that ensures a seamless transition of offender treatment and training from reception through the completion of community supervision" (2001, 47). He also urges, "We can't be afraid of change. In the corrections business, change is the only thing that is constant. Tackling reentry is not a destination. It is a journey. There is no reentry utopia. What we achieve will require continuous improvement processes coupled with a lot of hard work" (50).

Leading by example, Wilkinson has set about to transform his entire department into an agency that embraces the added mission of successful reentry. He terms his blueprint for organizational transformation the "Ohio Plan," short for the "Ohio Plan for Productive Offender Reentry and Recidivism Reduction." Under this plan, an internal planning committee and a council of community members reviewed the department's reentry approach and developed ways to address knowledge gaps, deficient practices, or nonexistent policies. Following this review, the department chose to dismantle all prerelease programs, which served only a few prisoners and had no measurable outcomes, and instead budgeted $1.7 million for a universal release-planning program, which includes a reentry plan for every returning prisoner. Under the fully implemented Ohio Plan, prisoners will reenter society with documentation of all training, educational, and other prison programs they participated in, information that will assist prospective employers and service providers in assessing the former prisoners' capabilities and needs more comprehensively. This new initiative will include, for the first time, measures of success on the outside. The Ohio Plan also calls for a review of all staff assignments, department policies, training, programs, and community initiatives to determine whether they support the new mission of successful reentry (Wilkinson 2001). In short, the Ohio Department of Rehabilitation and Correction has undertaken a top-to-bottom realignment of its central business processes, from staff training to program design, with the profound goal of ensuring that all procedures promote the successful reentry of individuals held in its prisons.

Work Opportunities

Using examples from the chapters in Part Two, we can construct some concrete goals that might accompany organizational realignments similar to those now under way in Ohio. For example, prisons should strive for full prisoner employment, as is the case in Oregon. However, the goal is more than reducing idleness. Consistent with the guiding principle to "prepare for reentry," these work opportunities should be evaluated for their connections to the outside world of work. Opportunities that are more likely to lead to work in the community are preferable to those that do not. Work opportunities that enhance skills, attitudes, and behaviors that are valued in the external labor market are more helpful than simple "make-work" experiences. Furthermore, some prisoners might better achieve their full employment objective by full-time participation in educational, treatment, or skill-building programs that are, in their cases, necessary employment prerequisites. Prisoners nearing their release dates should prepare packets including resumes, diplomas, and references to assist them with job interviews on the outside. To the extent feasible, those interviews should begin before release, and former employers should be contacted about their willingness to rehire former employees. Every effort should be made to provide employment on the outside. As a corollary proposition, prisons should be evaluated in terms of their former inmates' postrelease employment rates.

Health Care

Similarly, prison health services should be reengineered to prepare individuals for reentry. As was proposed in chapter 8, special attention should be paid to communicable diseases such as HIV/AIDS, tuberculosis, and hepatitis. In close collaboration with public health practitioners in the community, prison health providers should institute a systematic approach to screening, inoculation, detection, and treatment. Universal education programs should be launched within the prisons to cultivate awareness of the behavioral antecedents to these diseases, the risks they pose to intimate partners and others, and the precautionary measures that can be taken, both inside prison and back in the community. In short, the broader public health community on both sides of the prison walls should take advantage of the public health "opportunity" presented by imprisonment to prepare prisoners, particularly those with these diseases, in ways that promote positive health outcomes.

Beyond the special public health imperative regarding communicable diseases, prison health care providers adhering to the "prepare for reentry" principle should adopt new policies regarding discharge planning. Every effort should be made to ensure that prisoners have applied for benefits prior to their release so that payments for treatment and prescription drugs can commence immediately upon discharge. Appointments with community health care providers should also be made before release. Ideally, as in Rhode Island, those outside providers should establish contact with their inmate patients before they are released from prison. To ensure continuity of care, every prisoner should be discharged with a complete medical record. Finally, if the discharged prisoner has a history of addiction, then appropriate placement in outpatient or residential treatment facilities should be made prior to the release date. If this requires placing prisoners on waiting lists for drug treatment while they are still in prison, then prison and program staff should coordinate those processes.

Family Ties

Families face special challenges in adhering to the "prepare for reentry" imperative. As we discussed in chapter 6, current criminal justice policies seem designed to weaken, not strengthen, family ties during incarceration. Assisting prisoners' families for reentry requires a major transformation of correctional practice, as well as an increased commitment from communities to support prisoners' families during the prisoners' incarceration. Yet in the narrowest sense, this principle necessitates interventions designed to help families work through the issues associated with a family member's return. Correctional agencies have a role to play here; reentry counselors should speak with families about the release process, provide accurate information about the exact release date and any supervision conditions, and allow extra visiting time and phone contacts as the release date approaches so the family can work through any emerging issues. In addition, at the community level, community organizations and support networks should counsel families on the likely stresses and conflicts surrounding their relatives' return from prison.

Community Roles

As the Baltimore Reentry Partnership initiative demonstrated, the community can also play an important role in preparing for reentry. Community groups, working with local police and neighborhood organizations, should insist on the creation of a safety plan for each prisoner returning to live among them in order to minimize the recidivism risks and protect potential victims. As in the Baltimore project, these groups should contact returning prisoners to welcome them home while simultaneously encouraging them to avoid any further antisocial behavior. Community organizations can play a vital role in ensuring that resources such as transitional housing, health care appointments, and drug treatment are already arranged prior to release. This process helps ensure that ex-prisoners' critical first days, weeks, and months in society are times of smooth transition. In essence, the community should insist that the criminal justice system be held accountable for a simple checklist of reentry preparation—that every prisoner has made contact with family members, has housing lined up, has health care appointments (including drug treatment), has made arrangements for work or educational programs, and has a clear safety plan in place.

Personal Expectations

Finally, at the most basic level, each prisoner should observe the imperative to "prepare for reentry." This requires an internal process of developing the necessary resolve to meet the challenges of returning home. Often, prisoners are overly optimistic about the level of support that awaits them (Visher, La Vigne, and Farrell 2003), and their expectations need to be tempered with a dose of reality. The period of incarceration can be a time to develop a set of supportive networks, a new or renewed connection to one's faith, or a new commitment to a cause or career. Correctional administrators should validate and facilitate these activities because they are likely to improve prisoners' chances for success on the outside.

Build Bridges between Prisons and Communities

Prisons are social institutions that by their very nature are isolated and removed from the rest of society. Yet the individuals who are held in these institutions come from, maintain contact with, and return to the larger world. For that reentry journey to be effective, these institutions, the individuals and families affected by incarceration, and the broader society should strive to build bridges between prisons and the communities on the outside.

Among Criminal Justice Agencies

These bridges should connect many individuals and entities that are now poorly connected at best. The process should begin first with the agencies of the criminal justice system. Links should be established among corrections agencies and the courts that send offenders to these agencies, the parole agencies that supervise prisoners after release, and the police agencies that are responsible for public safety in the communities to which prisoners return. As is the case in Richland County (Ohio)'s reentry court, pre-sentence reports prepared for the courts should be transformed into reentry plans, identifying the issues that the offender should address while in prison (e.g., drug addiction, literacy, anger management). This reentry plan should then augment the prison's classification and program assignment process and also identify community-based resources available to the reentering prisoner following sentence completion. Should the prisoner be released to a reentry court, this reentry plan, now expanded to include progress reports from in-prison programs, should provide the foundation for a plan of action during supervision.

Even where no reentry court exists, corrections agencies should build extensive connections with the agencies that provide supervision on the outside, beginning with parole agencies. Often, prisons and parole exist under the same organizational umbrella, but too often they do not speak to each other. The fact that fewer than 25 percent of prisoners are now released by parole boards (see chapter 4) does not relieve prisons of their obligation to build constructive bridges with supervisory agencies—public and private—in the community. At a minimum, recognizing that about 80 percent of prisoners are released to supervision, corrections agencies should ensure a full transfer of relevant information to the supervisory entities. Even better, these institutions should conduct a series of prerelease conferences (by teleconferencing if necessary) in which the prison staff, parole staff, and prisoner meet to ensure that the probabilities of successful reentry are maximized.

Bridges should also be built between the police and the prisons. The lack of communication between these two major institutions in the criminal justice system is striking. Too often, the police consider that their job is done once an offender has been arrested, convicted, and sent to prison. Frequently, the police are not even notified when a prisoner is released and sent home. Too often, corrections agencies operate in total isolation from the police. As state agencies, they have little contact with local police chiefs or sheriffs. They see little connection between their missions and public safety, except that they provide custody for inmates, many of whom are dangerous. They resist the notion that they be held accountable for the failure rates of released prisoners.

A full partnership among police, corrections, and parole agencies could significantly improve reentry outcomes, particularly by reducing reoffending rates. Even before prisoners are released, however, these partnerships could use the incarceration period to reduce crime. While director of corrections in Connecticut, Larry Meachum launched a highly successful effort to break the hold street gangs had on life inside the state's prisons, and collaborated with local police to develop intelligence capabilities inside the prisons that led to successful criminal investigations of gang violence in the community (Leatherby 1996). The Urban Institute's research found that in Illinois, nearly a third (30 percent) of prisoners were involved in gangs prior to incarceration, but only 5.2 percent expected to remain involved with gangs after release (Visher et al. 2003). Based on this finding, the incarceration period should be viewed as an opportunity for police and corrections departments and other community groups to reduce the influence of criminal gangs and the violence they commit.

Between Prisons and Private Organizations

The bridges between prisons and the community must extend beyond the agencies of the criminal justice system, however. As in Oregon and Texas, businesses should be invited into the prisons, ideally to provide jobs that can be transferred to jobs on the outside, but minimally to provide job fairs so that prospective employers can interview potential job candidates before they are released from prison. Health care providers should also be invited into prisons, perhaps to provide prison health services, but minimally to ensure that health care is continuous during reentry. Faith institutions should be encouraged to come into the prisons to provide religious instruction and pastoral care to individual prisoners and to create mentorship relationships between prisoners and members of churches, mosques, and synagogues who agree to embrace the returning prisoners in the faith community. Journalists and other media representatives should be allowed access to the prison world, consistent with security imperatives, to shine a light on prison life, expose conditions in need of governmental attention, and provide a window on institutions too long closed to public view. Local colleges and universities should be encouraged to bring classroom instructors into the prisons. Family members should be encouraged, not discouraged, from visiting their loved ones in prison.

In all of these activities, individual prisoners should be encouraged to build bridges as well. Of course, not all bridges lead to constructive activities, so obviously connections with criminal associates for criminal purposes should not be allowed. Nevertheless, prison policies should facilitate connections to families, potential employers, service providers, ex-offender associations, faith-based institutions, and other organizations in the community that could smooth the transition home.

Between Correctional Agencies and the Community

These bridges are not just for the benefit of prisoners, however. Just as prisoners should be encouraged to establish contact with the outside world, so, too, should prison administrators. As they pursue their expanded mission of facilitating successful reentry, prison administrators need to engage the world outside the prison walls. When the Maryland Division of Corrections began planning the Reentry Partnership, Assistant Commissioner Jack Kavanaugh was directed to meet with community groups in the Baltimore neighborhoods that received the highest number of returning prisoners. Neither he nor any representative of his department had ever met with these groups before. The initial meetings were characterized by suspicion, anger, and skepticism on the part of the community members. These citizens basically asked Kavanaugh, "What took you so long? Why are you just now saying that you care about how prisoners return to our community? Why should we believe that you really want things to change?" Kavanaugh realized that his view of his responsibilities as a public official had been too narrow—he had not understood his obligations to the communities to which prisoners returned.

Twenty years ago, when I was involved in the first experiments in community policing carried out by the New York City Police Department, we told the community police officers assigned to newly defined beats in a Brooklyn precinct that they should build bridges with individuals and institutions in their beats. They were required to interview business owners, residents, neighborhood leaders, and others to learn more about the crime problems facing the community. Invariably, when these officers knocked on doors in an attempt to interview community residents, the precinct would receive phone calls complaining that someone was at the door impersonating a police officer. The callers could not believe that a police officer had come to them to discuss community problems and to ask how they thought the police were responding. Unfortunately, the same gulf that has long existed between the police and the community can also be found, in different form, between corrections/parole agencies and the community. In making the connections necessary for successful reentry, those agencies need to walk across these bridges; contact individuals, businesses, political institutions, and community groups; and find out the problems with prisoner reentry and how well we are doing in addressing those problems. Acting on the insights gained from these conversations could revolutionize American prison management.

Seize the Moment of Release

The criminal justice system is like an assembly line. Police hand off arrests to prosecutors who in turn bring cases to court; in court, judges impose sentences on the guilty who in turn are sometimes sent off to prison. At the back end of this assembly line, prisoners are released from prison. Ironically, this critical step in the assembly line receives the least attention in the world of criminal justice practice. Yet this is where hundreds of thousands of Americans each year make difficult and dangerous transitions in ways that affect their sense of identity, their relationships with family and community, and their chances of successful reintegration into society.

In many jurisdictions, the moment of release from prison seems designed to increase the odds of failure. Prisoners are often released in the early morning hours to locations where drugs, prostitutes, and alcohol are abundant. They are often discharged wearing prison gear, carrying their belongings in a plastic bag, with little money to buy new clothes or secure transportation home. Often, family members are not notified of the details of the release process, so they are not there to provide immediate connections. For mentally ill prisoners taking prescription drugs, a one- or two-day supply of medication may be provided, if they are lucky. For a large number of returning prisoners, the release process leads straight to a homeless shelter.

Too often, the moment of release is viewed as the end of the assembly line; the prisoner is simply shown the door and sent on his way. Too often, this moment becomes the correctional system's last opportunity to remind the prisoner of his degraded status in society. The challenge of building an effective reentry initiative is to reverse this worldview and to seize the moment of release as an opportunity to improve reentry chances, support the reintegration processes, and encourage the elevation of returning prisoners' status.

Simple things matter. In the Maryland Reentry Partnership program, community members and prisoners due to be released to those communities hold an "exit orientation" meeting once a month. The community members' first message is "Welcome home." At one exit orientation, an older prisoner commented that he had been released from prison twice before, but had never been welcomed home. An effective reentry partnership will find ways to increase the likelihood that someone—a family member, a friend, a mentor, a community leader, a police officer, or a pastor—will say "Welcome home" at the moment of release.

Beyond this symbolic and powerful statement, the moment of release should be marked by tangible connections to the community. Family should be involved, where appropriate—particularly the returning prisoner's children. Transitional housing, if needed, should be available. Mentors from community organizations of formerly incarcerated individuals should be part of the welcoming team. Benefits such as Medicaid should be restored, where available. Health care should be continuous. The ingredients of the safety plan, worked out prior to the prisoner's release, should be activated so that behaviors, associations, locations, and individuals that might elevate the risk of reoffending are identified and addressed.

The moment of release also provides opportunities for supporting a returning prisoner's new identity. In particular, this moment might provide an opportunity for reconciliation between the prisoner and the crime victim. Some returning prisoners might want to take advantage of opportunities to work on community projects or engage in other forms of redemptive service that would send a signal to society that they are indeed assets to the community. Some might work with young people in the community, demonstrating the importance of avoiding the life choices that can lead to prison.

Making these symbolic and tangible connections a reality may require additional resources. However, as we discussed in chapter 5, the risks of rearrest are highest immediately after release, so a simple risk-reduction goal definitely warrants investing additional resources during these early weeks and months. Furthermore, as we mentioned in chapter 3, there is something irrational about a criminal justice system that spends ten times as much on a prisoner's last day in prison as it does on his first day after prison. Shifting existing resources from prison to reentry management, and from the last months of supervision to the first months after release, would reflect a public acknowledgment that our current policies regarding the moment of release are highly counterproductive and that seizing that moment could significantly improve the reentry process.

Strengthen the Concentric Circles of Support

In April 2002, my colleague Michelle Waul and I conducted a two-day strategic planning session on prisoner reentry with a vibrant and eclectic group of community leaders in San Diego. Much like the Winston-Salem meeting described in chapter 11, this session's participants ranged from criminal justice officials to pastors in local churches. In struggling to describe the relationships they envisioned among returning prisoners, their families, community groups, and the government, the San Diego Reentry Roundtable came up with this imperative: strengthen the concentric circles of support. I am indebted to them for this insight; it captures an important principle about the proper interrelationships among individual, private, and governmental activities in improving reentry outcomes.

The Returning Prisoner

At the center of the concentric circles of support stands the individual leaving prison. If he or she can manage the reentry process well, reconnect with family and work, and navigate the pitfalls of the return from prison, then the role of other support systems, including parole and police agencies, will be minimal. For the successful returning prisoner, the supervision period (if any) should end as soon as possible, and lost rights should be restored. One goal of the reentry process—a goal embraced by prisons, prisoners, family members, and others—should be to strengthen the ex-prisoner's capacity to succeed without support.

Family

The first concentric circle is the family. Sometimes, however, the family poses a risk to successful reentry. As we observed in chapter 6, prisoners' families are often involved in criminal activity, substance abuse, and other risky behaviors. Sometimes there is no family ready to support the former prisoner. More typically, however, families represent important assets. An effective reentry strategy should discern whether, for every returning prisoner, the family structure contains these assets and, if so, should seek to strengthen this concentric circle. As the research on La Bodega de la Familia demonstrated, helping former prisoners' family members cope with reentry stresses can result in lower levels of antisocial behavior. However, these families need support and cannot be expected to shoulder this additional burden without help.

Peer Group

The next concentric circle is the returning prisoner's peer group. As with family members, some peers provide negative influences, while others offer positive pressure. Reentry planning should discern the risks and assets in the returning prisoner's peer groups. The safety plan may include directions to stay away from certain groups or gangs. The plan may also include new peer groups, such as mentors from a church or support networks of ex-offenders. An effective community-based reentry initiative, such as the community justice intermediary proposed in chapter 3, should have intimate knowledge of the dynamics of neighborhood peer groups in order to help the ex-prisoner steer clear of potentially negative influences.

Community Institutions

Outside peer groups lies a concentric circle of community institutions, the formal and informal associations that are the backbone for neighborhood social capital. Faith institutions, business organizations, tenant groups, homeowners' associations, elected officials, crime prevention coalitions, neighborhood watch groups, and fraternal groups all have a role to play in successful prisoner reentry. At a minimum, these community institutions should be educated about how incarceration and reentry impacts their communities. They can serve as helpful advocates for humane and effective policies on crime control, incarceration, and reentry. Furthermore, these institutions can provide important resources to support returning prisoners, families, and peer groups. Jobs, health programs, day care, drug treatment, and other resources require active investment by private- and public-sector institutions. Strengthening this circle of support can change a community's attitude about returning prisoners from one of denial and resistance to one of awareness and support.

Social Service Agencies

The next concentric circle is made up of the social service agencies in a jurisdiction. These agencies provide public assistance, job training, drug treatment, transitional housing, education, and other services to individuals in the community. Returning prisoners (and their families) are frequently eligible for those services; however, too often these service providers, consciously or unconsciously, shun these potential clients. Granted, returning prisoners are often difficult clients, with multiple problems and needs exacerbated by their transition from prison to community. Furthermore, guidelines from funding agencies often encourage service providers to accept clients with higher chances of success. To carry out effective reentry initiatives, however, this concentric circle of support must be aligned to provide services to every member of this unique clientele, particularly at the time of greatest need—the moment of release.

Criminal Justice Agencies

The agencies of the criminal justice system, particularly parole and police agencies, make up the outermost circle of support. These agencies do not typically think of themselves as providing "support," but they do in a very real sense. They act as agents of the justice system and can reinforce core values, such as the importance of the rule of law and the principles of fair treatment. In the ways they enforce the law or conditions of supervision, they can generate respect for the justice system. Moreover, these agencies can promote, in simple and powerful ways, the social goal of reintegration. This is very important. When I attended an exit orientation sponsored by the Maryland Reentry Partnership, the community coalition meeting with returning prisoners included the police officer assigned to that neighborhood. When the officer introduced himself to the prisoners, he said, "The police are a part of your community. We want you to succeed when you come home. I have a job to do and will enforce the law if necessary, but I also will work with this coalition to help you succeed." This was a powerful statement from an influential voice at a critical moment.

To strengthen the concentric circles of support requires an understanding of each circle's role and the connections among these circles. Those circles closest to the center can have the most powerful and enduring influence—the prisoner's individual sense of self, supported by family members and then by peers. Community groups and social service agencies can provide critical support and reinforce important social norms. The criminal justice agencies express the power of the state and the values of the justice system. As we strengthen these circles, we should establish a priority of strengthening those that are most likely to have long-term social value, and reserve for unavoidable uses those that involve the power of the state.

Promote Successful Reintegration

The final principle of effective reentry sets the context for all efforts aimed at improving returning prisoners' prospects for success. In addition to focusing on short-term programs that make transitions easier, proponents of successful reentry should also advocate for longer-term initiatives that reduce the divide between "us" and "them," between society and those who have broken society's laws. In addition to working to reduce the rearrest rates of returning prisoners, these advocates should also promote prisoners' reintegration into mainstream society. While mindful of the failures of the reentry process, attention should be paid to the successes.

Striking this new balance between short-term and long-term success, recidivism and reintegration, success and failure, is critical to the overall effort to reengineer the reentry process. It is quite natural for agency personnel and service providers to focus on the immediate needs of returning prisoners. Indeed, the third principle of effective reentry recommends explicit concentration on the moment of release. However, this short-term horizon will inevitably be populated with failures as prisoners struggle to handle this difficult transition. These failures will be evident in high rates of rearrest, relapse to drug addiction, homelessness, and unemployment. The clientele's needs will be more obvious than the clientele's successes.

Recognizing Milestones

To overcome this natural focus on failure, the reentry process should explicitly recognize the importance of successful reintegration. Completion of the milestones of the reentry journey should be commemorated. Drug treatment programs and reentry courts often have graduation ceremonies to mark program completion. Why not include similar ceremonies to mark parole completion? Why not celebrate the restoration of an ex-felon's right to vote by holding voter registration ceremonies? Why not celebrate that a woman recently released from prison has had her child returned from foster care? Why not end each period of supervision by applying to the court for the complete restoration of the ex-offender's rights?

As we discussed in chapter 10, these elevation ceremonies are important events in the ex-convict's life. The initial court hearing pronouncing guilt and imposing a sentence of imprisonment serves to diminish the convict's status. Reentry ceremonies, by contrast, formally recognize the restoration of full status. In addition, the prison experience for some individuals results in an added obligation of citizenship; namely, these ex-prisoners strive to work for criminal justice reform, to provide a helping hand to the next generation of returning prisoners, and to persuade young people to avoid involvement with crime. The voices and contributions of these "wounded leaders" are undervalued societal assets. Our reentry policies should particularly celebrate those former prisoners who want to help others to successfully reintegrate.

Successful ex-offenders should not be the only voices in the chorus, however. Corrections officials, law enforcement leaders, parole agents, elected officials, community leaders, and victim advocates should all promote successful reintegration. We should celebrate the accomplishments of former offenders, particularly those who have been imprisoned and then make good. They have overcome enormous odds and have put behind themselves a personal history marked with failure. We should, of course, pay attention to reentry's failures, but we do this already. To encourage more successes, and to reward those who have made it, we should also create a culture that rewards and values the successful reintegration of individuals who have broken the law.

A First Step

These five principles of effective reentry should provide guideposts for communities or agencies that are seeking to reengineer the reentry process. As Hammer and Champy (1993, 52) noted in their manifesto, reengineering "is about inventing new approaches to process structure that bear little or no resemblance to those of previous eras." Accordingly, it may be necessary to reject "the conventional wisdom and received assumptions of the past" (52). New partnerships and alliances will be necessary to complete this reengineering project. Resources will need to be reallocated. New performance measures will be required to gauge success. As the National Institute of Corrections (2002, 4–5) points out, this kind of reform represents a "sea change" and "is not for the short-winded or faint spirited." The first step, however, is to take apart our current reentry process, agree upon the principles that should guide the reconstruction effort, and then summon the fortitude to stay the course.

The reengineering initiative depicted in this chapter does not require any legislative changes. Even within our current sentencing structures, correctional practices, parole provisions, and supervision systems, a reengineering team could make significant progress toward a more effective reentry process. However, these efforts would be even more successful if the surrounding legislative framework also promoted the goal of social reintegration of former offenders. In the next and concluding chapter of the book, we turn our attention to a legislative reform agenda to create a jurisprudence of reintegration.

13

A Jurisprudence of Reintegration

For the past 30 years, sentencing policy in America has been in a state of turmoil. Before the 1970s, our country had demonstrated a strong consensus on sentencing policies and practices. Every state in the nation, the District of Columbia, and the federal system had adopted an indeterminate sentencing model as its statutory framework. Yet, beginning in the early 1970s, that consensus fell apart as the indeterminate sentencing model came under strong criticism from both liberal and conservative ends of the political spectrum.

Now, the national portrait of sentencing practices more closely resembles a patchwork quilt than a blanket. Some states have abolished parole as a release mechanism. Some have established sentencing commissions to fix permissible sentence lengths. Others have embraced "truth-in-sentencing" schemes, which require prisoners to complete a percentage of their prison sentence before release can be considered. Many states have enacted laws requiring that offenders convicted of designated crimes be sentenced to mandatory minimum prison terms. Even those states that have retained the classic indeterminate sentencing framework have witnessed significant changes in laws governing the imposition of prison sentences.

The landscape of punishment in America has also changed profoundly over the past 30 years. Incarceration rates have increased fourfold. Parole release rates have dropped dramatically. Parole supervision has increased significantly. Parole revocation practices now send hundreds of thousands of individuals back to prison each year. To some extent, these changes in punishment practices reflect the demise of the American consensus on indeterminate sentencing. For example, the decline in the nation's discretionary release rate partly reflects some states' decisions to abolish parole boards. But in a deeper sense, the changes in punishment practices and the end of the consensus on indeterminate sentencing can be traced to the same social forces. Both developments reflect a growing retributive sentiment, an increasing distrust of official discretion, and a fundamental shift in power as legislatures, not the judiciary, have become responsible for sentencing policy. In short, our sentencing jurisprudence has been held captive to a populist revolt. The indeterminate sentencing ideals of a generation ago were no match to the public's fear of crime, disdain for discretion, and distrust of judges.

Some reformers long for a return to the Golden Era when indeterminate sentencing reigned supreme. While some states have recently abandoned their mandatory minimum-sentencing statutes and others have modified their "truth-in-sentencing" formulas, it is hard to imagine a political scenario in which legislators would propose restoring parole boards, returning wide discretion to sentencing judges, and reaffirming prisoner rehabilitation. Other reformers propose that America should return to the level of incarceration we experienced in 1970. This also appears highly unlikely. Although prison populations are likely to decline because of low crime rates and tight state budgets, cutting the prison population to a quarter—or even half—of its current size would require profound changes in sentencing policy, particularly drug enforcement policy, that seem beyond the current realm of possibility.

This final chapter deals with these two realities as certainties—that we continue to live in a world of incongruous sentencing policies, and our incarceration rates remain high. I accept these realities not because I favor this state of affairs. On the contrary, I firmly believe that our sentencing philosophies are often unprincipled and that our excessive reliance on incarceration is profoundly misguided. Rather it is my hope that we can advance a new national focus on policies that support the successful reintegration of the millions of Americans who have spent time in our nation's prisons. In my view, this particular sentencing goal has been lost in the turmoil over punishment policy that our nation has experienced over the past 30 years. Furthermore, I believe it can be revived without a return to the Golden Era. The goal of promoting the reintegration of former prisoners (and other ex-offenders) can, in fact, be superimposed on all of the current sentencing frameworks. Finally, a focus on reintegration is imperative if we wish to reverse the social exclusion attributable to our high rate of incarceration. Large numbers of our fellow citizens have been damaged by their prison experiences. For each of them, the damage extends to networks of families, friends, and communities. Sadly, America is now at risk of creating a social class of damaged individuals. Our current realities of punishment, therefore, demand that we consider developing a jurisprudence of reintegration, a philosophy embedded in our sentencing statutes that seeks to minimize the social harm that results when we use prisons as our prevailing response to crime.

This chapter thus contains recommendations for Congress and our state legislatures. The legislative branch of government, not the judiciary, must create the architecture that supports a jurisprudence of reintegration. The previous chapter proposed five principles of effective reentry, recommendations that were addressed to corrections professionals, law enforcement, service providers, community leaders, and reform advocates as well as individuals held in our prisons. Using these principles to guide a reengineering exercise should significantly improve reentry outcomes in a jurisdiction. The greatest chance of success will come, however, when both sets of recommendations are implemented. Establishing a statutory framework of reintegration jurisprudence for the nation's sentencing policies would create an environment supportive of our reentry principles. Conversely, the outcomes of our proposed reengineering effort are more likely to be successful if our legislatures simultaneously enact sentencing reforms that reflect the reintegration objective.

Create Incentives for Reentry Preparation

The indeterminate sentencing model benefits society because it creates incentives for a prisoner to prepare for the return home. In theory, the chances that a parole board would grant an inmate early release depend, in part, on the extent to which that inmate has participated in vocational, educational, drug treatment, and other programs, as well as on the availability of housing, jobs, family support, and other connections to positive activities in the community. An inmate seeking early release would theoretically be more likely to participate in these programs and make these connections, thereby increasing the likelihood of early release and successful reentry.

Parole decisionmaking practices do not reflect this incentive model, however. Even in states that have retained parole boards, decisions on early release must also take into account other factors, such as the crime's severity, the victim's views, the prosecutor's position, and the need for prison space. These factors are not directly related to the likelihood of successful reentry. Some look backward to issues raised at the trial. Others, such as prison overcrowding, reflect administrative priorities. Rarely do they address preparation for the realities of reentry.

The challenge, then, to the legislative branch, is to construct a statutory framework that creates incentives for reentry preparation. Legislative reform would reflect a fairly straightforward proposition: an inmate could seek a reduction in the prison sentence by demonstrating (1) successful participation in prison activities that are demonstrably related to postprison success, and (2) verifiable connections to family, work, housing, and other support systems in the community. If those could be demonstrated to the appropriate authority (probably the corrections department), then the sentence reduction would be automatic.

The legislation proposed here borrows, of course, from the "good time" or "earned credit" statutes that exist in a number of states. Certainly a reentry preparation credit could be incorporated into those systems. However, it is important to keep two key principles in mind: prison activities *and* community preparation are required to gain the credit, and the credit is automatically awarded once the conditions have been met. Reentry preparation credit could not be awarded simply to reduce prison populations. Nor could the credit be denied for extraneous reasons, such as the objections of the prosecutor, the victim, or the media.

This piece of the reintegration architecture could be enacted in all states of the country, including those states that employ traditional indeterminate sentencing and those that have embraced determinate sentencing. In proposing this reform, legislators could make two arguments that would distinguish this early release mechanism from others. First, it places the burden on the inmate to make good use of prison time for self-improvement and to activate social networks in the community that will facilitate successful reentry. This requirement, in turn, demands accountability from individuals, families, and neighborhood organizations. Second, because the system is mandatory, the decision to grant early release cannot be contaminated by inappropriate considerations. This requirement appropriately addresses the public's distrust of discretion and preference for "truth" in our sentencing policies.

Of course, many details would require attention. The legislation would need to specify the period of first eligibility for reentry preparation credit and the exact criteria that would have to be met to receive the credit. Corrections departments would also be required to promulgate regulations governing the new program, including internal avenues for appealing adverse decisions. This legislation would also need to require annual reports on system implementation to promote transparency and public accountability. Legislatures should also authorize and fund a rigorous evaluation to test the underlying hypothesis—namely, that rewarding certain behavior with early release leads to improved reentry outcomes. But with well over a million people in prison, and 40 percent of them scheduled to be released each year, the opportunity to create effective incentives that promote the prisoners' active involvement in preparing for their return home is enormous.

Devolve Supervision to Local Jurisdictions

In the classic indeterminate sentencing model, a prisoner released before the end of his or her sentence still "owes" time to the state. The completion of this portion of the sentence is supervised by a state agency, the board of (or division of) parole. Yet, in reality, the level of government closest to the realities of life under community supervision is the local (city and county) government, not the state government. Crime prevention and control is a local, not a state, responsibility. The governmental functions that most directly affect successful reentry—health care, drug treatment, child welfare, public housing, job training—are functions typically carried out by local governments. In fact, other forms of community supervision—probation (both adult and juvenile) and pretrial release—that closely resemble parole supervision are usually managed by local agencies, not state agencies. With the high concentrations of prisoners returning to a small number of communities far removed from state capitols and other state executive branch functions, it seems illogical for a state agency to oversee reentry processes.

State legislatures could easily address this anomaly by devolving supervision functions and resources to local governments. The authorizing legislation could make local government responsible for supervising the remaining period of an ex-prisoner's state sentence; local government could then decide how best to carry out this new function. Most likely, an expanded probation department would handle parole supervision responsibilities. In chapter 3 we discussed the idea of assigning all community supervision functions to a newly created justice intermediary, tentatively called the community justice development corporation. This intermediary would oversee, on behalf of the courts, all community residents who have legal obligations to the criminal justice system.

The guiding principle for this legislative reform is the principle of devolution, defined in Webster's as the "transference (as of rights, powers, property, or responsibility) to another, especially the surrender of power to local authorities by a central government." Advocates for devolution frequently argue that government functions are best performed when they are carried out closest to the people being served. DiIulio and Nathan (1998) popularized the phrase "devolution" in their writing on the shift of Medicaid responsibilities from the federal government to the states. This movement exemplified "big devolution," in which one level of government, in this case the federal government, withdraws from a policy arena it has dominated and surrenders authority to a lower level of government. Justice devolution, particularly moving parole supervision to local governments, represents a particularly compelling argument for aligning government functions with the workings of families and neighborhoods. These institutions can play critical roles in reducing crime, facilitating reintegration, and promoting a sense of justice.

A state legislature could also expect efficiencies from this movement toward devolved supervision. It makes little sense, for example, for a parole officer (a state employee) to be supervising John Jones while a probation officer (a city or county employee) supervises his brother James. If the police have reason to believe John or James may have been involved in a crime, it is highly inefficient for them to consult with two different agencies. Similarly, it is simply wasteful for a state agency and a city agency to create two separate guides to community resources, meet separately with community groups to explain their functions, or negotiate separate data-sharing agreements with government agencies.

The most important benefit of a devolved supervision system is that it would support the reintegration of returning prisoners. The mayor or other local elected official would be held accountable for delivering reentry services and coordinating related activities. Community groups concerned about high-risk prisoners being released onto the streets without housing, medication, or family support could call upon local officials to use the supervision resources for those purposes. A combined supervision entity, whether public or private, would have a broader understanding of community risks and assets and could use that knowledge to assist prisoners in their return home.

Redefine the Purposes of Revocation

Legislative reform of our parole revocation system is critical to the success of a jurisprudence of reintegration. As we noted in chapter 3, the practice of parole revocation has created a system of "back-end" sentencing in America, a system that now sends hundreds of thousands of parolees back to prison each year. This form of sentencing should be subjected to the same analysis as has been applied to "front-end" sentencing, and this analysis should be conducted by the state legislature or by the state sentencing commission on behalf of the legislature. This review would determine, among other things, whether like cases are treated alike, racial minorities receive disparate treatment, and punishments are proportionate to offenses. Answers to these questions might well lead to legislation or sentencing guidelines that would create sentencing grids for parole violations, much like the grids used for front-end sentencing by judges in many jurisdictions.

Before conducting such an analysis, however, state legislatures must address threshold questions of sentencing jurisprudence: What is the purpose of this form of sentencing? Is there a distinction between the purposes of front-end and back-end sentencing? Is there a difference between revoking liberty for committing a new crime and revoking liberty for failing to abide by other conditions of supervision?

The answers to these questions can reveal a level of commitment to prisoner reintegration. If a state legislature (or sentencing commission) sees no difference between the purposes of front-end and back-end sentencing, then parole should be revoked whenever the parolee commits a serious infraction and the remainder of the sentence should be served in prison. Taken to this extreme, the release period represents an ex-prisoner's opportunity to comply with the rules of supervision, and failure to do so requires imposition of the full sentence. Alternatively, a state could view back-end sentencing primarily as a way to promote successful reintegration. The modulation of supervision conditions—from most lenient to most restrictive, including loss of liberty—would be geared to changes in parolee behavior. A parolee refusing to participate in required outpatient drug treatment, for example, might be required to receive residential treatment. A parolee found stalking a former intimate partner might be placed in a regime of electronic monitoring and orders of protection. In this highly flexible, behavior-focused system of community supervision, a new period of incarceration for violating a condition of supervision would be justified only if it was integral to the overall plan of increasing the individual's chances of prosocial behavior. As Tyler (1990) points out and the experience of drug courts confirms (Harrell et al. 1999), the severity of the sanction is less important in securing compliance with social norms than the consistency and predictability of a system of incentives and modest sanctions administered in a respectful manner. Thus, if postrelease supervision is designed to promote reintegration, then taking away liberty solely for punitive purposes is a waste of a valuable resource.

Some additional guidelines for parole revocation should also be established. Legislation reforming parole revocation policies should ensure that arrests for new crimes committed while under supervision are handled separately, with enhanced penalties. Statutory limits should be placed on the length of the new sentences that can be imposed for "technical" violations. Returning prisoners should be authorized to demonstrate, at regular intervals, that their reentry has been successful and they have avoided a return to crime and, therefore, should be released from supervision entirely. As with the reentry preparation credit proposed earlier, this requirement would create incentives for prosocial behavior and allow supervisory agencies to focus on individuals needing attention. Consistent with the devolution of supervision to the local level, this legislation should require that these sentences be served in local jails, not state prisons. Finally, as we have proposed throughout this book, the state should also create reentry courts (see below) to oversee the reintegration process so that, like drug courts, the imposition of these short stints in detention is part of a larger program using incentives and sanctions to promote prosocial behavior.

In short, new legislation should stipulate that, except for new crimes, the deprivation of liberty is warranted only if the person under supervision has consistently failed to engage in activities reasonably related to his or her reintegration. This approach requires, in turn, that legislatures create and fund a transparent, accountable regime of supports and sanctions that reward activities that foster reintegration and discourages those that do not. In these conditions, when a particular individual is failing to abide by the terms of his or her supervision, and all other sanctions have failed, the state is entitled to return him or her to jail (for a short period of time) to underscore the importance society attaches to the goal of reintegration.

Limit Collateral Sanctions

Chapter 4 described the new world of "invisible punishment" in which ex-offenders face a web of collateral sanctions that impede their efforts to reestablish themselves as productive citizens. In defining these sanctions, and distinguishing them from other collateral consequences of imprisonment, that chapter pointed out that legislation created them all. In some cases, these sanctions resulted from state legislation. In other cases, Congress passed laws that either denied federal benefits to categories of offenders or, through riders to appropriations, encouraged states to enact enhanced criminal penalties in order to receive federal funding. The net result is a network of statutory punishments over and above the traditional punishments of imprisonment, community supervision, fines, and penalties.

Consistent with a jurisprudence of reintegration, state and federal legislatures should take a fresh look at the laws creating these collateral sanctions. Some may be reasonable restrictions that are directly tied to the safety risk posed by the offender. For example, specifying that a child molester cannot work for a child care agency is a reasonable restriction, as is the suspension of the driver's license of someone convicted of drunk driving. Legislatures should require judges to make fact-based, individualized risk assessments as a predicate to imposing these sorts of collateral sanctions. However, the universe of invisible punishment is not currently defined by individualized risk assessments and the restrictions necessary to alleviate those risks. On the contrary, it seems this universe intends simply to continue imposing punishment well beyond the end of the criminal sentence, effectively hardening distinctions between "us" and "them." In short, because invisible punishment undermines reintegration, these sanctions should be significantly limited to those that are necessary to protect potential victims from future harm.

The full statutory articulation of a jurisprudence of reintegration would also provide methods for restoring rights lost by virtue of a felony conviction. As we discussed in chapter 10, the denial of voting rights to ex-felons, sometimes for life, is a profound expression of their diminished status. Similarly, the restricted legal avenues available for gaining certificates of relief from disabilities or certificates of good conduct allow ex-felons little opportunity to establish a new identity within society. By themselves, statutes providing ex-felons the right to vote and rights to legal relief will not significantly narrow the divide between "us" and "them." These statutes are, however, essential components of a jurisprudence of reintegration. The legal reinstatement of these rights would validate the restoration of social status, as we live in a society that values legal markers of identity. These reforms would also have practical value, giving avenues for political expression to a group of citizens who have been subjected to the most adverse actions of the state. Finally, by reducing arbitrary barriers to services, these reforms would provide tangible assistance for ex-offenders in search of employment, housing, and other supports necessary for successful reintegration.

Create Reentry Courts

Throughout this book, we have confronted different versions of the same question: "Who is responsible for prisoner reentry?" In a very real sense, the answer is, "Many people." Successful reentry depends, as we discussed earlier, on concentric circles of support—a strong and healthy returning prisoner; supportive family members, friends, and community institutions; effective social services; and a criminal justice system that balances its public safety mission with the mission to support prisoner reintegration. Yet, within that outer circle, we have choices with respect to the entity most directly responsible for prisoner reentry.

In 1999, I proposed that reentry courts oversee the reentry process. In this proposal, the functions currently performed by parole agents would be carried out under the auspices of the reentry court.[1] Reentry courts offer numerous advantages over our current system of reentry supervision. Judges command the public's confidence and, by contrast, our parole system is held in low public esteem. Judges carry out their business in open courtrooms, not closed offices, so the public, former prisoners, family members, and others can benefit from the open articulation of reasons for the government's decisions. Judges have been trained in the law, with experience in applying legal standards to facts and making tough decisions after weighing advocates' competing proposals. As is now true in some experimental reentry courts, the judges that oversee reentry could be the same as those who impose sentences, keeping track of a prisoner's progress on meeting the goals of a reentry plan, and possibly granting early release to a prisoner who has made significant progress. This alone would represent a profound departure from our assembly-line approach to justice in which sentencing judges are unaware of outcomes for offenders they send to prison.

However, the most compelling reason for moving toward a universal system of reentry courts is these courts' ability to promote reintegration. As proposed, reentry courts would build on the experiences of drug courts, which use incentives and sanctions to support the efforts of drug-addicted defendants in achieving long-term sobriety. Similarly, reentry courts would support returning prisoners' efforts to establish a prosocial identity, a step toward the goal of reintegration. Just as drug court judges celebrate every clean urine test, a significant passage of time since the last relapse, or the successful completion of a stage of treatment, a reentry court judge would celebrate a job offer, successful reunification with family, connection with transitional housing, or the completion of a community service project. On the other hand, the reentry court judge, like his drug court counterpart, would be able to order curfews, electronic monitoring, inpatient treatment, "stay-away" orders, or other increased levels of supervision when the situation demands it. In addition, as is true with drug courts, the reentry court would be authorized to order short periods of confinement in local jails when this sanction is necessary in order to make the prisoner understand the importance of the court-imposed conditions.

Finally, the reentry court should be empowered, by its authorizing legislation, to recognize progress on the road to reintegration by issuing appropriate judicial decrees. For example, the court should be able to shorten the supervision period following a period of compliance. The court should also be able to tailor or modify a collateral sanction—such as a driver's license suspension—when circumstances have changed. Similarly, the court should recognize when an ex-prisoner has completed a period of supervision by issuing that individual a certificate of relief from disabilities and, following a prescribed period of time with no arrests, a certificate of good conduct. Issuance of these legal instruments should become part of daily reentry court dockets.

If enacted by our nation's legislatures, these five proposals would constitute the architecture of a jurisprudence of reintegration. Certainly other ideas could find a comfortable place within this structure, but these five recommendations would imply a profound shift in our thinking about the challenges of prisoner reentry. Even without changes in basic sentencing reforms, enactment of these proposed reforms would demonstrate that, as a nation, we recognize the realities of prisoner reentry and the goal of reintegration. This architecture would also provide structural support for the reengineering activities proposed in the preceding chapter so that organizational reforms would be aligned with the operating principles of the jurisdiction's sentencing system. Finally, the enactment of these reforms would signal to the thousands of program administrators and government officials who work on issues involving prisoner reentry that their elected officials have embraced sentencing policies that are supportive of, not inconsistent with, their aspirations. Pursuing reintegration does not mean we have to resolve all of our nation's difficult debates over sentencing policy. Pursuit of this goal cannot simply be left to well-intentioned program administrators, innovative corrections directors, articulate community advocates, or dedicated policy analysts. This is a social challenge that requires the voice of the people, as expressed through their elected officials.

NOTE

1. A justice intermediary, proposed elsewhere in this book, could also perform the supervision functions of the parole agency.

Afterword

We have ample reason to be pessimistic about the state of justice in America. We currently imprison record numbers of our fellow citizens. We have constructed systems of supervision and extended sanctions that severely inhibit former prisoners' ability to regain their place at society's table. We have created a society with large numbers of former prisoners and other ex-offenders who live their lives in diminished status. Our experiment in mass incarceration has had a significant impact on the children, families, and communities of those we send to prison. We have weakened our democracy by denying millions of citizens the right to vote, undermined our pursuit of racial justice by incarceration policies with racially disparate outcomes, and created a society in which the stigma of a criminal conviction consigns large numbers of its members to a life at the margin.

This book has documented some of the consequences of this profound shift in criminal justice policy. In response to these new realities, we might conclude that America should reverse its course and dramatically reduce our reliance on prison as a response to crime. This proposal faces an enormous uphill battle in the political arena, however. Even if a political consensus were in place, achieving this goal would take a long time. This book has proposed that we simultaneously embrace a second goal—to reduce the harms associated with imprisonment, beginning with the reorientation of our philosophy to promote the successful reentry and reintegration of the hundreds of thousands of Americans leaving prison each year. This goal can be achieved immediately, without rolling back decades of sentencing reforms and dismantling the far-flung network of prisons in America. By creatively reengineering the reentry process and enacting laws promoting reintegration, we could set a different course for our justice system.

Over the past five years, the nation has witnessed a heightened interest in prisoner reentry. Beginning with Attorney General Janet Reno's 1999 call for the creation of reentry courts and reentry partnerships, and including President George W. Bush's 2004 announcement of a $300 million four-year reentry initiative, this focus on prisoner reentry has drawn support from the nation's highest public officials. Congress is now considering the Second Chance Act, an omnibus bill with bipartisan support that would represent a significant shift toward a reintegration philosophy. Within the federal government, the Office of Justice Programs has led an unprecedented consortium of federal reentry agencies implementing the first federal reentry funding program, which awarded money to each of the 50 states to develop new reentry programs. The National Institute of Corrections (NIC) has launched the Transition from Prison to Community Initiative, in which 9 states are reexamining the operating policies of various state agencies, including corrections, health, housing, employment, and family services, to support successful transitions from prison. The work of the Reentry Policy Council, established by the Council on State Governments (CSG), and the Reentry Policy Academy, created by the National Governors Association (NGA), has prompted state officials to undertake the hard work of designing new state policies to promote successful reentry. At the local level, some mayors in large cities have realized that the well-being of their communities is adversely affected by failed prisoner reentry, and have rallied city agencies and local stakeholders to improve those outcomes. Community groups, churches, ex-offender organizations, business leaders, journalists, and others have added their voices to the call for national attention to these issues.

These activities in the policy arena have been supported by a number of America's most respected foundations, which see the intersection between this criminal justice policy domain and their funding priorities in other domains, such as health, workforce development, racial justice, and family welfare. The academic community has played a critical role, conducting research on critical questions and releasing timely reports that fill some of the many gaps in our knowledge about how the era of mass incarceration has affected life in America.

As we come to a close in our discussion, it is impossible to predict whether the remarkable new national conversation on prisoner reentry is sufficiently broad and deep to mature into an agenda for systemic and statutory reforms such as those proposed in the two final chapters of this book. However, the outward signs are encouraging. The interest in the topic is broadly bipartisan, bringing together, as new allies, institutions from both ends of the political spectrum. The federal funding, combined with the work of the CSG, NGA, and NIC, has ensured that every state is undertaking a critical examination of its reentry policies. The leadership of corrections professionals has made "reentry" a topic of sustained importance, not a program of the moment. The high level of interest expressed by professionals in related sectors—health care, child development, housing, employment, community building, faith institutions—improves the likelihood that these issues will not be viewed simply as criminal justice issues. Finally, the growing awareness within communities, particularly communities of color, of the consequences of the four-fold increase in incarceration rates on their present realities and future prospects ensures that the voices of those most affected will lend urgency to the nation's deliberations.

The risk at this juncture is the allure of success. Implementing a new program, completing a new interagency memorandum of understanding, and lifting a barrier to ex-offender employment should all be celebrated, but they are merely drops in the bucket. In this era of intellectual ferment, overdue awareness, political support, and public understanding, we have the opportunity to understand the magnitude of the phenomenon, develop new ideas, and translate these ideas from concept to reality. We must not confuse superficial reforms with profound changes. Unless this generation squarely faces the challenges of reentry and pursues an agenda of deep and lasting reforms, the goal of prisoner reintegration will escape our grasp.

References

ABA. See American Bar Association.

Abadinsky, Howard. 1997. *Probation and Parole: Theory and Practice*. 6th ed. Upper Saddle River, NJ: Prentice Hall.

Adams, Wendy L., Kristen Lawton Barry, and Michael F. Fleming. 1996. "Screening for Problem Drinking in Older Primary Care Patients." *Journal of the American Medical Association* 276(24): 1964–67.

Adamson, Christopher R. 1983. "Punishment After Slavery: Southern State Penal Systems, 1865–1890." *Social Problems* 30(5): 553–69.

Allen, Scott. 2003. "Developing a Systematic Approach to Hepatitis C for Correctional Systems: Controversies and Emerging Consensus." *HEPP Report: Infectious Diseases in Corrections* 6(4): 1–4. Providence, RI: Brown Medical School, Office of Continuing Medical Education.

Amato, Paul R., and Fernando Rivera. 1999. "Paternal Involvement and Children's Behavior Problems." *Journal of Marriage and the Family* 61(2): 375–84.

American Bar Association. 1981. *ABA Standards for Criminal Justice*. Chicago: American Bar Association.

———. 1993. *ABA Standards for Criminal Justice*. Chicago: American Bar Association.

———. 1997. *ABA Standards for Criminal Justice*. 3rd ed. Chicago: American Bar Association.

———. 2004. *ABA Standards for Criminal Justice: Collateral Sanctions and Discretionary Disqualification of Convicted Persons*. 3rd ed. Chicago: American Bar Association.

American Correctional Association. 1977. *Standards for Adult Correctional Institutions*. 1st ed. Lanham, MD: American Correctional Association.

———. 1981. *Standards for Adult Correctional Institutions*. 2nd ed. Lanham, MD: American Correctional Association.

———. 1983. *The American Prison: From the Beginning . . .: A Pictorial History*. College Park, MD: American Correctional Association.

American Friends Service Committee. 1971. *Struggle for Justice: A Report on Crime and Punishment in America.* New York: Hill & Wang.

Anno, B. Jaye. 2002. "Prison Health Services: An Overview." Paper presented at the Urban Institute Reentry Roundtable: *The Public Health Dimensions of Prisoner Reentry: Addressing the Health Needs and Risks of Returning Prisoners and Their Families,* Los Angeles, December 11–13.

Aos, Steve, Polly Phipps, Robert Barnoski, and Roxanne Lieb. 2001. *The Comparative Costs and Benefits of Programs to Reduce Crime.* Olympia: Washington State Institute for Public Policy.

Associated Press. 2002. "Despite High Court Ruling, Three of Four Oakland Tenants Stay." April 5.

———. 2003a. "Homeless, Jobless Sex Offender Decides to Revoke Parole, Return to Prison." May 14.

———. 2003b. "Suit Filed to Relocate Sex Offender." May 1.

Atkinson, Robert D., and Knut A. Rostad. 2003. "Can Inmates Become an Integral Part of the U.S. Workforce?" Paper prepared for the Urban Institute Reentry Roundtable: *Employment Dimensions of Reentry: Understanding the Nexus between Reentry and Work,* New York, May 19–20.

Austin, James, and John Irwin. 2001. *It's About Time: America's Imprisonment Binge.* 3rd ed. Belmont, CA: Wadsworth.

Barnes, Harry Elmer, and Negley K. Teeters. 1959. *New Horizons in Criminology.* 3rd ed. Englewood Cliffs, NJ: Prentice Hall.

Barnhill, S., and Paula Dressel. 1991. "Three Generations at Economic Risk When Daughters Go to Prison." Paper presented to the Association of Black Sociologists, Cincinnati, August.

Bateson, Charles. 1974. *The Convict Ships, 1787–1868.* 2nd ed. Sydney, Australia: A. H. and A. W. Reed.

Bauer, Lynn. 2004. "Justice Expenditure and Employment Extracts, 2001." Bureau of Justice Statistics Bulletin. NCJ 190641. Washington, DC: U.S. Department of Justice, Bureau of Justice Statistics.

Bauer, Lynn, and Steven D. Owens. 2004. "Justice Expenditure and Employment in the United States, 2001." Bureau of Justice Statistics Bulletin. NCJ 202792. Washington, DC: U.S. Department of Justice, Bureau of Justice Statistics.

Beaumont, Gustave de, and Alexis de Tocqueville. 1964. *On the Penitentiary System in the United States and Its Application to France 1833,* edited by H. R. Lanz and translated by F. Lieber. Carbondale: Southern Illinois University Press.

Beck, Allen J. 2000. "Prisoners in 1999." Bureau of Justice Statistics Bulletin. NCJ 183476. Washington, DC: U.S. Department of Justice, Bureau of Justice Statistics.

Beck, Allen J., and Paige M. Harrison. 2001. "Prisoners in 2000." Bureau of Justice Statistics Bulletin. NCJ 188207. Washington, DC: U.S. Department of Justice, Bureau of Justice Statistics.

Beck, Allen J., and Laura M. Maruschak. 2001. "Mental Health Treatment in State Prisons, 2000." NCJ 188215. Washington, DC: U.S. Department of Justice, Bureau of Justice Statistics.

———. 2004. "Hepatitis Testing and Treatment in State Prisons." NCJ 199173. Washington, DC: U.S. Department of Justice, Bureau of Justice Statistics.

Beck, Allen J., and Christopher Mumola. 1999. "Prisoners in 1998." Bureau of Justice Statistics Bulletin. NCJ 175687. Washington, DC: U.S. Department of Justice, Bureau of Justice Statistics.

Beck, Allen J., and Bernard E. Shipley. 1989. "Recidivism of Prisoners Released in 1983." NCJ 116261. Washington, DC: U.S. Department of Justice, Bureau of Justice Statistics.

Becker, Howard Saul. 1963. *Outsiders: Studies in the Sociology of Deviance.* New York: Free Press.

Belenko, Steven. 1998. *Behind Bars: Substance Abuse and America's Prison Population.* New York: National Center on Addiction and Substance Abuse at Columbia University.

Berk, Richard A., Kenneth J. Lenihan, and Peter H. Rossi. 1980. "Crime and Poverty: Some Experimental Evidence From Ex-Offenders." *American Sociological Review* 45(5): 766–86.

Bernstein, Jared, and Ellen Houston. 2000. *Crime and Work: What We Can Learn from the Low-Wage Labor Market.* Washington, DC: Economic Policy Institute.

BJS. See Bureau of Justice Statistics.

Bloom, Barbara, and David Steinhart. 1993. *Why Punish the Children? A Reappraisal of the Children of Incarcerated Mothers in America.* San Francisco: National Council on Crime and Delinquency.

Blumstein, Alfred, and Allen J. Beck. 1999. "Population Growth in the U.S. Prisons, 1980–1996." In *Prisons,* vol. 26 of *Crime and Justice,* edited by Michael Tonry and Joan Petersilia (17–61). Chicago: University of Chicago Press.

Blumstein, Alfred, and Jacqueline Cohen. 1973. "A Theory of the Stability of Punishment." *Journal of Criminal Law and Criminology* 64(2): 198–207.

———. 1987. "Characterizing Criminal Careers." *Science* 237(4818): 985–91.

Blumstein, Alfred, and Joel Wallman, eds. 2000. *The Crime Drop in America.* New York: Cambridge University Press.

Blumstein, Alfred, Jacqueline Cohen, J. Roth, and Christy Visher. 1986. *Criminal Careers and "Career Criminals."* Washington, DC: National Academy Press.

Bonczar, Thomas P., and Allen J. Beck. 2003. "Lifetime Likelihood of Going to State or Federal Prison." NCJ 160092. Washington, DC: U.S. Department of Justice, Bureau of Justice Statistics.

Boober, Becky H. 2004. *Maine Reentry Network Serious and Violent Offenders Reentry Initiative: December 2003 Six-Month Report.* Augusta: Maine Department of Corrections.

Bottomley, A. Keith. 1990. "Parole in Transition: A Comparative Study of Origins, Developments, and Prospects for the 1990s." In *Crime and Justice: An Annual Review of Research,* vol. 12, edited by Michael Tonry and Norval Morris (319–74). Chicago: University of Chicago Press.

Bourdieu, Pierre. 1986. "The Forms of Capital." In *Handbook of Theory and Research for the Sociology of Education,* edited by John G. Richardson (241–58). New York: Greenwood Press.

Bowly, Devereux, Jr. 1978. *The Poorhouse: Subsidized Housing in Chicago, 1895–1976.* Carbondale and Edwardsville: Southern Illinois University Press.

Bradley, Katharine H., Noel C. Richardson, R. B. Michael Oliver, and Elspeth M. Slayter. 2001. "No Place Like Home: Housing and the Ex-Prisoner." Policy brief. Boston: Community Resources for Justice.

Braman, Donald. 2002. "Families and Incarceration." In *Invisible Punishment: The Collateral Consequences of Mass Imprisonment,* edited by Marc Mauer and Meda Chesney-Lind (117–35). New York: The New Press.

———. 2003. "Families and Incarceration." NCJ 202981. Washington, DC: U.S. Department of Justice. http://www.ncjrs.org/pdffiles1/nij/grants/202981.pdf. (Accessed December 1, 2004.)

———. 2004. *Doing Time on the Outside: Incarceration and Family Life in Urban America.* Ann Arbor: University of Michigan Press.

Breed, Allen G. 1999. "Couple Test Faith, Rile Neighbors by Taking Sex Offender into Home." Associated Press, September 2.

Bureau of Economic Analysis. 2005. "Gross Domestic Product: Fourth Quarter 2004 (Advance)." January 28 press release. Washington, DC: U.S. Department of Commerce.

Bureau of Justice Statistics. 1979. "Census of State Adult Correctional Facilities, 1979." 2nd ICPSR ed. [computer file]. Conducted by U.S. Department of Commerce, Bureau of the Census. Ann Arbor, MI: Inter-university Consortium for Political and Social Research [producer and distributor], 1997.

———. 1984. "Census of State Adult Correctional Facilities, 1984." ICPSR ed. [computer file]. Conducted by U.S. Department of Commerce, Bureau of the Census. Ann Arbor, MI: Inter-university Consortium for Political and Social Research [producer and distributor], 1997.

———. 1993. *Use and Management of Criminal History Record Information: A Comprehensive Report.* Prepared by SEARCH. Washington, DC: U.S. Department of Justice.

———. 1999. "National Corrections Reporting Program, 1999." ICPSR ed. [computer file]. Conducted by United States Department of Justice, Bureau of Justice Statistics. Ann Arbor, MI: Inter-university Consortium for Political and Social Research [producer and distributor], 2002.

———. 2000a. *Correctional Populations in the United States, 1997.* NCJ 177613. Washington, DC: U.S. Department of Justice.

———. 2000b. "National Corrections Reporting Program, 2000." ICPSR ed. [computer file]. Conducted by U.S. Department of Justice, Bureau of Justice Statistics. Ann Arbor, MI: Inter-university Consortium for Political and Social Research [producer and distributor], 2003.

———. 2002. "Summary of State Sex Offender Registries, 2001." NCJ 192265. Washington, DC: U.S. Department of Justice.

Bureau of Labor Statistics. 2001. "How the Government Measures Unemployment." Update of report 864, published March 1994. Washington, DC: U.S. Department of Labor.

Burnett, David. 2003. "Targeted Testing for Hepatitis C in Wisconsin DOC." Proceedings of the Management of Hepatitis C in Prisons Conference, San Antonio, TX, January 25–26.

Burnett, Ross. 1992. *The Dynamics of Recidivism: Summary Report.* Oxford, UK: University of Oxford, Centre for Criminological Research. Quoted in Maruna (2001, 136).

Bursik, Ronald J., Jr., and Harold G. Grasmick. 1993. *Neighborhoods and Crime: The Dimensions of Effective Community Control.* New York: Lexington Books.

Burt, Martha R., and Barbara E. Cohen. 1989. *America's Homeless: Numbers, Characteristics, and Programs That Serve Them.* Washington, DC: Urban Institute Press.

Burt, Martha R., Laudan Y. Aron, Toby Douglas, Jesse Valente, Edgar Lee, and Britta Iwen. 1999. *Homelessness: Programs and the People They Serve: Findings of the National Survey of Homeless Assistance Providers and Clients.* Washington, DC: The Urban Institute.

Burton, Velmer S., Jr., Francis T. Cullen, and Lawrence F. Travis III. 1987. "The Collateral Consequences of a Felony Conviction." *Federal Probation* 51(September): 52–60.

Bush, George W. 2004. "State of the Union Address." http://www.whitehouse.gov/news/releases/2004/01/20040120-7.html.

Bushway, Shawn, and Peter Reuter. 1997. "Labor Markets and Crime Risk Factors." In *Preventing Crime: What Works, What Doesn't, What's Promising.* Washington, DC: U.S. Department of Justice, National Institute of Justice.

———. 2001. "Labor Markets and Crime." In *Crime: Public Policies for Crime Control*, 3rd ed., edited by James Q. Wilson and Joan Petersilia (191–224). Oakland, CA: Institute for Contemporary Studies Press.

———. 2002. "Labor Markets and Crime Risk Factors." In *Evidence-Based Crime Prevention*, edited by Lawrence Sherman, David Farrington, Brandon Welsh, and Doris MacKenzie. New York: Rutledge Press.

Butterfield, Fox. 2001. "Inmate Rehabilitation Returns as Prison Goal." *New York Times*, May 20, sec. 1.

———. 2003a. "Infections in Newly Released Inmates Are Rising." *New York Times*, January 28, United States Section.

———. 2003b. "With Cash Tight, States Reassess Long Jail Terms." *New York Times*, November 10.

Cadora, Eric, and Charles Swartz. 1999. "The Community Justice Project at the Center for Alternative Sentencing and Employment Services (CASES)." For more information see http://www.communityjusticeproject.org.

Cadora, Eric, with Charles Swartz and Mannix Gordon. 2003. "Criminal Justice and Health and Human Services: An Exploration of Overlapping Needs, Resources, and Interests in Brooklyn Neighborhoods." In *Prisoners Once Removed*, edited by Jeremy Travis and Michelle Waul (285–311). Washington, DC: Urban Institute Press.

Cahalan, Margaret W., and Lee Anne Parsons. 1986. *Historical Corrections Statistics in the United States, 1850–1984.* Washington, DC: U.S. Department of Justice, Bureau of Justice Statistics.

California Department of Corrections. 1997. "Preventing Parole Failure Program: An Evaluation." Sacramento: California Department of Corrections.

Camp, Camille Graham, and George M. Camp. 2002. *The Corrections Yearbook 2001: Adult Systems.* Middletown, CT: Criminal Justice Institute, Inc.

Case, Anne C., and Lawrence F. Katz. 1991. "The Company You Keep: The Effects of Family and Neighborhood on Disadvantaged Youths." NBER Working Paper 3705. Cambridge, MA: National Bureau of Economic Research.

Cavanagh, Shannon E., and Adele V. Harrell. 1998. *The District of Columbia Drug Court 1997–1998.* Washington, DC: The Urban Institute.

Center for Sex Offender Management. 1999. *Sex Offender Registration: Policy Overview and Comprehensive Practices.* Silver Spring, MD: Center for Sex Offender Management.

———. 2001. "Community Notification and Education." Resource document. Silver Spring, MD: Center for Sex Offender Management.

Centers for Disease Control and Prevention. 1998a. "HIV Prevention through Early Detection and Treatment of Other Sexually Transmitted Diseases—United States." *Morbidity and Mortality Weekly Report* 47 (RR-12).

———. 1998b. "New Study Helps Explain How STDs May Increase Risk of HIV Transmission: STDs Damage Cells that Normally Protect against Infection." July 2 news release.

———. 2001. *HIV/AIDS Surveillance Report* 13(2).

Chin, Gabriel J., and Richard W. Holmes Jr. 2002. "Effective Assistance of Counsel and the Consequences of Guilty Pleas." *Cornell Law Review* 87(3): 697–742.

Citizens' Inquiry on Parole and Criminal Justice. 1975. *Report on New York Parole*. New York: Citizens' Inquiry on Parole and Criminal Justice.

Clear, Todd R. 2004. "Concentrated Incarceration and Social Justice: Hypotheses for a Research Agenda." Presentation to the Center on Social Justice, University of California, Berkeley.

Clear, Todd R., and Dina R. Rose. 1999. "When Neighbors Go to Jail: Impact on Attitudes about Formal and Informal Social Control." Research Preview. Washington, DC: U.S. Department of Justice, National Institute of Justice.

Clear, Todd R., Dina R. Rose, and J. Ryder. 2001. "Incarceration and the Community: The Problem of Removing and Returning Offenders." *Crime and Delinquency* 47(3): 335–51.

Clear, Todd R., Dina R. Rose, Elin Waring, and Kristen Scully. 2003. "Coercive Mobility and Crime: A Preliminary Examination of Concentrated Incarceration and Social Disorganization." *Justice Quarterly* 20(1): 33–64.

Coleman, James S. 1990. *Foundations of Social Theory*. Cambridge, MA: Harvard University Press.

Colledge, Maureen, Patrick Collier, and Sam Brand. 1999. "Programmes for Offenders: Guidance for Evaluators." *Crime Reduction Programme and Constructive Regimes in Prisons*. London, UK: Research Development and Statistics Directorate, Home Office.

Corporation for Supportive Housing. 2002. "Compact to End Long-Term Homelessness." http://www.csh.org/index.cfm?fuseaction=Page.viewPage&pageId=40. (Accessed February 16, 2004.)

Council of State Governments. 2005. *Report of the Re-entry Policy Council: Charting the Safe and Successful Return of Prisoners to the Community*. Lexington, KY: Council of State Governments.

CSOM. See Center for Sex Offender Management.

Culhane, Dennis P., Stephen Metraux, and Trevor Hadley. 2002. "Public Service Reductions Associated with the Placement of Homeless People with Severe Mental Illness in Supportive Housing." *Housing Policy Debate* 13(1): 107–63.

Cullen, Francis T., and Paul Gendreau. 2000. "Assessing Correctional Rehabilitation: Policy, Practice, and Prospects." In *Criminal Justice 2000: Policies, Processes, and Decisions of the Criminal Justice System*, vol. 3, edited by J. Horney (109–76). Washington, DC: U.S. Department of Justice.

Curry, Dan. 2001. "Education Dept. May Relax Provision Denying Student Aid to Those with Drug Convictions." *Chronicle of Higher Education*, August 14.

DeFao, Janine. 2003. "Jerry Brown's About-Face on Criminal Sentencing." *San Francisco Chronicle*, February 18, A-1.

Demeo, Marisa J., and Steven A. Ochoa. 2003. *Diminished Voting Power in the Latino Community: The Impact of Felony Disenfranchisement Laws in Ten Targeted States.* Los Angeles: MALDEF. http://www.maldef.org/pdf/LatinoVotingReport.pdf. (Accessed December 1, 2004.)

Demleitner, Nora V. 1999. "Preventing Internal Exile: The Need for Restrictions on Collateral Sentencing Consequences." *Stanford Law and Policy Review* 11(1): 153–63.

DiIulio, John J., Jr., and Richard Nathan. 1998. "Introduction." In *Medicaid and Devolution: A View from the States,* edited by Frank J. Thompson and John J. DiIulio Jr. (1–13). Washington, DC: Brookings Institution Press.

Ditton, Paula M. 1999. "Mental Health and Treatment of Inmates and Probationers." NCJ 174463. Washington, DC: U.S. Department of Justice, Bureau of Justice Statistics.

Drucker, Ernest. 2002. "Population Impact of Mass Incarceration Under New York's Rockefeller Drug Laws: An Analysis of Years of Life Lost." *Journal of Urban Health* 79(3): 434–35.

Durkheim, Emile. [1893] 1964. *The Division of Labor in Society,* translated by George Simpson. New York: Free Press.

Edin, Kathryn. 2000. "Few Good Men: Why Poor Mothers Don't Marry or Remarry." *The American Prospect* 11(4): 26–31.

Edin, Kathryn, and Laura Lein. 1997. *Making Ends Meet: How Single Mothers Survive Welfare and Low-Wage Work.* New York: Russell Sage Foundation.

English, J. 2003. "LAPD Sweeps." Los Angeles: City News Service Inc., April 14.

Erikson, Kai. 1962. "Notes on the Sociology of Deviance." *Social Problems* 9: 307–14.

eTc Campaign. 2003. "The Campaign to Promote Equitable Telephone Charges." http://www.curenational.org/~etc/. (Accessed April 5, 2004.)

Executive Leadership Institute. 2002. "Deschutes County Community Youth Investment Project." Portland, OR: Portland State University. http://www.eli.pdx. edu/legacy/deschutes_youth9-01.pdf. (Accessed June 2, 2004.)

Executive Office of the President. 2003. *Economic Report of the President.* Washington, DC: U.S. Government Printing Office.

Farrington, David P. 1986. "Age and Crime." In *Crime and Justice: An Annual Review of Research,* vol. 7, edited by Michael Tonry and Norval Morris (189–250). Chicago: University of Chicago Press.

Fellner, Jamie, and Marc Mauer. 1998. *Losing the Vote: The Impact of Felony Disenfranchisement Laws in the United States.* Washington, DC: Human Rights Watch and The Sentencing Project.

Finn, Peter. 1998. *Successful Job Placement for Ex-Offenders: The Center for Employment Opportunities.* Washington, DC: U.S. Department of Justice, National Institute of Justice.

Flanigan, T. P., J. Y. Kim, S. Zierler, J. Rich, K. Vigilante, and D. Bury-Maynard. 1996. "A Prison Release Program for HIV-Positive Women: Linking Them to Health Services and Community Follow-Up." *American Journal of Public Health* 86(6): 886–87.

Florida House of Representatives, Justice Council, Committee on Corrections. 1998. *Maintaining Family Contact When a Family Member Goes to Prison: An Examination of State Policies on Mail, Visiting, and Telephone Access.* http://www.fcc.state.fl.us/fcc/reports/family.pdf. (Accessed February 8, 2005.)

Frankel, Marvin E. 1973. *Criminal Sentences: Law Without Order.* New York: Hill & Wang.

Freeman, Richard. 1999. "The Economics of Crime." In *Handbook of Labor Economics,* edited by Orley C. Ashenfelter and David Card, vol. 3C (chapter 52). New York: Elsevier Science.

Friedman, Donna Haig, Michelle Hayes, John McGah, and Anthony Roman. 1997. "A Snapshot of Individuals and Families Accessing Boston's Emergency Homeless Shelters, 1997." Boston: The John W. McCormack Institute of Public Affairs, University of Massachusetts.

Friedman, Lawrence M. 1993. *Crime and Punishment in American History.* New York: Basic Books.

Furman, Edna. 1983. "Studies in Childhood Bereavement." *Canadian Journal of Psychiatry* 28(4): 241–47.

Furstenberg, Frank F. 1993. "How Families Manage Risk and Opportunity in Dangerous Neighborhoods." In *Sociology and the Public Agenda,* edited by William J. Wilson (231–58). Newbury Park, CA: Sage Publications.

———. 1995. "Fathering in the Inner-City: Paternal Participation and Public Policy." In *Research on Men and Masculinities Series 7,* edited by M. S. Kimmel and M. Marsiglio (119–47). Thousand Oaks, CA: Sage Publications.

Gabel, Katherine, and Denise Johnston, eds. 1995. *Children of Incarcerated Parents.* New York: Lexington Books.

GAO. See U.S. General Accounting Office.

Garfinkel, Harold. 1956. "Conditions of Successful Degradation Ceremonies." *American Journal of Sociology* 61(5): 420–24.

Garrison, Jessica, and Daniel Hernandez. 2002. "Seven More Shot in L.A." *Los Angeles Times,* November 20. http://www.latimes.com/. (Accessed January 5, 2003.)

Garvey, Stephen P. 1998. "Freeing Prisoners' Labor." *Stanford Law Review* 50(2): 339–98.

Gates, Gerald G., Timothy J. Flanagan, Laurence Motiuk, and Lynn Stewart. 1999. "Adult Correctional Treatment." In *Prisons,* vol. 26 of *Crime and Justice* edited by Michael Tonry and Joan Petersilia (361–426). Chicago: University of Chicago Press.

Gendreau, Paul, and Tracy Little. 1993. "A Meta-Analysis of the Effectiveness of Sanctions on Offender Recidivism." Unpublished manuscript, University of New Brunswick, Saint John, British Columbia, Canada. Quoted in Petersilia (1998, 6).

Genty, Philip M. 2001. "Incarcerated Parents and the Adoption and Safe Families Act: A Challenge for Correctional Service Providers." *International Community Corrections Association Journal,* 44–47.

Gerber, Jurg, and Eric J. Fritsch. 1994. "The Effects of Academic and Vocational Program Participation on Inmate Misconduct and Reincarceration." In *Prison Education Research Project: Final Report.* Huntsville, TX: Sam Houston State University.

Giardini, Giovanni Ippolito. 1959. *The Parole Process.* Springfield, IL: Thomas.

Gifford, Sidra Lee. 2002. "Justice Expenditure and Employment in the United States, 1999." Bureau of Justice Statistics Bulletin. NCJ 191746. Washington, DC: U.S. Department of Justice, Bureau of Justice Statistics.

Glaser, Jordan B., and Robert B. Greifinger. 1993. "Correctional Health Care: A Public Health Opportunity." *Annals of Internal Medicine* 118(2): 139–45.

Goffin Hanna, Marcia. 1978. *A Review of Temporary Release Programs in New York State.* New York: New York Commission of Correction.

Gonzalez, Juan. 1997. "A Revealing 'Capeman.' " *New York Daily News,* October 23.

Gottfredson, Don M., Leslie T. Wilkins, and Peter B. Hoffman. 1978. *Guidelines for Parole and Sentencing.* Lexington, MA: Heath/Lexington.

Greenfeld, Lawrence A., Michael R. Rand, Diane Craven, Patsy A. Klaus, Craig A. Perkins, Cheryl Ringel, Greg Warchol, Cathy Maston, and James Alan Fox. 1998. "Violence by Intimates: Analysis of Data on Crimes by Current or Former Spouses, Boyfriends, and Girlfriends." NCJ 167237. U.S. Department of Justice, Bureau of Justice Statistics.

Grinstead, Olga A., Barry Zack, Bonnie Faigeles, Nina Grossman, and Leroy Blea. 1999. "Reducing Postrelease HIV Risk among Male Prison Inmates: A Peer-Led Intervention." *Criminal Justice and Behavior* 26(4): 453–65.

Hagan, John. 1993. "The Social Embeddedness of Crime and Unemployment." *Criminology* 31(4): 465–92.

Hagan, John, and Juleigh Petty Coleman. 2001. "Returning Captives of the American War on Drugs: Issues of Community and Family Reentry." *Crime and Delinquency* 47(3): 352–67.

Hagan, John, and Ronit Dinovitzer. 1999. "Collateral Consequences of Imprisonment for Children, Communities, and Prisoners." In *Prisons,* vol. 26 of *Crime and Justice,* edited by Michael Tonry and Joan Petersilia (121–62). Chicago: University of Chicago Press.

Hairston, Creasie Finney. 1995. "Fathers in Prison." In *Children of Incarcerated Parents,* edited by Katherine Gabel and Denise Johnston (31–40). New York: Lexington Books.

———. 1998. "The Forgotten Parent: Understanding the Forces that Influence Incarcerated Fathers' Relationships with Their Children." *Child Welfare: Journal of Policy, Practice and Program* 77(5): 617–39.

———. 1999. "Kinship Care When Parents Are Incarcerated." In *Kinship Care Research: Improving Practice through Research,* edited by James P. Gleeson and Creasie Finney Hairston (189–212). Washington, DC: Child Welfare League of America.

Hairston, Creasie Finney, and James Rollin. 2003. "Social Capital and Family Connections." *Women, Girls & Criminal Justice* 4(5): 67–69.

Hammer, Michael, and James Champy. 1993. *Reengineering the Corporation: A Manifesto for Business Revolution.* New York: HarperCollins.

Hammett, Theodore M., Mary Patricia Harmon, and Laura M. Maruschak. 1999. *1996–1997 Update: HIV/AIDS, STDs, and TB in Correctional Facilities.* NCJ 176344. Washington, DC: U.S. Department of Justice, National Institute of Justice.

Hammett, Theodore M., Cheryl Roberts, and Sofia Kennedy. 2001. "Health-Related Issues in Prisoner Reentry." *Crime and Delinquency* 47(3): 390–409.

Hammett, Theodore M., Rebecca Widom, Joel Epstein, Michael Gross, Santiago Sifre, and Tammy Enos. 1995. *1994 Update: HIV/AIDS and STDs in Correctional Facilities.* NCJ 156832. Washington, DC: U.S. Department of Justice, National Institute of Justice.

Harlow, Caroline Wold. 2003. "Education and Correctional Populations." NCJ 195670. Washington, DC: U.S. Department of Justice, Bureau of Justice Statistics.

Harper, Cynthia C., and Sara S. McLanahan. 1999. "Father Absence and Youth Incarceration." Working Paper 99-03. Princeton, NJ: Center for Research on Child Well-being, Princeton University.

Harrell, Adele, Shannon E. Cavanagh, and John Roman. 1999. "Findings from the Evaluation of the D.C. Superior Court Drug Intervention Program." Washington, DC: The Urban Institute.

Harrison, Jeffrey L. 1999. "Repentance, Redemption, and Transformation in the Context of Economic and Civil Rights." In *Civic Repentance,* edited by Amitai Etzioni (3–44). Lanham, MD: Rowman and Littlefield.

Harrison, Paige M. 2000. "Incarceration Rates for Prisoners under State or Federal Jurisdiction, per 100,000 Residents" [computer file]. Bureau of Justice Statistics, National Prisoner Statistics data series (NPS-1). http://www.ojp.usdoj.gov/bjs/data/corpop25.wk1. (Accessed December 16, 2004.)

Harrison, Paige M., and Allen J. Beck. 2002. "Prisoners in 2001." Bureau of Justice Statistics Bulletin. NCJ 195189. Washington, DC: U.S. Department of Justice, Bureau of Justice Statistics.

———. 2003. "Prisoners in 2002." Bureau of Justice Statistics Bulletin. NCJ 200248. Washington, DC: U.S. Department of Justice, Bureau of Justice Statistics.

Harrison, Paige M., and Jennifer C. Karberg. 2004. "Prison and Jail Inmates at Midyear 2003." Bureau of Justice Statistics Bulletin. NCJ 203947. Washington, DC: U.S. Department of Justice, Bureau of Justice Statistics.

Harvard Law Review. 1989. "The Disenfranchisement of Ex-felons: Citizenship, Criminality, and 'The Purity of the Ballot Box.' " *Harvard Law Review* 102: 1300–17.

Hebenton, Bill, and Terry Thomas. 1993. *Criminal Records: State, Citizen, and the Politics of Protection.* Brookfield, VT: Avebury.

Heffernan, William. 1977. "State Prisoners in Escapist Mood." *Daily News,* April 20, p. 14.

Heintze, Theresa, and Lawrence M. Berger. 2004. "Employment Transitions and Housing Assistance." Paper presented at the 26th Annual APPAM (Association for Public Policy Analysis and Management) Research Conference: *Creating and Using Evidence in Public Policy Analysis and Management,* Atlanta, October 28–30.

Helfgott, Jacqueline. 1997. "Ex-Offender Needs Versus Community Opportunity in Seattle, Washington." *Federal Probation* 61(2): 12–24.

Hiller, Matthew L., Kevin Knight, and D. Dwayne Simpson. 1999. "Prison-Based Substance Abuse Treatment, Residential Aftercare, and Recidivism." *Addiction* 94(6): 833–42.

Hirsch, Amy E., Sharon M. Dietrich, Rue Landau, Peter D. Schneider, Irv Ackelsberg, Judith Bernstein-Baker, and Joseph Hohenstein. 2002. "Every Door Closed: Barriers Facing Parents with Criminal Records." Washington, DC: Center for Law and Social Policy and Community Legal Services, Inc.

Hirschi, Travis, and Michael Gottfredson. 1983. "Age and the Explanation of Crime." *American Journal of Sociology* 89(3): 552–84.

Holzer, Harry J., and Paul Offner. 2002. "Recent Trends in Employment of Low-skilled Young Men." Paper presented at the Extending Opportunities Conference, Washington, DC, May 13.

Holzer, Harry J., Steven Raphael, and Michael A. Stoll. 2002. "Can Employers Play a More Positive Role in Prisoner Reentry?" Paper prepared for the Urban Institute Reentry Roundtable: *Prisoner Reentry and the Institutions of Civil Society,* Washington, DC, March 20–21.

———. 2003. "Employment Barriers Facing Ex-Prisoners." Paper prepared for the Urban Institute Reentry Roundtable: *Employment Dimensions of Reentry: Understanding the Nexus between Prisoner Reentry and Work,* New York, May 19–20.

Horn, Martin F. 2001. "Rethinking Sentencing." *Corrections Management Quarterly* 5(3): 34–40.

Horney, Julie, D. Wayne Osgood, and Ineke Haen Marshall. 1995. "Criminal Careers in the Short-Term: Intra-Individual Variability in Crime and Its Relation to Local Life Circumstances." *American Sociological Review* 60(5): 655–73.

Hornung, Carlton A., B. Jaye Anno, Robert B. Greifinger, and Soniya Gadre. 2002. "Health Care for Soon-to-Be-Released Inmates: A Survey of State Prison Systems." In *The Health Status of Soon-to-Be-Released Inmates: A Report to Congress,* vol. 2 (1–11). Chicago: National Commission on Correctional Health Care.

Hubbell, Webb. 2001. "The Mark of Cain." *San Francisco Chronicle,* June 10.

HUD. See U.S. Department of Housing and Urban Development.

Hughes, Timothy A., Doris J. Wilson, and Allen J. Beck. 2001. "Trends in State Parole, 1990–2000." NCJ 184735. Washington, DC: U.S. Department of Justice, Bureau of Justice Statistics.

Human Rights Watch. 2003. *Ill-Equipped: U.S. Prisons and Offenders with Mental Illness.* New York: Human Rights Watch. http://www.hrw.org/reports/2003/usa1003/usa1003.pdf. (Accessed November 16, 2004.)

Hylton, Wil S. 2003. "Sick on the Inside." *Harper's Magazine,* August.

Iguchi, Martin Y. 2001. "Differential Drug Use, HIV/AIDS and Related Health Outcomes Among Racial and Ethnic Populations." Presented at NIDA (National Institute on Drug Abuse) workshop, Bethesda, MD, April 26–27.

Immerwahr, John, and Jean Johnson. 2002. "The Revolving Door: Exploring Public Attitudes toward Prisoner Reentry." Paper prepared for the Urban Institute Reentry Roundtable: *Prisoner Reentry and the Institutions of Civil Society: Bridges and Barriers to Successful Reintegration,* Washington, DC, March 20–21.

Inciardi, James A., Steven S. Martin, Clifford A. Butzin, Robert M. Hooper, and Lana D. Harrison. 1997. "An Effective Model of Prison-Based Treatment for Drug-Involved Offenders." *Journal of Drug Issues* 27(2): 261–78.

International Centre for Prison Studies, King's College London. n.d. "World Prison Brief." http://www.kcl.ac.uk/depsta/rel/icps/worldbrief/world_brief.html. (Accessed February 25, 2004.)

International Society for Traumatic Stress Studies. 2003. "Intimate Partner Violence." http://www.istss.org/terrorism/Intimate_Partner_Violence.htm. (Accessed April 5, 2004.)

Irwin, John. 1970. *The Felon.* Englewood Cliffs, NJ: Prentice Hall. Reprint, Berkeley: University of California Press, 1987.

———. 1985. *The Jail: Managing the Underclass in American Society.* Berkeley: University of California Press.

Jacobs, James B. 1982. "Sentencing by Prison Personnel: Good Time." *UCLA Law Review* 30: 217–70.

———. 1983. *New Perspectives on Prisons and Imprisonment.* Ithaca, NY: Cornell University Press.

Johnston, Denise. 1991. *Jailed Mothers.* Pasadena, CA: Pacific Oaks Center for Children of Incarcerated Parents.

———. 1992. *Children of Offenders.* Pasadena, CA: Pacific Oaks Center for Children of Incarcerated Parents.

———. 1993. *Intergenerational Incarceration.* Pasadena, CA: Pacific Oaks Center for Children of Incarcerated Parents. Quoted in Johnston (1995, 80).

———. 1995. "Effects of Parental Incarceration." In *Children of Incarcerated Parents,* edited by Katherine Gabel and Denise Johnston (59–88). New York: Lexington Books.

———. 1999. "Children of Criminal Offenders and Foster Care." Presented at the Child Welfare League of America National Conference on Research, Seattle.

———. 2001. "Incarceration of Women and Effects on Parenting." Paper prepared for a conference: *The Effects of Incarceration on Children and Families,* sponsored by the Program on Child, Adolescent, and Family Studies, Institute for Policy Research, Northwestern University, Evanston, IL, May 5.

Johnston, Denise, and Michael Carlin. 1996. "Enduring Trauma among Children of Incarcerated Criminal Offenders." *Progress: Family Systems Research and Therapy* 5: 9–36.

Joint Center for Housing Studies of Harvard University. 2001. "The State of the Nation's Housing: 2001." Cambridge, MA: Harvard University.

Jones, Greg, Michael Connelly, and Kate Wagner. 2001. "The Effects of Diminution Credits on Inmate Behavior and Recidivism: An Overview." http://www.msccsp.org/publications/diminution.html. (Accessed December 3, 2004.)

Judy, Richard, and Carol D'Amico. 1997. *Workforce 2020: Work and Workers in the 21st Century.* Washington, DC: The Hudson Institute.

Justice Policy Institute. 2002. "Cellblocks or Classrooms? The Funding of Higher Education and Corrections and Its Impact on African American Men." Washington, DC: The Justice Policy Institute.

Kalogeras, Steven. 2003. "Legislative Changes on Felony Disenfranchisement, 1996–2003." Washington, DC: The Sentencing Project.

Kandel, Denise B., Emily Rosenbaum, and Kevin Chen. 1994. "Impact of Maternal Drug Use and Life Experiences on Preadolescent Children Born to Teenage Mothers." *Journal of Marriage and the Family* 56(2): 325–40.

Kasarda, John D., and Morris Janowitz. 1974. "Community Attachment in Mass Society." *American Sociological Review* 39(3): 328–39.

Kennedy, Anthony M. 2003. Speech at the American Bar Association Annual Meeting, San Francisco, August 9. http://www.supremecourtus.gov/publicinfo/speeches/sp_08-09-03.html. (Accessed March 15, 2004.)

Keyssar, Alexander. 2000. *The Right to Vote: The Contested History of Democracy in the United States.* New York: Basic Books.

Kihss, Peter. 1977. "140 Prisoners Are Removed from Work Program as Controls Are Tightened Under New State Law." *New York Times,* August 26.

King, Ryan S., and Marc Mauer. 2004. "The Vanishing Black Electorate: Felony Disenfranchisement in Atlanta, Georgia." Washington, DC: The Sentencing Project.

Kling, Jeffrey R. 2002. "The Effect of Prison Sentence Length on the Subsequent Employment and Earnings of Criminal Defendants." Unpublished manuscript, Princeton University.

La Vigne, Nancy G., and Gillian L. Thomson. 2003. *A Portrait of Prisoner Reentry in Ohio.* Washington, DC: The Urban Institute. http://www.urban.org/url.cfm?ID=410891. (Accessed April 5, 2004.)

La Vigne, Nancy G., Christy Visher, and Jennifer Castro. 2004. *Chicago Prisoners' Experiences Returning Home.* Washington, DC: The Urban Institute.

La Vigne, Nancy G., Cynthia A. Mamalian, Jeremy Travis, and Christy Visher. 2003. *A Portrait of Prisoner Reentry in Illinois.* Washington, DC: The Urban Institute. http://www.urban.org/url.cfm?ID=410662. (Accessed April 5, 2004.)

La Vigne, Nancy G., Vera Kachnowski, Jeremy Travis, Rebecca Naser, and Christy Visher. 2003. *A Portrait of Prisoner Reentry in Maryland.* Washington, DC: The Urban Institute. http://www.urban.org/url.cfm?ID=410655. (Accessed April 5, 2004.)

Lamb-Mechanick, Deborah, and Julianne Nelson. 2000. "Prison Health Care Survey: An Analysis of Factors Influencing Per Capita Costs." NIC 015999. Washington, DC: U.S. Department of Justice, National Institute of Corrections.

Langan, Patrick A., and David Levin. 2002. "Recidivism of Prisoners Released in 1994." NCJ 193427. Washington, DC: U.S. Department of Justice, Bureau of Justice Statistics.

Langan, Patrick A., Erica L. Schmitt, and Matthew R. Durose. 2003. *Recidivism of Sex Offenders Released from Prison in 1994.* NCJ 198281. Washington, DC: U.S. Department of Justice, Bureau of Justice Statistics.

Laub, John H., and Robert J. Sampson. 2001. *Understanding Desistence from Crime.* Chicago: University of Chicago Press.

———. 2003. *Shared Beginnings, Divergent Lives: Delinquent Boys to Age 70.* Cambridge, MA: Harvard University Press.

Laub, John H., Daniel S. Nagin, and Robert J. Sampson. 1998. "Trajectories of Change in Criminal Offending: Good Marriages and the Desistance Process." *American Sociological Review* 63(2): 225–38.

Lawrence, Sarah, and Jeremy Travis. 2004. *The New Landscape of Imprisonment: Mapping America's Prison Expansion.* Washington, DC: The Urban Institute.

Lawrence, Sarah, Daniel P. Mears, Glenn Dubin, and Jeremy Travis. 2002. *The Practice and Promise of Prison Programming.* Washington, DC: The Urban Institute.

Leatherby, Drew. 1996. "Connecticut's Garner Correctional Institution Close Custody Phase Program." State Innovations brief. P013-9602. Lexington, KY: The Council of State Governments.

Legal Action Center. 2004. *After Prison: Roadblocks to Reentry: A Report on State Legal Barriers Facing People with Criminal Records.* New York: The Legal Action Center.

Leib, Roxanne. 1996. "Community Notification Laws: A Step toward More Effective Solutions." *Journal of Interpersonal Violence* 11(2): 298–300.

Lin, Jennifer, and Mark Fazlollah. 2003. "Test All Inmates at Risk for Hepatitis C." Washington, DC: Centers for Disease Control and Prevention.

Little Hoover Commission. 2003. *Back to the Community: Safe and Sound Parole Policies.* Sacramento, CA: Little Hoover Commission. http://www.lhc.ca.gov/lhcdir/172/execsum172.pdf. (Accessed March 25, 2004.)

Loeber, Rolf, and David P. Farrington, eds. 1998. *Serious and Violent Juvenile Offenders: Risk Factors and Successful Interventions.* Thousand Oaks, CA: Sage Publications.

———. 2001. *Child Delinquents: Development, Intervention, and Service Needs.* Thousand Oaks, CA: Sage Publications.

Lofland, John. 1969. *Deviance and Identity.* Englewood Cliffs, NJ: Prentice Hall.

Los Angeles Police Department. 2002. "Law Enforcement Community Conducts—Operation Enough." November 20 press release. Los Angeles: Media Relations Section, Office of the Chief of Police, Los Angeles Police Department.

Love, Margaret Colgate. 2003. "Starting Over with a Clean Slate: In Praise of a Forgotten Section of the Model Penal Code." *Fordham Urban Law Journal* 30(5): 1705–41.

Lynch, James P., and William J. Sabol. 2001. *Prisoner Reentry in Perspective.* Crime Policy Report, vol. 3. Washington, DC: The Urban Institute.

MacGowan, Robin J., Andrew Margolis, Juarlyn Gaiter, Kathleen Morrow, Barry Zack, John Askew, Timothy McAuliffe, James M. Sosman, and Gloria D. Eldridge. 2003. "Predictors of Risky Sex of Young Men After Release from Prison." *International Journal of STD and AIDS* 14(8): 519–23.

Manpower Demonstration Research Corporation. 2002. "Enhanced Services for the Hard-to-Employ Demonstration and Evaluation Project." Washington, DC: U.S. Department of Justice.

Manza, Jeff, Clem Brooks, and Christopher Uggen. 2004. "Public Attitudes Toward Felon Disenfranchisement in the United States." *Public Opinion Quarterly* 68(2): 275–86.

Marshall, Thomas H. 1950. *Citizenship and Social Class.* Cambridge: Cambridge University Press.

————. 1964. "Citizenship and Social Class." In *Class, Citizenship, and Social Development: Essays by T. H. Marshall* (65–122). Westport, CT: Greenwood Press.

Martinez, Mike. 2002. "Huge City Police Sweep Nets 60." *Oakland (CA) Tribune,* December 7.

Martinson, Robert. 1974. "What Works? Questions and Answers about Prison Reform." *The Public Interest* 35: 22–54.

Maruna, Shadd. 2001. *Making Good: How Ex-Convicts Reform and Rebuild Their Lives.* Washington, DC: American Psychological Association Books.

Maruna, Shadd, and Thomas P. LeBel. 2003. "Welcome Home? Examining the 'Reentry Court' Concept from a Strength-based Perspective." *Western Criminology Review* 4(2): 91–107.

Maruschak, Laura M. 2002. "HIV in Prisons, 2000." Bureau of Justice Statistics Bulletin. NCJ 196023. Washington, DC: U.S. Department of Justice, Bureau of Justice Statistics.

————. 2004. "HIV in Prisons, 2001." Bureau of Justice Statistics Bulletin. NCJ 202293. Washington, DC: U.S. Department of Justice, Bureau of Justice Statistics.

Mauer, Marc. 2002. "Mass Imprisonment and the Disappearing Voters." In *Invisible Punishment: The Collateral Consequences of Mass Imprisonment,* edited by Marc Mauer and Meda Chesney-Lind (50–58). New York: The New Press.

————. 2003. "Comparative International Rates of Incarceration: An Examination of Causes and Trends." Testimony presented to the U.S. Commission on Civil Rights, Washington, DC, June 20.

Mauer, Marc, and Meda Chesney-Lind, eds. 2002. *Invisible Punishment: The Collateral Consequences of Mass Imprisonment.* New York: The New Press.

Mauer, Marc, Ryan S. King, and Malcom C. Young. 2004. "The Meaning of 'Life': Long Prison Sentences in Context." Washington, DC: The Sentencing Project.

Mazurek, Gerald H., Philip A. LoBue, Charles L. Daley, John Bernardo, Alfred A. Lardizabal, William R. Bishai, Michael F. Iademarco, and James S. Rothel. 2001. "Comparison of a Whole-Blood Interferon Gamma Assay with Tuberculin Skin Testing for Detecting Latent *Mycobacterium Tuberculosis* Infection." *Journal of the American Medical Association* 286(14): 1740–47.

McLanahan, Sara, and Gary Sandefur. 1994. *Growing Up with a Single Parent: What Hurts, What Helps.* Cambridge, MA: Harvard University Press.

McLoyd, Vonnie C. 1998. "Socioeconomic Disadvantage and Child Development." *American Psychologist* 53(2): 185–204.

Meisenhelder, T. 1977. "An Exploratory Study of Exiting from Criminal Careers." *Criminology* 15(3): 319–34.

———. 1982. "Becoming Normal: Certification as a Stage in Exiting from Crime." *Deviant Behaviour: An Interdisciplinary Journal* 3: 137–53.

Menon, Ramdas, Craig Blakely, Dottie Carmichael, and Laurie Silver. 1992. "An Evaluation of Project RIO Outcomes: An Evaluative Report." College Station: Texas A&M University, Public Policy Resources Laboratory.

Metraux, Stephen, and Dennis P. Culhane. 2004. "Homeless Shelter Use and Reincarceration Following Prison Release: Assessing the Risk." *Criminology and Public Policy* 3(2): 201–22.

Michael, Robert T., and Nancy B. Tuma. 1985. "Entry into Marriage and Parenthood by Young Men and Women: The Influence of Family Background." *Demography* 22(4): 515–44.

Minnesota Department of Corrections. 2001. *2000 Performance Report: Adult Recidivism in Minnesota*. St. Paul: Minnesota Department of Corrections, Research and Evaluation Unit.

Morris, Norval. 2002. *Maconochie's Gentlemen: The Story of Norfolk Island and the Roots of Modern Prison Reform (Studies in Crime and Public Policy)*. New York: Oxford University Press.

Mumola, Christopher J. 1999. "Substance Abuse and Treatment, State and Federal Prisoners, 1997." NCJ 172871. Washington, DC: U.S. Department of Justice, Bureau of Justice Statistics.

———. 2000. "Incarcerated Parents and Their Children." NCJ 182335. Washington, DC: U.S. Department of Justice, Bureau of Justice Statistics.

———. 2002. "Survey of Inmates in State and Federal Correctional Facilities, 2001 Annual Survey of Jails, and the 2001 National Prisoners Statistics Program." Paper presented at the National Center for Children and Families, Washington, DC, October 31.

———. 2004. "Incarcerated Parents and Their Children." Presented at the annual Administration for Children and Families Welfare Research and Evaluation Conference, U.S. Department of Health and Human Services, Washington, DC, May 28.

Nathan, Vincent M. 1985. "Guest Editorial." *Journal of Prison and Jail Health* 5(1): 3–12.

National Advisory Commission on Criminal Justice Standards and Goals. 1973. *Corrections*. Washington, DC: National Advisory Commission on Criminal Justice Standards and Goals.

National Center for Policy Analysis. 2002. "Federal Prisoner Industries Need 'Work.' " July 22 media advisory. Washington, DC: National Center for Policy Analysis.

National Commission on Correctional Health Care. 1996. "Official Position Statement: Charging Inmates a Fee for Health Care Services." *Journal of Correctional Health Care* 3(2): 179–84.

———. 2002. *The Health Status of Soon-to-Be-Released Inmates: A Report to Congress*, vol. 1. Washington, DC: U.S. Department of Justice, National Institute of Justice.

National Commission on Law Observance and Enforcement. 1931. *Penal Institutions, Probation, and Parole*. Washington, DC: U.S. Government Printing Office.

National Correctional Industries Association. 2002. *National Correctional Industries Association Directory*. Baltimore: National Correctional Industries Association.

National Council on Crime and Delinquency. 1962. "Annulment of a Conviction of Crime: A Model Act." *Crime and Delinquency* 8: 97–98.

National Institute of Corrections. 2002. "Transition from Prison to Community Initiative." Washington, DC: National Institute of Corrections. http://www.nicic.org/pubs/2002/017520.pdf. (Accessed July 9, 2004.)

———. 2003. "Corrections Agency Collaboration with Public Health." NIC-019101. Longmont, CO: National Institute of Corrections.

National Probation and Parole Association. 1957. *Parole in Principle and Practice: A Manual and Report.* This report came out of the second National Conference on Parole, sponsored by the Federal Parole Board and the National Probation and Parole Association, Washington, DC, April 9–11, 1956.

NCCD. See National Council on Crime and Delinquency.

NCCHC. See National Commission on Correctional Health Care.

Needels, Karen E. 1996. "Go Directly to Jail and Do Not Collect? A Long-term Study of Recidivism, Employment, and Earnings Patterns among Prison Releasees." *Journal of Research in Crime and Delinquency* 33(4): 471–96.

Nelson, Martha, Perry Deess, and Charlotte Allen. 1999. *The First Month Out: Post-Incarceration Experiences in New York City.* New York: Vera Institute of Justice.

New York Times. 2002a. "Ending Chronic Homelessness." March 13. Editorial.

———. 2002b. "Former Felons Have a Right to Vote." October 17, A32.

NIC. See National Institute of Corrections.

Olivares, Kathleen M., Velmer S. Burton Jr., and Francis Cullen. 1996. "The Collateral Consequences of a Felony Conviction: A National Study of State Legal Codes 10 Years Later." *Federal Probation* 60: 10–17.

Pager, Devah. 2002. "The Mark of a Criminal Record." Paper presented at the annual meeting of the American Sociological Association, Chicago, August 16–19.

Paternoster, Raymond, and Lee Ann Iovanni. 1989. "The Labeling Perspective and Delinquency: An Elaboration of the Theory and an Assessment of the Evidence." *Justice Quarterly* 6: 359–94.

Pattillo, Mary, David Weiman, and Bruce Western, eds. 2004. *Imprisoning America: The Social Effects of Mass Incarceration.* New York: Russell Sage Foundation.

Petersilia, Joan. 1998. "A Decade of Experimenting with Intermediate Sanctions: What Have We Learned?" *Federal Probation* 62(2): 3–9.

———. 2003. *When Prisoners Come Home: Parole and Prisoner Reentry.* New York: Oxford University Press.

Petersilia, Joan, and Susan Turner. 1993. "Evaluating Intensive Supervision Probation/Parole: Results from a Nationwide Experiment." NIJ Research in Brief. Washington, DC: U.S. Department of Justice, National Institute of Justice.

Pettit, Becky, and Christopher Lyons. 2003. "The Consequences of Incarceration on Employment and Earnings Over the Life Course: Evidence from Washington State." Seattle: University of Washington.

Phillips, Susan, and Barbara Bloom. 1998. "In Whose Best Interest? The Impact of Changing Public Policy on Relatives Caring for Children with Incarcerated Parents." *Child Welfare* 77(5): 531–42.

Piehl, Anne M. 2002. *From Cell to Street: A Plan to Supervise Inmates After Release.* Boston: Massachusetts Institute for a New Commonwealth.

Piliavin, Irving, and Stanley Masters. 1981. *The Impact of Employment Programs on Offenders, Addicts, and Problem Youth: Implications from Supported Work.* Madison: University of Wisconsin, Institute for Research and Poverty Discussion.

Piven, Frances F., and Richard A. Cloward. 2000. *Why Americans Still Don't Vote: And Why Politicians Want It That Way.* Boston: Beacon Press.

Popkin, Susan J., Diane K. Levy, Laura E. Harris, Jennifer Comey, Mary K. Cunningham, Larry Buron, and William Woodley. 2002. *HOPE VI Panel Study: Baseline Report.* Washington, DC: The Urban Institute.

Positive Populations. 2000. "Correctional Systems Grapple with Dual Epidemics: HIV and Hepatitis C." *Positive Populations* 2(1). Cited in Anno (2002, 10).

President's Commission on Law Enforcement and Administration of Justice. 1967. *The Challenge of Crime in a Free Society.* Washington, DC: U.S. Government Printing Office.

Putnam, Robert D. 1993. *Making Democracy Work: Civic Traditions in Modern Italy.* Princeton, NJ: Princeton University Press.

Rafter, Nicole Hahn, and Debra L. Stanley. 1999. *Prisons in America: A Reference Handbook.* Santa Barbara, CA: ABC-Clio, Inc.

Raftery, Thomas. 1977. "Rape Rap Hits 3rd Con on Release." *(New York) Daily News,* May 6.

Raine, Harrison. 1977. "Woman Slain, Accuse Convict on Jail Leave." *(New York) Daily News,* May 4.

Raphael, Steven, and Michael A. Stoll. 2004. "The Effect of Prison Releases on Regional Crime Rates." In *The Brookings-Wharton Papers on Urban Affairs 2004,* edited by William G. Gale and Janet Rothenberg Pack. Washington, DC: Brookings Institution Press.

Reitz, Kevin. 1998. "Sentencing." In *The Handbook of Crime and Punishment,* edited by Michael Tonry (542–62). New York: Oxford University Press.

Rhine, Edward E., William R. Smith, and Ronald W. Jackson. 1991. *Paroling Authorities: Recent History and Current Practice.* Laurel, MD: American Correctional Association.

Rice, Coliece, and Paige Harrison. 2000. "Sentenced Prisoners Admitted to State or Federal Jurisdiction." National Prisoners Statistics Data Series (NPS-1). Washington, DC: Bureau of Justice Statistics. http://www.ojp.usdoj.gov/bjs/dtdata.htm. (Accessed April 8, 2004.)

Rich, Josiah D., Leah Holmes, Christopher Salas, Grace Macalino, Deborah Davis, James Ryczek, and Timothy Flanigan. 2001. "Successful Linkage of Medical Care and Community Services for HIV-Positive Offenders Being Released from Prison." *Journal of Urban Health* 78(2): 279–89.

Ripley, Amanda. 2002. "This Year the Nation's Prisons Will Release More Than 630,000 People—A New Record. Amanda Ripley Follows One Man's Struggle to Stay Outside the Gates." *Time,* January 21, 56–62.

Roberts, Cheryl, Sofia Kennedy, Theodore M. Hammett, and N. F. Rosenberg. 2001. *Discharge Planning and Continuity of Care for HIV-Infected State Prison Inmates as They Return to the Community: A Study of Ten States.* Report submitted to the Centers for Disease Control and Prevention by Abt Associates, Inc.

———. 2002. "Linkages between In-Prison and Community-Based Health Services." Paper presented at the Urban Institute Reentry Roundtable: *The Public Health Dimensions of Prisoner Reentry: Addressing the Health Needs and Risks of Returning Prisoners and Their Families,* Los Angeles, December 11–13.

Roberts, Victoria. 2003. Interview by Cathy Duchamp, *All Things Considered.* National Public Radio, June 10.

Rodriguez, Nino, and Brenner Brown. 2003. "Preventing Homelessness among People Leaving Prison." State Sentencing and Corrections Program brief. New York: Vera Institute of Justice.

Rollo, Ned. 2002. *99 Days and a Get Up: A Guide to Success Following Release for Inmates and Their Loved Ones.* 3rd ed. Dallas, TX: OPEN, Inc.

Roman, Caterina Gouvis, and Gretchen E. Moore. 2004. "Measuring Local Institutions and Organizations: The Role of Community Institutional Capacity in Social Capital." Washington, DC: The Urban Institute.

Rose, Dina, and Todd R. Clear. 1998. "Incarceration, Social Capital and Crime: Examining the Unintended Consequences of Incarceration." *Criminology* 36(3): 441–80.

Rose, Dina, Todd R. Clear, and J. Ryder. 2002. "Drugs, Incarcerations, and Neighborhood Life: The Impact of Reintegrating Offenders into the Community. Final Report." Washington, DC: U.S. Department of Justice, National Institute of Justice.

Rosenfeld, Richard. 2000. "Patterns in Adult Homicide." In *The Crime Drop in America,* edited by Alfred Blumstein and J. Wallman (130–63). Cambridge: Cambridge University Press.

Rosenfeld, Richard, Joel Wallman, and Robert J. Fornango. Forthcoming. "The Contribution of Ex-Prisoners to Crime Rates." In *Prisoner Reentry and Public Safety in America,* edited by Jeremy Travis and Christy Visher. New York: Cambridge University Press.

Rosenfeld, Richard, Joel Wallman, Robert J. Fornango, Jeremy Travis, and Karen Beckman. 2004. "Reentry and Recidivism: Defining the Public Safety Challenge of Prisoner Reentry." Presented at the Annual American Society of Criminology Conference, Nashville, TN, November 17.

Rossman, Shelli B., Caterina Gouvis Roman, Janeen Buck, and Elaine Morley. 1999. *Impact of the Opportunity to Succeed (OPTS) Aftercare Program for Substance-Abusers.* Washington, DC: The Urban Institute.

Rostad, Knut A. 2002. "Employing Prison Inmates: Does It Work?" Bethesda, MD: The Enterprise Prison Institute.

Rothman, David. 1980. *Conscience and Convenience: The Asylum and Its Alternatives in Progressive America.* Boston: Little, Brown.

Rottman David B., Carol R. Flango, Melissa T. Cantrell, Randall Hansen, and Neil LaFountain. 2000. "State Court Organization 1998." NCJ 178932. Washington, DC: U.S. Department of Justice, Bureau of Justice Statistics. http://www.ojp.usdoj.gov/bjs/pub/pdf/sco98.pdf. (Accessed December 6, 2004.)

Rousseau, Jean-Jacques. [1762] 1957. *The Social Contract or Principles of Political Right.* New York: Hafner.

Rovner-Pieczenik, Roberta. 1973. *A Review of Manpower R&D Projects in the Correctional Field (1963–1973).* Manpower Research Monograph no. 28. Washington, DC: U.S. Department of Labor.

Rubenstein, Gwen. 2001. *Getting to Work: How TANF Can Support Ex-Offender Parents in the Transition to Self-Sufficiency.* New York: Legal Action Center.

Rubenstein, Gwen, and Debbie Mukamal. 2002. "Welfare and Housing: Denial of Benefits to Drug Offenders." In *Invisible Punishment: The Collateral Consequences of Mass*

Imprisonment, edited by Marc Mauer and Meda Chesney-Lind (37–49). New York: The New Press.

Runda, John C., Edward E. Rhine, and Robert E. Wetter. 1994. *The Practice of Parole Boards.* Lexington, KY: Association of Paroling Authorities International.

Sabol, William J. 2003. "Employment and Recidivism of Offenders Released under Supervision from Ohio State Prisons During 1999 and 2000." Presented to the City of Cleveland Community Reentry Strategic Initiative, November 11.

Sabol, William J., and James P. Lynch. 1998. "Assessing the Longer-run Consequences of Incarceration: Effects on Families and Employment." Paper presented at the 20th Annual APPAM (Association for Public Policy Analysis and Management) Research Conference, New York, October 29–31.

Sabol, William J., Katherine Rosich, Kamala Mallik Kane, David P. Kirk, and Glenn Dubin. 2002. "The Influences of Truth-in-Sentencing Reforms on Changes in States' Sentencing Practices and Prison Populations." Report to the National Institute of Justice. Washington, DC: The Urban Institute.

Sack, W. 1977. "Children of Imprisoned Fathers." *Psychiatry* 40: 163–74.

Samenow, Stanton E. 1984. *Inside the Criminal Mind.* New York: Crown.

Sampson, Robert J., and John H. Laub. 1993. *Crime in the Making: Pathways and Turning Points through Life.* Cambridge, MA: Harvard University Press.

Santana, Arthur. 2003. "Locked Down and Far from Home." *Washington Post,* April 24.

Sard, Barbara, and Margy Waller. 2002. "Housing Strategies to Strengthen Welfare Policy and Support Working Families." Center on Urban and Metropolitan Policy and the Center on Budget and Policy Priorities research brief. Washington, DC: The Brookings Institution.

Schochet, Peter Z., John Brughardt, and Steven Glazerman. 2001. *National Job Corps Study: The Impacts of Job Corps on Participants' Employment and Related Outcomes.* Princeton, NJ: Mathematica Policy Research, Inc.

Schuck, Peter H., and John Williams. 1999. "Removing Criminal Aliens: The Pitfalls and Promises of Federalism." *Harvard Journal of Law and Public Policy* 22: 367–463.

Seiter, Richard P. 1975. *Evaluation Research As a Feedback Mechanism for Criminal Justice Policy Making: A Critical Analysis.* PhD diss., Ohio State University, Columbus, OH. Quoted in Seiter and Kadela (2003, 378).

Seiter, Richard P., and Karen R. Kadela. 2003. "Prisoner Reentry: What Works, What Does Not, and What Is Promising." *Crime and Delinquency* 49(3): 360–88.

Sentencing Project, The. 1997. *Intended and Unintended Consequences: State Racial Disparities in Imprisonment.* Washington, DC: The Sentencing Project.

Shafer, Dee NaQuin. 2002. "To Evict or Not to Evict." *Journal of Housing and Urban Development* 59(4): 12–16.

Shonkoff, Jack P., and Deborah A. Phillips, eds. 2000. *From Neurons to Neighborhoods: The Science of Early Childhood Development.* Washington, DC: National Academy Press.

Shover, Neal 1996. *Great Pretenders: Pursuits and Careers of Persistent Thieves.* Boulder, CO: Westview Press. Quoted in Maruna (2001, 136).

Simon, Jonathan. 1993. *Poor Discipline: Parole and the Social Control of the Underclass, 1890–1990.* Chicago: University of Chicago Press.

Sink, Lisa. 2002. "Judge Orders Release of Child Sex Offender." *Milwaukee Journal Sentinel,* April 25.

Skogan, Wesley G. 2003. *Community Policing: Can It Work?* Belmont, CA: Wadsworth.

Social Exclusion Unit, Office of the Deputy Prime Minister. 2001. *Preventing Social Exclusion.* Government Report. West Yorkshire, UK: Office of the Deputy Prime Minister.

Solomon, Amy L., Avinash Bhati, and Vera Kachnowski. 2005. *Does Parole Work? Analyzing the Impact of Post-Prison Supervision and Recidivism.* Washington, DC: The Urban Institute.

Solomon, Amy L., Michelle Waul, Asheley Van Ness, and Jeremy Travis. 2004. *Outside the Walls: A National Snapshot of Community-Based Prisoner Reentry Programs.* Washington, DC: The Urban Institute.

Spelman, William. 2000. "The Limited Importance of Prison Expansion." In *The Crime Drop in America,* edited by Alfred Blumstein and Joel Wallman (97–129). Cambridge: Cambridge University Press.

Stephan, James J. 1999. *State Prison Expenditures, 1996.* NCJ 172211. Washington, DC: U.S. Department of Justice, Bureau of Justice Statistics.

———. 2004. "State Prison Expenditures, 2001." NCJ 202949. Washington, DC: U.S. Department of Justice, Bureau of Justice Statistics.

Stephenson, B., D. Wohl, N. Kiziah, D. Rosen, D. Ngo, N. Merriman, and A. Kaplan. 2000. "Release from Prison Is Associated with Increased HIV RNA at Time of Reincarceration." Oral Abstract no. TuOrD323. Paper presented at XIII International AIDS Conference, Durban, South Africa, July 11.

Steurer, Stephen J., Linda Smith, and Alice Tracy. 2001. "Three State Recidivism Study." Lanham, MD: Correctional Education Association.

Stockett, Leah, and Helen Fox Fields. n.d. *Issue Brief: Prevention and Treatment of HIV, STDs and TB in Correctional Settings.* ASTHO White Paper. Washington, DC: Association of State and Territorial Health Officials. http://www.astho.org/pubs/IB-whitepaper.pdf. (Accessed April 6, 2004.)

Struckman-Johnson, Cindy, and David Struckman-Johnson. 2000. "Sexual Coercion Rates in Seven Midwestern Prisons for Men." *The Prison Journal* 80(4): 379–90.

Sullivan, Eileen. 2002a. "Trantino Left With No Home, No Work." *Courier-Post, South Jersey's Newspaper,* February 20.

———. 2002b. "Trantino Moves Back to Camden." *Courier-Post, South Jersey's Newspaper,* February 16.

———. 2002c. "Trantino Move Unnerves Collingswood Neighbors." *Courier-Post, South Jersey's Newspaper,* February 14.

Sullivan, Eileen, Milton Mino, Katherine Nelson, and Jill Pope. 2002. "Families as a Resource in Recovery from Drug Abuse: An Evaluation of La Bodega de la Familia." New York: Vera Institute of Justice.

Sullivan, Mercer L. 1993. "Young Fathers and Parenting in Two Inner-City Neighborhoods." In *Young Unwed Fathers: Changing Roles and Emerging Policies,* edited by Robert I. Lerman and Theodora J. Ooms (51–73). Philadelphia, PA: Temple University Press.

Thoennes, Nancy. 2003. "Child Support Profile: Massachusetts Incarcerated and Paroled Parents." Denver: Center for Policy Research.

Thompson, Frank J., and John J. DiIulio Jr., eds. 1998. *Medicaid and Devolution: A View from the States.* Washington, DC: Brookings Institution Press.

Thornberry, Terence P., Carolyn A. Smith, and Gregory J. Howard. 1997. "Risk Factors for Teenage Fatherhood." *Journal of Marriage and the Family* 59(3): 505–22.

Tonry, Michael. 1996. *Sentencing Matters*. New York: Oxford University Press.

———. 1999. "The Fragmentation of Sentencing and Corrections in America." *Sentencing and Corrections: Issues for the 21st Century*. Washington, DC: U.S. Department of Justice, National Institute of Justice.

Travis, Jeremy. 1999. "Prisons, Work, and Reentry." *Corrections Today* 61(6): 102–7.

———. 2000. *But They All Come Back: Rethinking Prisoner Reentry*. Washington, DC: U.S. Department of Justice, National Institute of Justice.

———. 2002. "Invisible Punishment: An Instrument of Social Exclusion." In *Invisible Punishment: The Collateral Consequences of Mass Imprisonment*, edited by Marc Mauer and Meda Chesney-Lind (1–36). New York: The New Press.

Travis, Jeremy, and Sarah Lawrence. 2002a. *Beyond the Prison Gates: The State of Parole in America*. Washington, DC: The Urban Institute.

———. 2002b. "California's Parole Experiment." *California Journal* 33(8): 18–23.

Travis, Jeremy, and Christy Visher. 2003. "Transitions from Prison to Community: Understanding Individual Pathways." *Annual Review of Sociology* 29: 89–113.

Travis, Jeremy, and Michelle Waul, eds. 2003. *Prisoners Once Removed: The Impact of Incarceration and Reentry on Children, Families, and Communities*. Washington, DC: Urban Institute Press.

Travis, Jeremy, Elizabeth M. Cincotta, and Amy L. Solomon. 2003. "Families Left Behind: The Hidden Cost of Incarceration and Reentry." Washington, DC: The Urban Institute.

Travis, Jeremy, Shelli Rossman, and Kamala Mallik Kane. 2004. "Prisoner Reentry in Illinois: Planning for a Neighborhood-level Reentry Demonstration Project." Presented to the MacArthur Foundation, Chicago, April 15.

Travis, Jeremy, Amy L. Solomon, and Michelle Waul. 2001. *From Prison to Home: The Dimensions and Consequences of Prisoner Reentry*. Washington, DC: The Urban Institute.

Travis, Jeremy, Sinead Keegan, and Eric Cadora, with Amy Solomon and Charles Swartz. 2003. *A Portrait of Prisoner Reentry in New Jersey*. Washington, DC: The Urban Institute. http://www.urban.org/UploadedPDF/410899_nj_prisoner_reentry.pdf. (Accessed December 6, 2004.)

Trice, Harrison M., and Paul M. Roman. 1970. "Delabeling, Relabeling, and Alcoholics Anonymous." *Social Problems* 17(4): 538–46.

Tucker, Susan, and Eric Cadora. 2003. "Justice Reinvestment." *Ideas for an Open Society* 3(3): 2–5. http://www.soros.org/resources/articles_publications/publications/ideas_20040106/ideas_justice_reinvestment_reduced.pdf.

Turner, Susan, and Joan Petersilia. 1996a. *Work Release: Recidivism and Corrections Costs in Washington State*. Washington, DC: U.S. Department of Justice, National Institute of Justice.

———. 1996b. "Work Release in Washington: Effects on Recidivism and Corrections Costs." *Prison Journal* 76(2): 138–64.

Tyler, Thomas R. 1988. *The Social Psychology of Procedural Justice*. New York: Plenum.

———. 1990. *Why People Obey the Law*. New Haven, CT: Yale University Press.

Tyler, John H., and Jeffrey R. Kling. Forthcoming. "Prison-based Education and Reentry into the Mainstream Labor Market." In *The Impact of Incarceration on Labor*

Market Outcomes, edited by Shawn Bushway, Michael Stoll, and David Weiman. New York: Russell Sage Foundation.

Uggen, Christopher. 2000. "Work as a Turning Point in the Life Course of Criminals: A Duration Model of Age, Employment, and Recidivism." *American Sociological Review* 65(4): 529–46.

Uggen, Christopher, and Jeff Manza. 2002. "Democratic Contraction? Political Consequences of Felon Disenfranchisement in the United States." *American Sociological Review* 67(6): 777–803.

———. 2004. "Lost Voices: The Civic and Political Views of Disfranchised Felons." In *Imprisoning America: The Social Effects of Mass Incarceration,* edited by Mary Pattillo, David Weiman, and Bruce Western (165–204). New York: Russell Sage Foundation.

Uggen, Christopher, and Melissa Thompson. 2003. "The Socioeconomic Determinants of Ill-Gotten Gains: Within-Person Changes in Drug Use and Illegal Earnings." *American Journal of Sociology* 109(1): 146–85.

Uggen, Christopher, Jeff Manza, and Angela Behrens. 2004. "Less than the Average Citizen: Stigma, Role Transition, and the Civic Reintegration of Convicted Felons." In *After Crime and Punishment: Pathways to Offender Reintegration,* edited by Shadd Maruna and Russ Immarigeon (258–90). Cullompton, Devon, UK: Willan Publishing.

Uggen, Christopher, Melissa Thompson, and Jeff Manza. 2000. "Crime, Class and Reintegration: The Scope of Social Distribution of America's Criminal Class." Paper presented at the annual meeting of the American Society of Criminology, San Francisco, November 18.

Uggen, Christopher, and Jeff Manza, with Melissa Thompson and Sara Wakefield. 2002. "Impact of Recent Legal Changes in Felon Voting Rights in Five States." Prepared for The National Symposium on Felony Disenfranchisement, Washington, DC, September 30–October 1.

U.S. Census Bureau. 2000. "Historical National Population Estimates: July 1, 1900 to July 1, 1999." Washington, DC: U.S. Census Bureau, Population Estimates Program, Population Division. http://www.census.gov/population/estimates/nation/popclockest.txt. (Accessed December 16, 2004.)

———. 2002. "National Population Estimates: April 1, 2000 to July 1, 2002" [computer file]. Table NA-EST2002-01. Washington, DC: U.S. Census Bureau, Population Division. http://www.census.gov/popest/archives/2000s/vintage_2002/files/NA-EST2002-01.xls. (Accessed December 16, 2004.)

U.S. Department of Housing and Urban Development. 1996. " 'One Strike and You're Out' Screening and Eviction Policies for Public Housing Authorities." Notice PIH 96-16 (HA). Washington, DC: U.S. Department of Housing and Urban Development, Office of Public and Indian Housing. http://www.hud.gov/offices/pih/publications/notices/96/pih96-16.pdf.

———. 1997. *Meeting the Challenge: Public Housing Authorities Respond to the "One Strike and You're Out" Initiative.* Washington, DC: U.S. Department of Housing and Urban Development.

———. 1999. *Waiting in Vain: An Update on America's Rental Housing Crisis.* Washington, DC: U.S. Department of Housing and Urban Development, Office of Policy Development and Research.

U.S. Department of Labor. 2002. "Labor Force Statistics from the Current Population Survey." http://data.bls.gov. (Accessed August 16, 2002.)

U.S. General Accounting Office. 2001. *Prisoner Releases: Trends and Information on Reintegration Programs.* GAO-01-483. Washington, DC: U.S. General Accounting Office.

———. 2003. "Formula Grants: 2000 Census Redistributes Federal Funding among States." GAO-03-178. Washington, DC: U.S. General Accounting Office.

Venkatesh, Sudhir Alladi. 2002. "The Robert Taylor Homes Relocation Study." Research report from the Center for Urban Research and Policy. New York: Columbia University.

Veysey, Bonita M., and Gisela Bichler-Robertson. 2002. "Prevalence Estimates of Psychiatric Disorders in Correctional Settings." In *Health Status of Soon-to-Be Released Inmates: Report to Congress,* vol. 2. Chicago, IL: National Commission on Correctional Health Care.

Vigilante, Kevin C., Mary M. Flynn, Patricia C. Affleck, J. C. Stunkle, N. A. Merriman, T. P. Flanigan, J. A. Mitty, and J. D. Rich. 1999. "Reduction in Recidivism of Incarcerated Women through Primary Care, Peer Counseling, and Discharge Planning." *Journal of Women's Health* 8(3): 409–15.

Visher, Christy, Nancy La Vigne, and Jill Farrell. 2003. *Illinois Prisoners' Reflections on Returning Home.* Washington, DC: The Urban Institute.

Visher, Christy, Nancy La Vigne, and Jeremy Travis. 2004. *Returning Home: Understanding the Challenges of Prisoner Reentry: Maryland Pilot Study: Findings from Baltimore.* Washington, DC: The Urban Institute.

Voelker, Rebecca. 2004. "New Initiatives Target Inmates' Health." *Journal of the American Medical Association* 291(13): 1549–51.

von Hirsch, Andrew. 1976. *Doing Justice: The Choice of Punishments.* New York: Hill & Wang.

Watson, Amy, Patricia Hanrahan, Daniel Luchins, and Arthur Lurigio. 2001. "Mental Health Courts and the Complex Issue of Mentally Ill Offenders." *Psychiatric Services* 52(4): 477–81.

Watson, Jamie, Amy L. Solomon, Nancy G. La Vigne, Jeremy Travis, Meagan Funches, and Barbara Parthasarathy. 2004. *A Portrait of Prisoner Reentry in Texas.* Washington, DC: The Urban Institute. http://www.urban.org/url.cfm?ID=410972. (Accessed April 5, 2004.)

Weiland, Carolyn. 1996. "Fee-for-Service Programs: A Literature Review and Results of a National Survey." *Journal of Correctional Health Care* 3(2): 145–58.

Weinbaum, Cindy, Rob Lyerla, and Harold S. Margolis. 2003. "Prevention and Control of Infections with Hepatitis Viruses in Correctional Settings." *Morbidity and Mortality Weekly Report* 52(RR-01): 1–33. Erratum at http://www.cdc.gov/mmwr/preview/mmwrhtml/mm5210a9.htm.

Western, Bruce, and Sarah McLanahan. 2000. "Fathers Behind Bars: The Impact of Incarceration on Family Formation." *Contemporary Perspectives in Family Research* 2: 307–22.

Western, Bruce, and Becky Pettit. 2000. "Incarceration and Racial Inequality in Men's Employment." *Industrial and Labor Relations Review* 54(3): 3–16.

Western, Bruce, Jeffrey R. Kling, and David F. Weiman. 2001. "The Labor Market Consequences of Incarceration." *Crime and Delinquency* 47(3): 410–27.

Western, Bruce, Leonard M. Lopoo, and Sarah McLanahan. 2004. "Incarceration and the Bonds Between Parents in Fragile Families." In *Imprisoning America: The Social Effects of Mass Incarceration,* edited by Mary Pattillo, David Weiman, and Bruce Western (21–45). New York: Russell Sage Foundation.

Wilkinson, Reginald A. 2001. "Offender Reentry: A Storm Overdue." *Corrections Management Quarterly* 5(3): 46–51.

Wilson, David B., Catherine A. Gallagher, and Doris L. Mackenzie. 2000. "A Meta-Analysis of Corrections-Based Education, Vocation, and Work Programs for Adult Offenders." *Journal of Research in Crime and Delinquency* 37(4): 347–68.

Wilson, William Julius.1996. *When Work Disappears: The World of the New Urban Poor.* New York: Alfred A. Knopf, Inc.

Wines, Enoch C., ed. 1871. "Declaration of Principles Adopted and Promulgated by the Congress." In *Transactions of the National Congress on Penitentiary and Reformatory Discipline.* Albany, NY: Weed Parsons & Company.

Wines, Enoch C., and Theodore W. Dwight. [1867] 1973. *Report on the Prisons and Reformatories of the United States and Canada.* Presented to the Legislature of New York, 1867. Albany, NY: Van Benthuysen & Sons' Steam Printing House. Reprint with a new introduction by Martha Youth Bouranel, 1973. New York: AMS Press, Inc.

Wisely, W. 2002. "Los Angeles Jail Condom Giveaway." *Prison Legal News,* September.

Wolff, Nancy. 2003. "Investing in Health and Justice Outcomes: An Investment Strategy for Offenders with Mental Health Problems in New Jersey." Prepared for the New Jersey Institute for Social Justice, Health, Mental Health, and Substance Abuse Reentry Roundtable, Newark, NJ, January 24. http://www.njisj.org/reports/wolff_report.pdf. (Accessed December 6, 2004.)

Wolff, Nancy, and Jeffrey Draine. 2003. "Dynamics of Social Capital of Prisoners and Community Reentry: Ties That Bind?" *Journal of Correctional Healthcare* 10(3): 457–90.

Women's Prison Association. 1996. *When a Mother Is Arrested: How the Criminal Justice and Child Welfare Systems Can Work Together More Effectively.* Baltimore: Maryland Department of Human Resources.

Wong, John B. 1999. "Cost-Effectiveness of Treatments for Chronic Hepatitis C." *American Journal of Medicine* 107(6B): 74S–78S.

Wool, Jon, and Don Stemen. 2004. "Changing Fortunes or Changing Attitudes? Sentencing and Corrections Reforms in 2003." Issues in Brief. New York: Vera Institute of Justice.

Wright, Lois, and Cynthia Seymour. 2000. *Working with Children and Families Separated by Incarceration.* Washington, DC: Child Welfare League of America Press.

Wu, Lawrence L., and Brian C. Martinson. 1993. "Family Structure and the Risk of Premarital Birth." *American Sociological Review* 58(2): 210–32.

Zevitz, Richard G., and Mary Ann Farkas. 2000. *Sex Offender Community Notification: Assessing the Impact in Wisconsin.* Washington, DC: U.S. Department of Justice, National Institute of Justice.

Zimring, Franklin E., Gordon Hawkins, and Sam Kamin. 2001. *Punishment and Democracy: Three Strikes and You're Out in California.* New York: Oxford University Press.

About the Author

Jeremy Travis became the fourth president of John Jay College of Criminal Justice on August 16, 2004. Prior to his appointment, Mr. Travis served four years as a senior fellow affiliated with the Justice Policy Center at the Urban Institute, where he launched a national research program on prisoner reentry into society and initiated research agendas on crime in a community context, sentencing, and international crime. While at the Urban Institute, Mr. Travis cochaired the Reentry Roundtable, a group of nationally prominent researchers and policymakers devoted to exploring the dimensions of prisoner reentry. From 1994 to 2000, Mr. Travis was the director of the National Institute of Justice (NIJ). A key figure in the development of new approaches to prisoner reentry, he pioneered the concept of the reentry court, designed the Department of Justice's reentry partnership initiative, and created the federal reentry program in President Clinton's FY 2000 budget. Before his tenure at NIJ, Mr. Travis was deputy commissioner of legal matters at the New York City Police Department, chief counsel to the House of Representatives Subcommittee on Criminal Justice, and special advisor to the mayor of New York City. Mr. Travis has received numerous awards for his contributions to the field of criminal justice, including the American Society of Criminology's August Vollmer Award, the Gerhard O. W. Muller

Award from the Academy of Criminal Justice Sciences, and the Margaret Mead Award from the International Community Corrections Association. He has taught courses on criminal justice, public policy, history, and law at Yale College, New York University's Wagner Graduate School of Public Service, New York Law School, and George Washington University.

Index